PIETY PROMOTED,

IN A COLLECTION OF DYING SAYINGS

OF MANY OF THE PEOPLE CALLED

QUAKERS.

WITH AN APPENDIX.

PIETY PROMOTED,

IN A

COLLECTION OF DYING SAYINGS

OF MANY OF

THE PEOPLE CALLED QUAKERS:

WITH

A BRIEF ACCOUNT OF SOME OF THEIR LABOURS IN THE GOSPEL, AND SUFFERINGS FOR THE SAME.

A NEW AND COMPLETE EDITION,

COMPRISING THE ELEVEN PARTS HERETOFORE SEPARATELY PUBLISHED.

EDITED BY

WILLIAM EVANS AND THOMAS EVANS.

IN FOUR VOLUMES.

VOLUME THIRD.

PHILADELPHIA:
FOR SALE AT FRIENDS' BOOK STORE,
No. 84 ARCH STREET.
1854.

INDEX

TO

THE THIRD VOLUME.

PIETY PROMOTED,

IN BRIEF MEMORIALS OF THE VIRTUOUS LIVES, SERVICES, AND DYING SAYINGS

OF SEVERAL OF THE PEOPLE CALLED

QUAKERS.

THE EIGHTH PART.

(CONTINUED.)

BY THOMAS WAGSTAFFE.

"Light is sown for the righteous, and gladness for the upright in heart." PSALM xcvii. 11.

"The righteous hath hope in his death." PROV. xiv. 32.

PIETY PROMOTED.

THE EIGHTH PART.

(CONTINUED.)

SARAH WAGSTAFFE, of Chipping-Norton, in Oxfordshire, widow of Thomas Wagstaffe, formerly of Banbury, in the same county, was born in the year 1695, and educated in the way of truth in the city of London, where her parents lived. Being faithful to the dictates thereof in her young years, she experienced its supporting influence under many exercises which fell to her lot through life, having often to remark to her children the benefit thereof; and by suitable instructions, endeavoured to lead their minds to regard its dictates when very young; and when remote from her, was often, by writing, reviving suitable counsel to them, being herself a good example, a tender parent, and well beloved among her neighbours and friends.

Towards the decline of her life she was afflicted with bodily weakness, which confined her to her chamber for some months before she died, which she bore with much resignation and patience, often desiring she might hold out to the end, for which she patiently waited. Before she became incapable, she employed her pen to such of her children as were at a distance from her, particularly to one of her sons. When she, by letter, took her last leave of him and his family, she expressed herself thus:

'That my children and grand-children may be so conducted through mutability, as that we may all meet in joy and bliss, I entreat (says she) in love, that thou and thine may mind your future state above all, and let not the hurry of this transitory world, with all its tinsel glare, pride, grandeur, and vanity, choke the good seed, which, as it is permitted to take root, will bring forth the good fruit, which will entitle you to discipleship, and give you a beauty and glory which all these things cannot give.

'Dear son, be on thy guard, and watch over thy children; repress all pride, ambition, and vain conversation in them as much as possible. O this world's fading enjoyments have overrun the major part of our Society! How few live up to what they profess! I write with a fervent desire for all your immortal souls, each of which is of more value than all this world, which with all its checkered pleasures and afflictions, must soon end as the bubble on the water, and then peace with our Maker will only stand us in stead.'

At another time, when to appearance she grew near her end, she expressed herself to this effect: that her trust and dependence was on her Almighty Protector, Saviour, and Redeemer, by whose grace she doubted not, but that she should close in peace.

After which she continued some weeks, in much quietness and patience, until the 5th of the First month, 1771, when she quietly departed without sigh or groan, and was interred in Friends' burial-ground at Chipping-Norton aforesaid, after a solemn meeting, the 13th of the same; aged near seventy-six years.

ABRAHAM SHACKLETON, born at Harden, in the parish of Bingley, Yorkshire, according to the best information, was the youngest child of Richard and Sarah Shackleton of that place. His mother died when he was about six years of age, his father when he was about eight. Though deprived so early of religious parents, the impression made by their careful education of him was not in vain; he used often to commemorate the tender care and concern of his pious father, how he followed him (his son) when very young to his bed-side, and on leaving him to his repose, awfully recommended him to seek the divine blessing. And this blessing remarkably attended him during the course of his life. When very young, and exposed to manifold dangers in his education afterwards, this blessing followed him, and by its precious influence, led him aside from his companions, and into solitary places to seek the Lord, and to witness the operation of his hand.

His employment being that of a school-master, he laboured in it with conscientious care for many years; in which he had not only the education of children of the members of our own Society, but also some of various denominations, some of whom fill conspicuous stations in the world, and retain an affectionate regard for his memory, and, from a remembrance of his diligence and care in their tuition, his living example of uprightness, temperance, and humility, a great regard for the Society.

Although in this arduous employment he met with many probations, yet keeping to a feeling sense of divine support, he grew from strength to strength, and became a very useful and valuable member of the Society; and in the station of an elder, had often to minister in his own house, in the families of friends, and in the church, in which counsel dropped from him in much tenderness and sweetness.

Thus, through a course of many years, he was conducted in great circumspection in a living travail for the prosperity of truth, and that the professors of it might be preserved out of hurtful things; had frequently to testify against such superfluities as sometimes came in his way, particularly a practice too prevalent among many, that of sitting long after dinner with bottles and glasses before them, as having a tendency to draw many into snares.

He was also much concerned at a custom too prevalent among Friends, of uncovering the head by way of ceremony upon entering into a room, and was pained when he saw the youth or others in that practice. He used to say, that when he was a young man, he durst not baulk his testimony in that respect, though the cross occasioned thereby seemed as bitter as death.

After a diligent discharge of his laborious employment for many years, he became in a greater degree separated from the cares of this life, and devoted much of his time in attending meetings for discipline in various parts of the nation of Ireland, where he was settled in his school, and also the yearly meeting in London, to the help of his brethren and his own peace.

After the death of his wife, who had been his beloved and faithful help-meet many years, and who departed this life in cheerful resignation, great composure and sweet peace, in the eightieth year of her age, he quitted house-keeping and retired to live with a relation in the same village where he was visited with his last illness, which he bore with great patience, saying he was mercifully dealt with.

During the course of his disorder, and while able, he got out to meetings, and when rendered incapable thereof, many friends visited him, to whom he was drawn forth in sweet counsel to the tendering of their spirits. Many were the seasonable opportunities of this sort, and many sensible, savoury expressions dropped from him, which showed his mind was often replenished with heavenly oil.

A little before his departure, he said to his relations about him, 'I have no cause to grieve, neither would I have you [to do so];' yet mentioned he had nothing to trust to but the mercies of the Almighty. His mind was often favoured with heavenly joy, and one night, after much pain, he expressed with a melodious voice, 'I am well, I feel no pain, I feel good. O the elders! the elders! they should dig for the arising of the well of life as with the staves in their hands. Spring up, O well, and I will sing unto thee!' At another time, in a manner similar to this, he uttered these words, 'Those that are faithful to the end shall receive a crown, a crown that fadeth not away; but rebellion is as the sin of witchcraft.'

Much more dropped from him, but not being taken down, could not be perfectly remembered.

He departed in great peace the 24th of the Sixth month, 1771, and was interred the 27th of the same; aged seventy-four years.

JOSEPH BEVINGTON, son of Timothy and Hannah Bevington, of the city of Worcester, was a young man, who from a child was sober and well-inclined, exemplary in his conduct, dutiful to his parents, and of a tender and loving disposition. As he grew up towards man's estate, he gave evident proofs of a suitable attention to that divine principle in his own mind, by which his conduct was so regulated, as to give ground of hope he would fill up his station with reputation to himself and comfort to all his friends.

He was taken ill about the 1st of the Sixth month, 1771, and his disorder gradually increasing, his father found his mind engaged to go and sit by him one evening on his going to bed sooner than usual, and in much tenderness expressed, that though he had hoped he might, in the appointment of Providence, have been his successor, both in the church and in the world, yet, when illness attacked even one so young and healthy as he, the issue might be doubtful, and therefore desired him to examine his accounts and meetness for a final change, if the Lord should please to remove him. He, in affectionate, lively terms, expressed the sense he had of his father's tender regard for him, and they parted that evening under a sweet sense of that love which unites beyond the ties of nature.

His distemper increasing, which proved to be a fever, he was mercifully preserved sensible. His father and mother being often concerned to wait on the Lord by his bed-side, he was frequently broken into tenderness, but did not say much.

Getting a little better, he went into the country for the air. In some conversation with a friend there who was in a declining state, he expressed, that he did not know how it might please Providence to deal with him; 'but,' said he, 'I had rather, if consistent with his will, go now, than live longer, and fall into anything that might bring dishonour to our holy profession.'

A near friend visiting him, found him in tears, and expressing her fears lest anything had grieved him, he answered, no, but he was looking towards another world.

He returned out of the country in about a week rather poorly, and on the morrow was seized with a shivering fit, and sending for his father, he with earnestness took him by the hand, and said, 'Dear father, I have already gone through a very trying time, but I believe this will be much more so;' and expressing his care for his parents, added, 'He that made me has a right to take me away when he pleases; and I desire, as he hath favoured me with much resignation of mind to his will hitherto, it may continue. I have not always been so careful and circumspect in my conduct as I ought to have been; but lately, and especially since my illness, I do not know that I could have done better, and trust it will be well with me.'

His indisposition increasing, all hopes of his recovery were removed, in which, he being in extreme pain and sickness, his parents were engaged to wait on the Lord with him, who was graciously pleased to comfort their minds; and under this broken, humble, contrite state before him, who sustains his people in every needful time, this beloved youth with an audible voice said, 'O what a dreadful day would this have been to me, if I had cause to fear I was going to meet an angry judge, that might say, Depart from me, thou worker of iniquity! but,' said he, 'I have hope in God, that I shall be admitted into his rest.' This much bowed the hearts of all his near connections present, and helped to bear up their spirits in that trying season.

Soon after, this dear object of paternal affection quietly departed this life in his father's arms, having, in a good degree, escaped the dangers, jeopardies, and temptations attendant on human life, and we trust was gathered with the beauty of innocency upon him, to the just of all generations, in the twenty-first year of his age, on the 9th of the Seventh month, 1771, and was buried in the city of Worcester, on the 14th of the same.

ANN GURNEY, daughter of John and Ann Gurney, of the city of Norwich, was a comely person, of quick parts, and a lively turn. Hence she early showed a natural inclination to height and gaiety, which brought a concern upon her parents on her account, lest she should be carried away with the common stream into liberties of a hurtful nature. But such was the gracious dealing of divine mercy towards her, that some time before she was taken with her last illness, an agreeable alteration was observed in her disposition and conduct, which undoubtedly arose from the cordial reception she had given to an heavenly visitation upon her spirit; for, in the sequel, it evidently appeared, a state of preparation was thereby effected, properly to endure the tedious illness and solemn event that ensued.

For many months, her usual state of health seemed, at times, to be broken in upon, and tokens of infirmity appeared, which increased upon her, and at length terminated in a settled decline.

Several weeks before her decease, she cheerfully said to her sisters, 'My little tenement is much shaken, and will soon be in decay.' A while after, her mother saying she should be very thankful if it pleased Providence to raise her up again, she replied, 'That must be as it pleases Providence, but I can never go with less guilt.'

She said, she believed divine goodness had often been very near to her, and supported her; for she could not have supported herself.

To her sister Lucy she said, 'My dear, I hope thou wilt never do anything to grieve thy father and mother, and be sure do nothing against thy own conscience. Do not grieve for me; for though we have loved one another, it is right we should part.'

She acknowledged she had sometimes gone contrary to the testimony of her conscience; but she had known sorrow for it, and, she believed, forgiveness; and made no doubt, but if it pleased Providence to take her away, she should go to heaven.

To her mother she said, 'I know it will be a loss; make it but a little one.' Her mother replying, 'It is a bitter cup, my dear,' she answered, 'But Providence will sweeten the bitter cup.' And on her mother's saying she believed a glorious mansion was prepared for her, she replied with much earnestness, 'I make no doubt of that, and I expect to see thee and my father there.'

Desiring her sisters to be called, she told them she was glad to see them; and, lying a while sweetly still, she awfully said, she hoped they would always live in the fear of the Lord, and never do anything against their consciences.

Being told her uncle Edmund Gurney said that she was in a sweet frame, and compared her to Mount Sion, that could not be moved, she answered, 'Then why does my mother grieve so?'

Her father going one morning into her chamber, she desired him to come by her bed-side, saying she was glad to see him, and that she thought herself not worse. On his saying he hoped her better parent, her heavenly Father, had been near to her that night, she answered, 'Yes, that he has, and I hope near thee too.'

Two days before her decease, she earnestly prayed the Lord would be with her to the end, and give her patience to the last; and that, if he pleased, he would mercifully grant her an easy passage, as her uncle Edmund had prayed for on her account. She declared she was very willing to go, with many other comfortable expressions.

She was composed and easy in her mind throughout her long and painful illness, and never once expressed a wish to live. She said she had many near and dear relations to leave; but she should not know the pain of losing them.

Thus having shown a steady example of faith, patience, resignation, and heavenly composure, in the bloom of youth, she departed the 19th of the First month, 1772; aged fourteen years and nine months.

WILLIAM HUNT, of New Gardon, in the province of North Carolina, in America, was born in the province of Pennsylvania; and, by accounts received, he was first reached by truth about the eighth year of his age, which continued to follow him from time to time, that when in company with his acquaintance, he has been often tendered and led to seek solitary places to vent his tears; although he then did not know what it was that so broke in upon his spirit.

Being situated in a part, at that early period of his life, where no religion prevailed, but the people lived rather dissolutely, he had no one to tell the distress and exercise of his mind to, for his mother dying when he was young, who he had been informed was a religious woman, and his father when he was about twelve, he was left quite alone. But after some time going to live with his sister, and those tender impressions continuing, the Lord in mercy showed him they were from the immediate operation of his own spirit, and that his growth in truth and experience of its pure virtue, lay in his being faithful to the dictates thereof; by which he was fitted for service, even in very early years, his mouth being opened in testimony before he was fifteen years of age; and through the heavenly influence of the Spirit, he became an able minister, rightly dividing the word of truth, to the great comfort and edification of the church where his lot was cast.

He was concerned to travel in truth's service before his twentieth year, and visited the provinces of Virginia and Maryland; and afterwards in the course of his Christian progress, all the provinces of America, and almost all the meetings therein. Although he had a large family, whose subsistence much depended on his industry and care; yet, when he found the requirings of truth, and became fully satisfied thereof, he cheerfully gave up all into the care of that hand which drew him into service, relying thereon for the preservation of himself and all his, in every dispensation of Providence, and which was mercifully afforded to him.

In the year 1771 he came to Great Britain on a religious visit, and travelled through most parts of the north of England, Scotland and Ireland, and after the yearly meeting, 1772, he visited the general quarterly meetings at Colchester, Woodbridge and Norwich. Soon after this he proceeded through Lincolnshire for Hull, whence, with his companion, Thomas Thornborough, our friend Samuel Emlen, Jr., of Philadelphia, and Morris Birkbeck, he embarked for Holland; and after visiting the few Friends there, he embarked in a vessel bound to Scarborough, but, by contrary winds, landed at Shields the latter end of the Eighth month, with a dedication of heart for further service if required; but was, soon after he landed, taken ill of the small-pox. In the course of this illness, his mind was preserved perfectly calm, and his patience and fortitude were truly great, as was also his resignation to the divine disposal, signifying to his companion that his coming there was providential, but that his sickness was nigh unto death, if not quite; 'for,' says he, 'when I wait, I seem enclosed, I see no further.'

To a friend who remarked that whatever affliction we may be tried with, we may yet see cause of thankfulness, he replied, 'Great cause, indeed; I never saw it clearer. Oh! the wisdom! the wisdom and goodness, the mercy and kindness, have appeared to me wonderful! And the further and deeper we go, the more we wonder. I have admired since I was cast on this bed, that all the world does not seek after the enjoyment of truth, it so far transcends all other things.'

At another time, to some Friends who came to see him, he said, 'The Lord knows how I have loved you from our first acquaintance, and longed for your growth and establishment in the blessed truth, and I now feel the same renewed afresh:' adding, that he much desired they might fill up the places Providence intended, and lay up treasure in heaven; 'for,' says he, 'what would a thousand worlds avail me now.' He also expressed his satisfaction that he had not spent his time idly since he came to England, nor neglected one meeting he could well attend; and that under so great a load of bodily affliction, what a treasure a quiet mind was.

At another time he said, with great composure, 'The Lord knows best. I am in his hand, let him do what he will.' Leaning on Morris Birkbeck, he said, 'Dear Morris, I have a request to make, which is, in case I am suddenly taken away, do thou write to my dear wife, and let her know all is well. Write also to my children, to improve the hints I frequently gave for their conduct while with them and since.'

At another time, a day or two before his death, he said to him, 'This is a trying time, but my mind is above it all;' and it was observable that a sweet melody was in his heart when few words were expressed.

A little before his death, he said triumphantly, 'Friends, truth reigns over all;' and soon after quietly departed this life, the 9th of the Ninth month, 1772, and was interred in Friends' burial-ground at Newcastle upon Tyne, the 11th of the same; aged thirty-nine, a minister twenty-four years.

ELIZABETH SMITH, of Burlington, in West Jersey, in America, was one whose deportment from a child was composed and steady. Frequently, while others sought recreation and amusements abroad, she chose to be at home, employing herself in the business of the family, or improving her mind by some useful application. As she grew up, the reproofs of instruction became the way of life to her, and she was governed by a meek and quiet spirit; her conversation and conduct seemed to be almost one continued example of child-like simplicity and innocence. Her mother dying while she was young, the care of her father's family devolved upon her for a considerable time before his death. Her duty to him, and behaviour in general, gained the love of a careful religious parent, and a blessing attended her, as her future life manifested. Her words were few, but savoury and instructive; she had a feeling heart, and the distressed were often relieved by her charity: happy in herself, she endeavoured to make all about her so. She had a great regard for the Holy Scriptures; on taking up a bible, she remarked to a particular friend, what a treasure it contained; and sought to inculcate the reading thereof, and to discourage the fashionable books of the times.

It was her concern frequently to retire to wait on the Lord, to know her strength renewed in him, and the effects were visible by a cheerful serenity in her countenance.

In her early youth she was called to the work of the ministry, in which she delivered herself in a clear, consistent manner; and it flowing from the right spring, was often attended with good effect. She was concerned to travel in the exercise of her gift as far to the northward as New England, and also to some of the southern provinces, and frequently to the meetings about home. But in her latter time she was greatly afflicted with a dropsical disorder, which subjected her to be tapped, by which she was so far relieved, that for several years she had a better state of health. In this interval she frequently attended meetings for worship and discipline; and the last summer before her death, though much enfeebled in body, had often very acceptable service in the ministry: alive and strong in the best sense, her company was greatly satisfactory to friends about her.

Her disorder returning, she waited for her change with a lively hope; and a serenity of mind attended her, being inwardly supported beyond mere human attainment.

She uttered many expressions during the conflicts of her illness, much to the comfort and satisfaction of those present. In solemn supplication to the Almighty on her own account, to be near and support her, she expressed herself in great reverence to the following effect: 'Thou who art the God of my life, who hast kept and fed me all my life long, be now near and support me by thy presence, and if it is thy will to put an end to my being here, I submit. Be graciously pleased to give me rest in thy mansion, with thy dear Son, the Lamb immaculate, for ever and ever.'

She often said she had nothing to do but to bear her pains with patience. Once in great extremity of pain, she remarked that she had reasoned, 'Why am I so afflicted?' and had received this answer in her mind, 'My beloved son, who never offended me, drank of the cup before thee.' 'Thus,' said she, 'I am helped along with one kind hint after another.' She frequently expressed the peace and consolation she felt in those trying moments, in having lived in the fear of her Creator.

A night or two before her departure, she said she thought it easier for her to leave the world than for those who had children to leave. A near and intimate friend replied, there were many who loved her; she said she did not know but it was so, and that love would be consummated hereafter. Towards the conclusion she said with great tenderness of spirit, that she thought she was going; and added, I would not have you to be troubled, it is to joy unspeakable and full of glory.

She died the 2d of the Tenth month, 1772; aged about forty-eight years.

Among other of her writings she left the following epistle, which is thought meet to be here inserted, viz.:

'To the Quarterly and Monthly meeting of Women Friends, held at Burlington and Chesterfield in West New Jersey, in America.

'Dearly beloved Friends,

'In a fresh remembrance of the many seasons of divine favour, we have been made partakers of together, in these meetings appointed for transacting the affairs of the church, does my spirit affectionately salute the living: and not expecting to have the like opportunity again, it rested with me to visit you after this manner, with fervent desires for the prosperity of truth and righteousness in general; and in a particular manner, I have a desire that our sex may not fall short in living up to the faithful performance of their respective duties, and discharging that trust which the Lord has committed to them, honestly, as in his sight. For this good end, I tenderly beseech you all, both elder and younger, who have known and may know the Master's will concerning you, that you may be obedient. Let not reasoning with flesh and blood, or pleading excuses because of unfitness, as you may think, prevail. Bear with me, if I observe, where that is the case, dwarfishness and weakness will be the consequence, and the best life is in danger of being quite lost, as it may with sorrow be remarked of some who profess with us, that a name to live and be accounted as wise virgins has seemed to suffice, whose case I have often lamented. It is the ardent prayer of my soul for such, while I am writing this, that they may awake to righteousness, and diligently attend to the teachings of the spirit of the Lord, who will not fail to fit and qualify for every good word and work. I am satisfied as that becomes the principal concern of individuals, the cause of complaining of misconduct would be much removed, and our Zion would more conspicuously shine, and there would be none found within her walls barren or unfruitful in the saving knowledge of God; but that the ancient promise made to Israel shall remain to be the portion of his people for ever, "That he would be as the dew of Hermon, and as the dew that descended upon the mountains of Zion, for there the Lord commanded the blessing, even life for evermore." Ps. cxxxiii. 3.

'My dear young friends, with love unfeigned do I affectionately salute you, whose company in these meetings I have been glad of; and I would encourage all who have a right to membership, to the steady attendance of them at the set time, as often as you can while health permits. We are, by nature, very short sighted, and know not when the times of refreshment may come from the presence of the Lord; and therefore it is good for us to endeavour patiently to wait and quietly to hope for his salvation, which I fully believe he is about to reveal in your hearts. If you are faithful to the discoveries of divine grace, your understandings will be more and more opened in the mysteries of God's kingdom, even that which was hid from ages and generations; and, as the apostle testifies, is now revealed by the spirit of the dear Son of God, our holy advocate with the father.

'I have hinted above and hope I shall die in the faith of it, that the Lord will form a people to himself, that shall show forth his praise, and will yet beautify the house of his glory. Under this prospect my spirit is at times deeply bowed in intercession for the descendants of faithful Friends, that they may not render themselves unworthy of so great a mercy, and other especial favours that they are blessed with beyond many; but that they may not only be the called, but chosen of the Lord. Now, in a degree of my heavenly Father's love, do I affectionately bid you farewell, desiring that grace, mercy and peace may be multiplied in and amongst you, and conclude your true friend,

'ELIZABETH SMITH.

'BURLINGTON, the 30th of the Third month, 1772.'

PRISCILLA GURNEY, wife of Edmund Gurney, of Norwich, was seized in the Sixth month, 1772, with a bleeding from the lungs, which to her appeared likely to end her days speedily. She laid quietly, and said calmly, she had not any thing criminal in outward things on her mind, and she hoped in the mercy of God.

For many weeks there seemed some flattering symptoms, she said not much about them, but appeared to be under a secret exercise of mind. As her husband was sitting by her one forenoon, she, in a very solid, humble frame of spirit, spoke to this effect: 'My dear, God is good indeed, a father of tender mercies. I feel his mercy renewed to me. I shall die of this illness; but I shall be happy, and I am quite willing to go. When I was visited with the truth, I had, as it were, an offer made me of a rich seat in the kingdom of heaven; but, O the world has been too much for me! and many have been my bitter baptisms for disobedience; and yet, O thou merciful Father! thou hast forgiven me, and I shall have a mansion with thee to eternity.'

Many, very many, were the comfortable expressions she uttered upon various occasions. One evening, on her husband taking leave of her, she said sweetly, 'I have an afflicted body, but an easy mind.' She frequently expressed her perfect resignation to her heavenly Father's will, who might justly be said to be long-suffering and forbearing to her, though very unworthy; but she had loved and served him in some degree, and further said, if it was his will to spare her life, and to require it of her, she would acknowledge him in the congregations of his people, or in any other way he pleased.

When her three brothers came from London to see her, observing one of them to be much tendered and affected, she desired they would not grieve for her, but for themselves, that they might experience the same comfort when the same awful visitation might be theirs, as it certainly in a little time would be: or to the same import.

The second visit her father paid her in her illness, she expressed herself thus: 'Dear father, I have always loved thee. No child could love a parent more than I have loved thee.' And after some pause, 'Dear father, I have been enabled to pray fervently to the Almighty for an easy passage, and that I might have a small mansion in the kingdom; and, O father, there never can be a stronger proof of the Holy Spirit, for the answer was, as if it was an outward voice, Thou shalt enter into a full fruition of joy.'

The divine mercy of God was indeed richly extended to her throughout her whole illness, and was her stay and support, by which, although her sufferings were great, her patience and meekness were wonderful. Such a calmness and composure covered her mind, that she disposed all her affairs, and directed things to be done after her decease without any visible discomposure to herself. She lay many weeks wishing for her dissolution, and when she thought her husband too anxious for her, she would say, 'I desire thee not to grieve for me. It would be cruel to desire my continuance in this affliction, as all will be well with me.'

The last day of her life, as he was sitting by her as usual, she desired every body to leave the room but him and the young woman that attended her; and after a pause of quietness, she uttered such expressions as these: 'My dear, it has for some time been a close trying season to me. Many deep conflicts have I passed through, and that heavenly peace I felt in weeks past has much left me; but yet I have a little hope I shall have a mansion in the kingdom.' In reply to this state of deep probation, her husband spoke a little to her as matter came before him, and she was very calm and humble, and after a considerable time in silence she called him again to her, and said, 'How gracious and merciful is God! I think I now see the seat I was first offered in my heavenly Father's house, and I feel an assurance I shall have it. This affliction has been a great refinement to my poor mind. My heavenly Father's arms are open to receive me, and I die rejoicing.'

After this unutterable favour she laid very quiet, and in divine sweetness fell into a doze. When she awoke, she expressed her fears lest she should have a hard passage, wishing it might be otherwise, and seemed revived. The family were ordered to go to bed, it being about nine in the evening, except a friend and Elizabeth Parkinson, the young woman who waited on her, who with her husband sat quietly by her. About ten o'clock, without any visible alteration to them, she departed, having had her desire granted, and no doubt is entered into everlasting felicity.

She died the 4th of the Tenth month, 1772, in the thirty-fifth year of her age, and was interred in Friends' burying-ground at Norwich, the 11th day of the same month.

JOHN WOOLMAN, of the province of West Jersey, in America, was born at Northampton, in that province, of parents professing with Friends, who had a tender care over him, and, being good examples themselves, promoted every appearance of good in him.

About the seventh year of his age, he became acquainted with the operations of divine love in his heart; and as he went from school one Seventh-day, whilst his companions were at play, he went forward out of sight, and sitting down, read the 22d chapter of the Revelations: "He showed me a river of water, clear as crystal, proceeding out of the throne of God and the Lamb," &c. In reading of which, his mind was drawn to seek after that pure habitation which he then believed God had prepared for his servants. The place where he sat, and the sweetness that attended his mind, remained fresh in his memory for many years afterwards. This and the like gracious visitations had such an effect upon him, that when he heard boys make use of ill language it troubled him, and through the continued mercies of God he experienced preservation from it himself; and the pious instruction of his parents would recur freshly in his mind, when he happened to be among wicked children, which was of use to him. His parents, who had a large family of children, frequently on the First-day of the week, after meeting, employed them in reading the Scriptures, or other good books, one after the other, the rest sitting by for instruction.

In some memoirs left behind, he records this as a good practice, and worthy of imitation by those who are entrusted with the care of children. Thus, in his very young years, through the renewings of divine love on his tender mind, he was preserved from many snares incident to youth, until he had attained about the sixteenth year of his age, when, as appears by his own account, through unwatchfulness he suffered his mind to be carried away by a love of improper company, and, though preserved from profane language or scandalous conduct, there was still a plant alive which brought forth wild grapes. Though at times he was brought seriously to consider his ways, which affected his mind with sorrow, yet, by an inattention to these reproofs of instruction, vanity was added to vanity, and repentance to repentance, and his mind became alienated from the truth, and hasted towards destruction. 'Whilst,' says he in his memoirs, 'I meditate on the gulf towards which I travelled, and reflect on my youthful disobedience, mine eyes run down with water.'

Nevertheless, afterward, his mind became more estranged from the enjoyment of real good, and he ran greater lengths in vanity, until it pleased the Lord to visit him with sickness, which appeared to be nigh unto death; in which state, darkness, horror and amazement seized his mind, and he thought it would have been better for him never to have had a being in this world, than to see such a day of confusion and affliction of body and mind. Herein he bewailed himself, and cries ascended to an offended God, who in his mercy at length heard him, and that word which is as a fire and a hammer, broke and dissolved his rebellious heart into a state of contrition, which was succeeded with inward consolation and desires, that if the Lord would be pleased to restore his health, he might walk humbly before him. Though the first part of his desire was granted, he again relapsed into folly and vanity; of one instance thereof I take his own account, viz.: 'I remember once having spent a part of the day in wantonness; as I went to bed at night, there lay in a window near my bed a Bible, which I opened and first cast my eye on the text, "We lie down in our shame, and our confusion covers us." This I knew to be my case, and meeting with so unexpected a reproof, I was somewhat affected by it, and went to bed under remorse of conscience, which I soon cast off again.'

But at length, through the powerful operation of divine love, he was enabled to take up the cross, and lived a very retired, religious life, until it pleased the great Author of our being, about the twenty-second year of his age, to commit to him a dispensation of the gospel ministry; through faithfulness thereto, he witnessed an increase of those talents committed to his care, and visited most of the American provinces at different times. About the year 1763, during the Indian war, he travelled about two hundred miles into the back parts of Pennsylvania, though attended with great fatigue of body and danger of his life, in order to pay a religious visit to an Indian settlement there, which was favourably received by the natives, and doubtless was attended with peace to his own mind, as he found many of them susceptible of divine impressions. He was for many years deeply exercised on behalf of the poor enslaved Africans, and both by word and writing, endeavoured to convince mankind of that unrighteous traffic, and injustice of keeping them in slavery.

In the year 1772, with the concurrence and unity of his brethren, he came over to England to visit Friends here, and landed in London about the 8th of the Sixth month. The yearly meeting being then sitting, he attended that meeting, in the course of which he had to drop divers weighty and instructive remarks. His mind being drawn towards the north, he soon departed from this city, and by the way of Hertford, Buckinghamshire, Northampton and Banbury quarterly meetings, he proceeded to the quarterly meeting at York, where, after having attended most of the sittings thereof, he was taken ill of the small-pox, in which disorder he continued about two weeks, at times under great affliction of body, and then departed in full assurance of a happy eternity, as the following expressions, amongst others, taken from his own mouth, plainly evidence.

One day being asked how he felt himself, he meekly answered, 'I do not know that I have slept this night. I feel the disorder making its progress, but my mind is mercifully preserved in stillness and peace.' Some time after, he said he was sensible the pains of death must be hard to bear, but if he escaped them now, he must some time pass through them, and did not know he could be better prepared, but had no will in it. He said he had settled his outward affairs to his mind; had taken leave of his wife and family, as never to return, leaving them to the Divine protection; adding, 'and though I feel them near to me at this time, yet I freely give them up, having an hope they will be provided for.' A little after said, 'This trial is made easier than I could have thought, by my will being wholly taken away; for if I was anxious as to the event, it would be harder; but I am not, and my mind enjoys a perfect calm.'

In the night a young woman having given him something to drink, he said, 'My child, thou seemest very kind to me, a poor creature, the Lord will reward thee for it.' A while after he cried out with great earnestness of spirit, 'O my Father! my Father! how comfortable art thou to my soul in this trying season.' Being asked if he could take a little nourishment, after some pause he replied, 'My child, I cannot tell what to say to it; I seem nearly arrived where my soul shall have rest from all my troubles.' After giving in something to be put in his journal, he said, 'I believe the Lord will now excuse me from exercises of this kind, and I see no work but one, which is to be the last wrought by me in this world. The messenger will come that will release me from all these troubles, but it must be in the Lord's time, which I am waiting for.' He said he had laboured to do whatever was required, according to the ability received, in the remembrance of which he had peace. Though the disorder was strong at times, and would come over his mind like a whirlwind, yet it had hitherto been kept steady, and centered in everlasting love; adding, 'And if that is mercifully continued, I ask or desire no more.'

At another time he said he had long had a view of visiting this nation; and some time before he came, he had a dream, in which he saw himself in the northern parts of it; and that the spring of the gospel was opened in him, much as in the beginning of friends, such as George Fox and William Dewsbury; and he saw the different states of people as clearly as he had ever seen flowers in a garden; but in his going on he was suddenly stopped, though he could not see for what end, but looked towards home, and fell into a flood of tears, which waked him.

At another time he said, 'My draught seemed strongest to the north, and I mentioned in my own monthly meeting, that attending the quarterly meeting at York, and being there, looked like home to me.'

Having repeatedly consented to take a medicine with a view to settle his stomach, but without effect, the friend then waiting on him said, through distress, 'What shall I do now?' He answered with great composure, "Rejoice evermore, and in every thing give thanks:" but added a little after, 'This is sometimes hard to come at.'

One morning early he broke forth in supplication on this wise: 'O Lord! it was thy power that enabled me to forsake sin in my youth, and I have felt thy bruises since for disobedience, but as I bowed under them thou healedst me; and though I have gone through many trials and sore afflictions, thou hast been with me, continuing a father and a friend. I feel thy power now, and beg that in the approaching trying moments, thou wilt keep my heart steadfast unto thee.' Upon his giving the same friend directions concerning some little matters, she said, 'I will take care, but hope thou mayest live to order them thyself.' He replied, 'My hope is in Christ; and though I may now seem a little better, a change in the disorder may soon happen, and my little strength be dissolved, and if it so happen, I shall be gathered to my everlasting rest.' On her saying she did not doubt that, but could not help mourning to see so many faithful servants removed at so low a time, he said, 'All goodness cometh from the Lord, whose power is the same, and he can work as he sees best.' The same day, after giving her directions about wrapping his corpse, and perceiving her to weep, he said, 'I had rather thou wouldst guard against weeping or sorrowing for me, my sister. I sorrow not, though I have had some painful conflicts; but now they seem over, and matters all settled; and I look at the face of my dear

Redeemer, for sweet is his voice, and his countenance comely.'

Being very weak, and in general difficult to be understood, he uttered a few words in commemoration of the Lord's goodness to him; and added, 'How tenderly have I been waited upon in this time of affliction, in which I may say in Job's words, "Tedious days and wearisome nights are appointed unto me." And how many are spending their time and money on vanity and superfluities, while thousands and tens of thousands want the necessaries of life, who might be relieved by them, and their distresses at such a time as this, in some degree softened by the administering of suitable things.'

An apothecary who attended him of his own accord, he being unwilling to have any sent for, appeared very anxious to assist him, with whom conversing, he queried about the probability of such a load of matter being thrown off his weak body, and the apothecary making some remarks implying he thought it might, he spoke with an audible voice on this wise: 'My dependence is on the Lord Jesus Christ, who I trust will forgive my sins, which is all I hope for; and if it be his will to raise up this body again, I am content, and if to die, I am resigned: and if thou canst not be easy without trying to assist nature, in order to lengthen out my life, I submit.' After this, his throat was so much affected, that it was very difficult for him to speak so as to be understood, and he frequently wrote when he wanted any thing. About the second hour on Fourth-day morning, being the 7th of the Tenth month, 1772, he asked for pen and ink, and at several times, with much difficulty, wrote thus: 'I believe my being here is in the wisdom of Christ; I know not as to life or death.' About a quarter before six the same morning, he seemed to fall into an easy sleep, which continued about half an hour, when seeming to awake, he breathed a few times with more difficulty, and so expired without sigh, groan, or struggle.

He often said it was hid from him whether he might recover or not, and he was not desirous to know it; but from his own feeling of the disorder, and his feeble constitution, he thought he should not.

WILLIAM YOUNG, son of William Young, of Leominster, in the county of Hereford, and Hannah his wife, she being deceased, was in his childhood of a sweet and sprightly natural temper, and although of a tender frame, seemed healthy, until he contracted a cold, which at length brought on a consumption.

In the course of his affliction his deportment was grave, and as he grew worse, he became more thoughtful, and made many sensible remarks of the uncertainty of visible things; and expressed a grateful sense of the kindness of Providence many ways, and particularly in the visits and good advice he received from friends. Although he had been preserved in a more innocent conduct than most young men of his age, he knew that would not entitle him to the felicity of the redeemed, and was therefore earnestly desirous of attaining such a state of inward purity and renovation of heart as would procure divine favour; and on this account had many painful conflicts. When his recovery was thought doubtful, he often lamented his having lost that tenderness and fervency of spirit towards God which he had formerly experienced.

For many weeks before his death he was apprehensive of his end being near, and said, 'If I die now in my youth, it may be all for the best, and may put other young people upon the consideration of their latter end.' On his father's saying it would be well for us to be resigned to the divine will, but intimating a reluctancy to part, he replied with much earnestness, 'Aye, do be resigned; let us all be resigned;' and frequently expressed a desire to be resigned either to life or death; but said, if it pleased the Lord to fit him for his change, and take him from the slippery paths of life at so early a period, he should think it a favour; for he had no desire to live, except it was to the glory of his Creator.

He several times showed great concern at hearing of the disorderly walking of some amongst us, and a deep sense of the wonderful goodness and condescension of Christ in suffering for mankind.

Some weeks before his death, observing his sister weep, he said, 'We must part. I must leave you; but I hope and believe we shall meet again.'

The 2d of the First month he was very ill, and seeing his father affected, he said, 'O father, what a mercy it would be if the Lord should be pleased to take me to himself! Do not grieve, for if I should be spared and turn out naught, it would be a greater affliction.'

The next morning, after having had a very bad night, he was weak and low, but appeared quite calm in mind; and on his sister's saying, after some other conversation, she hoped he was resigned, he replied with much sweetness, 'Yes, sister, I hope I am quite resigned to the Almighty's will; but surely if it is his will, it will be a mercy to be taken from this troublesome world to himself. And I have a hope he will take me to himself; he hath been pleased wonderfully to calm my mind.' She observed there was great room to hope, and that the sufferings of his friends would be greatest; he replied very earnestly, 'O my sufferings will be nothing in proportion to my offences! but I have a hope my offences will be forgiven. O how merciful is the Lord! How great is his goodness! How pure is his love! Mercy, goodness, purity, belong to him.' Seeing his sister much affected at what he said, he continued, 'We cannot tell, sister; some worse than I have been restored. He is able to raise me up, and if he should, and make me some sort of a member (meaning of his church militant), I hope I shall be careful to keep near to him; but I desire not to live, no, not a moment, as one of this world.'

That night he was so weak, those about him were apprehensive he could not continue long. The next day he seemed pretty free from pain, but drowsy, and his expressions rambling, but innocent; indeed, his countenance and conversation were sweet and lamb-like. The next morning he desired to be put to bed, being in great pain, but could not rest there; and being replaced in the easy chair and same posture he had lain in for many nights, he seemed much easier, and told his sister he was going; she said she hoped to a better inheritance; he replied, 'Aye, for I believe in one that can save me;' and repeatedly said the fear of death was taken away. And a day or two before his death, he said, 'I am going to leave an affectionate father, to meet the great Almighty Father.'

Another time, his sister saying it was a favour he was preserved so patient, he said, 'I hope I shall be kept so; I am under the Lord's care entirely; nothing else will do. I see nothing else will do.' The same day he uttered many sweet and lively expressions, but his voice was too low to be understood, so as to connect the sentences. The day before his decease it was so weak and broken, that he could scarcely articulate a sentence; but was meek and patient as a lamb, and once said something about rejoicing in the house of God, and when he could no otherwise express himself, would reach up to kiss his father and sister, his heart being full of love. When asked if he would have any thing sent to his eldest sister then in Cornwall, he said, 'Nothing but my love,' or dear love; adding, 'In that love I feel for all.' He frequently desired those about him not to grieve, and would sometimes say, 'Why, if you think I am going well, should you grieve?' and observed, that if he had brought on his illness by any bad course of life, it would be hard to bear; but added, 'I believe you have no reason to think I have.'

He took a most affectionate leave of his sister, bidding

her love and adore the Lord; and said something about his father, which could not be understood. His father then telling him he hoped there was a place prepared for him amongst the blessed, and that he loved to be with the good, he replied as well as he was able, 'Aye, dearly, dearly.' And in about two hours after, he departed so quietly, that those present apprehended him to be fallen asleep, the 7th day of the First month, 1773, in the nineteenth year of his age.

HANNAH DUDLEY, late wife of Robert Dudley, of Clonmel, in Ireland, was born at Woodbridge in Suffolk, and religiously educated, which was blessed to her. Through the prevailing power of divine love, she was brought to know a state of submission to divers near trials which fell to her lot; and having her heart weaned from the world and its delusive profits and friendships, she became more and more refined, being an example of humility, plainness, and self-denial.

About the year 1772 some symptoms of a consumption appeared, but for some time she attended meetings both for worship and discipline, in some of which she was enabled to bear a living testimony to the truth.

In the course of her illness many friends visited her, to whom she was enabled to drop some tender expressions, and it seemed to be her greatest joy to see and hear of the prosperity of truth; and at divers opportunities she had suitable counsel and instruction to give to those about her.

About a week before her departure, our friend Robert Willis, of West Jersey in America, being in the course of his religious visit at her house, had a comfortable and tendering opportunity with her, her husband and sister.

About two days before her decease, she dropped much excellent advice to her husband and sister, expressing her desire to be released; but added her hope she should be preserved patient to the end; and afterwards on some mitigation of her pain, signified her entire resignation to the divine will. Speaking to her husband's eldest son, in a very weighty manner, she advised him to remember her admonitions; saying also, 'Shun bad company, obey thy parent, and do not offend him; seek the Lord and he will be found of thee, but if thou forsake him, he will cast thee off for ever.'

To their apprentice she said, 'Jemmy, love plainness and continue in it, for truth leads to plainness. Thou hast been favoured with an education beyond many, therefore prize it, and hast known truth, therefore beware of trampling on the testimony, but be circumspect in all thy ways and conduct. Thou art just entering on the slippery part of life, the slippery paths of youth, and art no stranger to the temptations and allurements of the adversary. I have often thought it a great mercy that thou hast been preserved from (I believe) almost any vice.' Just after, she very affectionately took her leave of her brother and sister-in-law, saying, 'Our acquaintance has been short, but we have loved one another;' and then prayed very fervently that a blessing might rest upon their family.

Being pressed to try and take a little sleep, she replied, 'O that I could sleep in the arms of my beloved!' And with great fervency prayed, 'O Lord God, have mercy upon me! and let thy compassionate ear be opened. Lord God Almighty! send the guardian angel of thy presence to conduct my spirit.' After which she lay in great peace and serenity of mind, growing weaker and weaker, yet sensible to the last, and with her hand closed in her husband's, departed without sigh or groan, as one falling into a sweet sleep, the 25th of the First month, 1773; aged about forty-seven years, a minister about nine years. After a very large and solemn meeting, her body was decently interred the 29th, in Friends' burial-ground in Clonmel aforesaid.

SAMUEL FOTHERGILL, of Warrington, in Lancashire, was the sixth son of our worthy ancient friend John Fothergill mentioned in this treatise, see Vol. II., page 365, and of Margaret his wife, for an account of whom see Vol. II., page 186.

This their son being of an active and lively disposition, and during his apprenticeship mostly from under the watchful eye of his affectionate parent, he fled from the holy cross of Christ, and indulged himself in the gratifications of folly and licentiousness, violating the repeated convictions of divine grace in his own mind, which had been mercifully extended from his early years, thereby wounding the soul of his tender father, of whose religious care to form and lead the tender minds of his children to piety and virtue we have an account in the memoirs of his life. Yet his pious admonitions proved, nevertheless, as bread cast on the waters, which returned after many days; for about the twenty-first year of his age, the visitation of divine love was so powerfully renewed, that it proved effectual to turn his steps out of the paths of vanity; and, as he has expressed, with humble and awful gratitude to the Preserver of men, it then appeared clear to his understanding, that would be the last call the Heavenly Father would favour him with. He therefore consulted no longer with flesh and blood, but gave up to the holy visitation, devoting his whole heart and affections to seek reconciliation with God, through the mediation of Jesus Christ; and abiding in great humility under the purifying operation of the Holy Ghost and fire, he became thereby qualified for those eminent services he was called into. In a few months, by the constraining power and love of God, his mouth was opened to bear a testimony to the sufficiency of that holy arm that had plucked him as a brand out of the fire.

Thus a dispensation of the ministry being committed to his charge, he attended faithfully thereto, and moved therein at the requirings, and under the direction of, divine wisdom, by which means he soon became an able minister of the gospel, called thereto and qualified by the Holy Ghost. Under this influence he laboured with diligence, and devoted much of his time and strength, when health permitted, to the service of his dear Lord and master, for the continuance of whose favours he counted nothing too near or dear to part with, that he might be instrumental in gathering souls to God, which was the object he had in view in all his gospel labours. Being diligent himself, he endeavoured much to excite Friends to a due and constant attendance of meetings for religious worship, and those for the discipline of the church.

Through the course of his gospel labours, both in public and private, animated by divine love, he expressed an uncommon warmth of affection for the rising youth of this generation, with whom he was led into a deep brotherly feeling and sympathy for their present and eternal welfare; under which concern his love to this class of both sexes, under all denominations, was strong and ardent.

He travelled much in England and Scotland, several times in Ireland, and once through most of the North American colonies, in the service of truth; where, though singularly humbled in a sense of poverty, weakness and insufficiency on his first landing, he was, by accounts received, marvellously strengthened, both in public and private, in gospel authority and love, to the awakening and comforting of many.

In the fore part of the year 1769, he visited most of the families of Friends in the monthly meeting of Gracechurch-street, London; in which service he was divinely strengthened and enabled to extend a helping hand to many in close and necessary labour, for their increasing care, to live and act consistently with our holy profession, to the comfort and help of divers, and his own peace; and afterwards, at two different opportunities, he visited the families of Friends in Horslydown and Westminster monthly meeting in that city, to the same good effect.

He mostly attended the yearly meetings in London, and other places, when of bodily ability; in which his gospel labours were very acceptable and edifying; being particularly careful, when called from home, to return to his family and friends with as much expedition as the nature of his service would admit.

Having acquired a moderate competency by his diligence and industry, he declined trade for several years before his decease, devoting his time and talents to the service of the churches. As a pillar in the Lord's house he was steadfast, being actuated by a Christian and manly zeal; in deportment grave; his private conversation was savory and edifying, corresponding with his ministry, which at times went forth as a flame, piercing the obdurate, yet descended like dew upon the tender plants of our heavenly Father's planting, the true mourners in Zion; with these he travailed in a deep sympathy of spirit. In his gospel labours he was free from affectation; in doctrine, clear, sound and pathetic, filled with charity, allowing for the prejudices of mankind, being indeed a minister and elder worthy of double honour, speaking whereof he knew, and what his own hands had handled of the good word of life.

He endured a long and painful illness with much patience and resignation; and towards the close of his time, expressed himself to some of his relations, when they took leave of him, previous to their setting out for the yearly meeting in London, to the following effect:

'Our health is no more at our command than length of days: mine seems drawing fast towards a conclusion; but I am content with every allotment of Providence, for they are all in wisdom, unerring wisdom.

'There is one thing which, as an arm underneath, bears up and supports; and though the rolling tempestuous billows surround, yet my head is kept above them, and my feet are firmly established. O! seek it, press after it, lay fast hold of it.

'Though painful my nights, and wearisome my days, yet I am preserved in patience and resignation. Death hath no terrors, nor will the grave have any victory. My soul triumphs over death, hell, and the grave.

'Husbands and wives, parents and children, health and riches, must all go. Disappointment is another name for them.

'I should have been thankful had I been able to get to the ensuing yearly meeting in London, which you are now going to attend, where I have been so often refreshed with my brethren; but it is otherwise allotted. I shall remember them, and some of them will remember me. The Lord knows best what is best for us. I am content and resigned to his will.

'I feel a foretaste of that joy that is to come; and who would wish to change such a state of mind?

'I should be glad if an easy channel could be found to inform the yearly meeting, that as I have lived, so I shall close, with the most unshaken assurance, that we have not followed cunningly devised fables, but the pure, living, eternal substance.

'Let the aged be strong, let the middle-aged be animated, and the youth encouraged; for the Lord is still with Sion; the Lord will bless Sion.

'If I be now removed out of his church militant, where I have endeavoured in some measure to fill up my duty, I have an evidence that I shall gain an admittance into his glorious church triumphant, far above the heavens.

'My dear love is to all them that love the Lord Jesus.'

He departed this life at his house in Warrington, the 15th, and was buried the 19th day of the Sixth month, 1772, at Penketh, in the fifty-seventh year of his age, and the thirty-sixth of his ministry.

And now, Reader, before thou close the book, pause a little, and consider, what progress thou hast made in this heavenly race. The prophet Isaiah, after describing the coming of Christ, and very emphatically setting forth his office, the peaceable government of his power, and its glorious effects upon his followers, in chap. xi., in the next chapter declares what the faithful experience: "And in that day thou shalt say, O Lord! I will praise thee; though thou wast angry with me, thine anger is turned away, and thou comfortedst me. Behold, God is my salvation, I will trust and not be afraid, for the Lord Jehovah is my strength, and my song, he also is become my salvation.' Isaiah xii. 1, 2.

The same living, divine power, the same inexhaustible source of wisdom and goodness remains. The enjoyments of time are transient, its pleasures are delusive; let therefore all trust in his arm: this is the strength and beauty of men; their alone help and dependence is here, in all their exercises through time, that when they come to close, as has been the case with the just in all generations, in effect, to declare, "Behold, God is my salvation, I will trust and not be afraid; for the Lord Jehovah is my strength and my song, he also is become my salvation."

END OF THE EIGHTH PART.

PIETY PROMOTED,

IN BRIEF MEMORIALS AND DYING EXPRESSIONS

OF SOME OF THE PEOPLE CALLED

QUAKERS.

THE NINTH PART.

BY THOMAS WAGSTAFFE.

"Verily there is a reward for the righteous." PSALM lviii. 11.

PREFACE.

THE general approbation which publications of this kind have had, makes a continuance of the collection desirable. Memorials of the circumspect lives and dying expressions of such as finish their course well, show the efficacy of the divine principle [the holy spirit of the Lord Jesus] which we profess, and that obedience to its dictates yields the peaceable fruits of righteousness.

To promote an attention to this principle in the youth, to whom this is particularly addressed, the following accounts of many who have been faithful in their day, are recommended to their perusal; with the intent that, excited by the example, they also may fill up their duty as they go along, and partake of the same peace these had to rejoice in, when no human help could afford them comfort. The experience of those who are gone before, is as a waymark to those who follow after; and their example calls loudly, "Follow us, as we have followed Christ."

Those who in early youth are happily brought under the teachings of this divine principle, and are faithful to its precepts, are prepared to encounter the world and all its allurements. If prosperity be their lot, they can receive it as the bounty of an Almighty Father, and keep in that state of humility which becomes dependent beings, applying it to the honour of Him who hath entrusted them therewith. If afflictions attend, and it is sometimes the lot of good men to experience adverse winds and tempestuous seasons, they can look with an humble confidence to Him for protection in their conflicts, and bow to the hand which has permitted them. It was not the offering of any temporal things, according to the Psalmist; but, says he, "Offer to God thanksgivings; pay thy vows to the Most High; then call on me in the day of trouble, and I will deliver thee, and thou shalt glorify me." Psalm l.

This hath been the experience of those who have had their trust in God's power, in every age; and as they have gone along in this vale of tears, for such it hath been to many, they have, from time to time, had their faith renewed, and their hope confirmed, so as to set up their Ebenezer, "Hitherto hath the Lord helped us."

"We have," as saith the apostle, "no continuing city here;" neither have we any state of security beyond "Give us this day our daily bread." Whatever may be our growth and experience in religion, it will never go beyond that state of dependence. Our only safety is a truly humble state, wherein the mind is exercised in a daily watch, care, and travail, for the arisings of the divine life; under a sense of which, such have a hope that He who hath been their morning light, and hitherto conducted in safety, will, in the conclusion, be their evening song; and, in effect, adopt the language of the prophet, "I will greatly rejoice in the Lord; my soul shall be joyful in my God; for he hath clothed me with the garments of salvation."

T. W.

Stockwell, Surry, Eleventh month, 1795.

PIETY PROMOTED.

THE NINTH PART.

LUKE HOWARD, of Dover, was a serviceable man in the early breaking forth of truth in this nation, a faithful sufferer for its testimony, and preserved to the end in peace. The following account is extracted from a short journal and collection of his writings.

In his tender years he experienced in himself the appearance of the love and grace of God, reproving for evil; and when about fourteen years of age, he was bound an apprentice to a shoemaker in Dover. His master, being in a seeking state, and having forsaken the public worship and joined with some who were separated from it, treated him kindly; which so wrought on him, that he took a resolution to become more conscientious towards God, and more orderly to his master, than he had been, not daring to wrong him by neglecting his work. Thus he served out his apprenticeship to his master's content; and, a few weeks after his time was expired, he came to London to work, frequented a meeting in Coleman-street, and was admitted a member thereof. The war between the king and parliament being then very hot, and forts raising about the city, he sought to be entered in the army; but many pressing to go, 'It was my lot,' says he, 'to be left out; that so I might be clear of the blood of all men, as since I have seen it and rejoice, though then troubled at my dismission.'

He then returned to Dover, where there were several young men inquiring the way to Zion, with their faces thitherward, and searching the Scriptures, hoping to find the right way. 'There, and in that day,' says he, 'I was convinced that singing of psalms in rhyme and metre, was a lie in me as to my own condition, and a mock service as to the Lord; and was forced to sit silent under the cross, when others sung.' This, at that period, was so strange, that the priest took notice of him, and in a little time it was noised abroad as a great wonder, that he refused to sing psalms. His master, with whom he had served his apprenticeship, being also troubled at it, got Samuel Fisher, their priest, to come and discourse with him. Fisher had much to say to him: 'But,' said he, 'I said what was in my own conscience manifested, and I did not know another in the world of my mind; but so it was, my peace abounded, and knowledge increased.' Samuel Fisher returned home, and never dared to sing more in the steeple-house; but was soon after convinced of the everlasting truth, in which he ended his days in prison, for his testimony thereto.

Luke Howard, meanwhile, went among the Brownists, also the Presbyterians, and the Independents, and then among the Baptists, with whom he chose rather to join than with any other. He passed through their ceremony of water-baptism, but still knew not where to find a resting-place, not knowing he had a guide within him to keep him out of all evil; and in this state he mourned with tears. Nevertheless he got over his convictions, and went into liberties; 'In this great loss,' says he, 'I continued until I did, as too many do, gêt above the witness, and I sought to make merry over it, and to take my fill of the world, with all I could enjoy thereof.'

But soon after, coming to London on business he went to hear a preacher in Lombard-street; and afterwards a young man, named William Caton, stood up, and sounded an alarm out of Zion, and proclaimed the gospel of peace out of the

Lord's holy mountain; but L. Howard's mind being after visible things, he slighted it at that time. The next First-day, being at home, he was told a Quaker was preaching; and, going to see what manner of man he was, found him to be the afore-named William Caton. Luke was reached by his testimony, was a guard to him from the boys and others who offered him abuse, and in the evening went to visit him, where he found his companion, John Stubbs. He invited them to go home with him, which they did, and had several meetings there, and their testimony was to him as a pleasant song, and he bore them company out of town. Then exercise fell to his lot, but he was led along in safety under the teachings of truth, so that he expresses himself thus, after giving an account of the exercises he had to pass through: 'My experience hath been, and is, as I abode in obedience to the Lord, in waiting on him, which I hope I shall ever do; the word of the Lord opened to me when in a great strait, saying, "I will cleave the rocks and mountains, that the redeemed of the Lord may come to Zion;" at which I felt and saw a little light, and a hope sprung up of getting over and through those rocks and mountains of thick and black darkness in me, which the enemy presented to be so great, that it was impossible to get over. So then, and ever since, in that grounded hope, as an anchor to my soul, I have cast my care upon the Lord, and have rode through many bitter storms, and, I bless the Lord, my flight hath not been in the winter, and now, I hope in the Lord, it will not be in the Sabbath-day. Even so, amen.'

In the course of his pilgrimage it was sometimes his lot to be imprisoned. Once he was sent to Dover castle, with three more, and detained sixteen months, because he could not forbear meetings. At this time he employed six men in his trade, but he was obliged to shut up his shop for six months, neither could he work in prison for a time; but obtaining the liberty of an entry to the grate, where they drew their meat up with a cord, he worked a little there, and his wife kept cows and sold milk, to assist in supporting his family; 'and,' says he, 'I had perfect peace, joy, and content, in it all; and the Lord made it all good to me, both within and without. It also appears he suffered a long imprisonment in the castle, in 1684; during which, he often pleaded with the magistrates on account of their cruel and unjust treatment of him.

Thus persevering, he was preserved in greenness to old age. The following expressions were taken down during his illness by a friend present, as delivered, viz.:

'God, the Lord of heaven and earth, appeared to me in an acceptable time, in the year 1655, by his word, through his servants John Stubbs and William Caton, in the gift of his grace, the Son of his love, Christ Jesus, whom he sent out of his own bosom, and by the sword of his own mouth, and by the brightness of his arising, cut me off from the wild olive tree, which I was rooted in by transgression, and grafted me into the true olive root, the life of which is the light of the world, and by his love and spirit in my heart, raised me to worship him in spirit and truth. Then the cross appeared so great, that if it had been his will, I would rather have parted with my natural life, if I could have had peace, than to have taken it up; but in the day of his love and power, through the word of life, and the arising thereof, I was made willing to do his will, and to take up the cross, not for a little while, but with a resolution as long as life continued. And though many temptations have attended, yet the Lord hath delivered me out of them all, and hath engaged my soul and all within me, to serve him in newness of life, and begot and continued a breathing, that he would never give more knowledge than he would give me power to obey, and in the day thereof hath made me willing to serve him, and deny myself, and his reward is and hath been in my bosom. He is worthy to be worshipped, obeyed, and feared for ever, for he speaks peace to his children, that they turn not again to folly. In his peace stands my rest, which rest remains for the people of God, and in this, I take my leave of the world, with soul, body, and spirit, given up to the Lord, in and through his grace, the life of Christ Jesus, in whom all the promises are yea, and amen.'

He departed this life the 7th of the Eighth month, O. S. 1699.

The Morning Meeting of London, in a testimony concerning him, dated the 26th of the Sixth month, 1704, say, he was preserved to the end, and died in the faith of our Lord and Saviour Jesus Christ; and we doubt not that he received the crown of righteousness, from God the righteous judge.

MARGARET FOX, widow of our ancient Friend and elder George Fox, was convinced of the principle of truth, on his first coming into that part of Lancashire where she dwelt, in 1652; being then the wife of Thomas Fell, one of the Welsh judges, a man much esteemed in his country for his wisdom, moderation, and mercy, being also a tender husband and loving father, and one who sought after God in the best way it was made known to him. He frequently entertained those who were accounted serious and godly men; and had often prayers, and religious exercises in the family; and in this manner also Margaret was seeking after the right way for many years, though often afraid she was short of it.

She was born in the year 1614; her parents were of honourable repute in that country, and her father, John Askew, was of an ancient family and estate, and a pious charitable man. It was in the seeking state before-mentioned that it pleased divine wisdom to move the heart of George Fox, to visit the family of the judge, who was then in London, and to open to them the eternal truth; by which means the minds of herself, children, and a great part of the servants, were convinced and turned to God. When the judge returned home, and found the great change wrought on them, he was much surprised, and appeared to be troubled; but Richard Farnworth, and some other friends, who came to the house soon after George Fox had been there, had some discourse with him, and he was still and quiet, and weighed things. George Fox returning in the evening, and being admitted, spoke so powerfully and convincingly, that the judge was so far satisfied that it was the truth, that he offered his own house as a meeting-place, and was kind to Friends, on every occasion, to his decease: which was about the year 1658, being then sixty years of age.

His widow laboured to promote the cause of truth, applied frequently to the king, on behalf of her suffering friends; and visited them in various parts of the nation, sometimes accompanied by one of her daughters. About the year 1661, she was sent for from her own house, and carried to Lancaster castle, because she would not swear; was premunired, and sentenced to forfeit her real and personal estate to the king, and to be imprisoned during life; but after having been in prison about four years, she was set at liberty by order of the king and council. Soon after this she was married to George Fox, but was again, on the old premunire, taken from her house, and carried to prison; where she continued another year in a sickly state, till her husband obtained her discharge under the great seal. All these sufferings she endured with much patience, and neither fainted nor murmured; but was kept so cheerful and easy under them, that her enemies were amazed to see it; and several of them that persecuted her came to nothing; whilst, as she denied and despised the glory of this fading world, for Christ's and truth's sake, God gave her honour and a name among the righteous; and qualifications, many ways, for considerable service in the church. In this she shone as a morning star, being filled with real wisdom and understanding, for the propagation of truth and righteousness; of a clear discerning of spirits, and the working of the enemy to draw from the life and power of truth, into a liberty that genders to bondage, and to separation and breach of unity among friends; appearing firm and zealous against the same. She was fervent and living in her ministry, and in supplication and prayers to Almighty God; to the edifying and building up many in that most precious truth, which gives victory over the world.

She was not only a great and exemplary sufferer for truth, but a visitor and a sympathizer with the faithful in their sufferings; zealously interceding for their relief, with such as were in authority; as being afflicted with the afflicted, and mourning with those that mourned.

She never spared herself in her manifold labours on truth's account, both in her ministry abroad, in most places in this nation, and other services; but approved herself as one that needed not to be ashamed of her work and service for the Lord, his truth, and people; which she performed with all sincerity, while God was pleased to give her strength and ability.

She was preserved in a good understanding to the last; and in the time of her sickness, she was in a sweet frame of spirit. She uttered many heavenly expressions near her conclusion in this world, some of which are as follows:

'Come, come,' said she, 'let us join to the Lord, and be of one spirit; let us join to the Eternal God, and be of one spirit.' A friend visiting her, who had been acquainted with her upwards of forty-five years, she said, 'The Lord is with me, and I am with the Lord, and in him only will I trust, and commit all to the divine providence of the Lord, both concerning my children and grandchildren, and all things they do enjoy from him, both in spirituals and temporals; who is the God of all the mercies and blessings to his people throughout all generations; to him be glorious praises for ever, amen.' At another time she said, 'Oh, my sweet Lord, into thy holy bosom do I commit myself freely, and not desiring to live in this troublesome, painful world, it is all nothing to me, for my maker is my husband.' At another time she said, 'Come, Lord, I am freely given up to thy will.' Again she said, 'I freely forgive all people upon the face of the whole earth, for any wrong done to me; as freely as I desire to be forgiven:' and seeing those about her sorrowful, she said, 'Be quiet, for I am as comfortable in my spirit as ever I was.' A little before she departed, she said to one by her, 'Rachel, take me in thy arms: I am in peace.'

She departed this life at Swarthmore-hall, the 23d day of the Second month, 1702, being near the eighty-eighth year of her age; and was buried in the burial-ground at Simbrooke, belonging to Swarthmore, the 27th of the same, attended by many Friends and others.

Her writings were collected and printed in an octavo volume, from which the foregoing account is extracted.

LUCY CHOPPING, of Stebbing, in Essex, whose maiden name was Wait, was born in Worcestershire, in the early part of the last century. She was soberly and religiously educated by her grandmother, who lived to a great age, being in her one hundred and fourteenth year when she died; and who often informed her of the hard sufferings many of the family had gone through, on account of religion, in Queen Mary's days. After her death, she was left under the care of an uncle, who was a Puritan, and had a tender care over her. He gave her good advice, and cautioned her to shun idle company, never to learn to dance or to read ballads, nor to wear lace nor ribbons on her clothes; but to go and hear the best men that preached at that time: so that she acknowledged that it was good for her that she had been so warned.

She came to London in the time of the civil wars, and lived in a religious family, who wanted her to learn to sing psalms, which she was not easy to do, but returned back into

Worcestershire. About this period, many were going to New England, and thinking that all who went thither at that time, to enjoy the liberty of their consciences, were good and religious people, and that it must be pleasant living in such a land, where all were such, she inclined also to go thither; but, communicating her mind to Vavasor Powel, an eminent preacher among the Puritans in that day, he told her that the word was nigh in her heart and mouth, that she might hear it and obey it; and that she need not go beyond the seas on that account. This stopped her journey; but she still earnestly sought to hear those preachers who were accounted gifted men. She went to hear Humphrey Smith in particular, who was esteemed to have an excellent gift, and did not think it lawful to take money for preaching. He, being once at a meeting, sat a great while in silence; at which the congregation wondering, he stood up, and told them that he had formerly spoken what was opened to him, 'But now,' says he, 'my mouth is stopped, and I believe, whenever it may please the Lord to open it again, it will be more to his glory than ever it hath been.' This made her very desirous to know where he went; but soon after it pleased the Lord to send one of his servants, called a Quaker, by whom Humphrey Smith was more fully convinced, as she also was herself.

In a little time it pleased the Lord to qualify him for the ministry; and he travelled abroad, in the service thereof, into the west of England, where he, with many more, was imprisoned. She then found it her concern to visit them in prison; and went from one prison to another, doing them service in mending and making their clothes; and many of them being far from their homes, she went and visited their families. She spent many years in this service, which was very acceptable to those that could not have liberty to see their families themselves; and great was her labour of love, in that she did it freely, although she travelled on foot: besides which, she frequently attended the yearly meeting, when established.

Having, at the request of her friend Humphrey Smith, conducted his son into Essex, where he was bound an apprentice, she often went to visit him. At length she became the wife of John Chopping, of Stebbing; with whom she lived but about two years, and survived him about twenty-eight years. She was a mother in Israel, of a good understanding, a visitor of the afflicted in body or mind, and often had a word of advice and comfort to them. She particularly exhorted the young convinced to faithfulness; and when any were grown careless, she was tender in advice and exhortation; and often to so good effect, as to reach the witness in them.

About two weeks before her death, she walked six miles to a meeting, in order to visit a woman, who, being overcome with the cares of the world, neglected meetings: whom she warned of her danger, and who became more careful afterwards in her duty.

The day following she was taken ill, when she expressed herself thus: 'I cannot say that what I feared is come upon me, but that which I have long desired; for I am very ill, and do think it will be my end. But it will be well with me. I shall go to my mansion which is prepared for me and all the faithful followers of the Lamb; and I have nothing to do but to die. The Lord has been with me, even as with Jacob, and I knew it not; and, blessed be his name, he has been with me, and made known the way of life and salvation to me, and preserved me through many hard exercises and deep afflictions, and sorrowful travails in spirit. He hath been with me through my pilgrimage, and kept me safe through many long journeys, in which I have walked many hundred miles, to serve my friends in the truth, and for the truth's sake, and mostly alone; and the Lord preserved me, so that none were suffered to do me any harm: for which I have often been humbly thankful, and now I feel peace, and shall in a little time rest with Him in everlasting joy and peace.'

At another time she said, 'It is good to have nothing to do but to die: for now I feel it hard to bear the pain and sickness of this body.' She often expressed her concern for the churches, that good order might be kept up; and for the poor, for whom she always had a great care. A woman in high station visiting her, she advised her to prepare for such a time; telling her she had peace, and that was of more worth than all the pleasures of the world; and advised her to mind the gift and manifestation of the Spirit in her, which would lead her also into the way of life and peace. The woman, filled with admiration, said she never heard the like, that any person could have such a satisfaction and victory over death, for that there was no terror or fear of death in her; to whom Lucy Chopping answered, 'Perfect love casteth out fear. I have loved the Lord with all my heart, and served him with all my strength, and I have peace: the Lord is with me, and it will be a glorious change.' Again she said, 'The Lord has been with me in many hard afflictions, and given me hope, which hath been as "an anchor to my soul." I can say with David, "He hath plucked my feet out of the mire and clay, and set them upon a rock," and I shall not be moved.'

Growing weak, and having many sick fainting fits the day before she died, her niece, Elizabeth Wyatt, offered her something to take; she answered, 'I want nothing; the Lord is with me, and his Spirit comforts me. I have bread to eat which the world knows nothing of, and the wine of his kingdom refresheth me, and I desire no more of this. Do not endeavour to keep me here, for to die will be my gain, and though my body grows weak, my inward man grows strong. Speaking to her niece, and giving her good advice, she said, 'The Lord is with me, and I have an earnest of that which I shall in a little time launch into the full enjoyment of.'

She departed this life, being sensible to the last, the 6th of the Sixth month, 1705, and was buried in Friends' burial-ground at Stebbing.

THOMAS WILSON, of Ireland, was born in Cumberland, and educated in the profession of the church of England. While a youth he had great hungerings after righteousness, and the true knowledge of the living God, and his son Jesus Christ; and went with great diligence to hear the priests, and carefully minded what was spoken. If he heard of a priest that was noted for a good man, and preached two sermons in one day, he would go sometimes eight miles on foot, after hearing the morning sermon, to hear another in the afternoon; and the more he sought to hear, the more his hunger and thirst increased, so that he was sensible of great poverty of spirit. In the time of singing psalms a thoughtfulness came over him, that men should be made holy before they could rightly sing to the praise and glory of God; and he was stopped from singing them, through a godly sorrow which was in his heart, with secret cries and humble prayers to the living God of heaven and earth, for the knowledge of the way of salvation. In this state he travailed in great godly sorrow, weary of the heavy load of sin, as also of the doctrines and worships of men's making; and many texts of Scripture being opened to his understanding, he began to see that which was not of faith was sin, even in points of worship, and the pretended service to the great God.

Being thus made sensible that too many of the doctrines of the church, in which he was educated, were precepts of men's making; and that "God is a spirit, and they that worship him, must worship him in spirit and truth;" this worship he greatly longed to know; and conversed with priests thereon, but they could not direct him where to find it. But, after long travail of spirit, and great concern of soul, the Lord was graciously pleased to make him sensible, that what was to be known of God, was manifested in man. About this time he went into an evening meeting of the people called Quakers, with strong desires in his mind to the Lord, that if it was the true way of salvation which this people preached, he might have some inward feeling and testimony thereof in his own heart. After sitting some time in silence, a friend began to speak, directing and exhorting to an inward waiting upon the Lord in faith, to receive power from him over every unclean thought, by which heavenly power they might glorify and praise the name of the Lord, through the ability of his own free gift. This Thomas understood to be the holy word of grace, which the apostle preached, and to which he turned the minds of the people; and he felt his soul much in love therewith, saying in his heart, 'This is what I greatly wanted.' The Lord's power arose in the meeting to the breaking and tendering of his heart; and inward cries were raised in him to this effect, "O Lord, create in me a clean heart."

Now his heart was opened, and he felt the Lord's fierce anger because of sin; and he was made willing to love, and dwell under, his righteous judgments, being truly convinced that was the way to come to the mercy-seat. He saw he was to cease from the doctrines of men, and mind the gift which was in him, and sit down among friends in their silent meetings, to wait on the Lord in retiredness of mind, for his heavenly teachings and holy leadings; in the performance of which inward, divine, and heavenly worship, he, with many more young people, was convinced of the inward work of God, and turned to the Lord with all their hearts. Those who attended this meeting from time to time, became very tender and heavenly-minded, and in great love with each other: the heart-tendering power of the Lord being renewedly felt, inwardly revealed, when no words were spoken.

This our friend being thus raised up and qualified, came

forth in a public testimony; and was concerned not only to travel and visit many parts of this nation, Scotland, and Ireland, but also America; which he visited twice, in company with James Dickinson. He left there many seals of his ministry, which was sound, plain, and powerful, frequently attended with a heavenly sweetness, as he was divinely enabled to open the mysteries of life and salvation. He was also richly endowed with the spirit of supplication, in which he was drawn forth in great tenderness and fervency of spirit; not only on behalf of Christ's church and people, but for mankind in general.

After more than forty years' labour, his natural strength decayed; and towards the close of his time, having not long been returned from a journey of ten months through many parts of England, he expressed himself thus, 'Now I rejoice in that I have served the Lord in my day; and as I have laboured to promote the truth in my generation, I feel great peace from the Lord flowing in my soul, and am thankful that I have been made willing to serve him.'

He was taken ill about the Eleventh month, 1724, and continued weakly for several months; in which time he uttered many weighty expressions, and at several times was concerned in fervent prayer for the young and rising generation, that they might be faithful witnesses for the truth in their day. He expressed his concern that Friends should live agreeably to the doctrine of Christ; and that the good order established among us might be kept up and maintained, and that all differences and disorders might be kept out of the church. Among many weighty expressions, he said, 'The Lord's goodness fills my heart, which gives me an evidence and assurance of my everlasting peace in his kingdom, with my ancient friends, who are gone before me, with whom I had sweet comfort in the work of the gospel.' Notwithstanding our friend had been eminently attended with the power of truth, and had great service several ways, he would speak very humbly of himself, ascribing all the honour to the

Lord; saying, 'Although the Lord hath made me serviceable in his hand, what I trust in is the mercy of God in Jesus Christ;' and added, some friends sitting by him, 'The Lord visited me in my young years, and I felt his power, which hath been with me all along, and I am assured he will never leave me, which is my comfort.'

Near his conclusion, he often desired that he might be favoured with an easy passage, which was granted, and he was preserved sensible to the last: passing away without sigh or groan, as if he was going to sleep, the 20th of the Third month, 1725. His remains were buried the 22nd of the same; aged about seventy-one years. He was a minister about forty-five years.

ANDREW JAFFRAY, of Kingswell, in Scotland, was born in 1650; being the son of Alexander Jaffray, of the same place: for an account of whom, see Vol. I., page 159.

He gave his son, Andrew Jaffray, a liberal education; who, becoming convinced of truth about the time of his father's death, quickly came to esteem learning but as dross and dung, compared with the learning and knowing Jesus Christ, in his inward and spiritual appearance in the heart, and being thereby purified from dead works, to serve the living God; of which learning he soon became a zealous, faithful, and able teacher.

He cheerfully underwent great sufferings on account of truth; and was a constant fellow-prisoner in Aberdeen, with David and Robert Barclay, Alexander Forbes, Patrick Livingstone, and other early Friends, in the long sufferings they underwent for the truth. He was cheerfully given up to any service to which he found himself called; particularly going through the streets of Aberdeen, and to many places of worship therein, exhorting the people to repentance; and it was particularly remarked, that in the same streets where he had been reproachfully pointed at for the truth, and his testimony's sake; he, in his latter years, was looked upon with affection, and blessed as he passed along. He went through many deep, bitter, and severe exercises of spirit, by being made the butt and mock of people, because of his zeal against a man-made ministry; yet the Lord supported him through all, and he was preserved to bear a clear and faithful testimony for the truth in the meeting of Friends in Aberdeen, the very day before his illness.

He was confined to his bed for months, under the infirmity of old age, weakness, and distress of body. In the course of his illness, he bore a very clear testimony to the goodness of God to his soul, and mentioned the satisfactory remembrance he had, of his being separated for the work of the gospel; and that he had dedicated himself for that service, ever since his being called thereto.

He departed this life the 1st of the Second month, O. S. 1726, aged seventy-six years, and was buried in his own burying-ground at Kingswell the 4th of the same.

THOMAS THOMPSON, of Saffron Walden, in Essex, was born in a small village in the East Riding of Yorkshire, and received a dispensation of the gospel ministry in or about the twenty-fourth year of his age; which, as he received freely, he preached freely, travelling in England, Ireland, and twice in America, visiting Friends and labouring for the promotion of truth.

In the year 1727, it pleased the Lord to visit him with a consumption, under which, after a time, he was kept in patience and resignation to the divine will. A few days before he died, being under great weakness of body, he was concerned to supplicate the Lord on account of his church and people; which prayer was delivered under a tender sense and frame of spirit, and affected those present.

A few minutes after, he expressed himself in this manner, 'To those who inquire what end I make, let them know, I die in the faith that saves and triumphs over death and hell; through the mercy and goodness of God, finding no cloud in my way; but perfect peace with God through Jesus Christ, the presence of whose glory is with me; and I feel the comforts of his spirit attending me every day. I never felt the like comfort before. I may say, as was said of old, "Comfort ye, comfort ye my people, saith your God: speak ye comfortably to Jerusalem, say to her, her warfare is accomplished, her iniquity is pardoned, for she hath received double at the hand of the Lord for all her sins." Thus hath God dealt with my spirit; by his judgments refined me, and prepared me for an habitation with himself, in his heavenly kingdom; so that I may say, as David did, "Although I walk through the valley of the shadow of death, I fear no evil, because thou art with me; thy rod and thy staff comfort me. Thou preparest a table for me in the presence of mine enemies; thou anointest mine head with oil. My cup runs over" with praises to thy glorious name, thou glorious Fountain of brightness, who took notice of me in my childhood, in thy love and mercy. Thou compassest me about with the bands of thy salvation, and thou hast made me thine forever: O, glory, glory, to thy divine name and power, thou infinite Fountain of light and immortality. My soul blesses thee, and my spirit magnifies thy name, in the sense of that eternal word and wisdom that was in thy bosom from eternity, that intellectual light which shone everlastingly, and will be a glory and crown to all them that believe and walk therein: and in the faith of that I live and die.'

At another time, being under the sense and power of truth, he said, 'Glory, glory, to the excellent name of the Lord; the sweetness of his love can never be told; the rays of his beauty shine upon me; I am filled with the power of his love; glory be to his name for ever!'

A little before his departure he said, 'I have fought a good fight; I have finished my course. Henceforth is laid up for me a crown of glory, which God the righteous judge shall give me at the last day; and not to me only, but to all those who love his appearance.' And, just as he was dying, he said, 'Rejoice with me, rejoice!' and so departed this life in peace, the 30th of the Ninth month, November, O. S., and was buried the 3d of the Tenth month, 1727.

GEORGE CHALKLEY, son of Thomas Chalkley, of Frankford, in Pennsylvania, was a lad much inclined to read the Holy Scriptures, and other good books; and was obliging and dutiful to his parents, and ready and willing to do any service he could for his friends; diligent in going to religious meetings, and an entire lover of religious people. He was, in an uncommon degree, affectionately concerned for his mother, doing whatever he could freely and cheerfully to serve her; and told her not to do divers things which he thought too much for her; saying, 'Mother, let me do it, for, if I was a man, thou shouldest not do any thing at all, meaning as to labour. And she, affected with his filial love and care for and towards her in her husband's absence, would sometimes turn about and weep.

If this dear and tender youth, when reading, met with any thing which affected him, either in the Scriptures or other good writings, he would write it down, and get it by heart. One passage, which he had written down, and got by heart, much affected his father. It was the 15th verse of the lvii. chap. of Isaiah, viz.: "For thus saith the High and LoftyOne, that inhabiteth eternity, whose name is Holy, I dwell in the high and holy place, with him also who is of a contrite and humble spirit: to revive the spirit of the humble, and to revive the heart of the contrite ones."

It was usual for his father to advise his mother, not to set her affections too much upon him, thinking he was too ripe for heaven to stay long on earth. He was taken sick the 5th of the Eighth month, 1733; and in his sickness behaved himself more like a wise man than a child of ten years of age. His father was in another part of the world, and he would gladly have seen him; but he said that he should never see him more, and desired his mother to give his dear love to him, and to tell him that he was gone to his heavenly Father. He was very fervent in prayer, in the time of his sickness; and entreated that God would preserve his people all the world over.

One time, when in great pain, he prayed thus: 'Sweet Jesus, blessed Jesus, give me patience to bear my misery and pain, for my misery is greater than I can well bear. O come, sweet Jesus, why art thou so long in coming? I had rather be with thee, than in the finest places in the world.' One day he said, 'My misery and pain are very great; but what would it be, if the wrath of God was in my soul.'

His heart was full of love to his relations, acquaintance, and friends, who came to see him in his illness; and he took his last leave with a tenderness and sweetness which greatly affected many.

He departed this life the 13th of the Eighth month, 1733, and his remains were carried to the Bank meeting-house in Philadelphia, and buried from thence the First-day following, being accompanied by many friends and others. He was ten years and seven days of age when he died; and, as he was greatly beloved for the sweetness of his disposition, he was greatly lamented by many who were acquainted with him.

His father returning home, and meeting with this trial, said, 'Although it was a great and sore exercise and deep affliction to me to lose this promising youth, my only son, yet it was made tolerably easy to me; for he departed this life in much brightness and sweetness, more like an old Christian than a youth of ten years of age.'

JAMES DICKINSON, of Cumberland, was born in the year 1659. His parents, Matthew and Jane Dickinson, being convinced of the principles of Friends, educated him in the way of truth; and the Lord, by his power, reached him when very young, and often his heart was broken into true tenderness, so that many times he had a secret delight in being inwardly retired to feel the virtue thereof, which was the cause of true gladness to his parents, whose delight was in the enjoyment of the Lord's presence. They were good examples to their children, educating them in the way of righteousness, often exhorting them, with tears, to fear the Lord.

The following account of the first moving of the divine principle, or spirit of Christ, on his mind, is extracted from a short journal of his, long since out of print. 'My father,' says he, 'died when I was ten years old, and I not taking the counsel of the wise man, viz., to take counsel of my father, which was, to mind the light or measure of grace given unto me, my mind was drawn out after the vain plays, customs, and will-worships of the world, in which state I continued some time. Yet the Lord, by his power, did many times reach my heart, and, by the Spirit of his dear Son, the Lord Jesus Christ, reproved me for my vain conversation; many times calling me to return to him, from whom I had gone astray; whose power, in some measure, I had felt to tender my heart. But I, not minding to turn at the reproofs of wisdom, but going on in rebellion against his blessed spirit, ran, as with a multitude to do evil, into wildness and vanity, until the Lord in his mercy did visit my soul by his righteous judgments, and thereby turned my mirth into mourning, and joy into heaviness, and deep sorrow was my portion.

'Being warned to repent and turn to the Lord, a godly sorrow was begun, which I experienced to lead to true repentance. Then my familiars became my enemies, and I was a taunt and a by-word to them; yet still, as I loved the Lord in the way of his judgments, and waited upon him to know the way of them, I found the Lord to give victory, and saw my greatest enemies were those of my own house; and the war was begun there. As I was careful to keep in the light, I came to see the kingdom rent from Saul, and given to David, though there was a long war between the house of Saul and the house of David, yet as I kept my eye unto the Lord, I came to see the house of Saul grow weaker and weaker, and the house of David to grow stronger and stronger. Yet many were the days of mourning and nights of sorrow my soul went under, that I may say it was the day of Jacob's trouble, and of Joseph's affliction. Many times I cried unto the Lord, O that I had a cave in the ground, that I might mourn out my days, that in the end I might find peace with thee. In those deep afflictions and exercises, the Lord was very near, and often mixed mercy with judgment, so that my soul began to delight to wait upon him in the way of his judgment, seeing it was by the spirit of judgment and burning that the filth of the daughter of Sion must be done away. As I kept here, I felt the love of God to increase in my soul, which deeply affected me, and a hunger was increased in my heart, after the enjoyment of the Lord's power, and the operation of it, whether it was in mercy or judgment. So I knew my faith to be increased in the sufficiency of the power of God; then I saw "it was good for me that I was afflicted, for before I was afflicted I went astray." I found, as David said, "his rod and his staff comforted me;" and the Lord did often overcome me with his love.'

When about eighteen years of age, he was first concerned to bear a public testimony. 'Great,' says he, 'then was my exercise. Seeing the work to be very weighty, and looking at my own weakness, made me unwilling to give up to answer the Lord's requirings. But the Lord, in his great love filled my soul with the emanations of his power, which strengthened and encouraged me, that I was made willing to give up in obedience to his divine will. In great dread and fear I stood up and bore a public testimony in our own meeting, warning Friends to be more inward and faithful to the manifestations of his light and grace in their souls; and, after I had answered the requirings of the Lord, I found great peace flowing in my soul; which so prevailed upon my spirit, that I was bowed down under the sense of the Lord's goodness, and the weight of the exercise which I had felt upon me was removed.'

He visited Ireland twelve times, and was three times in America, once in Holland and Germany, and laboured much in his native country of England, and many were convinced through his ministry. He was very tender to the youth, a nursing father to the least, and full of charity to all rightly anointed, yet not hasty to join with forward spirits. He was also careful not to join in party, but was greatly concerned for the promotion of truth.

About a year before his death he was struck with the palsy, which deprived him of the use of one side, and his speech was in a great measure taken from him; yet he seemed to surmount the decays of expiring nature, and, in a sweet and heavenly disposition of mind, intimated his day's work was done, and that God whom he had served was still with him, and that he had the evidence of peace and future felicity sealed upon his soul, and was only waiting to be removed; but was fully resigned unto the Lord, to wait his time.

To a friend who visited him, he expressed himself to the following purport: 'I have served the Lord and his truth in my generation, and now I feel the blessed reward thereof. The accuser of the brethren is cast down as to me, and my peace with God is sealed for ever.'

He departed this life on the 6th of the Third month, O. S., 1741, and was buried the 8th of the same, aged about eighty-three, and a minister sixty-five years.

BENJAMIN HOLME was born of parents professing with Friends about the year 1682, who, as he grew up, took him along with them to meeting. Nevertheless he exceeded many in wildness and vanity, until it pleased the Lord so to touch his heart with his divine power and love, as to bring him under a concern in his very tender age, for peace with God. His exercise was great at that time, and he walked often alone in fields and secret places, seeking the Lord, that he might not miss peace to his soul. As the love of God prevailed in him, his love to God and his people increased, and he grew zealous for meetings, and was often bowed and tendered in them. His mouth was opened in supplication to the Lord, and in testimony, when about fourteen years of age; and, growing in the ministry, he travelled abroad to visit Friends when about seventeen years of age, accompanied by Joseph Kirkbride of Pennsylvania, and Leonard Fell.

He was a man devoted to the service of truth, and laboured almost incessantly in the work of the ministry, in this nation, Wales, and Scotland; was several times in Ireland, twice in Holland, and some parts of Germany; and in the year 1715, he took shipping for America, and visited Friends on that continent, and most of the West India Islands. In the course of his labours and travels, several were convinced by him; many, through his innocent carriage, as well as by his ministry, which was delivered in that plainness which becomes the simplicity and purity of truth, have been reached and brought to judge and speak favourably of Friends, and their Christian principles. In the latter part of his time, he was concerned to hold meetings in many places where no meetings of Friends had been.

His ministry was adorned with good conduct. He sought the good of all with sincerity, and was engaged to speak his mind with prudence and caution, both to old and young, and had a persuasive faculty in his exhortations beyond many, and was strictly careful not to divulge what he saw amiss in any, to others. He envied not, nor detracted from any; but lived in universal love and goodwill to all. It was his daily food to be found doing the will of God.

In his way to Haverfordwest, to the yearly meeting for Wales, being in a poor state of health, he was prevailed on to stay at Paul Bevan's, at Swansea, and attended two meetings there on a First-day; but being soon after taken with a fit of the ague, he was confined to bed, and proper care was taken of him. He appeared to be quite easy and resigned, and told Friends there in his illness, that it was a fine thing to make a right use of time, both with respect to this life and that which is to come; and often desired that Friends in that place might be good examples to their neighbours; that they might be brought from their forms of will-worship to the divine counsel, and then all would be safe and well.

He reached Swansea the 8th of the Second month, 1749, and died the 14th of the same, aged about sixty-seven years, and a minister about fifty-three years; and as he lived so he died, a pattern of meekness and innocency.

BENJAMIN HOLME'S Last Legacy, or Serious Advice; recommended by him, a little before his decease, to the youth under the tuition of several schoolmasters.

'Dear Children,

'I hereby tenderly salute you, with desires that as you advance in years, you may in grace, that so like good Samuel, you may grow in favour with the Lord and good men. Virtuous and pious living will not only very much recommend you to the better part of mankind, but it is the way to obtain the blessing which maketh rich, and adds no sorrow with it. Live in love and peace; speak lovingly and meekly one to another; and if you behave well, you will be a credit to your master and to your friends. Make good use of your time; strive to excel in learning, and in the best things. If you live in the fear of God, and take good ways, and it should please the Lord to spare you, you may be serviceable in your generation. The holy man of God, viz., John, told the elect lady, whom he wrote to, that he rejoiced greatly, that he found her children walking in the truth; and to be sure it would be a great comfort to many of your parents and good friends, to have you take good ways. If any of you should be put out to trades, if you are honest, peaceable, and careful to speak the truth, and to make a good improvement of your time while you are at school, so that the master can give a good account of you, his good recommendation may be a means to help several of you to good places.

'Dear children, "remember your Creator in the days of your youth," and consider the obligations which you are under to serve him, who is the author of your being, and the fountain from whom all the good things which you receive come. As the wise man saith, that "God hates a proud look, a lying tongue, and him that soweth discord amongst brethren," be sure that you hate to tell an untruth, and have a care of being proud; because we read that "Pride goes before destruction, and an haughty spirit before a fall." I would have you to guard against a quarrelsome spirit and temper, and if at any time any ill-natured people should call any of you unbecoming names, be sure that you do not give one harsh or unhandsome word for another, nor render reviling for reviling; but remember that the wise man saith, that "A soft answer turneth away wrath;" neither give flattering titles to any. Remember Elihu said, that "he accepted no man's person, nor gave flattering titles to man, lest his Maker should soon take him away." Now, although I advise you not to give these compliments, which may tend to gratify a vain and proud mind; yet I would have you learn to speak handsomely and becomingly to every body, even to the poorest servant or apprentice about any of your parents' houses, or to the beggar who asketh alms.

'Seek and pray, like good Jabez, that the Lord may keep you from evil; and we read that God granted him that which he requested. The fear of the Lord is a great blessing to all them that live in it. It is a fountain of life, which preserves from the snares of death; and if you would not be drawn into any evil or hurtful things, I would have you be very choice of your company, which often has great influence upon youth. Remember the wise man's counsel, "My son," saith he, "if sinners entice thee, consent thou not." Many good-natured people have been ruined, to a great degree, through hearkening to the enticements of sinners; but they are wise, who learn by others' harms to beware. Love to read the Holy Scriptures, and other good books, avoiding such as are pernicious, which may tend to corrupt, or make bad impressions on your tender minds. I very much desire that you may be prevailed upon by the power of divine life, to bear the yoke and cross of Christ in your youth; that in the end you may witness that peace which the world can neither give nor take away. That you may make a right and good application of this friendly admonition, and have the benefit hereby intended, is, with true love to you, the sincere wish of

'Your Friend,

'BENJAMIN HOLME.'

JOHN HAYWARD, of London, was born of reputable parents, not of our Society, who gave him an education suitable to the station in which they intended to place him. When of proper age, he was put under the care and tuition of an eminent surgeon. During his apprenticeship, he was favoured with a powerful visitation of divine love, which eclipsed the prospects of temporal greatness; and things permanent, objects of an higher nature, were presented to his view; and to seek after durable riches and righteousness, became the principal bent of his mind. Being thus in an earnest pursuit of substantial good, an external show of religion, in an observation of ceremonies, afforded him no solid peace; nor could he reap any benefit under a ministry not attended with divine power and authority. His understanding being opened, his inward conflicts and exercises increased, and the language of his disconsolate soul was, 'Can ye tell me where the beloved of my soul feeds his flock, or where the fold of true rest is to be found?'

About the twentieth year of his age, he was made willing to take up the cross, and sit down in silence among a despised people, to worship the Father in spirit and truth. He was effectually convinced, and having attained to some degree of establishment in religion, it became his duty to confess Christ before men, and to express the religious sentiments he had embraced, by the reformation of his whole conduct and demeanour.

Such a visible alteration caused him to become a wonder to his acquaintance; but his conversation being very circumspect and truly religious, accompanied with great modesty and affability, their prejudices and misapprehensions were removed, and upon all occasions they manifested an affectionate regard for him.

Having lived near the divine principle, or Spirit of truth, and under the forming hand of the Lord, who prepares for service in his church, he appeared in a public testimony about the thirtieth year of his age, which was well received and truly acceptable. He did not find it his concern to travel much abroad, yet visited some of the western and southern counties, and some neighbouring ones, to his own satisfaction, and the comfort and edification of Friends.

He early declined the profession of surgery, and with great caution entered into the concerns of trade, keeping a watchful care that he should not dishonour his high and holy profession. But a few years before his death he removed to Plaistow, in Essex, where he lived, not to himself alone, but to his friends and the public, seldom omitting proper opportunities of promoting love and good works by precept and example.

He gradually declined, without much pain, and at times he was cheerful and easy, discovering to those who were about him a mind occupied about a better world; occasionally mentioning, yet with due fear of presuming, that though nature might shrink, and be apprehensive for the dissolution of the frame, yet he felt nothing beyond it to give him pain, but a steady hope of the reward of, "Well done."

A few days before his decease, a friend visiting him, he signified to him, that all was easy, and that his day was nearly over.

He departed this life the 20th of the Second month, 1763, and was buried at Bunhill Fields the 27th of the same, aged eighty years. A minister about fifty years.

He left a considerable part of his substance to trustees, as a permanent fund, the interest whereof to be given to poor Friends, at their discretion; which proves a comfortable relief to a considerable number.

ELLIS LEWIS, an ancient Friend of Tyddin y Garreg, near Dolgelly, in Merionethshire, North Wales, was born of parents professing the truth as held by the people called Quakers; and in his very tender years was favoured with a visitation of divine love, which had such an effect on him that he appeared in a public testimony, about the thirteenth year of his age, in the English language, to which he was not accustomed, in a remarkable and tendering manner.

He continued faithful, and travelled in the work of the ministry divers times, through the principality, and likewise in divers parts of England, adorning the doctrine he preached by an innocent life and conversation, and well esteemed by Friends in many parts where he came.

A few years before his death, the infirmities of age rendered him incapable of travelling; yet he retained a lively sense of truth, and love to his brethren; having that ornament of a Christian mind, a meek and quiet spirit. Being patiently resigned to the divine will, he laid down his head in peace, the 23d of the Eleventh month, 1764, and was buried in Friends' burial-ground, at Tyddin y Garreg, the 28th of the same, aged eighty-seven, and a minister seventy-four years.

JOHN GOUGH, son of James Gough, was a young man of a good natural disposition and capacity, well furnished with useful learning; and as he grew up, being favoured with deep religious impressions, he sought after and attained best wisdom, to a degree in general exceeding his age.

On his entrance into active life, a propriety and steadiness of deportment, that might adorn advanced years, attracted the notice and respectful regard of the best Friends who had the opportunity of observing or being acquainted with him.

He was a dutiful son, an affectionate brother, an exemplary pattern of plainness, sobriety, and circumspection of life, giving evident indications he was early acquainted with the grace and truth which came by Jesus Christ.

He was, for a season, an assistant to his father in his school, but meeting with an opportunity of engaging with a Friend of London as a clerk, he removed thither; in which station he conducted himself with fidelity and honour during the short time he continued in it.

Being taken ill of a fever, which terminated his life, he said, a little before his departure, 'I have done all that I had to do, and must now go home.'

He departed this life about the Tenth month, 1769, aged nearly twenty-one, and was buried in Friends' burial-ground, at the Park, Southwark, after a very large and solemn meeting, in which the hearts of many were tendered.

His father, writing concerning him, says, 'Through divine favour and assistance, I freely give him up; thankful for having such a son, who hath left behind him too few like him in pure unmixed goodness, which diligently exerted itself to do well.'

RACHEL MOXHAM, daughter of John and Esther Moxham, of Melksham, in Wiltshire, was of an innocent and mild disposition, but fond of company, so that it appeared needful to her mother to be watchful over her on that account. About the fifteenth year of her age, religious impressions were observed to fix on her mind, so that she became sedate, loved retirement, and was mercifully taught how to wait, and what to wait for. One evening, after a silent opportunity of mental introversion, she said to her mother nearly as follows: 'I have thought it my duty to thank thee for thy care in preventing and restraining me from unsuitable company, which I took hardly. I believe, had I had the liberty I coveted, I should not have known the peace and comfort I now feel in obedience to the principles of truth; but should have gone in the broad way that leadeth to death.'

She continued steadily serious, looking towards the recompense of reward; and a few days before her decease, expressed a desire to attend the quarterly meeting. She accordingly went; and a Friend had there to mention the uncertainty of time, and the comfort of having, in a dying hour, hope towards God. This she took to herself, and said, that evening, her work was nearly finished. The quarterly meeting was on a Second-day; and the Sixth-day morning following she complained of illness. In about two hours after, her parents were so apprehensive of danger, as to be affected with sorrow, which she observing, said, 'Do not grieve for me, but rejoice evermore, and give thanks that I am going to everlasting rest;' then said, 'I hope,' paused a little, and added, 'I am going to everlasting rest and peace.' She expressed to a friend the sense she had of her departure; and hoped the Almighty would be near, and sustain the spirits of her parents under the trial, as he did hers at that time. She settled herself in the bed, and took leave of her friends, under the influence of such a sweet and awful solemnity as much affected the minds of those present, no words being spoken, except her saying, 'Lord receive my spirit.'

Thus she quietly departed, after about eight hours' illness, on the 20th of the Third month, 1772, aged nearly eighteen years, and Friends were favoured with a remarkably solemn meeting at her interment, the 24th, at Melksham aforesaid.

JOHN HASLAM, of Handsworth Woodhouse, in Yorkshire, was of a sober and innocent disposition from his infancy. His parents dying when he was young, the care of his education devolved on Gilbert Heathcote, a physician. Early giving up to a precious visitation from on high, he was prepared for service, and called to the work of the ministry about the 25th year of his age. He was soon drawn forth in the love of the gospel frequently to visit the churches in various parts of this nation. He visited Ireland twice, and Holland once, and paid a general visit to Friends in most of the colonies in America. He was exemplary in a deep inward exercise of spirit, and in patient waiting for the arising of the divine life, as a necessary qualification for service either in ministry or discipline, 'Being,' to use his own words addressed to ministers in an epistle found among his papers, 'a strength to a living, edifying ministry, and a check to that which was forward or floating; either not duly anointed, or not waiting truly for the resurrection of that life which reaches the witness in others, and opens into the treasury, where wisdom to divide the word aright is received.' He had a clear discerning of the opening of the heavenly gift, and was careful to give way to the requirings thereof, and was well accepted therein, yet he was often proved with deep inward poverty; and in imparting something of his experience in that respect to a friend, who remarked it was a safe state, he replied, he knew it to be so, but that it was possible sometimes to be depressed too low for the gift.

He was remarkably endued with patience and resignation in the loss of his wife, and, in some years after, of an only daughter, whom he survived about six years; and though her tender care over him was well supplied, yet, being far advanced in years, his bodily strength and memory gradually declined. He became incapable of attending meetings for about three years before his decease; yet he expressed great satisfaction with the visits of his friends, and appeared to be in a patient, resigned, and innocent frame of mind.

As his natural strength was thus worn out by almost imperceptible degrees, he was divested of this state of mutability, without much appearance of pain, the 4th of the Tenth month, 1773, and interred on the 6th of the same, in Friends' burial-ground at Handsworth Woodhouse, aged eighty-three years, and a minister about fifty-seven years.

SOPHIA HUME was born in South Carolina, and was descended, on her mother's side, from the stock of friends. Her grandfather was William Bayley, formerly a Baptist preacher at Poole, but was early convinced of truth, and became a living, powerful minister; for an account of whom see Vol. I. p. 72. Her grandmother was Mary Fisher, who was one of the first friends that visited New England in the year 1656, and who also, before her marriage with William Bayley, viz., about the year 1660, under a great concern of mind, went to Adrianople, to visit the Great Turk: the particulars of which are related in Sewel's History.

Her mother continued in profession with friends, but marrying out of the Society, this, her daughter, was educated agreeably to her father's mind; and for a considerable time took great delight in the pleasures and delusive amusements of this world. About the thirty-eighth year of her age her judgment was opened to see the vanity and folly of these practices; and she, in measure, forsook them, but was not fully convinced of the principle of truth in her own mind until about the year 1741, when, having Barclay's Apology by her, she looked into it, as she often expressed, to furnish herself with matter for conversation; but in the perusal of it her judgment was convinced of the truth of friends' principles: she joined the Society, and became a steady, exemplary member.

She came afterwards from South Carolina to reside in London, and about the year 1747, a concern came upon her to visit the inhabitants of her native country, from whence she sent the following account in a letter to a friend.

'A concern I had often felt in my soul for the happiness and eternal welfare of my native country revived in my breast; when I was to return and abase myself, by telling what God had done for my soul, and to call them from those things, in which I had often run to an excess of riot with them; and from which I had been, by the great love and powerful hand of God, brought and redeemed. When I arrived in Carolina, I found it my place and duty to keep meetings, with those few that professed with me; and though, at first, the meetings were sometimes interrupted by the rude and uncivil treatment of many, we met pretty quietly, and some of the inhabitants would now and then come and sit with us, to whom my mouth was opened at times in rehearsing what God had done for my soul.'

During her continuance there, she wrote a short account of the dealing of the Lord with her, which was soon after published. From thence she went by land to Philadelphia, a journey of between eight and nine hundred miles; and after her return from America, under a tender concern, she laboured, both by word and writing, to bring people to believe and live under that divine principle, the spirit of truth, which she had found, by happy experience, to be as a fountain of life.

In her private station she adorned the gospel by a life of humility and self-denial, and was zealous against all superfluity, both in dress and furniture. Thus preserved through a course of many years, towards the close of her time she appeared in remarkable tenderness, and, as if she were sensible that her dissolution was approaching, she gave directions, in divers respects, relating to her burial, with much composure.

On the 26th of First month, 1774, she was suddenly taken ill, and, being seized with an apoplexy, in about twelve hours departed this life. After a very large and solemn meeting at Gracechurch-street meeting-house, London, her remains were interred in Friends' burial-ground near Bunhill Fields. She was nearly seventy-three years of age, and about twenty-five years a minister.

ANN CROWLEY, daughter of Thomas Crowley, of Gracechurch-street, London, being seized with illness, which continued for several months, was preserved in much patience, and uttered many expressions which showed the fervency of her mind. At one time she expressed herself thus: 'The pains of death are hard to bear, but I am sensible they are not on me now, but they are near approaching; death is no terror to me. O death, where is thy sting? O grave, where is thy victory? My dear tender mother, it will be a bitter cup; but it is the Lord's preparing, and therefore drink it willingly.' Being removed into the country for the benefit of the air, she expressed herself to the following effect: 'This is hard work; it is indeed hard to bear, but the Lord is with me in these trying moments. I did not think my dissolution was so near, but I am ready, Take me, Father, take me to thyself this evening, if it be thy will, for I long to be with thee in paradise. Though I have endured so many moments of agonizing pain, the Lord has been my support through the whole, and, I doubt not, will continue to be with me to the end. Oh, Father! Father! Father! bow the heavens, and come down; be thou with thy people universally all the world over. Why do ye weep? Weep not for me, but give me up to the Lord, for I am happy; far happier than I can express. I wish every one of you could feel what I feel at this time, for it is beyond expression. Oh, it is like a heaven upon earth; it hath not entered into the heart of man to conceive what good things God hath in store for them that love him.'

To one of her sisters she said, 'Oh! my sister, give up, give up now, in the days of thy youth; for the Lord loves an early sacrifice. Oh, prepare thyself! lest it should please the Lord to cut thee down in the flower of thy youth.'

About two weeks before her departure, she earnestly prayed that it might please the Almighty to take her that night, and expressed herself as follows: 'Thou hast been pleased to give me a taste of thy goodness, and a sight of thy glory, and it is glorious indeed; but, oh, Father! I long to be with thee, that I may enjoy it in a more plentiful manner. The gates of heaven are open to receive me.' She said, 'I have never murmured at what it is the Lord's will I should suffer; but I was content if the pain had been much greater, if it was the will of my heavenly Father. Oh, Lord! I long to be with thee, where my soul shall join the angels and archangels that are in heaven.' She further added, 'It is my desire that you, my tender brothers and sisters, may come to the same experience. I was nearly visited, long before I was laid on this bed of sickness; if I had not been, it would be miserable indeed:' and a little after, 'My spirit was warmed in the renewing of thy love.'

About six days before her close, she sent for her three brothers separately to her bed-side; and, in a most affectionate and tender manner, cautioned them against the gaiety, riches, and grandeur of the world; and exhorted them to walk in the path of virtue, to keep close to divine instructions, and likewise to watch and pray continually: adding, 'I feel it needful, even on my death-bed.' To one of them she said, 'Give up, O give up; remember the fear of the Lord is the beginning of wisdom. Seek thou that wisdom now in the days of thy youth. Step gently along, and keep thy mind low and humble before him.' After lying still a little time, she said, 'Though painful my nights, and wearisome my days, as Samuel Fothergill said, yet I am preserved in resignation and patience.'

Some friends visiting her, she expressed to them, 'My pains of body are great, but my dependence is on the Lord, and my only comfort is in him. I thought from the beginning that I should not get over it; but within these three weeks I have seen clearly I shall not.' She further observed, that she had been visited long before her illness, and had found great uneasiness in wearing things that were gay, and also in speaking in the plural language to one person; and added, that she found it difficult to take up the cross, but when she did, her satisfaction was great. 'Oh! what I feel for those whose minds are involved in the world,' with much more; all importing the happy state of her mind; saying to one friend, 'I am ready, I have nothing to do but die.'

She particularly requested of her father, that after her decease, her body might be buried from Devonshire-house meeting; and desired, that the young folks of that quarter, in particular, might be invited to attend; hoping it might prove a profitable time to them.

The evening preceding her departure, she spoke to one of her sisters to the following effect:—'Gaiety proceeds from pride, and pride is the root of all evil:' and she fervently exhorted against it.

In the night her pains were exceedingly great, and she felt the approach of death; and in the last two hours continued uttering ejaculations. Calling for her mother, on her coming to her she said, 'Farewell:' and expired, the 12th of Second month, 1774, being not quite seventeen years of age.

THOMAS ROYLANCE, of Newton, near Middlewich, in Cheshire; was born of parents professing truth; who, having been weightily concerned for its promotion, and sufferers for its testimony, had a great care of his education; which had a good effect on his mind, as appears by his own account in manuscript, viz., 'I was through divine favour, early inclined to the love of truth, and to seek after it to the best of my understanding, often seeking places to pray, and pour out my soul to the Lord, in beseeching him for wisdom and strength to enable me to persevere in well-pleasing to him. And blessed, magnified, and eternally praised be his holy and most worthy name; he hath many times, in his own time, answered, and caused my cup to overflow in praises to his name, and admiration of his goodness. My soul, being as a well watered garden, hath rejoiced in his love; and, in abasedness of self, hath largely ascribed praises and glory to him, who, with the Son of his love, through the Holy Spirit, is eternally worthy. Amen.

'I early loved good men, and had a desire to go to meetings; so that while I was but very young, if any thing offered to let or hinder my going, I can remember I have wept to go, though four miles distant from us. I can also remember, that in my very young years, I loved to be speaking of good things; and often found it my place to reprove boys that were my companions, and sometimes others, for unsavoury words, or any thing unseemly. The Lord always sufficiently helped me, though it was with persons of greater age and capacity, as to the outward, than myself, when I found my mind engaged to converse with them on religious subjects; and as I grew up, I had great love to truth, and honest, sincere friends; in whose company and good conversation I much delighted.'

He was much given up to the service of truth; and much concerned that the discipline of the church might be managed in a weighty and proper manner. He was an example of plainness, and zealously concerned to warn those who took undue liberties, and was helpful in opening the understandings of many.

About the sixtieth year of his age, he came forth in a few words in the ministry, which was acceptable and edifying. He left a few remarks on that subject, worthy to be preserved.

'Although,' says he, 'there have sometimes been words in my heart, and, as it were, in my mouth, which I do not know but they might have been of ease to myself, and of service to others, had I delivered them; and I have been spoken to by some Friends, both in a private and public capacity, or station, thereon; but was always forbearing and backward that way, and have been afraid of too much forwardness in some, who, I have been and still am afraid, have not edified thereby. [I had] always a fear of, and a dislike to, the noise of the tool, the working of self and the creature, in our meetings, as it was not to be heard in the building of the Lord's house or temple of old. But that ministry which comes with a true flow from the divine spring, having its evidence and authority with it, I still loved, and greatly do love, and the vessel it flows through, for its sake, whether it be in rebukes or consolation, as the Almighty is pleased to give, and the case may require. Whether it may be more or less, it is beautiful; and if rightly received, it is comfortable and edifying.'

He died the 25th of the Second month, 1774, in the

seventy-third year of his age, at his house at Newton, after about two weeks' illness, which he bore with patience; expressing, near his conclusion, that all was well.

AMBROSE WILLIAMS, of Pont-y-pool, in Monmouthshire, was educated in the national way of worship; but, being dissatisfied therewith, and humbly desiring to be rightly directed, he came to a meeting of Friends, in which, though held in silence, his heart was replenished with divine love; and, through the teachings of this divine principle, he came to experience that the work of righteousness is peace; and in a few years had his mouth opened to testify to the sufficiency thereof.

He was a constant attender of meetings for worship and discipline; and a diligent labourer therein on his own account and that of others, that none might live as in ceiled houses, and let the house of the Lord lie waste.

By his exemplary life and conduct, and great love to his friends and neighbours, it may be justly said, that he was "An Israelite indeed, in whom there was no guile."

The First-day before his departure, he attended the morning meeting at Pont-y-moil, though weak in body; and, in a solid, weighty frame of mind, earnestly recommended all to do their day's work in the day time; signifying, that perhaps he might be the first called from works to rewards; that he had nothing lay in his way, but had done his day's work, having set his house in order.

He departed this life the 16th of the Third month, 1774; aged sixty-two, and a minister about thirty-three years; and his body was decently interred the 20th of the same at Pont-y-moil.

HANNAH LUDGATER, of Coggeshall, in Essex, wife of Robert Ludgater, of the same place, was born in Hampshire, and had her education among Friends; but in her early days she left the Society, and frequented other places of worship. In this unsettled state, it pleased the Father of mercies to enlighten her understanding; so that through the powerful operation of his love, she saw wherein she had missed her way, became again united to Friends, and in due time her mouth was opened to tell others what she had felt, and to invite them to come, taste, and see how good the Lord is. In this service she was engaged to travel both before and after her marriage with Robert Ludgater.

She resided for some time in the Isle of Wight, and afterwards, on her first coming to London, lived as housekeeper with a person not in religious profession with Friends; where her innocent and virtuous deportment gained her much esteem, and the Society for her sake. She was an affectionate wife, and much concerned to promote the discipline of the Society among her own sex, and was a true helpmeet to her brethren; of a weighty and discerning spirit, accompanied with diligence in labouring for the advancement of truth; though often pressing through great discouragements arising from bodily infirmities; which frequently rendered her incapable of attending meetings. She suffered great pain of body for the last six months of her time, under which probation her patience and resignation manifested the happy effects of faithful labour in the day of ability. Being steadfast in her dependence on the author of her faith, she had at times access to the fountain of life; under the sensible enjoyment whereof, she said, 'O how I long to be relieved; I have no doubt but I shall be mercifully relieved.' To a friend who visited her, she said, 'I have been in a good degree faithful in our meetings, and have not to charge myself with omitting one journey, when it was made known to be my duty. O how have we gone forth, poor and empty; yet have not lacked! the Supporter hath been near, and richly furnished.'

She departed this life the 28th of the Third month, and was buried at Coggeshall, the 3d of the Fourth month, 1774, aged about sixty-five years.

SARAH MARCH, of Durham, was born in London; and taking heed to the divine light, which shone in her heart, she had to bear testimony thereto, about the year 1753; in which service she laboured faithfully to promote the same principle in others; and gave evident proofs of the efficacy thereof by an exemplary deportment.

A little before her death she wrote the following paper, which she desired might be read in the several meetings in the county, which was done accordingly.

'Dear friends

'Under great weakness of body, my concern remains strong for your growth and prosperity in the blessed truth. In that love which I feel shed abroad in my heart doth my spirit salute you; beseeching you to meet as in the presence of God; in reverence and humility wait upon him, who is indeed the dread of nations; and I trust our God will graciously condescend to overshadow your assemblies with his power, which brings salvation; and to crown them with his blessing, which makes truly rich, and adds no sorrow with it. Let me entreat that no restlessness or impatience may prevail, although the Lord of life and glory should tarry; for he will most certainly arise in his own appointed time, with healing in his wings, for the sake of his own wrestling seed, that are waiting for Israel's consolation. If this be your situation before the Lord in secret, he will reward openly, and you will be enabled to praise God acceptably, and to magnify his great and worthy name; as doth my soul at this season, because I feel the same divine goodness that was my morning light is now my evening song, which makes me rejoice in the Lord; and my joy no man can take from me.'

She departed this life the 29th of the Fifth month, and was buried on the 2d of Sixth month, 1774, in Friends' burial-ground in the city of Durham; in the forty-fifth year of her age, and a minister about twenty years.

SARAH HARRIS, of Chipping Norton, in Oxfordshire, widow of Nicholas Harris, of the same place, was born about the year 1704; but no account is come to hand of her early youth, except that while she was a servant to a Friend at Banbury, in the same county, she was a sober, religious young woman. Through obedience to the principles of truth, she became useful in her day; and was of a gentle, affable, kind, and charitable disposition; a true lover of the religious of all denominations; and one who liberally administered, in proportion to her circumstances, to the poor and afflicted.

About the forty-sixth year of her age, she was concerned to bear testimony to that hand which had supported and preserved her in the various dispensations she had to pass through in life. She discovered a deep humility and sensibility of her own weakness and unfitness, as she thought, to be employed in the important work of the gospel ministry; as she knew and felt it to be an awful undertaking, and not to be performed in the policy, strength, and wisdom of man; but in the power and wisdom of God. Her calm and contented waiting and resignation, before she appeared in meetings, indicated her keeping invariably in remembrance the injunction of her Lord to his disciples, viz., "Tarry ye in the city of Jerusalem until ye be endued with power from on high." This laudable diffidence, Christian circumspection, and resignation of soul, rendered her services very acceptable to such as could taste and feel that the source of her ministry was the spring of life.

In her last illness, it was apparent to divers who visited her, that she had made provision for a blessed eternity; and that a lively feeling of divine refreshment was her support under bodily infirmities and decay. The visit of death was not unexpected, nor was she unprepared to sustain it. A sense of dependence and of gratitude, the foundation of true piety, continued with her to the last; and many comfortable expressions were uttered by her, in the course of her illness.

She often advised against too anxious a care about the business and things of this world; and often desired she might be favoured with patience to bear her affliction.

One day, after lying still some time, she said, "They that wait upon the Lord, shall renew their strength." At another time, to those of her family and friends present, she said, 'I have desired for you now, as well as at many other times, that the blessing of heaven might attend; but there must be a living up to what you know.' At another time she said, 'Let it be the business of your lives to be prepared for such a time as this.' Speaking to a person who made inquiry after her welfare, she said, 'The Lord is my shepherd, I shall not want.'

It being meeting-day, she said, 'Go to meeting all that can; and O that my spirit may be refreshed with yours!' She also advised not to let business hinder from going to week-day meetings.

She signified that when she gave up to speak a few words in meetings, it was in great simplicity and fear; and that she witnessed peace in it, being very careful to wait for divine qualification; and she humbly trusted, and could say in humility and thankfulness, she never was confounded.

She departed this life in great calmness and peace the 22d

of the Sixth month, 1774, and was buried the 30th of the same in Friends' burial-ground at Chipping Norton; aged seventy-one, and a minister twenty-five years.

SAMUEL WARING, of Alton, in Hampshire, was the son of Jeremiah Waring of Witney, in Oxfordshire: for an account of whom, see Vol. I., page 39. Being favoured with the benefit of a religious education, and yielding to the sanctifying operation of truth, the Lord was pleased to prepare and qualify him for his service. He came forth in a public testimony about the 25th year of his age; and being faithful in the exercise of his gift, he grew therein, and became an able minister of the gospel. He was exemplary in his attendance on meetings for worship and discipline; a diligent attender of the yearly meeting in London upwards of fifty years; and though not forward in speaking, yet his retired and awful sitting therein, furnished an edifying example to the attentive observers. At different periods of his life, he visited friends in South Wales, the west of England to the Land's End, all the southern, and divers of the midland and eastern counties in this nation; and some of them several times. In these visits we have cause to believe his service was acceptable; for being humbled into a deep sense of his own weakness and insufficiency, as well as the weight and importance of such services, he was not hasty in moving, but waited for a clear evidence, both as to the concern itself, and also the proper time for engaging therein.

Having the weight of a large family, and a considerable share of business upon him, he was steadily concerned that he might not be overcharged therewith, to the hinderance of his services; and with that view purposely shunned some flattering prospects of gain, desiring nothing more than to provide things honest in the sight of all men, that the ministry of which he had received a part, might not be blamed. Thus having, through the blessing of Providence, made a comfortable, though moderate, provision for a numerous family, he quitted business when in a flourishing state, more than twenty years before his death; spending much of the latter part of his time in reading and retirement. He was much given to hospitality, his heart and house being always open to receive the friends of truth, in whose company he took great delight. After having laboured in word and doctrine for a long series of time, he was, some years before his decease, gathered into humble silence, seldom appearing in public testimony in meetings; but the patient, resigned frame of his mind under this dispensation, and his close inward travail in spirit, made it evident beyond all doubt, that he retained his integrity, love, and zeal, to the end. Conversing with some friends a few weeks before his departure, he with great sweetness intimated, that his peace was sure.

During his last illness, which he bore with remarkable patience and composure, he said repeatedly, that he had no desire either for life or death, but felt his mind resigned to the Lord's will. After meditating some time in silence, one evening he said, 'I have been thinking of faithful Abraham, humble Isaac, and wrestling Jacob. Abraham was called the friend of God, because he was found faithful.' Among other weighty and affecting expressions, he mentioned more than once, that he believed a time of great calamity was coming over the nations, and that afterwards there would be a gathering of the people to the principle of truth, when they would flee to it, as doves to their windows.

The day before he died he took a solemn leave of divers friends who visited him, and the monthly meeting being next day, desired his love might be remembered to friends, saying that he expected he should sit with them no more.

Two of his daughters sitting up with him the last night, and asking how he did, he replied, 'I have fully as much pain as I can well bear; but I have thought the Lord can cut the work short in righteousness; and I hope to bear the portion allotted me with patience.' Soon after he added, 'It is all mercy I receive, through Jesus Christ our Lord. I hope I may say I have endeavoured to do nothing against the truth, and what little I have been enabled to do for the truth, I have done in a degree of sincerity and uprightness.'

He was preserved perfectly sensible to the last, and quietly departed this life, full of days and full of peace, on the 13th of the Second month, 1775, at Alton aforesaid, aged nearly eighty-four, and a minister about fifty-nine years. His corpse was interred in Friends' burial-ground there, the 19th of the same.

RACHEL WILSON, late wife of Isaac Wilson, of Kendal, in Westmoreland, was the daughter of John and Deborah Wilson of the same place, who gave her a religious education. Influenced by their example, and being favoured with the company and conversation of many valuable friends travelling in the work of the ministry, her mind was happily seasoned, and much profited; and being also early favoured with a visitation of divine love, she was enamoured therewith, and weaned from the fallacious pleasures and amusements which captivate too many of our youth.

Thus prizing the privileges she enjoyed, and the dawnings of divine wisdom in her soul, she was much led into solitude and secret retirement before the Lord, only choosing such company and conversation as might be profitable to her; and carefully dwelling under the forming hand, she witnessed a growth in virtue and piety, and became fitted for the work of the ministry, into which she was called about the eighteenth year of her age.

Being faithfully devoted to the service of her Lord and Master, she experienced a growth and increase in heavenly wisdom; and, by the constraining power of divine love, was drawn forth to visit the churches, not only in divers parts of this nation, but also in Ireland, Scotland, and America.

She also laboured much among those not in profession with us, who flocked to hear her testimony in the course of her travels; and was eminently qualified for that service, explaining the way of life and salvation in a manner that reached the witness in the hearts of the hearers, whereby many were brought to an acknowledgment of the truth.

She was remarkably diligent and exemplary in the attendance of our religious meetings, both for worship and discipline; and, when called forth to service, though she had many children and a large family under her care, she did not suffer these to prevent her from pursuing what appeared her manifest duty; but what she found in her hand to do, that she did with her might. She was a loving wife, an affectionate parent, a kind and helpful neighbour, tenderly sympathizing with the afflicted, and frequent in visiting the sick, in which visits she was very serviceable, often administering comfort to the drooping, distressed mind. In which service she found the reward of peace.

In the course of her religious duty she came to London, about the First month, 1775; and on delivering her certificate to the morning meeting, she expressed, in much tenderness, a desire, that after her being engaged in the service of truth from her youth, she might be preserved from those rocks and shoals which some had split upon, and that her sun might go down in brightness.

She entered into her service with great humility, visited most of the meetings in the city, and finding her mind concerned for the inhabitants of Gravesend, having had two meetings with them when she embarked for America, she went again to visit them. She was gladly received, and held two meetings in the town-hall, where, through divine favour, she was helped through her service to her own peace, and the comfort of many present.

After her return she attended several week-day meetings,

in the last of which, at Devonshire House, she was clothed with divine love, in an encouraging testimony to the honest hearted.

The next day, being the 4th of the Second month, she was taken ill, and was confined wholly to her chamber, and mostly to her bed, for six weeks; during which time she was favoured with quietness of mind, expressed her resignation either to live or die, and requested her husband, who attended upon her a great part of the time, that he would tell their children, it was her great desire they might, above every consideration, mind the one thing needful, which having been her care, was her unspeakable consolation in that time of close conflict.

She also in the course of her illness expressed to a friend that she was quite easy, and to some others remarked the necessity of doing what appeared to be our duty, while opportunity was afforded. She said her Master was kind to her, and at times favoured with his presence, which bore up in days of trial, and nights that were wearisome. She was often retired in mind, and remarked to some who attended her, that though no one loved her friends' company more than herself, yet she had now no desire to see them, but was quite resigned, though so far separated from her near connections.

She was a pattern of patience, and always appeared satisfied with those about her, who rendered her any little services. The last words she was heard to say were, 'Good tidings,' which no doubt the summons of death proved to her, as it appeared to have no sting, nor the grave any victory.

She quietly departed this life on the 18th of the Third month, 1775, at the house of Richard Chester, at London; and her remains were interred on the 23d of the same, in Bunhill Fields, after a meeting held at Devonshire House. She was about fifty-four years of age, and thirty-six years a minister.

MARY PRIDEAUX, wife of William Prideaux, of the county of Cornwall, was a pattern of meekness and piety; and as she grew in years she grew in grace and in the knowledge of our Lord Jesus Christ. She had a part of the ministry committed to her, in which she was a faithful steward and a bright example to others, not being forward to appear in ministry, as well knowing that true silence never shames the gospel. But when under the constraining power of truth, her ministry was with the demonstration of the spirit, and with power, greatly to the refreshment and strength of the honest hearted; and when she felt the drawings of truth, she was ready to leave her near connections in life. She visited some parts of the west when her name was Mary Davies, and after her marriage, several times. Not long before the close of her life, she found a concern to visit some of the midland counties, which service seemed near to accomplish her day's work, having soon after her return publicly to declare, happy would it be for all, in the conclusion of their time, to have to say with the apostle, "I have fought the good fight, I have finished my course, I have kept the faith; henceforth is laid up for me the crown of righteousness, which the Lord the righteous judge shall give me at that day; and not to me only, but to all those that love his appearing."

A short time after she was taken ill with a fever, which continued about four weeks; during which she behaved with patience, meekness, and yet with Christian fortitude; and many heavenly expressions dropped from her, at a meeting in her own house. She had to commemorate the goodness of the Lord to all those who put their trust in him, and humbly petitioned that he would be with them to the end; that they who lived in his fear, might die in his favour; requesting his protection in every trying season, with fervent desire that all who were present might know a thorough resignation of will; for the Lord our God requires obedience from all his servants. The same evening she signified that she thought her time was near a conclusion. Some days after she said, 'Humility is a qualification I desire my children may be endued with;' and signified to them her hope, that her advice in times past might be remembered, saying, 'I hope it may be as bread cast on the waters, that may return after many days. I have endeavoured to do my duty by you.'

Her disorder increasing, she desired she might endeavour to bear it; and that those in health would improve their time whilst health and strength were afforded, saying, 'I can do but little now; it would indeed be bad if I had my peace to make with the Lord. I have dedicated my health and strength to his service, according to my ability.' Finding herself growing weaker, she desired that her family might be resigned to the will of Providence, adding that she enjoyed great peace and tranquillity of mind, for which she was thankful; and further added, 'Oh, this is a favour indeed, to enjoy such tranquillity! All seems serene, and the streams of life flow freely; the river seems clear as crystal. Oh, that none may put off repentance till confined to a sick bed!' On seeing one of her daughters, she said, 'Oh! be good, be good, and fear the Lord, my dear child;' and again said, 'Then shall ye know, if you follow on to know the Lord, his going forth to be as the morning: he shall come unto us as the rain, as the latter and former rains upon the earth. Oh! the cunning foxes have holes and lodging-places, but the dear Son of God hath not where to lay his head. Lamentable, indeed, where this is the case!'

The same evening, finding herself in much pain, she expressed, that she felt the mercy of the Lord, who had forgiven all her offences; her omissions and commissions would be remembered no more; and said she found a pardon for all. Being in great agony, she desired that patience might have its perfect work, and often prayed that the Lord would cut the work short in righteousness, but desired that not her will, but His should be done. At another time she expressed herself thus: 'O that I were relieved from this world of peril and difficulty! I have nothing to encounter with but death, and this is no terror to me. O that I were safely arrived in the kingdom of heaven, where I shall be comfortably spoken to by my God!' When the agonies of death were upon her, she said, 'Is this the last fit? O that it was! Lord, dear Lord, come quickly. O death, where is thy sting? O grave, where is thy victory?' adding, 'What love I feel, what love I feel; my love is to all universally in the Lord.'

She quietly departed this life the 16th of the Sixth month, 1775; aged about fifty-six, and a minister thirty-four years.

JOSEPH OXLEY, of Norwich, was born at Brigg, in Lincolnshire; and being left an orphan when about eight years of age, he came under the guardianship of his uncle, Edmund Peckover, who educated him in the principles of Friends. But, according to an account left by himself in manuscript, for the information and caution of his offspring, he was led away by the influence of irreligious associates into an indifference towards religion, a neglect of the due attendance of meetings, and divers unprofitable and disorderly practices. 'But,' says he, 'at that time I was under such inward convictions, that my heart was often filled with grief and horror; however joyous I might appear outwardly, I was inwardly smitten and condemned.' Yet not sufficiently seeking to take up the cross, but rather to gratify his youthful inclinations, the power of evil so far prevailed over him, that he became the means of trouble and sorrow to his relations and friends. In process of time it pleased the Lord to meet with him as in a narrow place; for in the year 1739, he unexpectedly fell into a most distressing and alarming situation, wherein his life appeared in immediate danger from the surrounding pressure of a great crowd, he being low of stature. Confusion and terror instantly seized him, and made him cry aloud for help; upon which, some near him afforded such speedy assistance as, through divine mercy, extricated him from the great danger he was in.

After his deliverance, he became deeply humbled in thankfulness that he was not taken away in that unprepared hour; and being also sensibly favoured with a renewed visitation from on high, his heart was made to rejoice in admiration of the gracious abounding of divine love which he felt in his soul.

From this time he closely attended meetings, associated with experienced Friends, and embraced their advice; humbly submitting to bear the cross, and to follow the leadings of truth in its progressive manifestations. Abiding under a daily concern that, as he had believed in the truth, he might walk in it, he in time experienced a good degree of redemption, and resignation to the divine will.

About the year 1742 he found his mind baptized for the work of the ministry, which weighty service, he, after some time of deep trial, in great fear and reverence, gave up to, and appeared in public as a minister, to the satisfaction of Friends.

He travelled in the service of the gospel, at divers times, through many parts of this nation, Scotland, and Ireland; and in 1770 he passed over the great deep, and paid a religious visit to friends on the continent of America. He returned from there in 1772, with the reward of peace in his own bosom, and the approbation of friends, as amply expressed in their certificates from various provinces.

He was a man exemplary in conduct, and agreeable in conversation, honest in advice, charitable in sentiment, universal in benevolence, deservedly esteemed by his neighbours, and beloved by his friends.

A few months before his decease, he was impressed with a sense that his departure was at no great distance; and sometimes hinted to some nearly connected with him that it would be suddenly; yet, not as fearing it, but rather in a serious and pleasing acquiescence with the prospect.

Accordingly, after attending two meetings on First day, the 22d of the Tenth month, 1775, which were held in silence; and spending the evening with his family, in a disposition more than ordinarily pleasant; he went cheerfully up to bed: where he laid but a few minutes, before it pleased Almighty goodness to take him from the vicissitudes of mutability without a struggle, or passing through the tedious and afflicting pains commonly incident to nature: no doubt to him an easy passage to a heavenly mansion.

His remains were interred in Friends' burial-ground, at Norwich, the 26th of the Tenth month, 1775, in the sixty-first year of his age, and thirty-fourth of his ministry.

DEBORAH WARING, widow of Samuel Waring, before mentioned, was a native of Alton, in Hampshire; and being religiously educated in the principles of truth, and favoured with an early visitation of its sanctifying influence, was, by yielding obedience thereto, qualified for public service. About the 18th year of her age, it pleased the great Lord of the harvest to call her into the work of the ministry; in which service she was an unwearied labourer; and under the renewing of heavenly virtue, her doctrine frequently dropped like dew to the consolation of the right-minded, and edification of the body in love. She was often led, in an awful manner, to press the necessity of a reverent waiting for the fresh opening of the spring of all good; that every individual might be brought from all exterior dependence, to know the Lord for themselves; and witness the revelation of his dear son, the minister of the sanctuary, in their own hearts: and she recommended this doctrine to others by her own example.

She was a very diligent attender of meetings, both for worship and discipline; and not only at home and in her own county, but under the prevailing influence of divine love, her mind was engaged at sundry times to visit friends in divers other counties, having the unity of her monthly meeting in that weighty service; and, by some remarks of her own, it appears, that the Lord's blessed presence was with her, and strengthened her from day to day.

She was of a tender, sympathizing disposition, and was enabled to fill up the several relative duties in life with great propriety, and to continue fresh and lively in old age.

It having pleased the Lord to remove her husband (with whom she had long lived in much unity and affection) about a year before her, she was divinely supported under that great trial, beyond her expectation, as she expressed in sundry living testimonies, which she delivered in the family at that solemn season.

But her health soon after began to decline, and her faculties suffered an abatement of their usual strength; yet, during six months' gradual decay, she was preserved in much innocence; frequently aspiring after that which, from her youth up, she had preferred to all created excellence, and desiring to be preserved to the end, in a sense of that power which had been her morning light, and her guide through the vicissitudes of life.

Being one day observed to be unusually anxious, and one of her daughters asking her how she did, she replied, 'My poor mind is tossed, and I long to be fixed, fixed, fixed. There is one who can walk upon the sea, and command a calm.' She afterward wished to be lifted up, to be new-clothed, and go home; and prayed, 'Gracious and merciful Father, look down upon me, if it is thy blessed will.'

She departed this life without sigh or groan, at Alton, the 3d of the Second month, 1776, and was interred in Friends' burial-ground there, the 11th of the same; aged seventy-eight, and a minister about sixty years.

WILLIAM FRY, of the city of Bristol, was favoured with the visitation of divine love in early youth, and was helped thereby to walk circumspectly. At that time, he stood much alone among the youth; nevertheless, continuing faithful, he became a good example of watchfulness and self-denial. About the twenty-seventh year of his age, he first appeared in the ministry, but for several years seldom; being not only then, but always, as he expressed himself a little before his death, 'more desirous to feel than to speak.' As he was often led into a deep travail of spirit, that the ministry might be kept living, and that nothing might be offered in the will of the creature, he was himself careful in this respect, and waited for the holy anointing, the only true qualification, before he opened his mouth in testimony.

He travelled in the service of truth through Ireland, Wales, and many parts of this nation; concerning which, he spoke to a friend who came to visit him, to this effect; that he had ever found great peace and satisfaction in giving up to those services, the remembrance of which was very lively with him, particularly during his last sickness.

During this illness, which was painful, and of several months' continuance, he uttered many weighty expressions. Being asked by a friend one evening if his pain was then great, he replied, 'I have been in great pain this day, but my mind is favoured with a calm, which I desire to be thankful for.' Observing he was dipt into very low seasons, he remarked that it had been the case with many favoured servants of the Lord, some of whom he named, and added, it was not to be wondered at that it was so with him; saying, 'Oh! how have I longed, and do long, to feel the arisings of that life which is more desirable to a remnant in this day, than the increase of corn, wine, or oil.' He mentioned also that he had a view of a gathering day in Bristol, and, though he might not live to see it, he should die in the faith of it.

Some days afterwards he expressed himself in the following manner:

'I think I have been favoured, during my illness, to experience what I have often had to declare; that it is a good thing to dwell near the truth, that inexhaustible fountain and ocean of divine love. The sweet streams issuing therefrom sweeten the bitter cup. This it is that has supported me under the present afflicting dispensations, and the deep baptisms which it hath been my lot to pass through, wherein I may say I have been dipped as into the bottom of Jordan.' He afterwards added, 'I have been favoured with a calmness; may I not say, a holy calmness; what if I say, a foretaste of that joy which shall be known when this mortal part puts on immortality; and have been enabled to bear with patience and resignation, the present trying afflictions, without murmuring or saying, Lord, what doest thou; or why dealest thou so with me? It is comfortable to witness that which hath been our morning light to be our evening song. May those present, who have been acquainted with the visitation of truth in the morning of their day, continue to abide under it, and prize it above every thing else. It was excellent advice, to buy the truth, and sell it not: it is these that will find support under every trial; and though we may have to say, as our blessed Lord in his agony said, "If it be possible, O Father, let this cup pass from me," which was the effect of his humanity; but oh, how soon did the divinity appear in him! "Nevertheless, not my will, but thine, be done." You who have known the place where true prayer is wont to be made, remember me, and desire for me, that I may be preserved, without murmuring or repining, to the end. It is these, and these only, that dwell near the rock, that are fitted for an habitation in that city, the walls whereof are salvation, and the gates stand open all the day; and there is no night there. It needs not the sun by day, nor the moon by night; for the Lord God and the Lamb are the light thereof.'

At another time he said, 'I remember when on board ship, it was a comfortable sound in the night season, to hear the watchmen say, "All is well." I have a hope I shall know the good Pilot, to steer me into that port, where I may with patriarchs, prophets, and apostles, and those already gathered like sheaves of corn fully ripe, enter into the garner of rest and peace.'

About a month before his death, he said, 'Though many and severe trials come upon us, yet a little while and they will be over; a short period will put an end thereto. I have many times thought, and at this time, how comfortable a thing it is to be able to say with confidence, as one formerly, "Thou shalt guide me with thy counsel, and afterwards receive me into glory. Whom have I in heaven beside thee, and there is none upon earth that I desire but thee. My flesh and my heart faileth, but God is my strength and my portion for ever."'

Many other lively expressions dropped at different periods from him, but his voice becoming broken, it was with difficulty he could speak so as to be understood for a whole sentence together. He continued sensible, and in a quiet frame to the last; and went off as one falling asleep, the 9th day of the Fifth month, 1776, aged nearly fifty-three, and a minister about twenty-six years. His remains were interred in Friends' burial-ground, near the meeting-house at the Friars, Bristol, the 15th of the same month.

JOSEPH JACKSON, of the county of York, was born about the year 1697. He was convinced of the principle of truth about the year 1740; and, under its influence, was concerned to bear testimony thereto, about the year 1746. He was zealous for its promotion, dedicating most of his time to the service thereof, having left trade to be at liberty for it, and was diligent in attending meetings for worship and discipline, visiting most of the meetings in Great Britain. This concern remained with him until the summer of 1775, when, returning home, he was visited with sickness. In the course of his illness, a Friend asking him how he did, he replied, 'I am very weak in body, but the Lord is good to me, as I have but little pain. Yet I could wish to be gone, that I might be at rest; but am willing to wait all my appointed time, until my change come, as I am favoured with peace.' He added, 'My time of labour is now over. I have completed my work within the day, and am now ready to return home to my rest. O Lord, I long to be with thee; yet not my will, but thine, be done.'

A little after he said, 'Oh! how precious is the truth; how little is it sought after by many, for want of knowing its value! I have often wished, and been moved to pray in secret, that those who have once known and witnessed it, may never depart from it; for if they do they will lose their birth-right, and the blessing attending it; but that they may keep it to the end. It is the pearl of great price, and worth more than all we are possessed of in this world. It will purchase us an everlasting inheritance in the world to come; and this is what I have been concerned to labour for, both for myself and others.' It being time for going to meeting, he bade the Friends farewell, saying, 'My mind will accompany you.'

Sundry other Friends visiting him at different times, found him in the same lively disposition, often expressing his desire that all who made profession of the truth might live under its holy government. Such love to his friends, and peaceful serenity of mind, attended him all along, as contributed much to the satisfaction and refreshment of those who visited him.

He quietly departed this life the 16th, and was buried the 18th of the Twelfth month, 1776, at Gildersome, in Yorkshire, aged about seventy-nine years, and a minister about thirty years.

ANN MERCY BELL, of York, was born in London. She had her education in Friends' school and workhouse, being admitted soon after its establishment, and afterwards continued there as a school-mistress for many years. Being early favoured with divine visitations, she was not only preserved from the gross pollutions of the world, but was, in a good degree, enabled to renounce vain and youthful pleasures and amusements, which she frequently confessed with humble thankfulness and gratitude.

In the year 1731 she married Nathaniel Bell, of York, and became a member of that meeting. While in a private capacity, she was well esteemed as a Friend of circumspect life and conversation, a pattern of plainness, and therein, as well as in other respects, a good example. At length, steadily adhering to the divine teacher in her heart, and under the influence of the spirit of truth, she had, from a well-grounded experience, to declare to others the way of life and salvation. In this service she faithfully laboured, according to ability received, at home and in adjacent parts; and, in the course thereof, found drawings, in the love of the gospel, to visit various other parts of England: also, when engaged in family visits, she found it her concern not to overlook those who, by misconduct, had incurred the censure of Friends.

Her labours were not confined to those of the Society of Friends; but, in the course of her travels, she had compassionately to call and direct people of other denominations to the unerring teacher in themselves, and had meetings among them in divers places where no friends were settled.

In the year 1753 she found a concern to visit friends in London; and during her stay in that city, under the influence of love to mankind, had to exhort the inhabitants thereof, in the streets, markets, and many places in and about London, Westminster, and Southwark, calling them to repentance and amendment of life. In this service she was signally furnished with ability to labour, to the tendering many of their minds, and acknowledgment of her goodwill to them; and such was the ardour of her mind, and the flowing forth of love to them, that she frequently preached three or four times a day, in different parts. On her return home she had to acknowledge that she was favoured with the return of peace; which she esteemed a sufficient reward for the various exercises which attended that laborious service.

Towards the conclusion of her time, she expressed her fervent desire, that he who had been her morning light might be her evening song; which there is no doubt she mercifully experienced. Being suddenly seized with an apoplectic fit, at the approach of the stroke she was heard to say, 'Sweet Jesus,' with some other expressions, which, through the hurry and surprise those about her were in, are not now remembered.

In a few hours after, she departed, without sigh or groan, the 30th of the Twelfth month, 1775; and was interred in Friends' burial-ground in York, the 4th of the First month, 1776; aged about sixty-nine, and a minister about thirty years.

REBECCA SHEWELL, daughter of Edward and Sarah Shewell, of Camberwell, in Surry, was a child adorned with meekness, innocence, and humility; dutiful to her parents, and affectionate to her brothers and sisters; a lover of the servants of Christ, fond of reading the Holy Scriptures, and often so tendered in reading them, that those who were present and heard her, were edified by it.

Being taken with an illness, which continued for twelve months, she bore it with much patience and resignation of mind. She was not confined to her chamber more than about three weeks; in which season she told her mother, that she believed she should die, and requested her to pray for her; which her mother being enabled to do, it seemed much to ease her mind. A few days after, she said, 'I have often been desirous of recovering; but I find desires will not do, I must have patience;' and expressed her thankfulness to her sisters for their tender care over her; and said, 'O, that I could keep from groaning, that it might not make them uneasy.' She signified her apprehensions that her complaint increased; not that she wished to live, but it was a fear she should not obtain future bliss. One time some remarks being made to her on the pleasing things of this world, and what she might enjoy, she answered, 'I have no desire for these things. I had rather die and go to Christ.' She was frequent in prayer by herself, and often wished to be left alone, and the curtains to be drawn about her. Her sister observing her to be in much pain, asked her to take something; she answered, that none of these things would do her good; but it being observed the Lord could do her good, she answered, 'He can, but none of these things can.'

Her mother asked her, the day before she died, if she thought she should die; she said, 'Yes;' she had rather die than live, but was afraid she was not good enough. Her mother encouraging her, and intimating that she believed there was a mansion prepared for her; the child expressed her willingness to go to it, desiring her mother to pray for her; and the mother answering, 'I do; dost thou do it thyself?' the child said, 'I do, I do;' and being asked if it was with outward words, she replied, very fervently, 'No, no, in my heart.' She also intimated that she was quite easy; and frequently bade them farewell. Soon after, her speech failed her; but she appeared to retain her senses to the last.

She departed, without sigh or groan, the 17th of the Second month, 1777, aged only eight years and four months.

ANN LEAVER, daughter of John and Mary Leaver, of Nottingham, being taken ill, signified her belief that her time would not be long, and said, that the prospect of eternity was awful; and that though she had not committed any bad thing, yet she had found it difficult, when at meeting, to get to that steady watchfulness and settled composure she longed for. She expressed thankfulness for the opportunities she was sometimes favoured with in the family, in their sitting together at home; and added, that she hoped the Almighty had blotted out her transgressions; and prayed that she might be enabled to bear with patience the trying dispensation she had to pass through, which she believed was allotted for her further purification; and begged for a certain evidence, that her conclusion might be happy, and her passage easy; which was mercifully granted.

In the course of her illness she dropped many expressions, which show that she looked forward to a glorious inheritance; some of which are as follow.

After having given her sisters some tender advice, she said, 'How awful to look at eternity, and few young people in time of health think so much of their latter end as they ought to do, though they have as much cause as those more advanced, having no more certainty of life.' She plainly saw that those of a cheerful disposition were in danger of going too far in company; adding, 'Those who are taken away in youth escape many snares and temptations, that such as live longer are in danger to be hurt by.' Several times she expressed her humble thankfulness for the last week's illness, saying, that it had been a profitable, though painful, dispensation to her. At another time, when in great pain, she spoke thus: 'O, it is hard work! how needful when in health so to live as to be in readiness! for it is enough to struggle with the pains of the body.' She also said, that she plainly saw it was as necessary for us to watch over our thoughts, as words or actions; desiring the prayers of those present, that she might be supported under her affliction with patience.

After a painful day, being in the afternoon favoured with

stillness and composure of mind, she thought herself going; and took a solemn farewell of her near connections and friends; desiring all present might make due preparation for that solemn and awful time, when the soul must be separated from the body; saying, that she did not expect to have had any thing of that sort to deliver, but as it came into her mind, she dropped it; and added, 'I want to be gone, I seem to have no business here.' Her pain returning, she found she should not go so soon as she expected; but begged for patience, saying, 'The Lord's time is the best time.'

The day she died, the doctor proposing to lay on some blisters, she said she was out of the reach of blisters; 'No mortal can help me; there is but one who can help me;' yet she was willing to submit, if her father desired it. But she added, 'O, that we might be a little still, and sit comfortably together!' Being, in some degree, free from her sharp agonies for nearly an hour, she said, 'We are pure and comfortable now;' and talked pleasantly, saying, that the unwearied enemy had been endeavouring to trouble her, but she found him a liar.

The same evening she said, 'No one can think what I feel; but if it is to purify me for an admittance into that holy place, where no impure thing can enter, I am willing to bear ten times more; and, I hope, with a tolerable degree of patience too. I hope I am not impatient; but really the conflict is so sharp, at times, that I cannot forbear crying out. O Lord, keep me, keep me: my God help me, and please to release me this night. I long to be gone. Although I have had many pleasant prospects in view, I have resigned them all, and would not return again to the world for any consideration.' Much more she said to the same effect.

She at times lamented that people, advanced in years, should be so closely attached to the world, as too many appeared to be, saying that they must soon leave it.

Her mother retiring to supper, she soon sent for her again, and told her, with a sweet composure and calmness, 'My dear mother, I am now going, and would have my father and sister to come and sit with me a while, and take a final leave;' adding, 'My prayer is granted; for I have earnestly begged I might not see the light of another morning.' She took a solemn and affectionate leave, saying that she wondered she could part with her near connections so easily; 'For,' said she, 'I have no tears to shed. It is not hardness of heart, for I know I love you all as well as ever; but it is to me an earnest that I am going to something greater.' She desired her affectionate love to many of her absent relations, and particularly to some nearly her equals in years, saying, 'Let them be admonished from me how they spend their time.'

After some time, she said, 'It is all over, and I am perfectly happy. I have no pain. The conflict is at an end. Farewell, farewell;' and pausing a while, she said, 'I am now going to join saints and angels, and the spirits of just men made perfect;' adding, 'I have no more to say. I would have you to leave me, for I am going to sleep.' Then laying her head quietly on the pillow, she expired, without a sigh or groan, the 22d of the Third month, 1777, aged twenty years.

Her corpse was carried to Friends' meeting-house in Nottingham; and, after a solemn meeting, was interred in their burial-ground there.

MARY BUNDOCK, of Manningtree, in Essex, was religiously inclined from her childhood; and as she grew up delighted in the company of solid friends; endeavouring, amidst the various trials and exercises to which her situation exposed her, to walk in simplicity and awful fear before the Lord, who graciously preserved and prepared her for service.

About the thirtieth year of her age she appeared in public testimony; in which she had the unity of Friends, and continued to labour therein, both at home and abroad; frequently travelling into different parts of this nation in the service of truth.

She was of a grave deportment, and of sound judgment, earnestly concerned to discourage all undue liberties. The benevolence of her mind appeared in many instances towards her neighbours, by seasonable advice, and frequently administering to their necessities. She was a diligent attender of the meeting she belonged to, in which her travail in silence was helpful and comfortable, till prevented by bodily infirmities.

In her last illness, which was at times very painful, she uttered many comfortable expressions. A friend who came to visit her, saying, 'She is sensible;' she replied, 'Yes, I am sensible who has been my preserver from the earliest time of my life, and has helped me along, and supported me in weakness, so that I have been revived through his goodness, from time to time. There is but one power to help. The last time I attended a public meeting, it was the fervent desire of my mind for my friends, as well as for myself, that we might seek to experience this only help near.' To another friend she said, 'Dear friend, trust in the Lord; he never leaves his little ones; no, never, never. Though outward afflictions happen to the righteous, as well as to the ungodly, yet light is sown for the righteous, and gladness for the upright in heart.'

It was no small cause of comfort to observe the lively frame of her spirit, by which it appeared that, though her outward strength decayed, her inward strength was renewed day by day.

She departed this life at Colchester, on the 8th of the Tenth month, 1778, and was buried the 15th of the same, in Friends' burial-ground there; aged eighty-three, and a minister about fifty-three years.

CUTHBERT WIGHAM, of Cornwood, in Northumberland, was educated in the way of the Church of England, and was in his youth addicted to many youthful follies, and some gross evils. But it pleased God, who is rich in mercy towards sinners, to call him by his grace, and reveal his Son in him; whereby, about the year 1734, he was convinced of the blessed truth, as it is in Jesus, and received it.

Being thus brought into deep judgment for his transgressions, and sensibly feeling God's wrath poured forth, he durst no longer follow his old courses and ways of living, nor durst longer associate with his old companions, but joined in society with the people called Quakers; and, several of his neighbours being about the same time convinced of the truth, he was made instrumental in settling a meeting in Cornwood, in the year 1735.

About a year after his convincement, a dispensation of the gospel was committed to him, in which he laboured faithfully according to the ability given. His ministry was not with the enticing words of man's wisdom, but in the power and demonstration of the spirit; and he often had to magnify that power that had redeemed his soul out of the horrible pit of everlasting darkness. Having known, as he expressed, the terrors of the Lord for evil-doing, he was earnestly engaged to warn others to take heed to their ways, lest they should bring themselves under such terrors as he had felt, but now, through infinite mercy, was released from, and come to the enjoyment of that peace which the world cannot give or take away.

In the year 1753 he took a journey on foot, accompanied by a friend, and had many meetings among a people who were strangers to Friends and their principles; and also visited various other parts of the North, and some parts of Scotland; having meetings in his way at several places where no Friends resided. He was as a nursing father to the young convinced in that day; and open in love to receive all in whom any tenderness appeared, whether their station in the world was high or low.

He met with some exercises and cross occurrences in his own family, which grieved him much, yet he was favoured to outlive all his sorrows. Though, through age and infirmity of body, his natural faculties were much impaired, yet his mind appeared to be redeemed out of all evil; and he was brought to the innocency of a little child. Being perfectly sensible of his approaching dissolution, he seemed to meet it with cheerfulness, saying, 'I will wait in patience till my change comes. Oh! it is a fine thing to be ready;' and, indeed, the patience and resignation which appeared in his countenance evidently denoted the calmness and serenity of his mind.

Thus, in innocency, he finished his course the 9th of the Second month, 1780, and was buried in a piece of ground given by himself for a burial-ground, in Cornwood; aged about seventy-seven years, and a minister about forty-three years.

JONAH THOMPSON, of Compton, near Sherborne, in Dorsetshire, was born near Penrith, in Cumberland, about the year 1702. He was grandson of Thomas Lawson, who, in the early times of the Society of Friends, was a zealous advocate for their principles, as his writings testify. His parents dying while he was young, he came under the care of a relation not in religious fellowship with Friends; who left him entirely at his own liberty respecting his attendance at places of worship, and the choice of his religious profession. But being, at that early period, impressed with divine fear, and a sense of the nature of true religion, he was mercifully preserved. Though he had little or no expectations from his relations, or view of subsistence but by his own industry, yet, relying on the protecting care of Providence, he had the fortitude, at about the age of fourteen, to withstand offers which were repeatedly made him of an education at school, and at the university, with a view to qualify and provide for him as a minister of the established worship. This is the more remarkable, as his mind was strongly attached to literary pursuits. He has since frequently remarked, that he was then fully convinced of the impropriety of such a mode of making ministers; believing none could be truly so, but those who were of Christ's making, by the call and qualifications of his holy Spirit. He therefore put himself apprentice to a Friend, at Kendal, in Westmoreland, to learn the trade of a weaver, with whom he faithfully served his time. At leisure hours he prosecuted his studies, and acquired such a share of learning as qualified him to undertake the care of a school at Grayrigg in that county. From thence he removed to Yatton near Bristol; and on his marriage a few years after, he settled in Dorsetshire, where he mostly resided the remainder of his time.

There is reason to believe that he was, whilst at Grayrigg, made sensible of a call to the work of the ministry, on that foundation which in early life had appeared to him so necessary; and for which there is no doubt but he was in good measure duly prepared and qualified, through the operation of grace upon his own heart; and he soon became an able minister of the gospel of Christ. In the year 1728, he paid a religious visit, in company with William Longmire, to most of the counties in this nation, to his own peace and the satisfaction of his friends.

In the year 1750 he visited the meetings of Friends in America, where his labours of love were generally acceptable; and some years after his return, he embarked again for the same continent, on which, for some time, he took up his residence.

After his second return from America, he resumed the employment of a schoolmaster; and travelled no long journeys from home, but was a diligent attender of the meeting he belonged to, and frequently attended the yearly meeting.

His ministry was acceptable to persons of various denominations, being often led to declare the truths of the gospel with great calmness and deliberation, and with such convincing clearness as frequently to occasion many to acknowledge the truth of his doctrine.

For some time before his decease he frequently expressed his apprehensions of his approaching end, and particularly on a public solemn occasion, when, after a clear intimation that the time of his departure was at hand, he added, in nearly the following words: 'I may say with humility, and a degree of Christian boldness, I have fought a good fight, I have finished my course, I have kept the faith; henceforth there is laid up for me a crown of righteousness incorruptible in heaven.'

In his last illness he remarked to some friends who visited him, that he had lived long enough, his services being over, and had nothing to do but to die, having a well-grounded hope that the change would be to his advantage. That on reviewing his past life, he could find but few instances in which he could have acted better, was he to live his time over again; and that he had a great advantage during his illness, in having a quiet, easy mind, and no accuser there. For a near friend and fellow-labourer in the gospel, who took leave of him a few days before his departure, he wished a portion of the same peace in the decline of life which he then experienced.

He was preserved in great composure and resignation, and, for the most part, retained his faculties to the last; and on the 21st of the Fifth month, 1780, quietly departed this life. His body was interred in Friends' burial-ground at Yeovil, on the 27th. Aged nearly seventy-eight, and a minister about fifty-five years.

ROBERT HAYWARD, of Suffolk, in the early part of his life, embraced the tendering visitation of the day-spring from on high, and, according to the discoveries thereof to his understanding, gave up in obedience; and being prepared to declare what God had done for his soul, he invited others to taste and see how good the Lord is to all those that put their trust in him.

His labours were often favoured with general acceptance where his lot was cast, which was for the most part confined to the county where he dwelt, and places adjacent. He was industrious in his business, a plain and inoffensive man in life and conversation, endeavouring by precept and example to be instrumental in promoting the welfare of all.

This continued to be the humble engagement of his mind to his conclusion, in which the same godly simplicity seemed to attend him.

During the time of his illness he was favoured with exemplary patience and resignation, which were the means of his support under the excruciating pain which at times he felt; and he would frequently say, 'The Lord is my shepherd, I shall not want. Grace, nor truth, nor any good thing, will he withhold from them that put their trust in him. I find him near to help me in this the time of my affliction, and nothing to stand in my way. Oh, what a comfort it is to those that have done their day's work in the day-time. I have endeavoured to discharge my duty to the best of my knowledge. I feel peace, sweet peace, such as the world cannot give, nor take away.'

At times, many Friends coming to see him, he frequently had a word of encouragement to drop among them and those about him, and to tell what God had done for his soul. He likewise had several comfortable opportunities with his children and grandchildren. His earnest desires and prayers were put up for the young and rising generation, that they might be preserved in the fear of the Lord.

The nearer the time of his departure approached, the

stronger his memory grew; and he seemed to experience more of the incomes of divine favour; and, like a well-watered garden, he was fresh and green to the last.

A few hours before his close he had a fainting fit, and those about him thought him gone; but after a while he revived, and, like good old Jacob, gave his children his blessing, and said that he should sleep that night in the arms of his heavenly Father.

He was sensible to the last, and departed this life with great composure, and full assurance of happiness, being full of days and full of peace, the 24th of the Tenth month, 1780, and was buried in Friends' burial-ground at Lynn, in Norfolk; aged eighty-five years, and a minister nearly fifty years.

ELIZABETH HOLME, of Newcastle-upon-Tyne, was the daughter of Anthony and Dorothy Wilson, and born at High-wray, near Hawkshead, in Lancashire. She was favoured with a religious education, and in her youth her mind was impressed with the fear of God. She was often drawn into retirement and a watchful state of mind. Thus she attained a growth in religious experience, and about the thirty-fourth year of her age, was concerned to bear testimony to the efficacy of that divine principle [the Spirit of Christ] which she herself had felt: in which service she grew, and, in company with Lydia Lancaster, visited the meetings of Friends in Ireland and Scotland.

After her marriage with Reginald Holme, she visited various parts of England; and in her station of a wife, she conducted herself with prudence and propriety; and, being preserved in watchfulness, suffered not her temporal concerns to hinder her services in the church.

Her last illness was short, scarcely ten days, most of which time she kept her bed, appearing to be under great bodily weakness, but not much pain, and bright in her understanding to the last.

To a friend who came to see her, at parting she said, 'Remember me affectionately to thy husband, and let him remember me when he draws near [the throne of grace], that I may pass through the valley of the shadow of death, and be enabled to put off the robe of mortality and put on immortality, full of glory. I trust to enjoy a part of that portion that is laid up for the faithful; for such I have endeavoured to be, according to the ability given. I have nothing stands before me. I do not clearly see that this is the finishing stroke, but every stroke draws nearer and nearer. In this I have no will, but stand ready, and in patience wait till his own time.'

Her daughter sitting by her, she said, 'Oh, sweet peace, what an enjoyment it is in this weakness. I have discharged my duty to God and his people in this place.'

A near friend calling to see her, he said, 'Thou hast laboured faithfully amongst us, and we shall have a great want of thy company.' She said, 'I have so. I hope it may be as bread cast on the waters, that may arise many days hence.' At another time she said, 'I thought I had been going, but it seems as if the people held me, not so willing to let me go as I am myself. Oh, that every link of this chain was broken, that I might lie down in peace for evermore.'

The morning before she died, being Fifth-day, her daughter sitting by her, she said, 'I may say with king Hezekiah, the hand of the Lord is upon me, I am waiting for my change.' After asking, 'Is thy husband gone to meeting?' she added, 'I wish it may be a refreshing season to him, and all the living members assembled this day, with whom my spirit unites, and craves the canopy of divine love may overshadow their minds, and strengthen for the work's sake.' After a pause, she said to her daughter, 'My dear, thy company is precious to me in this affliction, and thy husband's, which I dearly love. O Lord, let us taste of thy goodness, that we may be refreshed.'

She quietly departed this life the 9th of the Second month, 1781, and was interred on the 12th, in Friends' burial-ground in Newcastle: aged nearly seventy-eight, and a minister forty-four years.

THOMAS GAWTHORP, of Preston Patrick, in Westmoreland, was born of honest parents, of our religious profession, at Skipton, in Yorkshire, in the year 1709. His father dying when he was young, he was put apprentice to a man near Leeds, not of our profession; and, meeting with severe treatment during his service, to free himself therefrom, he was induced, towards the conclusion of the term, to enlist in the army, in which he continued about five years.

Whilst in that service, being, by permission, on a visit to his relations at Skipton, he attended a meeting there, at which he was effectually reached, by the powerful testimony of Mary Slater; and from that time attended Friends' meetings, when opportunities offered. Though he laboured under great exercise of mind on account of his situation, yet he was not free to have his discharge purchased, fearing how he might stand his ground. One of his officers, observing his dissatisfaction with the way of life he was in, made him an offer of his discharge, on his returning the money he had received when he enlisted, which, after solid consideration, he accepted; and paying the money so soon as he had earned by his industry sufficient for that purpose, he obtained his discharge, and returned to Skipton, the place of his birth.

During his residence there, which was not long, he came forth in public testimony. From thence he removed to Kendal, and soon after accompanied a friend on a religious visit into Scotland.

After his return, he married a young woman of a respectable family, belonging to Preston Patrick monthly meeting, and settled within the said meeting, a few miles from Kendal, where he continued to reside when at home, to the time of his decease.

His mind being devoted to the service of his great Master, and obedient to the manifestations of [the spirit of] truth, he grew in the gift received, and became a deep and able minister of the gospel; diligently labouring in the openings of life, for the exaltation of truth in the hearts of the people; unto whom, from an inward sense of their states, he had often close, pertinent doctrine to deliver; not in the wisdom of man, nor the eloquence of words, but in the simplicity of the gospel, and with the demonstration of divine authority, reaching the witness in the hearts of many. He, nevertheless, often found it his place not to feed, but to famish, the eager desire in the minds of the people after words; by setting them an example of humble and awful worship in solemn silence.

He was exemplary in his diligent attendance of our religious meetings, and in a circumspect conduct among men in the necessary management of his outward concerns.

He was frequently engaged to leave his family and worldly affairs, to pay religious visits to Friends in different parts, having several times visited divers parts of England, Scotland, and Ireland. He also visited Friends in America four different times. In all these labours of love we have reason to believe he discharged his duty honestly, and was made instrumental in the great Master's hand to the stirring up the pure mind in many.

He was also frequently engaged in visiting Friends' families, and enabled to speak pertinently to the states of individuals.

In his third visit to America, he was particularly concerned on account of the hard and suffering state of the poor negroes, and we believe his labours on behalf of that oppressed people were of service.

Upon his return from his last visit to America, he was much reduced in his bodily strength; but his mind seemed centred in peace, being covered with innocency and sweetness, and patiently waiting for his change; having an evidence that his day's work was nearly accomplished.

He attended the meeting to which he belonged, under great bodily infirmity, though at a considerable distance, until he was wholly confined. He departed this life the 29th of the Ninth month, 1781, and was interred the 4th of the Tenth month following, in Friends' burial-ground at Preston Patrick; aged about seventy-one, and a minister forty-seven years.

His friends of Westmoreland, in their testimony concerning him, say, 'We doubt not but his conclusion was a happy release from the conflicts and deep exercises attending his pilgrimage here; and that he is gathered to the just of all generations, to reap the reward of his labours.'

MABEL WIGHAM, a member of Newcastle meeting, was the daughter of Cuthbert Wigham, of whom an account has been given at p. 112, and was about six years of age when her parents were convinced, and a meeting settled at Cornwood, the place of her father's abode.

In her youth she discovered a warm affection for Friends, and, as she expressed to some of her near friends, tender desires were raised in her mind, after an inward acquaintance with that life and virtue which she was favoured to hear livingly testified of, by her worthy father and many other Friends, who at that time were concerned to visit that meeting. Being in a good degree preserved in an innocent frame of mind, and attending to the reproofs of instruction, that she might be favoured to find the way of life, she was often drawn into solitary places to pour forth her supplications before the Lord, that he would in mercy, make himself known to her as the good Shepherd of Israel; whose voice she might hear and distinguish from the voice of the stranger.

The fruit of her humble, seeking state of mind soon discovered itself in her growth in ardent love to truth and Friends, and in her great desires to attend our religious meetings and opportunities of worship at home, as also monthly and quarterly meetings. In all these she was a good example, by her silent, humble waiting upon the Lord; where often, in much brokenness of spirit, she dropped her silent tears, and the good effects thereof were manifested in the reach it had on others present.

A few years after her marriage to Thomas Wigham, of Limestone, in Cornwood, she appeared in testimony in a few words, which were sweet and savoury. By humbly depending on the Lord for renewed strength, she came to experience a growth in her gift; and was drawn forth to visit the churches, for which service she was qualified in a particular manner, being truly a daughter of consolation. For notwithstanding her temporal concerns, having a large family, and being only in low circumstances, she firmly trusted in the Lord who called her, and freely left all and followed him; often saying, 'The Lord is my Shepherd, I shall not want.'

After her return from visiting the meetings in London, about the Sixth month, 1779, her health became impaired, and a gradual decay took place, so that she was confined for many weeks. Her strength reviving, she got out to meetings again for some time, where she had close and deep service; and, for change of air, she went into her native county, which gave her an opportunity of visiting her near relations, much to their satisfaction and her own peace and comfort, and of taking a last farewell of her friends and neighbours in that county.

After her return from Cornwood, her disorder made great progress, and wasted her fast, and she was not able to get to meetings.

During her confinement, several of her friends went to visit her, in which many precious opportunities were witnessed, to the melting and humbling their spirits before the Lord, so that they could truly say the Prince of Peace was there.

She bore her illness with exemplary fortitude and resignation; and with a cheerful composure she mentioned her dissolution, and often said, 'The way seems clear, and I have no doubt, if the last conflict was over, but I shall be admitted to my Master's rest, and the joy of the Lord.'

Much seasonable and tender advice she gave to her children, encouraging them to seek and serve the Lord in their youth; and that, if they were chiefly concerned to attain heavenly treasure, the Lord would provide for their bodies; adding, 'Oh what satisfaction and peace I feel, in having dedicated my youthful days in seeking the Lord, and freely spending myself in his service.'

As she lived, so she died; in love, peace, and unity with her brethren. She departed this life, without a sigh, the 9th of the Eleventh month, 1781; and her remains were interred at Newcastle-on-Tyne, the 13th of the same; aged fifty-two, and a minister twenty-five years.

ROBERT PRYOR. — Expressions of the late Robert Pryor, of London, committed to writing by his brother, John Pryor, who attended him in his last illness.

For some months before his death, his usual state of health was altered, and signs of infirmity appeared, which continued to increase upon him, and at length terminated in a settled decline.

One day, speaking to me about his will, he said that some might think he had given a great deal away from his children; but he was more afraid of their having too much than too little, as he had seen great riches do much hurt, especially in our Society. He wished his children to be brought up plainly, and the boys to be put apprentices to sober, honest Friends.

One time, on taking leave of his son Robert, who had been up to see him, he desired him to be a good boy, and to speak the truth, and to keep to the plain language, and not to associate with bad boys, but choose the best for his companions. At another time he said, 'Brother, I hope I do not repine, though I am afraid lest I should. I have my low times, lest it should not be well with me. Sometimes I think it may be the enemy that strives to disturb me.' Speaking of his being resigned to the will of Providence, he said, 'What signifieth it, whether I die now, or twenty years hence? though if I look back, my time appears to have been very short.'

One day he said, 'Dear brother, do not be too anxious after the things of this world, for my inordinate desire to accumulate wealth, has been a heavy burthen to me: no one knows what I have suffered on that account.' He further said, that his having been so solicitous after the world, had made him but a dwarf in religion; and that if it had pleased the Lord to spare his life, he thought he should have found it his place to endeavour to be a more useful member in the Society; and to expend more of his income in charitable uses: that the love of money, and an inordinate desire after wealth, had pierced him through with many sorrows.

One afternoon his nephew came to ask him how he did: upon his taking leave, after sitting some time in silence, he desired him to keep constantly to meetings, to love friends' company, and not to launch out into the vanities of this world, or associate with those that were likely to draw him aside; reminding him that there would be an end, which would overtake us all; and that we ought always to be prepared.

One time, going to bed, he desired me to shut the door, saying that it was his desire to supplicate, which he did on his knees, begging the Lord not to leave him, but be with him in the trying moment, and grant him a safe and easy passage into his glorious kingdom; hoping he would accept his late repentance, which he trusted was sincere, though upon a dying bed. The next morning, as I stood by his bed-side, he spoke to me as follows: 'Brother, I have been in a quiet sleep, and had a comfortable vision. I thought I had a foresight of that glorious kingdom, where all is peace, serene, and quiet! Such a prospect as I had never before seen, and such as no tongue can express, the glory of that kingdom!'

At another time, expressing the satisfaction he had in my being with him, he desired that I would not leave him when the event happened; and requested to be buried in a plain way, and to be carried into the meeting-house; as he had seen the use of those meetings.

One morning asking him if he was free from pain, he answered, 'that he felt only violent oppression; that when the Lord pleased to release him, he believed he was ready; but hoped to wait the appointed time with patience: adding, he was as clear in his intellect as ever. What a favour! and that he was permitted to get home, and settle his affairs, was a great favour; but above all, that which he saw in his vision!'

He said that it appeared clear to him, that the less Friends talked about news and interfered in politics, the better. He thought they did not belong to them. He used to read the newspapers when at Bristol, to divert himself, but left it off, finding his time better employed in reading the Scriptures.

On taking a little refreshment, he said, 'What a favour it is thus to be waited upon, and to have every thing this world can afford, to alleviate or still the pains of the body! We have so much the more to be accountable for.' One evening, upon my asking him how he did, he said that he lay pretty easy, and was quiet in his mind. He thought he had a well-grounded hope, that all would be well with him; and that if it should please the Lord to take him into his glorious kingdom, what a happy change it would be!

One evening he said, that he did not know what to think of that night. He had prayed so often to be released, he was ready to fear lest he had offended. He should be very thankful to be released from his sufferings; yet hoped he could say, as that good man Isaac Sharples had expressed in prayer, at his bed-side, "Thy will be done, O Lord, in earth, as it is done in heaven." After this he continued remarkably still and calm, with much serenity in his countenance, taking little notice, but appearing wholly fixed on the greatest of all objects.

On the seventh day before his decease, he noticed those about him more than he had done some days before; and his sister coming in the afternoon, whom he had often expressed a desire to see, he mentioned it to me, as a great favour, to be permitted to see all his near friends; which being done, it seemed as if every wish was gratified.

He continued in the same calm, composed state of mind, growing weaker and weaker, yet sensible to the last; having his desire granted of an easy passage, I have no doubt, into that glorious kingdom, of which he expressed he had a foretaste.

He departed this life at his house in Budge-row, the 16th of the Seventh month, 1782, aged about thirty-seven years; and, after a solemn meeting at Gracechurch-street, was interred in Friends' burial ground, Bunhill-fields, the 21st of the same.

JOHN SCOTT, of Amwell, in Hertfordshire, was favoured with strength of body, and an active and vigorous mind. He was esteemed regular and moral in his conduct, and extensive in his knowledge, being remarkably diligent and attentive in promoting works of public utility; in assisting individuals in cases of difficulty; and in the conciliation of differences. Notwithstanding these qualifications, there is reason to believe, he frequently experienced the convictions of the Spirit of Truth, for not faithfully following the Lord, and adhering to the cross of Christ; by which true believers are crucified to the world; and the world to them.

During the yearly meeting at London, in the year 1783, he attended many of the meetings for worship, and appeared to be more religiously concerned than for some years preceding.

On the 1st of the Twelfth month he was seized with a fever, and expecting it would bring on his end, he was greatly humbled in spirit, expressing a sense of the happiness of the righteous in futurity; but being convinced of his own low and unprepared state, he said he was unworthy of the lowest place in the heavenly mansions, but hoped he should not be a companion of accursed and wrathful spirits.

In the early part of his illness, he discoursed with his wife concerning some outward affairs: particularly desiring that his only and beloved daughter might be brought up among Friends.

Notwithstanding the severity of the distemper, he was favoured with a clear and unimpaired understanding; and the exercise of his spirit seemed to be almost continual for peace and reconciliation with his Maker; having a hope, that if it should please the Lord to spare him, he should become a new man; but in much diffidence he expressed a fear, lest the old things should again prevail. He also said to the person who attended him, that he had been too proud; yet he had been remarkably easy of access to persons in low circumstances.

Speaking frequently of his brother Samuel Scott, and expressing a desire to see him, on the 9th of the Twelfth month, a special messenger was sent to Hartford from Ratcliffe, where he lay ill, requesting his attendance there. His brother, on being informed next morning by letter of his continued solicitude to see him, reached his house at Ratcliffe about four that afternoon. Being introduced to his bed-side, on asking him how he did, he answered, 'Very bad. I wanted to see thee, I had a great deal to say to thee, but I fear now I cannot.' What afterwards passed between them was as follows: After a short space of silence, John Scott began to speak with a voice full of power. 'I wanted to see thee, to tell thee, that I have nothing to trust to but the blessed Jesus; and that if I die, I do not die an unbeliever. If I die, I die a believer, and have nothing to trust to but mere unmerited mercy.'

Finding him brought down as from the 'clefts of the rocks, and the heights of the hills, into the valley of deep humiliation,' his brother rejoiced in spirit, and spoke comfortably to him; expressing the deep humiliating views he frequently had of his own state. John Scott replied, 'Oh! if it is so with thee, how must it be with me, who have been the chief of sinners!' The insufficiency of self-righteousness being mentioned, 'Oh!' said he, with great earnestness, 'righteousness! I have no righteousness, nor any thing to trust to but the blessed Jesus and his merits.'

Pausing awhile he proceeded, 'There is something within me which keeps me from despairing. I dare not despair, although I have as much reason to despair as any one; were it not for him who showed mercy to the thief upon the cross. The thief upon the cross, and Peter who denied his master, are much before me.' Being advised to trust in the Lord, he replied, 'I have none else to trust in.' 'Oh!' said he, 'the Saviour, he is the way, and there is no other. I now see there is no other. Oh the Saviour! I have done too much against him; and if I live I hope I shall be able to let the world know it, and that in many respects my mind is altered. But I dare not make resolutions.' His brother mentioning former times, and the days of his youth, in which they frequently conversed about, and were both clearly convinced of the necessity of inward and experimental piety, he answered, 'I was then very deficient, but I have since been much more shaken.' Visiting the sick in a formal customary manner being represented as unprofitable, he replied, 'Oh! it is not a time to be solicitous about forms! Here is a scene indeed, enough to bring down the grandeur of many, if they could see it. I buoyed myself up with the hope of many days.' Recommending him to the great object, Christ within, the hope of glory, to which his mind was measureably turned, his brother seemed to withdraw, on which he clasped his hand, and took a solemn farewell.

He continued in mutability about two days longer, altogether in a calm and rational state. About twelve hours before his decease, his speech much faltered; but by some broken expressions it appeared that the religious concern of his mind was continued.

On the 12th day of the Twelfth month, 1783, he departed this life, in remarkable quietness, without sigh or groan; and was buried in Friends' burying-ground at Ratcliffe, on the 18th, being nearly fifty-four years of age.

ISAAC SHARPLES.—A short narrative of ISAAC SHARPLES, late of Hitchin, written by himself some time before his decease: to which are added some of his expressions a little before his end.

'Being now about the eightieth year of my age, it is in my mind to leave some few hints of the Lord's tender dealings with me from my youth to this time, for the information and encouragement of those I may leave behind me. I was born near Prescot, in Lancashire, about the year 1702; my parents, William and Phœbe Sharples, being members of that meeting. My mother died about three years after, leaving six children, who, by her removal, were subjected to much hardship. My father, for want of keeping his place, forfeited his unity with Friends, by which the family became dispersed, and none of us continued in the Society.

'When I was about twelve years of age, by the persuasion of some of my father's relations, I was sprinkled at Ormskirk; from which time I continued to frequent the public worship, until I joined Friends. At about fourteen I was placed out apprentice to a tailor, where I suffered much; but my master, to whom I was bound, not having sufficient employment for me, after I had served about half my time, turned me over to a Friend for the remainder of the term, whereby I got some relief. In this family they would often be speaking of my mother, who was esteemed a valuable Friend.

'Having now frequent opportunity of being in Friends' company, and observing their regular lives and conversation, it gave me a secret liking towards them; but looking upon myself to be a settled member of the established church, so called, and there being most liberty [in it] for worldly indulgence, I endeavoured to satisfy myself in that way as long as I could, being often strongly tempted by youthful lusts after the common evils that are in the world; yet I was mercifully preserved from the grosser part thereof. At length it pleased the Lord, who had long followed me by his secret rebukes, to break in upon my soul by his powerful love and awakening visitations, to show me that was not my rest, because it was polluted. My present state and condition being now clearly laid open to my view, by the light that shined into my dark heart, I saw sin to be exceedingly sinful, and that it was this which separated me from my God, and caused him to withhold good things from me. I was also favoured to see my great loss of time and neglect of duty, and how far I was behind in my day's work. Although the Lord was pleased to wink at the time of ignorance, yet now I found his call and command was to repentance and amendment of life. When I set my heart to seek him, I met with great inward opposition from the world, the flesh, and the devil, who assaulted me with manifold temptations. But for ever magnified be my gracious God, he made good the saying of our blessed Saviour, "My Father is greater than all, and none shall be able to pluck you out of my Father's hands." Thus, although I was like one cast out and forsaken, and in great measure destitute of those natural advantages many are favoured with, my education being low, yet, in this state of weakness and ignorance, the Lord took me under his care and protection.

'When out of my apprenticeship, having but few friends or relations that took much notice of me, I concluded to travel in the way of my trade, and went to London, where I worked some time. Afterwards I proceeded westward, by way of Oxford, Cirencester, and Bristol, intending to travel through the western counties, and return again to London. But I had not gone far from Bristol, before kind Providence, watching over me for my good, mercifully interposed, directing my way in his wisdom. He was pleased to put a stop to my roving mind, and to convince me of the truth of that saying, "It is not in man that walketh, to direct his own steps."

'Meeting with employment in my trade in the county of Somerset, and being convinced of the blessed truth, I settled amongst Friends, and continued in that part of the country some years. About the year 1724, my mouth was first opened in the work of the ministry at a meeting at Claverham, in the said county, which I attended for some years, before I went much abroad. After my stay here about twelve years, I entered into a married state with Esther Thurston, of Thornbury, in Gloucestershire, widow, where I then settled. We lived together in true unity about five years, when she was removed from me by death. During my residence here, the Lord laid a concern upon me to pay a religious visit to divers northern counties, and Scotland, also South and North Wales; with which I acquainted my friends, and had their concurrence and certificate. I set forward, endeavouring to look with a single eye to my good guide, who was pleased to enable me to perform this service to my own comfort, and the satisfaction of my friends. For this, and for his preservation and care over me every way unto this time, I bow my soul to my gracious and merciful God. Although I sometimes set out in great inward poverty, yet I was secretly supported by an invisible hand, that I could truly say, the Lord was my shepherd, and bountifully supplied all my wants, so as many times to make my cup run over, filling my heart with his love; that I can now say, What shall I render to the Lord for all his benefits, who has been my morning light, and I humbly hope will be my evening song?

'After this journey, I continued at Thornbury about five years longer, visiting the meetings of my friends in most of the western and northwest counties, as the Lord was pleased to open my way. About the year 1743, a concern was laid upon me to visit the principal towns in the county of Devon, where there were no Friends; and notwithstanding the undertaking looked difficult and arduous, yet as I was preserved in a faithful obedience to the Lord's requirings, He who put me forth was pleased to go before me in such a manner, that notwithstanding it was sometimes attended with very close exercise, yet through his divine assistance I was enabled to perform this service to a good degree of satisfaction, and to meet with no opposition; except in one place from an angry priest. At several towns I had meetings in the streets and market-houses. I afterwards went into Dorsetshire and Hampshire, and passed over the Isle of Jersey, in company with my friend Jeremiah Waring.

'1744. This year I visited Ireland.

'1745. Visited several western counties as far as Cornwall, and the circular yearly meeting there.

'1746. This year I entered a second time into a married state, with Mary, daughter of Joseph and Mary Ransom, of

Hitchin in Hertfordshire, where I then settled. She has been a true help-meet to me, we having now lived together in great unity about thirty-six years.

'After my marriage, I visited most of the counties of England and Wales, at different times, as the Lord was pleased to open my way, and enable me for it; through all which I have to acknowledge with thankfulness to my God, in whose service I went forth, that I lacked nothing, but was wonderfully preserved and supported; yet have nothing to glory in but that arm which was made bare for my help, and have done no more than was my duty to do. I have had many public services in barns and other places, where there were no Friends settled, and have attended many marriages and burials not herein particularly noticed. Under an humbling sense of the Lord's goodness, I can now look back with satisfaction and thankfulness to him who has enabled me so far to do my day's work in the day-time; and am now favoured in my old age to drink of that rock, out of which flow the issues of life; so that now, through his merciful aid, I can set up my Ebenezer, and say, Hitherto the Lord has helped me.

'I was called into the vineyard when young, and have ever since found work enough to do, either in digging, watering, or pruning: it not being a time for slothful servants, nor will it do to put that candle, which has been lighted in us, under a bed or a bushel. The Lord did not find me out amongst the wise and prudent of this world; but he took me from the stones of the street, whence, in his wisdom and goodness, he has often raised up children to Abraham. I have now to rejoice that my day's work is so near a happy close, having only patiently to wait my appointed time, until my change come.'

Here ends the account our dear friend gives of himself: what follows is extracted from the testimony of Baldock monthly meeting concerning him.

When, through the infirmities attending old age, he was

rendered incapable of going far from home, he diligently attended his own and neighbouring meetings, frequently appearing therein in short but lively exhortations, endeavouring to stir up the minds of friends to a faithful attention to their duty. He had a spirit of discerning beyond many, and an excellent gift in the discipline of the church, having a clear sight of the insufficiency of the outward form, without the influence of the divine power to support it to edification. His ministry was plain and powerful, often reaching the witness of truth in the hearts of his hearers.

In supplication he was inward and weighty, an awful solemnity covering his spirit, whereby he was frequently favoured with near access to the throne of divine grace.

An innocent cheerfulness, tempered with gravity, adorned his conversation, and his conduct was a pattern of meekness, moderation, and love, which gained him general esteem. Thus persevering in true watchfulness, the language of the apostle, which he was known frequently to repeat, may be truly adopted concerning him, "Our rejoicing is this, the testimony of our conscience, that in simplicity and godly sincerity, not with fleshly wisdom, but by the grace of God, we have had our conversation in the world."

In his last illness, being sensible his end was approaching, he expressed himself after this manner:

'I feel my natural faculties fail much. I desire to be content with the Lord's will, and to wait all the days of my appointed time, until my change shall come. It is pleasant to think I draw so near the end of my race, and can now set up my Ebenezer, and say, "Hitherto the Lord has been my shield, and exceeding great reward."'

At another time a few friends sitting by him, he said, 'I find my body advancing apace towards its dissolution; but death is no king of terrors to me. I hope I shall be ready for my final change. Although our meeting in this place is but small, it affords me a secret satisfaction to see the forming hand at work in some of our youth, and that they are measurably called into service; to which I hope they will give up. The world, and the things of it, have lain too near, and hurt the growth of some who might have made further advances, had they not been hindered thereby.'

He was favoured to feel very little pain, his complaint being a gradual decay of nature. He kept his bed about two or three days, during which time he said but little, although he seemed quite sensible to the last. About an hour before his end he turned himself in his bed, and seemed to fall into sleep; departing quietly without sigh or groan, the 18th day of the Fifth month, 1784, about the eighty-second year of his age, and a minister about sixty years.

Thus, our dear and worthy friend, after a long and well-spent life, finished his course, and we doubt not, hath entered that glorious immortality of rest and peace prepared for the righteous. His remains were interred in Friends' burial-ground at Hitchin the 23d.

JOHN FISHER, of Youghall, being taken unwell, and his disorder increasing, he had two friends called up early on Second-day morning, the 14th of Second month, 1785, to get his will made, and to give some directions about his affairs; which, when done, he seemed to give himself up, and lament leaving his poor wife and children. A friend asking him about the state of his mind, whether he had any uneasiness that way, he answered, 'Indeed he had, and would not conceal it.' He bewailed his neglect while health was afforded, to make the necessary preparation, for such a time as that; and an uneasiness on the latter account increasing, he dropt many expressions, lamenting his backwardness in duty. He also particularly regretted losing his father so young, and the want of the tender tuition of a religious mother; which if he had been favoured with, he thought he should have done better; that he had not been undutiful to her; nor did she want natural affection to him; yet he plainly saw he had been left too much to himself when young, and kept a stranger to his best friends, whom he said he did not know till lately. He spoke several times of his children, fearing they would suffer loss for want of his care, if he should be removed from them; recommended the care of them to some friends then present; and repeatedly desired that they might be brought up in plainness, as it was his choice to have them decent and plain.

On Fourth-day morning he was earnest to have a doctor sent for, who had attended him and was gone to the country, after which he appeared to be more alarmed and uneasy at his own state, and said, 'It was sounded in my ears, "Set thy house in order for thou shalt die, and not live;"' and continued in great distress for some time. Being desirous to see as many of his relations as were in the house, several were called to him. When they came he said, 'My dear friends and relations, I love you in the bowels of affection, and have called you to tell you that I am summoned to appear before the great Judge. I have been negligent in my duty, and desire that you with me may beseech him to have mercy on me. I have a ray of hope that he will admit me into some corner of his kingdom.' The doctors coming in, interrupted him, and he said, 'I had rather they would let me die in peace, I hoped to have a comfortable little meeting with you; but perhaps we may have it when they are gone.'

He still seemed in great distress, and on friends coming into his room, he said to several of them, with a voice that denoted much uneasiness and fear, that he was going before the great Judge; and uttered many things, lamenting his backwardness in duty, and neglect in seeking an acquaintance with God. He desired friends present to retire inward, and pray for him; and after a short pause addressed himself to one, and asked what he thought of him, desiring he would speak his mind. He answering that he did not then find any thing particular to express further than a desire to seek for mercy and peace for him, which he had a good degree of hope he would attain; he answered, 'That is what I want, and not life,' and added, 'that gives me some ray of comfort.' He asked again, whether he did hope it for him; going on in prayer and earnest entreaties to the Lord, several times requesting his friends to pray for him. He was recommended not to look too much for, or depend on, their prayers, but to look to the Lord; he answered, that was quite his mind, his dependence was on him alone, and on his dear Son. On his uncle's coming into the room, he said, 'I am going before the great Judge, which is a serious thing;' and lamenting his state much as before, said that if he had submitted to his dear uncle's advice, it would have been better for him; but yet he apprehended his uncle did not use as much authority over him as he might have done.

Several friends coming into his room, he lamented his state much as before, and seeming to be in a great strait, said that he was not yet without a ray of hope. After many more expressions and fervent prayers, he said he had a good degree of hope that he should be received in mercy. After a while he came to say, he had a well-grounded hope, and that death would be no king of terrors to him. That this was a glorious day to him, the most glorious he had ever seen; that he had a wonderfully kind, merciful master, beyond what he could expect, and that he could sing for joy of what he then felt of God's mercy; 'but,' said he, 'warn all not to trust to that, by neglecting and trifling away their time;' with many more sweet and comfortable expressions. He also begged his wife to resign him, adding, 'Charge the rich in this world, that they be not high-minded, nor trust in uncertain riches.'

His voice growing strong, it came to be raised almost to a melody, with prayers and praises to the Lord for his merciful dealings to him, in sparing him that day. He said the Lord had lifted up the light of his countenance on him, which was indeed beautiful, and that he had a hope, a well-grounded hope, that he should find mercy; and at many times after, expressed a desire of being released, and asked his friends present to pray that he might be taken away.

On seeing his nephew come in, he called him, and gave him much suitable advice and caution, desiring he would leave off some superfluities, and not be ashamed to do so, and say his dying uncle bade him, who he knew loved him well, and that he should never be sorry for it. He recommended him to mind and submit to Friends' advice, and not do as himself often had done, when he got good advice, let it in at one ear and out at the other; adding, that the last friendly visit was very beneficial to him, that he had treasured up some hints he got, which seemed to be in particular a solemn warning to prepare for the time then approaching, and said these were the right sort of visits, and not those of the world.

He had his sister called, saying, his love to her was strengthened. When she came, he said, 'My dear sister, I believe I was sent back with a message to thee in particular, to shake thyself from the filth of the earth. Rise up early and work, lose no time. Do not be deceived, as I was many times.' In particular, he advised her to the constant attendance of meetings, and not to miss those on First-day afternoon, nor week-days.

On seeing his wife much afflicted, he said to her, 'My dear Mary, did I not desire thee to be strong? Be strong in the Lord, for he is good and kind.'

He showed much satisfaction at seeing so many of his friends and relations about him; and recommended them not to neglect or despise the day of small things, as he too much had done. His mother having died the evening before, and lying dead in the house, he said, 'My friends, you are come to the house of mourning, death below stairs, and death above; but it is a joyful day to me.' At another time he said, 'Dear uncle, I have had a precious meeting here to-day.'

He repeated advice several times to Friends to live in love and unity, and to avoid all breaches, saying, 'It is a beautiful thing for brethren to dwell together in unity;' and that he thought it made something towards the unity of the brethren hereafter, and was a mark of the Master's. A physician coming in, and offering him his hand, he answered that he had no occasion for him; that he was near going, and was very easy and well; and that this was a glorious day to him, far the most so of any he had seen in this life; describing the Lord's goodness and merciful dealings with him.

His wife being present, he said, 'I think it was divine wisdom that led me first to see her, in goodness to me, as she proved a blessing to me; and I do not doubt but she will be blest.' He recommended her to the kind care and attention of his friends, and said he had a hope that his children would be preserved, and that the great Master would take them under his care; desiring his wife again to be strong, and take what was to come with cheerfulness.

He advised Friends to give no sleep to their eyes till they have found an acquaintance with God; and said, 'This is a warning from a tongue you did not expect; but a new song is put into my mouth, even a song of praise. Oh that I had a tongue that could ring through the streets. Beware that you do not attribute these sayings to me; they were never bred in me, they are all from the great Master. He can make the stones of the street speak, and I am one of them.' After some time he said, 'My outward man grows weaker, but I perceive my inward man to grow stronger,' and he rejoiced in the Lord's goodness.

To a young man, not of our Society, he said, 'I am glad to see thee, and am obliged for the trouble thou hast taken. There is something good about thee. I believe thou art well inclined, but, like many others, willing to go on in the old beaten track; but when thou feelest any of the inward breathings of truth, or its discoveries, attend thereto, for I know thou hast a sufficiency of it to begin upon, in order to make a good ending.'

To his sister's husband he said, 'I have loved thee as a brother, and I know thou art an honest man, and hast something good in thee; but there is also something of shame. Remember, if thou dost not acknowledge God before men, he will not acknowledge thee.'

After a while, his wife being so full that she gave a little vent to her grief, he said, 'Keep silence;' and repeated, 'Keep silence before me, O islands, and let the people renew their strength.'

On seeing a religious inoffensive man, one of his friends, come into the room, he called out, 'O, John, I am glad to see thee. There is one,' said he, 'that has minded the day of small things;' and he spoke something of the Lord's goodness to himself, and how well it was with him.

To one of his servants he said he hoped he would be faithful to his mistress; and recommended him, and all of his profession, not to trust to the priest, or the ringing of a bell, to do the work for them, but to seek for themselves. That whatsoever was to be known of God was made manifest in man; and, blessing the Lord, said he had not sent bishop or priest to him to touch him, or engage his attention; but had come and touched him himself, and done the work for him.

On speaking to a Friend about the want of regularity in some of his accounts, by which he thought his family would sustain loss, he said it was no wonder these accounts should be neglected, when he had neglected his own great account.

He afterwards uttered many sweet expressions, a few of which, that could be remembered, were as follow:

'It is better to be here, though in the house of mourning, than in the house of rejoicing. O Lord, as I have found thee, I will not, I intend, let thee go. O beautiful is his countenance! he hath lifted up the light of his countenance on me, and it is beautiful indeed.'

On hearing the clock strike six, he said he had lived twenty-four hours longer than he expected, and that it was the most glorious, happy day that ever he had. Though he greatly regretted putting off the work so long, yet he rejoiced in the Lord's goodness, and hoped in that twenty-four hours he was enabled to find acceptance, as well as if he had been in the front of the battle. He also exhorted others not to trust to that, but to begin early, saying it is a fine thing at such a time to have nothing to do but to die, and that it was the Lord alone that did the work for him.

He signified his satisfaction in being, in a good degree, preserved in resignation since the beginning of his sickness, and that he had not used any angry expressions to those about him, nor in word or thought murmured at the great Master.

He lamented the pride and vanity of foolish people, in spending so much time and pains to deck their poor bodies, an example of the vileness of which he thought was in himself, and said, 'I believe I am thus strengthened for some good purpose for your sakes, and wish you may attend to the advice of a dying friend, and think of me sometimes, that there was such a one. I am going but a little before you.'

To a friend he said, 'I remember thou gave me some advice several years ago, which was good advice, though I did not then think it so, nor did thou speak it to me as thou shouldst have done; yet I have often thought of it since, and believe it was of use to me.'

To his wife he said, 'I do not belong to thee nor thou to me, now. It is a great mercy that this was not the sickness or death of a day or two, for I was not ready; but since this warning, I think I have not been idle one hour.' He also said, 'I have been enabled since my sickness, to give up wife, children, and all, and set no value on them, in comparison of what is before me.'

The doctor who was sent for, having returned from the country, when he was informed of it, his dependence and expectation being taken off from such helps, and even from the desire of life, he said, 'Give my love to him; I have no occasion for him now.' On a relation expressing a desire that the doctor should see him, as he was sent for, he consented, and was likewise prevailed on to consent to putting blisters on his legs, which were exceedingly troublesome to him for two days, and caused a severe conflict, which himself, and those about him, much lamented, after the fine easy state of mind he had before attained. He said he thought they delayed his passage, and that, but for them, he would have been in his Master's house before; and often prayed to be enabled to hold out to the end, and that his faith might not fail.

When he observed the light appear on Fifth-day morning, he desired to be kept quiet that day, as he must mind his own business; and not to let many come to see him, lest he should be disturbed, or in anything miss the mark.

Sixth-day evening, by his own desire, there was some blood taken from him, after which he lay more composed, and turning himself, said, 'Come, who knows but I may get a little of the great Master's company now before I go.' After a while, he said, 'Never fear, never fear; I hope all will be well.'

He said the Lord had greatly favoured him many times, when none knew it but himself, though he had too much neglected it; that he had an evidence the kingdom was open to receive him.

That night, being very uneasy, he many times prayed to the following purpose: 'O thou most gracious and merciful God, help me! O! leave me not in the hour of trial. O, my God! help me, and be with me, and grant me patience.'

To a friend, a little before his departure, he said, 'The sting of death is sin, and that is, through the Lord's goodness, taken away from me.'

Third-day afternoon, the 22d of Second month, 1785, he

quietly departed with a composed countenance, aged thirty-three years. His remains were interred in Friends' grave-yard the 25th of the same.

ROBERT WALKER, of Gildersome, in Yorkshire, was educated in the profession of truth; and being favoured with the visitations of divine love in his youth, was, by yielding obedience to its heavenly teachings, redeemed from the follies and vanities incident to youth, and gradually fitted for being a useful instrument in the church. About the year 1751 he first appeared as a minister, in much brokenness of spirit. He kept mostly to meetings about home, till the year 1756, when his heart being enlarged in gospel love, with the concurrence of Friends, he visited, at different times, most parts of this nation and Ireland; and in the year 1773 was engaged in a general visit to the meetings in North America, and laboured among them in much fervency of spirit. Being favoured with a sense of the approaching troubles in that part of the world, he delivered many faithful warnings, suitable cautions and instructions, greatly to the encouragement of the upright-hearted.

He was much devoted to the Lord's service, of an humble mind, and exemplary upright conversation, accompanied with innocent cheerfulness; was properly concerned that his temporal affairs might be conducted reputably; and was greatly esteemed by Friends and others.

The exercise of his gift in the ministry was attended with a striking and persuasive simplicity, and being in the demonstration of the Spirit, carried its own evidence with power to the hearts of the people; directing them from all outward dependence to the everlasting foundation, Christ Jesus, the rock of ages.

With a mind replenished with love, he engaged in a visit to the meetings of Friends in London and some of the southern counties; and was favoured to perform the same, in which he expressed he felt great peace; but his complaints increasing upon him, he retired to a Friend's house at Tottenham, and attended the meetings there on the First-day following, being the last public meeting he was at, and in which he bore a living testimony.

During his sickness he was mercifully preserved in a tender frame of mind, and expressed himself thus: 'I have seen my way into London, but not back; but am quite resigned to the Lord's will. I have laboured honestly and uprightly in my great Master's cause, and have peace. I am gradually sinking away. I desire some of you, if I should be removed, to write to my wife, and remember my very dear love to her, and to my children. It will be a close trial to them; but it will be well with me, and it is my earnest desire for my children, far above all other considerations, that they may seek the God of their father.'

He desired his love might be remembered to friends in the north; and said, 'I have looked towards home with a degree of anxiety, but it was soon taken away, and now I feel my mind quite easy, and resigned to the will of him who has been with me all my life long, and who knows what is best for me.'

At another time he said, 'People may think of putting off repentance to a dying hour; but what should I do now, if I had my peace to make. It is enough to bear the afflictions of the body:' and added, O Lord, preserve me in patience, to wait thy time.'

To a friend going into the room, when he had been in great pain, and requesting to stay with him, he said, 'Thou may go to thy rest; leave me to my Maker, who knows what is best for me. All will be well; if I be restored, I hope it will be for his service.'

To a friend who expressed some hope of his recovery, and said that his removal would be a great loss in these low times, he said, 'A stripping time must come, and it will come, to take the dependence of men from each other;' and he expressed that it had often been the fervent exercise of his mind, that the Almighty would be with him in his concluding moments.

The morning before his departure, taking a solemn leave of those about him, he said, 'Weep not for me, I am going home; and shall be gathered as a shock of corn fully ripe:' begging to be preserved from murmuring till his change should come, which, he said, would be a glorious change to him.

Thus, in a sweet frame of spirit, being sensible to the last, he departed this life, at the house of Thomas Phillips, at Tottenham,the 24th of the Ninth month, 1785, aged about sixty-eight years, and a minister thirty-four years.

His corpse was carried to Devonshire House meeting-house, London; after which it was interred in Friends' burial-ground, near Whitechapel, the 29th of the same.

REBECCA SUMMERS, wife of Thomas Summers, of Horsham, in the county of Sussex, was visited with a painful illness, which continued on her for about two years before her decease. She bore it with exemplary patience, having been all her life remarkable for the meekness of her spirit, and innocence of her conversation. She was a sincere lover of her friends, a diligent attender of our religious meetings when her health permitted, an affectionate wife, a tender parent, and a kind neighbour; and of a remarkably forgiving temper to those from whom she had received injuries. Nevertheless, towards the conclusion of her time, she was very low and poor, and unsatisfied about her future state; which her husband tenderly observing, said to her, that however the Lord's favour and acceptance might be hidden from her, he had no doubt but it would be well with her, if she was now removed; and expressed his fervent desire, that it might please the author of all good to make known his love to, and acceptance of, her, before her removal hence; which desire seemed fully answered.

She frequently said, 'Oh merciful Father, if it please thee, cut the thread of my life, and let me dwell with thy peaceable ones; yet not my will but thine be done.' At another time she said, 'O merciful Father, which art in heaven, thine is the kingdom, the power, and glory for ever. Hallelujah to the Lamb for ever.' Being lifted up in bed, she bowed her head, and said, 'My soul is reverently bowed down, I trust, under a sense of the Lord's mercy and goodness.' At another time she audibly and fervently said, 'I am upon the banks of deliverance. I shall dwell with my merciful Father to all generations;' adding, 'it is of no merit to me.' She also frequently said, 'Come, sweet Jesus, come.'

She was favoured with her wonted understanding; except at some intervals, for about three days before her departure, she was somewhat wandering; yet she perfectly knew those about her; and at times as clear and collected as at any time during her illness; by which she felt to the utmost the excruciating pain of body; but evidently partook of that which the eye of man has not seen, by which she was sustained through all. Desiring to be lifted up in bed, not long before her end, those about her intimating a fear it might be too much for her, she answered, 'What matters it whether I sit up or lie down, if I die in the arms of my Redeemer?'

Seeing her sister grieve, she said, 'Dear sister, do not do so, we shall meet again.'

A little time before her end, her speech failed very much, yet her senses seemed evidently clear; for on being asked what should be done for her, she said, 'Pray without ceasing;' and indeed it appeared to those present, her practice at that time.

She departed this life the 13th of the First month, 1785, and was buried the 16th of the same, in Friends' burial-ground at Plestow, near Capel in Surry.

ISAAC WILSON, of Kendal, in Westmoreland, was the son of Anthony and Dorothy Wilson, of Highwray, near Hawkshead, in the county of Lancaster, by whom he was religiously educated; and being favoured with an early visitation of Divine grace, and obedient thereto, he was preserved amidst the various temptations and allurements to which youth is exposed.

Having with fidelity served his apprenticeship in Kendal, he settled in business, and married Rachel, the daughter of John and Deborah Wilson, of the same place; to whom he was united in a mutual engagement for the promotion of truth and righteousness, and the welfare of his family, particularly in their best and endearing interests; in his conduct towards his children, beautifully uniting the authority of a parent, and the familiar persuasive influence of a friend. His wife (of whom see an account in this collection) was much engaged from home in the cause of truth; and though the separation was a close trial to him, yet he freely gave her up, encouraging her to follow the pointings of duty; being sensible that obedience to divine requirings brings peace, and an increase of light and strength.

Although he was zealously concerned for the support of our Christian testimony in all its branches, yet his zeal was so tempered with charity, that he retained the esteem even of the unfaithful. A care rested on his mind to preserve love and unity, and where any breach appeared, he laboured to have the occasion timely removed; and also was much engaged to give private admonitions.

About the fortieth year of his age, he was concerned publicly to testify to the efficacy of that divine principle which had been the guide of his youth; in the exercise of which duty his labours were edifying, and he was lively and fervent.

Although his family was large, and his engagements of a public and private nature many, yet he so ordered them, as not to interfere with his religious duty, being concerned constantly to attend meetings both for worship and discipline; frequently attended the yearly meeting in London; and, in company with other Friends, visited the monthly and quarterly meetings of Friends in Ireland, Scotland, and some parts of England. His disposition was hospitable and charitable; his conversation was informing and edifying, accompanied with affability. Being of sound judgment and integrity, he was often applied to by Friends and others for his advice, which he freely communicated, and to be an arbitrator in differences, by which means he contributed to the peace of many families. Notwithstanding his industry for the support of a numerous family, he was earnestly and constantly concerned to limit his pursuits in number and extension, agreeably to the circumscribing rule of truth.

Having been thus diligently concerned, through Divine assistance, to fill up the religious, relative and social duties of life; he experienced the gracious power that had been the stay of his youth, and a support under every trying dispensation of Providence, to be his evening song, and a staff to lean upon in declining age.

The last two years of his life he was much tried with indisposition; but the following expressions show the situation of his mind, which he delivered the day before his death, in the presence of some of his children, with great power and energy, though under much bodily weakness, viz.:

'I know not how it may be; I may remain with you a while longer, or be removed at this time; but I am easy as to the event. If, at times, I breathe a sigh, or a groan, it is not from a troubled mind. I feel no weight upon my spirit; but all seems clear. The world, and all that is in it, are nothing to me. Though I have been tried with pain of body, and deep inward poverty, yet now the Divine presence is near, and I am thankful to feel I am not forsaken. The Lord has been with me all my life long, and poured down his blessings upon me; and he will, my dear children, be with and support you, if you are concerned to seek him. Oh the matchless loving-kindness of our God! The tongue of men and angels is too short to show forth his praise.' And, after making a kind of melody, which cannot be expressed, he sweetly added, 'Peace! Peace! Peace!'

Thus, with a well-grounded hope that his day's work was finished, he died the 18th of the Eighth month, 1785; and was interred in Friends' burial-ground, at Kendal, on the 23d of the same, after a large and solemn meeting held on the occasion: aged seventy, having been a minister thirty years.

KEZIA MERRYWEATHER, wife of John Merryweather, of Ringwood, in Hampshire, was the daughter of Benjamin and Elizabeth Evens, of Woodbridge in Suffolk; who were careful to train her up in a godly conversation, which was blessed to her, for she gave early proof of an attachment to virtue. After her marriage it pleased the Lord to permit weakness of body frequently to attend her, which, at length, terminated in a settled decline. In the course of her illness, she gave good advice to divers who came to see her; dropped many comfortable expressions; and was preserved in much patience and resignation.

Her husband and sister being with her, she expressed to them, 'I would not have you sorrow as without hope. Oh, what a difference there is between those who have endeavoured to come up in the path of duty, and those who have followed lying vanities, when they come to such a time as this. Now I know the difference. When I first felt that I was taken for death, I seemed to have a little fear; but it was soon removed, and now I long for it. Oh! how I long to be in the full enjoyment of what I now feel. Lord, hasten thy messenger, if consistent with thy will. I believe the Lord, who has been with me in six troubles, will not forsake in the seventh.'

Her husband going into her room about two hours before her departure, she said, 'My dear, I sent for thee to see thy poor dying wife; but I would not have thee hurry thyself, but come and sit down by me. I feel so comfortable, I cannot express it; no pains; only cold!'

She soon after prayed to this effect: 'Oh! Lord, thou hast been a gracious God to me; be with me at this time; and if it be thy blessed will, grant me an easy passage from this troublesome world to the mansion of rest, where all sorrow is at an end, and all tears are wiped away.' Soon after, 'I feel so sweet and easy, that it does not seem as though I could be dying; if I am, it is a mercy I cannot be sufficiently thankful for. I did not think it possible for one in such a situation to be so easy.' On the apothecary coming in, and asking how she did, she answered, 'Very comfortable; waiting to go to rest, which I believe will be soon.' Soon after, desiring to be turned on her right side, she said she would have a little sleep, and then go to rest; which she did, lying as in a comfortable sleep about a quarter of an hour; when, awakening, she breathed a few times, and expired, without sigh, groan, or struggle, the 29th of the Ninth month, 1785, aged twenty-eight years; and was buried in Friends' burial-ground the 6th of Tenth month following.

JUDITH HILL, wife of John Hill, late treasurer of Ackworth School, was the daughter of Andrew and Judith Leaper, of London, who educated her in the profession of the Church of England, and brought her up in the practice of dressing, singing, dancing, and other vain customs of this degenerate world. These she was often made uneasy with; and about the twenty-third year of her age, her understanding being further enlightened, she gave up in obedience to the visitations of truth in her own mind, joined in profession with Friends, and became a diligent attender of their meetings, and, under a sense of duty, declined the customs of the world in speech, dress, and deportment.

This brought much suffering upon her from her parents, especially from her mother; but, being supported by that divine power that had convinced her judgment, she bore with much patience the reproaches with which it was her lot to be tried, which resignation was attended with peace; and in time she experienced the regard of her near relations, her mother expressing great satisfaction and full reconciliation with her. After her convincement she entered into a married state, and having in time a numerous family, she was concerned to educate them religiously.

In the year 1779, a suitable friend being wanted to superintend the institution of Ackworth, on its being proposed to her husband, he, after due consideration, engaged to go and reside there, and she occupied the station of mistress of the family.

About a year before her departure, her health gradually began to decline, and, the last three months of her confinement, she underwent great bodily affliction, but was enabled to endure it with exemplary patience and resignation to the will of the Lord, whom she found to be her abundant support.

In the fore part of her illness, one night, being seized with a fainting fit and much pain, her husband, daughters, and some others being present, being a little recovered, she expressed herself as follows: 'How it may please the Lord to deal with me I know not; but if he should be pleased to remove me this night, I am fully resigned to his divine will, come what may. I can truly say, I have not desired for myself or children, either riches or length of days, but that they might be nurtured in the fear of the Lord, and inherit a portion in the blessed truth.'

At another time, her husband questioning with her, 'Hast thou any word of comfort for me?' After a short pause, she answered, 'How it may please the Almighty to order it concerning my life, is at present hid from me; but this I know, the Lord brought us together, and hath supported through many deep trials and afflictions. When I have to look back to my childhood and education, I have cause to acknowledge with great thankfulness, that his preserving hand, in the time of ignorance, kept me from joining with the many evils and temptations which were in my father's family. When greater light and understanding were given, I gave up in obedience thereto; and now, on a strict search, find nothing stands in my way to eternal happiness.'

When she drew near her end, among other expressions, she said, 'I hope and believe, when the Lord is pleased to remove me, to be favoured with a place in his glorious mansions. I can truly say, if I die now, I die in peace with all men. I have not done many mighty acts, or been a conspicuous character in the world; nor have I desired it, but, I hope, endeavoured, according to knowledge, to live up to what was manifested to be my duty.'

The morning before she departed, her daughter hearing her speak, thought she wanted something, and went to her bed-side; she said, 'Didst thou not hear me? I said the sting of death, which is sin, is taken away. The pale horse and his rider will have no victory, for the guardian angel of the Lord's presence encompasseth about.'

After expressing that her time here was near closing, she desired to see her husband and children, and took a solemn leave of them, with some tender exhortations and remarks; signified that her mind was covered with the universal love of God; and added, 'I feel my little strength weaken apace, but my faith in the Lord grows stronger and stronger. I have a firm hope, and an unshaken assurance of entering everlasting happiness.' A solemn pause ensued; then she broke forth in manner following: 'Awful, solemn silence, how comfortable! It has been refreshing to my mind at this time. O seek after it, dear children; keep low and humble, for all that is exalted shall be brought down; yea, the sturdy oaks of Bashan, and the tall cedars of Lebanon, will the Lord lay low.' Then taking her husband and children each by the hand, she kissed them, bidding them Farewell, farewell in the Lord.

She quietly departed this life without sigh or groan, the 26th of Tenth month, 1785, aged nearly sixty years, and was interred the 30th of the same, in Friends' burial-ground at Ackworth, in Yorkshire.

THOMAS ROSS, of Wrightstown, in Bucks county, Pennsylvania, having, with the near sympathy and unity of his friends and brethren, come over to England to pay a religious visit to Friends there, arrived a few days before the yearly meeting in 1784, which he attended, and afterwards visited Ireland that summer. On his return, he joined his friend John Pemberton, of Philadelphia, in visiting the quarterly meetings at Woodbridge and Norwich, and proceeded forwards to Lincoln, York, and, by Durham, into Scotland. They had many meetings among those of other societies, which were generally large and satisfactory; but his bodily indispositions increasing, he was under the necessity of resting at sundry places; and, taking a few meetings by the way, he reached York the 2nd of the Eleventh month, 1785, and attended their monthly meeting the day following, which was the last meeting he was at.

During the course of his travels, his religious labours were truly acceptable to Friends, and well received by others; for, having an especial eye to the putting forth of the Divine hand, his ministry was attended with living virtue and deep instruction; and though not in the words which man's wisdom teacheth, yet in godly simplicity, and with a zeal becoming true religion.

In meetings for business, he was particularly serviceable; his remarks being mostly short, pertinent, and very instructive; exciting to a steady attention to divine counsel in the transacting of our Christian discipline, and therein to exercise true judgment, without partiality or respect of persons.

During the course of his illness he was preserved in a heavenly frame of mind. On many occasions dropping instructive counsel and advice to the friends who attended on and visited him; of which the following collection is but a small part. He frequently said that he knew not why he was continued in such an exercised state of bodily weakness; yet doubted not but that it was all in wisdom, and for some good end; adding, it was not for the clay to say to the potter, 'Why hast thou made me thus?'

Sitting in the family where he was, during the fore part of his illness, he expressed himself thus: 'Dear young people, keep to your first love; the bridegroom of souls will not be unmindful of the bride while she remains chaste; some of you, I believe, are espoused to Christ. O, the ardent desire which I feel for the youth! "Thy name is as ointment poured forth, therefore do the virgins love thee." '

The same day, 'I have not sought mine own honour, but the honour of Him who first drew me from my habitation, and have great reason to praise his name. One thing which inclines me to think my work may be nearly done is this; that it never appeared to be laid upon me to pay a general visit to England.' At another time he said, 'O the harmony there is in the Lord's family! "Ephraim shall not envy Judah, nor Judah vex Ephraim; nothing shall hurt or destroy in all thy holy mountain." '

Again he remarked, on his being under bodily oppression, 'I find no relief but when I feel a revival of that which is the healer of breaches; but that is not at my command. My mind was last night much drawn out to my fellow-labourers; O, that they [may] keep little! I have remembered that saying, "There are a few names even in Sardis who have not defiled their garments," and I hope there are a few in York. Dear friends, what a people should we be, did we dig deep enough. Our lights would shine before men; we should be as the salt of the earth. How many, who have begun well, have had their garments defiled with the world, and are become like the salt that has lost its savour. These are as dead weights in our assemblies, so that the living are scarcely able to bury the dead. O, Friends, keep to the truth, for it shall rise above the heads of gainsayers."

At another time, 'I could not be more at home any where. It revives me to see the children about me. I tell you, young people, the hardest thing I ever found in my passage was, when I was right, to keep so. Oh, the desire I felt to get here! The love I feel for you is like the love of Jonathan and David. It extends over sea and land; it is like the precious ointment; so that some can say with one formerly, "Neither heights nor depths, principalities nor powers, things present, or to come, shall ever separate us from it." The least sun casteth a lustre, as the glorious luminaries in the outward creation; so that we may say, "Great and marvellous are thy works, Lord God Almighty; just and true are thy ways, thou King of saints!"

Again, '"Commune with thine own heart, and be still;" this is doing business. Oh, how precious is truth! It may employ us on the highway, and in our outward engagements. Dear friends, let us prize it.' Speaking to the physician, he said, 'The outward man grows weaker; yet inward support waxeth stronger and stronger.' The same day he said, 'It is a great favour to have a brook by the way! Oh! I see my way over all! It is like a foretaste of what is to come. "Blessed are the dead that die in the Lord!" When he breaks in upon us it is like balm. "There is balm in Gilead." There are many not willing to go to the house of mourning; but there is occasion for it; it being high time to repair the breaches. I have thought for many weeks past, the curtain was nearly drawn. There seemed but few sands left in the glass; and yet I sometimes feel such a travail for Zion's prosperity, and the enlargement of her borders, that

I am ready to think the day's work is not yet done; and at other times, I feel so feeble and weak, that all seems nearly over. The event I cannot tell, but am favoured to be resigned.'

At another time, 'Think nothing too near, or too dear, to part with, dear young people, to purchase the truth. Your parents cannot give it you, though they may give you all they can. It is the Lord's prerogative. I have thought it was a great favour to have an education in the truth; but I have been grieved to see many born in the Society, like Esau, selling their birthright. Be not ashamed of the cross, dear friends, deny Him not before men.'

Again he added, 'Beware of lawful things; these lawful things are the strongest bait Satan ever laid for our society. Oh, these lawful things, they have hurt many. What a testimony would it be, if Friends were to shut up their shops on week days, to go to meetings, which ought to be the main concern; though many consider worldly things as such. When we have done all we can, we are but as unprofitable servants; we can add nothing to Him who is the fountain of goodness. Oh, that ocean of ancient goodness! I seem at times as if I was swallowed up in it. I have cause to be thankful, that I am favoured with a resigned mind, and have no will, either to live or die. Oh, Father, receive me into thy bosom.' At another time, 'Oh, my heart is knit to you, my friends; and to the seed which is in bondage in many hearts; and though you may have to go with it into the wilderness, yet be not discouraged.'

Feeling himself easier, and his mind favoured, he said, 'Oh, when he puts his hand in, as at the hole of the door, how does it smell of sweet myrrh. I hope I am not insensible from whence my help comes. He sometimes hides himself as behind the curtain, yet we must not awake or disturb our beloved until he please.'

Speaking on the general state of mankind, he said thus: 'Oh, how has my mind been oppressed, in observing that profaneness which abounds among the people; many of whom draw iniquity as with cords of vanity, and sin as with a cart-rope. Yet I have this satisfaction, that I have not failed to reprove many of those I have seen in this state; and have often advised inn-keepers and others, to discourage all kinds of wickedness in their houses. My advice hath been generally received without gainsaying, and I have comfort in the discharge of this duty. Oh, the vileness of the land of Ireland! Surely if any nation ever had occasion to mourn because of oaths, that has.'

Being under much bodily affliction, he said, 'How can one die better than in the Lord's service; for he has been indeed a wonderful counsellor; he has many times opened a way, when I could see no way; he will never leave nor forsake those who trust in him.' Again, 'It is a trying time, and yet, I believe I have a well-grounded hope of having done my duty. I feel no condemnation. O, dear friends, what a favour indeed, that we have an unction from above! Keep to the truth and its testimony, whatever may be the consequence, for it will rise over the heads of gainsayers.'

At another time, 'It will not do for any to rest contented with having known the Lord in days past, and years that are over and gone. We must follow on to know him; a supply of daily bread is requisite; and if there is not an hunger and thirst after righteousness, we may be sure the mind is distempered. But oh! how have I been pained to see and feel, many of the professors of the truth, going after the world and its spirit; who, instead of being way-marks, are as stumbling-blocks to honest inquirers: the state of these is lamentable. I have been comforted in the prospect of a rising generation, if they are not hurt by those who ought to be helpers, loving this present world. I have, in my time, met with many cross winds and boisterous waves; but have been preserved in a care to keep near the point, that guides to the harbour of rest. For these fifty years I have been endeavouring to fight the good fight of faith. O, dearest Father!

not my will, but thine, be done. Oh, when will the curtain be drawn; that this mortal may put on immortality, and eternal life, which will, I do believe, be my happy portion!'

He would often, in thankful commemoration of the goodness of God to him, break forth in these words, 'What shall I render unto thee, O Lord, for all thy benefits.'

A few days before his decease, on a friend returning from meeting, he said he had been favoured with such a sweet calm, that he hoped he should have passed away. A day or two before he died, he broke forth sweetly in these words; 'Oh joy! joy! joy!' Again, '"O death, where is thy sting? O grave, where is thy victory? The sting of death is sin!" I see no cloud in my way. I die in peace with all men.'

He departed this life the 13th of the Second month, 1786, at the house of Lindley Murray, at Holgate, near York; and was interred in Friends' burial-ground, in that city, the 16th of the same, in the seventy-eighth year of his age.

CLAUDE GAY, of Barking, in Essex, was a native of France, being born in the city of Lyons, about the year 1706, and was educated in the church of Rome, of which he continued a zealous member till about the thirty-sixth year of his age, when, being at Morlaix on account of business, he came under a religious exercise of mind. During this season, perceiving a New Testament in a room, he took it up, and observing it was licensed by two popes, he concluded he might lawfully read it. On opening the book, the first words he read were these; "God, that made the world, and all things therein, seeing he is Lord of heaven and earth, dwelleth not in temples made with hands, neither is he worshipped with men's hands." Acts xvii., verse 24, &c.

On the perusal of this passage, he was convinced in his judgment of the errors of the Romish doctrine of transubstantiation; and he saw clearly, that the adoration of the bread and wine, as the body and blood of Christ, was idolatrous, and contrary to the doctrine of the gospel; but, at the instance of a person who persuaded him not to forsake the public worship at once, he went to one of the smallest mass-houses in that town, and placed himself at the greatest distance from the priest. He did not keep kneeling steadily as was customary, but first on one knee and then on the other, with great restlessness; till the priest elevated the host, that the congregation beholding it, might prostrate themselves as usual before it.

This query strongly impressed his mind, 'Wilt thou also prostrate thyself?' Being affected therewith, he could continue there no longer; but, putting on his hat, with fear and trembling he arose, and hastily left the place; and confessed to his former adviser, he felt great condemnation for conforming that day against his conscience; and that being clearly convinced of the errors of the doctrine of that church, he ought to forsake them.

He continued about one year longer in France; but desiring to dwell with Protestants, he went to Jersey, and resided there; where meeting with Robert Barclay's Apology; he was, on perusing it, convinced of the truth of the doctrine contained therein, and embraced the principles of Friends.

About the year 1741, he was imprisoned by order of the magistrates there; and, after nine months' confinement, was banished to England; but returning, he was again imprisoned, and banished under pain of corporal punishment if he returned. He was afterwards relieved by order of the king and council, and left at liberty to return to Jersey; but being thus liberated, he settled at London about the year 1745.

In the exercise of his ministry he travelled much, chiefly on foot. In 1763 he visited Holland, some parts of Germany, and Switzerland, where his labours in the cause of piety seem to have been well received.

When not engaged in travelling his time was employed in attending meetings, teaching the French language, and tranlating several religious treatises into French. His diligence in attending meetings for worship and discipline was exemplary, even when suffering under the weight of age and infirmities; and he was also an example of humility, self-denial, and charity. Being careful in his ministry not to go beyond his guide, his appearances were seldom long, but lively, sound, edifying, and pertinent to the states of the people. He was fervent in prayer, and evinced a deep knowledge and experience in the things of God.

He endured a lingering and painful disease with much patience and resignation; his mind appeared abstracted from earthly things, and centred in the enjoyment of divine peace, declaring to those about him and with whom he conversed, that all fear of death was removed.

He departed this life at Barking, the 19th of the Second month, 1786, and was interred in Friends' burial-ground there, aged nearly eighty; and a minister about forty years.

MARTHA WILLIAMS, of Neath, in Glamorganshire, was the daughter of John and Abigail Binns, of Carleton Biggin, near Skipton, in Yorkshire, and was born in the Fifth month, 1710. She was educated in Friends' principles, but in her youth was prone to vanity. Nevertheless, by divine grace, she was effectually enabled to turn her back on the pleasures and allurements of this world, and her mind became engaged to seek an inheritance incorruptible.

About the twenty-eighth year of her age she found it to be her duty to bear a public testimony to the sufficiency of that power which had visited her; and great were her sufferings and conflicts under a sense of her unworthiness and inability for so great a work; but being renewedly helped and instructed by the extendings of divine love, she was strengthened to yield obedience to the requiring.

In 1746, she married Ambrose Williams, and settled at Pont-y-pool, in Monmouthshire. They were true helpmeets, giving up each other freely to the service of truth, trusting in the Lord, and, making it their principal care to seek first the kingdom of heaven and the righteousness thereof, all things necessary in this life were added unto them.

Under this devotedness of mind she was frequently concerned to visit Friends in most parts of England and Wales, and was twice in Ireland. She was a great encourager of the weak, a seeker after the scattered, and a sympathizer with the afflicted; and her cheerful temper gained her much place in the affections of young people, who were the particular objects of her tender care, and her advice often proved the means of drawing them nearer to the pure witness within.

The latter part of her life she lived with her son-in-law and daughter, Evan and Elizabeth Reese, of Neath. She was chiefly confined at home for about six months, and in the last two months suffered great pain; but was preserved in quietness and peace of mind, and was at times strengthened to express her thankfulness, that she was waiting the Lord's time to remove her to an everlasting rest. She tenderly advised her children to do their day's work in the day-time; putting up her prayers to the Father of mercies for their preservation, with great fervency; and praising the name of the Lord, who had been the stay of her youth, was the staff of her declining age; and who graciously favoured her with his presence to her latest moments.

She quietly departed this life at Neath, the 19th of the Second month, 1788, and was interred in Friends' burial-ground, at Swansea, the 24th of the same; aged seventy-eight, and a minister about fifty years.

MARY GURNEY, of Norwich, was the daughter of Edmund and Mary Gurney, of that city; Friends well esteemed, and religiously concerned to educate their children in the way of truth; and their care herein was the means of her being, in a good degree, preserved from the vanities of the world, in the time of her youth.

About the thirty-third year of her age she was favoured with a close humbling visitation of divine love, under which she was concerned to bear testimony thereto, by way of public ministry, in which Friends had unity with her; and though she did not travel much abroad, she visited some of the meetings in her own, and some adjacent counties. In the year 1788, she visited the meetings of Friends in Bristol, Worcestershire, and in divers other places, in which her public ministry, and religious services in Friends' families where her lot was cast, were to the comfort and satisfaction of many.

In the close of her visit she staid a short time in London, and attended some meetings there; and having visited the week-day meeting at Plaistow, and had acceptable service therein, she was soon after taken ill, and was conveyed to the house of Joseph Cockfield, at Upton, where, her indisposition rapidly increasing, she said that she hoped she should be favoured with patience to bear all. The following day, her disorder continuing to gain ground, and a person present saying, she might still live to do further good, she replied to this effect, that she endeavoured to make such matters easy to her mind, by thinking, "Shall not the Judge of all the earth do right?" and that she believed, if it pleased him to remove her, it would be in mercy, and that she might never go better.

Her quiet composure of spirit and resignation to the divine will during her illness, which, although short, was attended with much bodily pain, were truly edifying to those about her. She said to her companion, 'Oh! what greater happiness, than to enter into the fulness of joy;' and that she felt no guilt. Other comfortable and instructive expressions dropped from her at different times. About an hour before her dissolution she appeared to be engaged in supplication; but her voice failing, she could not be clearly understood. Her last words, which were distinctly heard, a short time before she expired, were, 'Ready, ready, ready! Jesus Christ, my Lord!'

She departed this life on the 2d of the Eleventh month, 1788, aged sixty-one; a minister about twenty-seven years; and was buried on the 9th of the same month, in Friends' burial-ground, near Bunhill fields, after a meeting in Gracechurch-street meeting-house.

ROBERT HARVEY, of Old Meldrum, in Scotland, having been a faithful labourer for the promotion of piety and virtue, in his time, that his example should not be lost, the following short account of him seems to claim a place in this collection. He was a man of exemplary conduct, a diligent attender of meetings, and an upright labourer in them, his ministry being sound and edifying. He visited most of the meetings in England and Wales, between the years 1754 and 1757, and soon after Ireland, returning by the north of England, to general satisfaction, and his own peace: and, although we have no further account of his travels in truth's service, yet it is evident he retained his integrity to his conclusion; as he signified a little before his departure, that all his accounts were clear, and that he found nothing but peace of mind.

He departed this life on the 21st of the Twelfth month, 1788, and was buried in Friends' burial-ground at Acquorthies the 23d of the same, aged seventy-seven years, and a minister fifty years.

DANIEL BURNS, of Lewes, in Sussex, was convinced of truth about the twentieth year of his age, whilst a soldier in the army; and being faithful to what was made manifest to be right, he bore his testimony against bearing arms. By the interposition of some friends of Hampshire, he was discharged in 1752, at Chichester, where he remained a short time, and then removed into the compass of Lewes monthly meeting. Abiding under the influence of the spirit of truth, he experienced a growth therein, and, after a while, had a few words to declare in meetings, by way of testimony.

He was exemplary in conduct and conversation, and laboured according to his ability in the service of truth; and many times, in much brokenness of spirit, would endeavour to strengthen and encourage the weak and sincere in heart, to come up in faithfulness to the manifestations of life and grace within. He was a pattern of meekness and tender affection for all in distress, whether friends or others, and used his endeavours for their relief; which many times were blessed with good success.

In his last illness, which was but short, he appeared perfectly resigned, and expressed himself somewhat after this manner; that he believed his day's work was done, all was well, and he felt peace.

He departed this life the 9th of the Third month, 1789, and was buried in Friends' burial-ground at Lewes, the 15th of the same, aged fifty-eight years.

THOMAS FINCH, of Brentford, in Middlesex, was born at Winkfield, in the county of Berks, of pious parents, under whom he had a guarded education; and, about the eighteenth year of his age, was favoured with an heavenly visitation, to which, if he had given way, he has since told an intimate acquaintance, he thought he should then have been called to the work of the ministry. But neglecting to live under the influence of this divine principle, and turning his attention to the reading of deistical authors, his understanding became so darkened, that his mind seemed closed up, in an unbelief of the truth of inward revelation; and he thought there was nothing greater than reason to be known in man; but, as he has said, he continued with friends, among whom he was educated, because he believed them the best moralists.

Although he continued many years disputing against the truth, yet it pleased the Most High, about the latter end of the year 1756, to favour him again with a fresh visitation of divine love. He now no longer consulted with flesh and blood, but gave up to its heavenly instructions; and being humbled under the mighty hand of God, he, in due time, received a part in the ministry of the gospel of Jesus Christ; in whose spiritual as well as outward appearance, he now firmly believed. Having tasted of the Lord's judgments and mercies, he laboured to persuade men to let their conversation be as becometh the gospel. He was diligent in attending meetings for worship and discipline, till near his decease; zealous for the promotion of righteousness, and of a benevolent disposition, which endeared him to friends and others of his acquaintance.

During his illness, which was long and painful, he was favoured with that resignation and peace which bespoke a mind elevated above earthly things. To some friends, not many days before his decease, he expressed himself thus: that although, during his indisposition, he had felt great poverty of spirit, and at times as though deserted, yet he trusted in the Lord's mercies; believing that he should be favoured, before the closing scene, to feel the Lord nigh, as in days past. This there was good cause to believe he experienced; for, the First-day evening before his decease, he broke forth in a living testimony to the mercy and loving-kindness of the Almighty; encouraging all who had known something of his goodness, to trust in him; saying, 'There is no shortness in him. If there is any shortness, it is in us, not in him. I bear this my last testimony to his goodness.'

At another time, being asked how he did, he said, 'I have been praying for help to carry me through with that patience which I love to see in myself and others.' To one who attended meetings, he observed, 'How comfortable a thing it is, to have nothing to do but to die;' that nothing stood in his way; and that the way to die the death of the righteous, was to live the life of the righteous.

He departed this life at Brentford, the 5th of the Fourth month, 1789; and his corpse was interred in Friends' burial-ground near that town, the 12th of the same: aged seventy-seven years, and a minister about thirty years.

The following remarks were dictated by him to a friend, whom he desired to write them down, in the course of his illness.

'As surely as things are in their places, the best things will be uppermost. Now, as we read, "The king's daughter is all glorious within," so there is something truly beautiful in the regulation made by true religion, where the objects of our affections are rightly regulated. It is of great consequence what we love best, because our lives and conversations are generally according to the order or disorder within.

'Notwithstanding the increase of knowledge among men, it seems but little of the best sort. There seem to be many who understand Latin, Greek, and Hebrew, who know but little of themselves. It must be allowed to be a material point whether a man has liberty or not; and if he has, wherein it consists, and which is the way to make the right use of it. This, well considered, may help us to discern the great importance of spiritual-mindedness. The carnally-minded world seems to know little of these divine things. Men, in common, seem but little aware how necessary a good state of mind is, in order to live a good life. Accordingly we see few men in much care about the state of their minds.'

WILLIAM RATHBONE, of Liverpool, was born there in 1726, of parents who were members of the national church. His mother died before he was two years old, and his father being, soon after, convinced of Friends' principles, he was carefully educated therein; and, being in a good degree obedient to the visitations of divine grace, he became while young an example of sobriety and industry.

About the seventeenth year of his age, being under discouraging circumstances, he formed the intention of going abroad, with a view to acquire wealth; but when he thought himself on the point of carrying this design into execution, his mind was brought under a weighty exercise, and he was impressed with a persuasion that his appointed station was in his native place, where a field of religious labour was opened before him; and, that if he persevered in his intention, his religious interests would be subverted, and the divine will concerning him be opposed. In this state of conflict he was convinced that, if his sole dependence was fixed on the Almighty arm, it would supply all his wants, and be an unfailing support in the various trials that might be allotted to him.

Through the continued extension of divine regard, he was enabled to yield obedience to these convictions; to enter into covenant with a covenant-keeping God; to limit his desires after perishing riches, and to bear the turning of his hand upon him. As he was favoured to enter on the active scenes of life with faith and dedication of heart, so he was supported, in his passage through it, to bear his portion of disappointment and affliction with Christian fortitude.

The gracious Being, who had directed his feet into the right way, was mercifully pleased to be with him, from step to step: so that he increased in stability and usefulness; and about the forty-ninth year of his age, he was concerned to bear a public testimony to the sufficiency of this divine grace, which had been the stay of his youth.

For some time before his decease, he was more than commonly enlarged in his public testimony; and accompanied two women Friends in visiting the families of Friends in his own and a neighbouring meeting. The minds of some of his friends were singularly impressed with the exercise he was under the First-day preceding his illness, when he had to express, in the morning meeting, the necessity of having oil in our vessels, and our lamps trimmed; calling upon some present to remember in what awakening manner this exhortation had been sounded in their hearing; saying, it was given him afresh to believe that there were those present who, when the solemn summons should be issued, "Behold the Bridegroom cometh; go ye forth to meet him;" however diligent they might have been in having their vessels replenished, would find they had nothing to spare.

The following day he was a little unwell, but cheerful; on Third-day, complained of a violent cold that affected his head; and in the afternoon was obliged to go to bed. He was confined to his chamber about a week, during which his patience and fortitude were exemplary; and although, through the extremity of his bodily illness, he was at times delirious, yet at intervals his understanding returned; in one of which he expressed audibly, 'Who would not love and praise thy name, thou King of saints;' and continued with solemn prostration of soul, for a considerable time, and then said, very intelligibly, 'O, poor creatures; called upon to offer an offering in righteousness; who can but, who dare but, obey the call.' It was a season of awful quietness; his spirit was again powerfully engaged in fervent prayer, for full two hours, except once or twice, when raised up to take something, he let fall a wandering expression, but when he was laid quietly down, he was again favoured with the renewed influence of the spirit of supplication.

Through the weight of his illness, his voice was much interrupted, but sundry expressions were at times distinctly heard, 'Most Holy Father;' 'Lord, God, Almighty;' 'I have known the rod, and bless the hand.' What followed could not be distinctly heard, but it is not easy to set forth the awful solemnity of the season.

In the evening, his wife and children being in the room, and one of his daughters beside him, he took both her hands in his, looked at her with a most sensible expression of affection, then closed his eyes, and, without a sigh or struggle, breathed his last.

He departed this life the 11th of the Eighth month, 1789, and was interred in Friends' burial-ground the 14th of the same, in the sixty-fourth year of his age; and a minister about fourteen years.

ELIZABETH MERRYWEATHER was the daughter of Samuel and Deborah Waring, mentioned before in this collection, and widow of Joseph Merryweather, all of the county of Hants. She had the advantage of a religious education, and was, through the influence of divine grace, enabled to escape many of the corruptions, follies, and vanities, incident to youth; and, in a good degree, to preserve an irreproachable character, from childhood to mature age. As she advanced in years, she gradually grew in grace, and in that saving knowledge which prepares and qualifies for service.

About the fortieth year of her age she came forth in a lively and edifying testimony; was very cautious not to enlarge beyond the limits of her gift in the ministry, and the present concern; and was desirous and careful that her conduct and conversation might be such as becomes a gospel minister.

She visited the meetings of Friends in Oxfordshire, Dorsetshire, and London; likewise the families of Friends in her own county, to general satisfaction, and her own peace, and retained her love and zeal for the cause of truth, unabated to the end. She was, for many years, frequently afflicted with long and painful attacks of illness; which, with some other very trying dispensations, she was enabled to bear with exemplary patience and resignation.

A short time before her decease she gave her daughter a strict charge that her funeral might be very plain, and free from all unnecessary expense; and also desired her relations and friends might be informed of her death, that if any of them should incline to attend her burial, they might have the opportunity of doing it, but that no invitation should be given; intimating that she had done nothing to deserve any extraordinary marks of regard.

About ten days before her close, she apprehended it was required of her to visit a Friend's family; which, with some difficulty, through great weakness, she was enabled to perform to good satisfaction; and on her return home, signified that she was favoured with an evidence that this was the last public service that would be required of her.

The same evening, on going to bed, she was seized with something like a fit; which, being followed with her old complaint, the gout in her stomach, she was confined to her bed for the last time; and said to her daughter that she had often thought the time of her release was nigh, but never saw it so clearly before; and now she had an evidence that the time was come, and charged her not to mourn for her, but rather to rejoice: adding, 'I have nothing to do; all is quietness and peace.' At another time, 'I am sweetly and peacefully passing away. The Lord is my support. The great Physician is near.' And soon after said, 'I have had a twelvemonth's conflict, and now, I believe, my heavenly Father hath pronounced it finished.'

Some friends sitting one day in the chamber, she was engaged to speak nearly as follows: 'I have been thinking many times what John said of those who had "come through great tribulations, and had washed their garments, and made them white in the blood of the Lamb." I have been brought through many, and have desired that my garments might be washed, that all might tend to my sanctification; and, under all, the Lord knew my integrity, and has given me a sure evidence of a resting-place with him, where sorrow cannot reach. And this is all I want my friends to know. I want no other testimonies to be borne of me.'

She then was led to praise and magnify that good hand, which, she said, had been with her all her life long, and would not forsake her in her last hour. To a friend in the ministry she spoke very encouragingly, exhorting her to be faithful to the least discovery of duty, saying, 'The widow's mite hath often been a comfort to me; though but a mite, it was not overlooked by the great Master:' adding, 'I have ever found that obedience to the smallest requirings brings peace, but disobedience will bring poverty.'

While she retained her speech and faculties she had a suitable word of exhortation or advice to most who visited her; and took an affectionate leave of her relations and friends.

Thus, favoured to close a life of much pain and sorrow in great peace, she expired without a struggle or a sigh, at Alton, the 7th of the Twelfth month, 1789, and her remains were interred in Friends' burial-ground there the 13th of the same; aged nearly sixty, and a minister about twenty years.

MARY LEAVER, wife of John Leaver, of Nottingham, was born in the year 1720, of parents professing with Friends. She was endowed with a good natural understanding, and had the advantage of a religious education. Through faithfulness to the humbling visitations of divine grace, she was raised up to bear testimony to the efficacy and sufficiency thereof about the year 1753.

She loved retirement, yet found it her concern to visit

Friends in most counties in England; and, in the year 1773, divers provinces in North America, where her service was very acceptable. Some time after her return, she met with a trying dispensation, her three daughters being removed from her by death in the space of a few years; all of them grown up to women's estate, and hopeful; which affliction she appeared to bear with becoming resignation to the Divine will.

Her last illness was very short, and part thereof attended with considerable pain, which she bore with truly Christian patience, saying to one of her near relations, the evening before her departure, 'I am content:' to which he replied, 'That is a favour:' she said, 'A great one;' and added, 'It has put me upon thinking every way; but I feel no condemnation; I am easy.'

She was mostly favoured with her understanding till near her conclusion; and quietly departed this life the 15th of the Twelfth month, 1789; and was interred in Friends' burial-ground, at Nottingham, the 18th of the same, aged about sixty-nine years; and a minister about thirty-six years.

SARAH TAYLOR, of Manchester, was the daughter of John and Margaret Routh, of Wensley-dale, in Yorkshire. She was religiously educated, and through the merciful visitations of the day-spring from on high, divine impressions were made on her tender mind; through faithfulness to the manifestations whereof, in patient resignation, she was fitted for further service, and appeared in the ministry about the nineteenth year of her age, and visited London, in company with Mary Slater. About the twentieth year of her age she removed to Manchester, and resided with her brother John Routh. In the year 1748 she was married to William Taylor. He survived but a few months, but she often expressed that they were united in a bond of heavenly fellowship. After his decease she continued unmarried.

In testimony she was lively, clear, and pertinent, reverently careful to wait for the opening and authority of the word of life, and skilful in dividing it to the people; and in her addresses to the Almighty, her mind was sensibly clothed with that which gives access to the throne of grace. Under the engagement of divine love, with the full concurrence of her brethren, she visited at several times the meetings of Friends in most parts of this kingdom, Wales, and Ireland. She was diligent in visiting the widows, fatherless, and afflicted, and exemplary in attending meetings for worship and discipline.

When the infirmities of old age attended, and she was, by a dropsy, confined to her house, and mostly to her bed, she expressed herself to a friend nearly as follows: 'I was never more sensible than in this time of my confinement and separation from my friends, of the various ways in which the Lord's work is marred, and his merciful designs, with respect to individuals, frustrated, through the reluctance of the creature to become as passive clay in the hands of the potter, vessels of the Lord's own forming, without any mixture. Some hesitate; some are too forward; but all this is from unreduced self, and all tends to mar the Lord's work. We are to be formed into pure vessels, quite emptied, that the divine word may have free course; no hesitation, no activity or contrivance of the creature, to choose or to refuse.' After a little pause she added, 'But he knoweth human weakness, who is a God of infinite compassion, and he stands ready to help us, if we look to him in sincerity. A sigh, a tear, arising from true contrition, is a sacrifice well pleasing in his sight; because it is of his own preparing, and will arise as incense from the temple of our hearts, if we are dedicated to him.'

The same friend going to her early in the morning, she mentioned a person who desired to be remembered to her, and by her. Sarah said, 'I have been thinking much of him in the night, and would have thee say, when thou seest him, that in looking at me, and the probability of my being nearer the solemn close than some others; and having been in a good degree preserved through many exercises, he may think there is a cause to rejoice. But I never passed through more proving conflicts than at present, nor ever had greater need of watchfulness, lest the enemy should get any advantage over me; or had at any time more distressing fears of losing ground, and the great work of redemption falling short, and receiving damage, by my poor mind being turned aside to objects of inferior importance, and so the victory not be obtained. Day and night, to be solicitous for preservation, was never more needful.'

'Oh, that great work of redemption! "I pray not," said our blessed Redeemer, "that thou shouldest take them out of the world, but that thou shouldest preserve them from the evils." We are called to victory. All depends upon keeping close to him who can alone preserve us in the hour of temptation. I will keep thee in the hour of temptation; then is the trying time, when the grand enemy endeavours to gain his end; it is his work to draw the mind into captivity; he wants to keep us in bondage.'

Some months before her removal, she said, 'I am not apprehensive my close is very near, though I feel nothing to stand in my way. I am quite resigned, and desire to be preserved in the patience; for though so feeble, and nearly worn out, a natural quickness about me, often under my sufferings, prompts to disquietude; but when thus tried, I invite patience; and also pray to the Giver of every good and perfect gift for it, and am favoured to feel its return.'

She also mentioned, that as her bodily strength became more impaired, her understanding was more opened to prospects which no language was copious enough to express; in which she experienced a freedom from all the fetters of earthly connections, or objects of sense. It was as the place of broad rivers where were no storms or tempests; neither galley with oars, nor gallant ship could pass; no work nor invention of man; but as in the ocean of divine love, her mind was filled with silent worship, and adoration of the Supreme Being. She added, few of her early acquaintance were now remaining in this life; yet, she said, there were situated in several parts of the nation, those whom her mind often visited in near love, and she felt them near in the covenant of truth.

She expressed, with much tenderness, her desires that those who were entering upon a situation, surrounded with dangers, might seek after the pearl of great price; and be willing to sell all, to purchase the field where the treasure was hid; for it would remain when all other supports failed.

On two friends visiting her, she said that she knew not how it might be with her, in respect either to life or death; nor did she desire to know; but it was abundantly made up by a prospect that was frequently laid open, and enlarged into a scene of ineffable glory and brightness, that at times it seemed too vast for her to bear; but as it was mercifully continued, her capacity for receiving it increased. She had been favoured to behold a state so glorified, in perpetual union with glorified spirits, that at seasons she seemed enclosed in a scene of universal brightness, glory, and beauty, too great for human comprehension. But she soon added, with awfulness, 'Yet this has not always been the case; there was a time when the heavens were as brass, and the earth as iron, and my soul encompassed as in clouds of impenetrable darkness; but since, that is mercifully removed, and the before-mentioned prospect has graciously succeeded.'

She had been made to view the past errors of her life, and also to feel that judgment must pass over the transgressing nature, and even upon every wrong impulse of the mind, though it might not break forth into action; by giving way to which, she had often prepared herself a cup of sorrow unknown to others. She said, what she felt for her friends in religious profession, was not to be expressed; nor the strength of her desire, that those who had yielded themselves into the purifying hand of judgment, might be preserved under it steadfast and immovable.

Nor could she set forth in words her ardent solicitude, that those who had been, and were wandering from the fold of rest, might be given to see their dangerous situation; adding, 'O, what I feel for those wanderers! Could I but gather them, could I open one of these prospects to their view, how would it stain all their worldly pursuits. Surely it would make them covet an establishment on this immutable foundation. I have often thought of those expressions, "If the righteous scarcely be saved, where shall the ungodly and the sinner appear?" What my mind has felt for some of you of late, has indeed exceeded any thing that I ever experienced before.'

Another time she said, 'I have had deep sufferings and baptisms to pass through, but I now see, with indubitable clearness, that there is a rock and fortress at the bottom; which, if we cleave to, no power of darkness, however great, shall be able to move us from it long together.' To a friend who sat with her, she said, 'The body is weak, but my mind is preserved in quietness, and seasons of consolation come unsought for; when clear prospects are opened to my view, of "the spirits of the just made perfect," and of the church triumphant, which words are insufficient to describe. It appears like a boundless expanse, an ocean of love, a river clear as crystal, which the vulture's eye cannot see; no galley with oars, nor gallant ship, can pass thereby. There the spirits of the just, the church triumphant, enjoy full fruition; are gathered into the place of pure prayer, adoration, and worship. Precious in the eyes of the Lord is the death of his saints; because in these crusts and shackles of the body, they cannot enjoy perfect, uninterrupted blessedness; and he wills and loves that those whom he has redeemed by his power, should enjoy, perfect, unmixed happiness.'

She added, 'I have learned with the apostle, that it is not by works of righteousness that I have done, but of his mercy that he hath saved me, by the washing of regeneration, and the renewing of the Holy Ghost. O, I would not change my situation for all the possessions of this world; nor for all the knowledge and speculation that the wise system-builders of the present age can acquire; and, whatever they may vainly suppose, it is not a delusion, nor the workings of imagination, nor of prejudice; but solid, enduring, substantial truth.'

After a solemn pause, before some friends took leave of her, she signified, with a sweet calmness, the probability of its being a final farewell; then added, 'But there is one thing of more importance, that I feel my mind pressed to fix upon yours; which is, that you may be gathered into entire resignation, to abide with your great Master on Mount Calvary. Remember what he declared, that "Where I am, there shall my servant be;" and this you know was under suffering. What I have wished for you is, that you may travail for a willingness to be kept here; for what can we desire more or greater, than to be where our great Lord and Master is. He knows your state and your weaknesses, and his eye is over you for good. But if, like Peter, you slide from his testimony, he may bring it to your remembrance; and though your trials may be many and severe, and you may be beset and buffeted on every hand; yet he is omnipotent, all powerful to preserve and keep you. It is the Father's good pleasure to give his adopted children the kingdom: for his regard is to his little flock, and all the combined powers of darkness shall not be able to pluck any of his lambs out of his hands.'

On the 19th of the Sixth month, to a friend, she spoke to the following import; "On looking over my past life, I cannot charge myself with being presumptuous; but I know I have not at all times been as honest as I should have been; especially in our large public meetings for worship. When things have arisen with clearness, that I should have communicated to the people, I have let the right time slip, by deliberating on my own unfitness. This is indeed consulting with flesh and blood; listening to an enemy. I have not only hereby increased my own portion of sorrow and conflict; but the blessed cause has suffered. The free circulation of life has been obstructed, when I have had reason to believe it would have flowed as from vessel to vessel.'

After sitting a while under the covering of a sweet and solemn quietness, she said, 'O, what an awful thing is pure gospel ministry! How few understand, or are sufficiently baptized into the true nature and spirit of pure, living, powerful, gospel ministry!' The following day, to the same friend, when taking leave of her, she said, 'Thou seest, dear child, how I am carried on from day to day; neither seeing, nor desiring to see, how the present dispensation is to terminate; but faith and patience are mercifully vouchsafed to sustain; though sometimes it seems as if they were ready to fail; and then, I am deeply tried. It is a great thing to be able to say, "I have fought the good fight; I have kept the faith." O, this keeping the faith, this cleaving close to him, who has indeed loved us freely! If some of you will keep the faith, you will be strengthened more and more, to make war in righteousness against the enemies of your own houses; and be able to lift up a standard against wrong things in others.' She afterwards added, 'I often visit you in that love which is wider than the ocean, and extends over sea and land, and do thou remember to keep the faith, in him who is invisible and invincible too.'

On Second-day preceding her departure, she was much afflicted with pain and shortness of breath; when a relation expressing her reluctance to leave her, to attend the monthly meeting, she said, 'I would have thee go; for though I have a trying putting on, I do not quite see the end; but it may not be long before it comes. Thou may tell Friends, I do not expect to see any of them again; and give my dear love to all, for it spreads universally.'

On Sixth-day morning the symptoms of approaching dissolution were more apparent; and her outward sight much gone, so that she did not seem to know those about her, but by their voices; yet her religious exercise did not cease. She frequently expressed much care and concern for a young woman in the family, earnestly entreating her to do all she could to inherit eternal life; with many other expressions of strong solicitude for her preservation.

About eight o'clock in the evening she took a little wine and water, but found it difficult to swallow; and when she had taken a small portion, said, with a strong and clear voice, 'No more;' and soon after dropped the following expressions: 'Be still, be still, and thou shalt soon see the salvation of thy God;' which were the last words uttered. They were accompanied with such an evidence that they were spoken concerning herself, and that it was her own blessed experience, as greatly bowed the spirits of those present, in resignation to the divine will. About ten she quietly breathed her last, the 19th of the Eighth month, 1791; and was buried in Friends' burial-ground, the 21st of the same, aged seventy-four years, and a minister fifty-four years.

MARY POOLEY, daughter of William and Mary Pooley, of Tooley Street, Southwark, was born the 11th of the Fifth month, 1772. Her parents were concerned to bring her up in plainness and sobriety; and their endeavours for her preservation therein, and from the many evils which are in the world, were not ineffectual. Although of a lively disposition, she was religiously inclined in very early life; she loved the truth, and the friends of it, and was of a steady deportment.

About the eighteenth year of her age, she seemed more frequently indisposed than heretofore; and, although it did not appear unlikely to others that she might still live to see many days, yet she seemed to have a sense given her that her stay in this world would not be to an advanced age; and her indisposition increasing, became a settled decline. During this trying season her patience was remarkable; she was preserved from murmuring, and seemed cheerful in spirit, saying, 'Through mercy I do not repine.'

Many expressions she uttered in the course of her illness, tending to show the resignation of her mind, and quiet acquiescence with divine permission. About a month before her decease, her father asking her how she did, she replied, 'I seem to be gradually going. I have remembered the words of Job, "The Lord giveth and the Lord taketh away, blessed be the name of the Lord." It is best to be resigned. Do not grieve, dear father; the Lord be with thee;' and again advised her parents to give her up freely, saying, 'We must part some time or other, and I cannot go better than well.'

About two weeks before her decease, after having made divers solid remarks, she said to this effect, 'There is a language that I have often thought of in the time of health, which is, O, that I might walk in all things consistent with the truth I make profession of.' And at another time, nearer her end, she said, 'I think I may truly say, I have not murmured in all this illness. The Lord is my refuge. I am comfortably resigned to his divine will, and seem to have nothing to do but to die.'

She continued a few days longer, during which she uttered many expressions to the same effect as the foregoing. The day she died, she desired that her father and brother might be sent for, with whom she had a solemn season; and afterwards appeared serene, and given up to the Lord's will. She quietly departed, the 12th of the Eleventh month, 1792, aged about twenty years and a half; and was interred the 18th, in Long Lane burial-ground, after a meeting held at Horslydown.

RALPH BAIMBRIDGE, a member of Newcastle meeting, having, through a variety of dispensations, been convinced that all outward and ceremonial worship was unavailing, and that nothing short of the pure, living, eternal substance, Christ Jesus, the Rock of ages, would truly profit the soul, he became a lively example of the efficacy of the Divine principle as professed by us, joined our Society about the twenty-fourth year of his age, and after a short time received a gift in the ministry.

It does not appear he was much engaged out of the compass of his own quarterly meeting; yet he sometimes went to the half-yearly meeting in Scotland, the yearly meeting in London, and the meetings in some neigbouring counties in his way to and from the yearly meeting. By some minutes which he left behind, it appears he was deeply baptized into the states of the people as he passed along, and was generally enabled to discharge his duty faithfully, and to reap the reward of peace.

His last illness was tedious and painful, but he bore it with exemplary patience and fortitude. He saw with composure the period of his life approaching; and though preserved in a calm resignation to the Divine will, he sometimes expressed a desire to be dissolved, being enabled to look forward with an humble confidence, from the retrospect of a well-spent life, to the enjoyment of its sure reward, an incorruptible inheritance with the saints in life.

He was favoured to the last with the use of his mental faculties; and at different times uttered weighty and edifying remarks. He signified, near the beginning of his confinement, that he had endeavoured to discharge his duty faithfully, and said he saw nothing more for him to do or to undo. At one time he expressed himself as follows: 'Though we hear and read of people at these times having great openings, sights, and revelations, seeming to be enraptured with Christ's love, and his meeting them, it has not been so with me, but I have been in a quiet rest, in a composed waiting state, feeling a covering of that which was my morning light; that which called and created me anew, and placed me in a state of sonship. He is yet with me, and I know that where he is, I shall be also, even as he is. As it is not likely I can do it myself again, I would wish my friends to be informed, that I rest in the same faith in that which gathered us to be a people. I feel him to be yet with me, who hath redeemed me out of all distress; the God who hath fed and kept me all my life long.'

He departed this life the 27th of the Fourth month, 1793, and was buried the 3d of the Fifth month following, aged about sixty-four, and a minister about forty years.

HENRY KITE, of Norton, in Hertfordshire, was but little known to Friends in his early life, being brought up in the National Church, and for some time frequented the meetings of the Methodists. Being favoured with an awakening visitation, he was brought to see the exceeding sinfulness of sin, and to feel judgment on the transgressing nature in him; and by obedience to these discoveries he became measurably reformed in life and conversation.

In the year 1768 he frequented our religious meetings, sitting therein in a weighty, solid frame; and his general conduct being consistent, he was in the year following received as a member. A faithful discharge of the duties of his station, which was that of a servant, procured the esteem of his employers; who readily made way for his attendance of meetings for worship and discipline, wherein he was very exemplary.

He was a man of a meek and humble spirit, and although not large in testimony, yet he grew in his gift, in the exercise whereof he was plain, lively, and edifying, reaching the witness of truth in the heart. He was useful also in the discipline of the church, having been frequently engaged therein to the satisfaction of his friends. It was his lot to meet with divers close trials, which he bore with Christian fortitude.

During his last illness, he said, 'My poor body is much afflicted, but I am comfortable in mind, which I esteem a great favour. I have paid my visit to the yearly meeting, and have no cause to repent, for I believe I was in my place in so doing.' And at another time, to his wife, 'My dear, do not weep for me, although my body is in a suffering state, my mind enjoys a perfect calm, and I have no fear of death.' On being asked by one of his sons how he was, he replied, 'Thou seest thy poor father labouring under great bodily affliction, but I am preserved with a still, quiet mind, and I feel the Lord's goodness graciously extended to me.

To his daughter he said, 'My dear, a few words have sprung in my mind, very comfortably; which are, "The Lord is risen in his holy temple, let all the earth be silent before him." What can the temple be but the body? O, what a comfort to feel the Lord's goodness so graciously extended to me, a poor creature. I can truly say, I have given all up. I have committed all into the hands of a merciful God, to do with me as he pleaseth: either to take me, or restore me to health; I have no will in it. O, what a favour is this, to be resigned either to life or death!'

At another time, 'I have to remember that "the Lord is a strong tower, whereunto the righteous flee, and are saved." I can with great thankfulness say to my God, "I have fought the good fight, and have kept the faith, henceforth there is laid up for me a crown of righteousness."' The day before he died, amongst other things, he said, 'I am clear of the blood of every one. I feel my disorder making its progress, and it appears to me that I shall be removed in a little time. My bodily affliction is great, but the sweet peace of my mind is far greater. O, how I feel the sweet influence of heavenly love!'

He departed this life the 15th of the Sixth month, 1793, at Norton, aged about fifty-five years, and was buried on the 21st of the same, in Friends' burial-ground at Baldock; and a minister about twenty-four years.

DOROTHY OWEN, of Dewispren, near Dolgelly, in Merionethshire, was the daughter of Rowland and Lowry Owen, of the same place. She was educated in the profession of Friends, notwithstanding which, she in her youth accompanied other young people in vain and unprofitable amusements. But about the sixteenth year of her age, being favoured with a visitation of divine love, she became sensible of the errors of such ways; and, by a strict attention to the reproofs of instruction, and submission to the operation of truth, she experienced redemption from the love and spirit of this world.

About the twenty-third year of her age, she appeared in a public testimony; and her conduct being consistent therewith, she was made instrumental to the convincing and gathering of divers to the principle and profession of the truth in the neighbourhood where she resided; where, from removals and defection, the members of our Society were reduced to a very small number.

The sweet savour of her zealous, humble, meek example, and her dedication of time, faculties, and property, though in low circumstances, to the glory of God and the good of her fellow-creatures, had a powerful tendency to enforce the doctrine she preached. She was remarkable for her diligence in the attendance of meetings for worship and discipline, from which neither distance nor weather kept her back, while of ability; and she frequently went nearly forty miles on foot in that mountainous country, to attend the monthly meeting: even when the inclemency of the season rendered it not only difficult but dangerous.

She contented herself with the least expensive manner of living and dress, in order to have the more to distribute to the necessities of others; tenderly sympathizing with the poor inhabitants around her: and so bright was her example, that one, not in profession with us, declared, 'Her conduct preaches daily to me.'

Her last illness was lingering and painful, which she bore with exemplary patience, and was eminently favoured with divine peace, so as sensibly to affect and gather the minds of those who visited her, into a sense of the same blessed influence. Her prospect of future happiness was unclouded; and she said very near the conclusion, 'The arms of divine mercy are wide open to receive me.'

She died the 12th, and was buried in Friends' burying-ground at Tyddyn-y-Gareg, the 17th of the Seventh month, 1793, aged about forty-two years; and a minister about nineteen years.

JOB SCOTT, of Providence, in Rhode Island, was removed by death while on a religious visit in Ireland. He was a man of strong understanding and quick discernment; but still more remarkable for having experienced the vigorous faculties of his mind reduced, in no common degree, under the humbling power of truth. When young, he was, according to his own account, much addicted to levity of conduct; and it is probable that the close exercises which he afterwards passed through, and the scrupulous disposition of mind in which for some time he appeared to live, were as the necessary inflections of the crooked wand to the contrary side, in order, at length, to reduce it to perfect straightness: wisdom even tormenting with her discipline, and at length returning the straight way.

He arrived in London in the First month, 1793, and laboured diligently in the occupation of his talent as a gospel minister, in and near the city, until the latter end of the Third month; when he proceeded leisurely to the Welsh yearly meeting, held at Carmarthen. On this occasion, as well as at the succeeding one of the Bristol yearly meeting, his business seemed to be that of leading the people from a reliance on preaching, by becoming himself, throughout, an example of humble silence.

He afterwards attended the yearly meeting in London, in the last sitting of which, he delivered some memorable hints respecting the commotions then prevailing in the earth; and pointing to the path in which the righteous, in such seasons of overturning, might tread with safety. After this he went, without much delay, to Ireland; to the meetings of which he paid a general visit, and returned to Dublin in the Eleventh month; but not finding himself clear of a belief of more service in that country, he went to Ballitore, at which place he fell sick with the small-pox. He asked several questions respecting that disease; and afterwards very emphatically declared, 'It is no matter what is the disorder;' and in a little while added, 'Its being that or any other, does not at all alter my feelings.'

A friend observing that his getting well through it would be a great favour, he replied with a smile, 'Whichever way it is, I hope I shall get well over it.' He also said, 'There is an eternal arm underneath each of us, which is sufficient to bear up and support; and will do it, as far as it is needful we should be supported; and I have long been confirmed in this sentiment, that nothing could possibly happen that would harm or injure me, while I kept under the divine influence.' Some time after he said, 'Though I am not without some considerable bodily pain, yet I feel such a portion of that good which is infinite, that it does not seem worth mentioning. If there was no greater enjoyment hereafter, the present would be a state truly desirable, through a never-ending eternity: and yet, the fulness is still more desirable.'

To relate all the instructive and comfortable expressions which he uttered, would swell this account beyond the proposed limits. A week before his close, dictating a letter to his relations and friends, after mentioning that his distress of body, through extreme difficulty of breathing, had for a short time been almost equal to any thing he could suppose human nature capable of supporting, he said,

'Just now, and for several hours past, I have been almost as easy as at any time in my life; I think certainly, never more so in my mind. I feel no kind of alarm; but the issue is certainly very doubtful. I feel easiest to address you in this manner, principally that you may know that my mind enjoys a fulness, in that which removes beyond the reach of all sorrow.

'I suppose my love was never in a state of greater enlargement, or less tinctured with selfishness, to all my relations and friends the world over. My desire for my children's substantial growth in the truth, and strict adherence to all its discoveries, to the close of their days, is by far the principal wish I have for them. Out of the enjoyment of a good degree of this precious inheritance, I know of nothing in this world worth living for. Ye that know it, suffer nothing, I most cordially beseech you, ever to divert your minds from an increasing and fervent pursuit after the fulness of it, even unto "the measure of the stature of the fulness of Christ."'

Afterwards, in addition to the foregoing letter, he added, 'My spirits are under little or no depression at all. Perhaps I never saw a time before, when all things not criminal, were so nearly alike to me, in point of any disturbance to the mind. I do not know, but that when awake, and capable of contemplation, I nearly rejoice and give thanks in all. When I verge a little towards sleep, I am all afloat, from the state of my nerves; and, from the extreme irritation, forced almost immediately, and with very unpleasant sensations, from beginning repose; but, through all, the soul seems deeply anchored in God.

'Many and painful have been the probationary exercises of this life to me. Ah! were there probability of strength, how I could enlarge; for my heart seems melted within me in retrospective view. But all the former conflicts, however grievous in their time, are lighter now than vanity; except as they are clearly seen to have contributed largely to the sanctification of the soul; as they are remembered with awfulness and gratitude before him, who has not been wanting to preserve through them all; and as they seem likely to introduce, either very shortly, or before a very long time, to an exceeding and eternal weight of glory.

'My very soul abhors the idea, that a Christian can ever be at liberty, while under the influence of heavenly good, to seek, or even desire, much wealth; though this disposition, in direct opposition to the life and doctrine of Christ, has gone far towards the destruction of true spiritual religion, I believe, in almost every religious society in the world.'

As nature became more oppressed with the disease, he observed it, and said, that if ever he rose above the present weight which he felt, and seemed sinking under, it would be through the marvellous display of eternal power and influence. He requested that if he were removed, some further particulars might be transmitted to his friends at home; adding, in substance, 'The Lord's will is blessed, and I feel no controversy with it. It is the Lord that enables me to coincide with his will, and to say amen to all the trials and conflicts he permits to attend us. I do not expect to have much to communicate in the course of this disorder, or that my strength will admit of it; but my mind is centred in that which brings into perfect acquiescence. There is nothing in this world worth being enjoyed out of the divine will.'

Two days before his decease, he said, 'I have no fear; for

"perfect love casteth out all fear; and he that feareth is not perfect in love." The same day he prayed thus; 'O Lord, my God, thou that hast been with me from my youth to this day, if a man who hath endured, with a degree of patience the various turnings of thy holy hand, may be permitted to supplicate thy name, cut short the work in righteousness, if consistent with thy holy will. Thou who hast wrought deliverance for Jacob, evince that thou art able to break my bonds asunder, and show forth thy salvation, that so my soul may magnify thy name for ever and ever.' And after a short pause, wherein he seemed to feel the earnest of his petition, he added, 'So be it, saith my soul.'

He frequently gave a word of caution to such as visited him; and after affectionately addressing one Friend he said, 'I am waiting patiently for the salvation of God; do you wait with me. I have no desire, nor the shadow of a desire, to be restored. I hope the doctors will soon find they have done their part.'

The evening before his decease, he said, 'You may tell my friends in New England, and every part of the world, that never did my soul bless the Lord on account of any worldly enjoyments, as I do now, in the blessings felt by me to be contained in the prospect of a very speedy release.' At another time he said, 'Some of my wishes are centred in as speedy release as may be consistent with the will of our heavenly Father; and an admission, which I have no doubt at all, not in the least degree, of obtaining, into that glorious kingdom, where the wicked cease from troubling, and the weary soul is eternally at rest.'

After another lively declaration, he added, 'I feel, and I wish you to feel for and with me, after the eternal rock of life and salvation; for as we are established thereon we shall be in the everlasting unity, which cannot be shaken by all the changes of time, nor interrupted in a never-ending eternity. I do expect considerable derangement will now take place. It is no discouragement to me, and ought to be none to those who trust in the Lord, and put no confidence in the flesh.'

Early in the day in which he was removed, under much suffering, he petitioned, 'O, Lord, if it be consistent with thy holy will, let loose my bonds, and send the moment of relief to my poor body and soul.' Afterwards he said, 'We cannot approve or disapprove, by parts, the works of Omnipotence rightly; we must approve the whole, and say, "Thy will be done," in all things.' And a short time after, his bodily afflictions being great, he said, 'I find all things must be endured.'

The extremity of his pain sometimes occasioned him to fear lest he should be impatient; and he said to the physician, 'Make great allowance for me, my distress is nearly as much as is supportable by human nature.' The physician saying there was a probability of his being very soon released, perhaps in an hour or two, he replied, 'If so, the Lord's name be blessed and praised for ever. I had much rather it were so than otherwise; for some time I perceived it hastening fast;' adding, 'The desire of my heart is the great blessing of time, and the consolation of eternity.' After a while he said to a friend, 'Guard against right hand errors. Let self be of no reputation; trust in the Lord, and he will carry thee through all.'

He died the 22d of the Eleventh month, 1793, at the house of Elizabeth Shackleton, at Ballitore; and was buried the 24th in Friends' burial-ground there. He was about forty-three years of age.

ABIGAIL KNIGHT, daughter of Joseph Knight, of Messing, in Essex, being taken ill, it was soon perceived that her disorder tended to her dissolution. Her father tenderly acquainted her with the prospect. She expressed that she had not much desire to live; that she did not see any thing here to stay for; and, if she might go well, that she was willing to die. She was under great exercise of mind for some days, doubting her future happiness; saying to her father she had done so many things she ought not to have done, and wishing she had minded more the hints he had frequently given her.

On his telling her he had no doubt from the feeling of his mind, that if she was removed by the present illness, it would be well with her, she expressed her doubts and fears, continuing under great exercise for some time, saying, 'I feel so much pain, that I cannot continue long, and I do not feel easy.' But after some days she signified she felt some ease, and hoped her sins would be forgiven her; and that she did not fear death, but hoped to be favoured with a more clear evidence before she departed.

Desiring to be with her father alone, she told him of the exercise of her mind, which she had felt for attending religious meetings so carelessly. That she thought it was mockery to sit in such an indifferent manner, and let the things of the world take up the attention of the mind; for which she had felt uneasiness, as much, she thought, as for any thing she had done amiss. She signified that when at times she endeavoured to be more gathered in her mind, the enemy got in and obstructed it; and that she found herself so weak through unwatchfulness at other times, as not to be able to withstand his suggestions. After this conversation she said she felt herself more easy.

Observing what a fine day it was, she said she had thought of one who said, 'How gloriously the outward sun doth shine! So doth the Son of righteousness shine this day on my soul;' and hoped she could in measure adopt the language as her own; that the things which stood in her way seemed gradually removed; and that she hoped to be favoured with a more clear evidence before she departed. To her sister she said, 'I have but little time, but if I had my time to spend over again, I should spend it very differently;' and that if she might have the least place in the kingdom of heaven, it was all she desired; which she thought would be granted.

In the evening, a lad, a member of our Society, coming into the room, she desired he would take warning by her, saying, 'I little thought, three weeks ago, I should be so near death as I am; and thou dost not know how soon thou mayest be so near;' asking him if he did not think he should be in great trouble if he was brought unto such a situation. She advised him to use the plain language, and plainness of dress; that she had been too much inclined to dress, but felt great uneasiness, and hoped for forgiveness; but she added, 'I believe I shall be happy. I feel so easy in my mind;' and added, 'What a fine thing it is to have peace of mind upon a dying bed. The nearer I am to the close, the more easy and clear my way seems. I do not dread death, but seem as if I could meet it with a smile;' that it was a great favour, for which she could not be thankful enough; and that she could not have thought it possible for her to find forgiveness in so short a time.

Towards the conclusion she signified the sting of death was taken away, and added pleasantly, 'I think to-morrow, or next day, will finish here.' The next morning her father going to speak to her, she seemed quite calm, and in a sweet frame of mind; and said, she loved to be still; she felt her heavenly Father near, as an arm underneath, and often admired the goodness and mercy of the Almighty to her, in so soon removing things which stood in her way.

About ten o'clock the same day she was taken with the pains of death, which being hard to bear, she besought the Lord to give her patience to bear them. About fifteen minutes before she departed, when it was expected she would have spoken no more, she said, 'Lord Jesus, receive my spirit. Lord, take me to thyself.' Soon after, she said, 'Farewell all, in the Lord; my pain will soon be over, the gates of heaven are open to receive me; the time is almost come.' Soon after she departed, on the 24th of the Second month, 1794, in the nineteenth year of her age.

ELIZABETH DRINKER, wife of Daniel Drinker, of the city of Philadelphia, being drawn in gospel love to visit the meetings of Friends in this nation, arrived here about the Seventh month, 1793. After visiting the meetings in the city of London, she proceeded into Kent, Sussex, and the western counties, as far as Falmouth, returning through Bristol to London. Though frequently tried with indisposition of body, she was strengthened in her gospel labours to the comfort and edification of many, being concerned to wait for, and move under, the fresh arisings of divine life.

In the Fourth month following, though in a declining state of health, she visited the meetings of Friends in Hertfordshire, &c., but her complaints increasing, she stopped at Staines, in Middlesex, nearly six weeks. While at this place she expressed to a friend an apprehension that her time would not be long in mutability, and at the same time mentioned, that as she sat in the meeting on First-day morning, though she had nothing to communicate to others, and part of the time felt low and discouraged, yet, towards the close, her mind was comforted in the fresh revival of those expressions of the prophet Habakkuk: "Although the fig-tree shall not blossom, neither shall fruit be in the vine; the labour of the olive shall fail, and the field shall yield no meat; the flocks shall be cut off from the fold, and there shall be no herd in the stall; yet will I rejoice in the Lord, I will joy in the God of my salvation." '

She reached London the 18th of the Sixth month, where for some time she appeared under great conflict of spirit; being very desirous, if consistent with her Master's will, to return to her beloved connections and native land. But this trying dispensation was permitted to pass over; and, some time before her dissolution, she seemed relieved from much anxiety respecting them; and was favoured to bear her suffering with great patience, evincing true Christian resignation and acquiescence in divine appointment.

She attended several meetings under great bodily weakness; and her last public testimony was at Westminster meeting, where she stood up with these words, 'Precious, very precious, in the sight of the Lord is the death of his saints;' on which she enlarged instructively and encouragingly.

During her confinement she was led to speak instructively to those about her; at one time nearly in these words: 'To look back, the world appears trifling and vanity; and if fresh trials come, and the storm be permitted to beat as against the wall, it is good to trust in the Lord, who, in gloomy seasons, is the protector of those that fear him. After encouraging those present to greater dedication, she said that the highest anthem that could be sung was, "Thy will be done." At another time she said she believed it was right that she had given up all and left home; whether for life or death, she must leave.

The last few days of her life she was much engaged in supplication, uttering many broken sentences, which, though not fully gathered, were expressive of the state of her mind, and breathed the language of consolation and praise.

When near the close, her spirit seemed supported above the last conflict; and, with an animated countenance, she said, 'Oh, the beauty! the excellent beauty! the beautiful prospect in view!' Then lifting up her hands, she appeared for some time in sweet silent adoration; after which she spoke but little, and with difficulty; yet she appeared sensible. She expired in the evening of the 10th of the Eighth month, 1794, so quietly, that it was scarcely known when she breathed her last; and her remains were interred at Bunhill-fields the 15th.

SAMUEL SPAVOLD, of Hitchin, in Hertfordshire, was born at Bawtry, in Yorkshire, and had his education among

Friends; and at a suitable age was bound apprentice to a carpenter and joiner in that county. In the forepart of his time he was much addicted to the follies of youth; but through the merciful visitation of divine grace, he became so effectually reached as to be stopped in his career of vanity about the nineteenth year of his age, and a short time after-terwards received a gift in the ministry.

When out of his time, he came to London, and worked as a ship-joiner at Deptford, and continued in that employment there and at Chatham for several years; during which time he was frequently exercised in his gift, and grew therein. Afterwards he removed to Folkstone, where way was opened for his further service in the church. In 1750 he settled at Hitchin, and during a long series of years laboured much in the work of the gospel, in this and other nations; and was at times baptized into deep exercises, which much excited the sympathy of his friends; to whom he approved himself an exemplary pattern of condescension.

He travelled four times through Wales, and as many through Ireland. He was once in America, and once in Scotland; and was often engaged in family visits as he passed along; and an universal love and charity accompanied his gospel labours. Notwithstanding he was at times large in testimony, he was a lover of silence; and had often to recommend a reverend humble waiting on God, saying, 'Oh, how I love this silent waiting, to feel my mind humbled before that great power. We want to be more inward; the Lord's people are an inward people.' His life and conversation spoke the same language.

He was remarkably diligent in the attendance of his own meeting, even in old age, and when bodily infirmity rendered it difficult. The latter part of his time he was afflicted with divers complaints, which brought on great weakness, and for many months confined him wholly at home; and at times in much pain, which he bore with fortitude and Christian resignation, often saying, 'It is all well, I am content:'

he was also at times weightily led in testimony to some who visited him. He would sometimes make mention of the love he felt towards his fellow-creatures; and once in particular signified it was so great, that if he had strength, he could go and preach to them on his crutches; and he often declared that the Lord had been wonderfully good to him.

Under great bodily affliction, two days before his death, he said to his wife, 'My dear, I cannot express the joy I feel; the Lord is very good.' A little after, 'Eternity is exceedingly solemn and awful to my mind; a state of eternal duration;' adding, 'It rejoices my heart that there are many fellow-travellers going, as with their hands on their loins, towards the heavenly Jerusalem and land of rest.'

'Man is made to glorify God whilst here, and enjoy him for ever in a glorious eternity; glory and honour be to his great name and power, and that for ever.' And afterwards to the following import; 'I rejoice in my heart, and am glad, that the Lord has enabled me to follow him in the straight and narrow way of the cross, which he hath prepared for his children and people to walk in.'

On the day he departed, amongst other things uttered in great weakness and difficulty, but evincing the sweet and heavenly state of his mind, he said, 'The truth is a precious thing; it is worth seeking for.' He seemed pleased with the company of those about him, affectionately saying to some, on taking leave, 'Farewell, I love you all.'

He quietly departed this life on the 9th of the First month, 1795, at Hitchin, in the eighty-seventh year of his age, and was interred there on the 15th; having been a minister about sixty-five years.

THE END OF THE NINTH PART.

PIETY PROMOTED,

IN BRIEF MEMORIALS AND DYING EXPRESSIONS

OF SOME OF THE SOCIETY OF

FRIENDS,

COMMONLY CALLED QUAKERS.

THE TENTH PART.

TO WHICH IS PREFIXED, A HISTORICAL ACCOUNT OF THE PRECEDING PARTS OR VOLUMES, AND OF THEIR SEVERAL COMPILERS AND EDITORS.

BY JOSEPH GURNEY BEVAN.

A HISTORICAL ACCOUNT

OF THE WORK ENTITLED

PIETY PROMOTED,

AND OF THE COMPILERS AND EDITORS OF THE NINE PRECEDING PARTS.

As the Volumes entitled PIETY PROMOTED, have met with a very general acceptance, and I believe have often proved incentives to a pious life, by recounting so many instances of happy death, I have thought that a concise relation of their origin and continuation, and of the friends who formed the several compilations, would be a proper introduction to this additional volume; attempted, as it is, after an interval of more than a century since the publication of the first.

John Tomkins, a Friend, of London, was the author of this volume, which was published in 1701. The narratives are arranged according to the dates when their respective objects departed this life; and as they begin with 1656, and end with 1700, this volume contains relations of the peaceful close of many of our early predecessors: in all, about fifty-nine names, the first being that zealous youth and patient sufferer, James Parnel, who died of sheer ill usage, in Colchester Castle.

To this volume the author has prefixed a copious preface; from which the following lines, explanatory of his purpose, which is the same with that of succeeding compilers, may, not inaptly, be inserted here. "The design," says he, "of this collection is, that godliness and holiness may increase and prevail amongst men, that they might have fruit unto holiness, that their end might be everlasting life. Having, in the course of my reading, met with many excellent sayings of our dying friends, that afforded much satisfaction of mind, I have collected some of them together for the benefit of others: knowing that usually the words of dying persons make deeper impression on the minds of men, than words spoken at other times. Some account I was obliged to give, concerning some of our dear friends' sufferings and labours in the gospel, the better to let the reader into the understanding [of] the weight, and indeed [the] meaning of some of their expressions: not with purpose to exalt men; but to exalt the great God, and his grace in Christ Jesus, by which they were what they were. The Lord give them that read, a heart to understand the things which belong to their peace: and if these shall be any means to stir up any to more faithfulness and diligence, in making their calling and election sure, my design is answered; and God shall have the praise of all; who is worthy forever."

The second part or volume appeared the following year, also published by John Tomkins. It contains upwards of nine sheets, and about forty-five names, but they are not so methodically arranged as in the former volume. It has a preface by another hand, without a name, but Whiting's Catalogue has the initials J. R.

John Tomkins, having thus engaged in an acceptable service, seems to have persevered in it to the last; for, the first volume having been reprinted in 1703, in 1706 he published a third, containing ten sheets, and about forty-eight names, rather promiscuously placed as to date. This volume also is prefaced by a friend of the author, namely, Christopher Meidel. John Tomkins did not long survive this last publication, but died in the Seventh month of the same year. He was born about 1663. His parents were both of them Friends. His father died when he was very young; and, as he grew up, he not only assisted his mother in her business, but was helpful to another family of children which she had by a second husband, who survived her, and afterwards fell into poverty. Tomkins was a diligent peruser and searcher of the Scriptures, a zealous promoter of the discipline of the Society, and was also esteemed a skilful minister. He was about forty-three years of age at the time of his decease, and left a widow and children. There is a copious account of some of his dying expressions in the fourth part of Piety Promoted, and also in J. Kendall's revised collection, Vol. II. p. 77. Besides these three parts or volumes of Piety Promoted, he was author of the following works:

1. The Harmony of the Old and New Testament, and the fulfilling of the prophecies, concerning our Lord and Saviour Jesus Christ, and his kingdom and glory in the latter days —with a brief Concordance of the names and attributes given to Christ, &c.

2. A Brief Testimony to the Great Duty of Prayer, showing the nature and benefit thereof; with above one hundred instances of God's answering prayer.

3. A Trumpet Sounded, or a Warning to the Unfaithful, to prize the day of their visitation before it be over: with a collection of the dying sayings of sundry persons.

John Whiting informs us, that John Tomkins died at Maryland Point, near Stratford: probably at the house of his friend and preface-writer, Christopher Meidel; who, from the title of one his pieces, seems to have lived at Stratford. Christopher Meidel was a Dane, or, more accurately, a Norwegian by birth, and educated at Copenhagen. Coming to England, in the station of chaplain to Prince George of Denmark, the husband of Queen Anne, he became preacher to the Danish church in London, and afterwards pastor to an independent congregation in Nightingale-lane, East Smithfield. He was convinced and joined the Society of Friends about 1699. He seems to have been intimate with Richard

Claridge, whom, in 1706, he attended to the burial of a woman-friend at Barking, at which town R. Claridge then lived, which, by means of her son, who was not a member of the Society, was conducted according to the accustomed rites, in the public grave-yard. Claridge testified against the superstition and pageantry; and, after the curate had read the service and was gone away, Meidel preached at the grave. I have not found the time of his decease, but it appears from a letter of his, dated 22d of Sixth month, 1708, to our historian, William Sewell, that he had been taken prisoner in France, probably on his return to his native country. An extract from this letter may be acceptable to the reader, viz.:

'Paris, 22d 6th mo., 1708.

'Dear Friend:

'That blessed God who is pleased sometimes to lead his poor travailing children into paths of straits and difficulties, to try their faith and patience, and to show his power and goodness in bringing them out again, has brought me along hitherto, blessed be his name, and kept my poor soul from fainting, and is still upholding and providing in time of need.

'This day two weeks I was brought prisoner hither, having been stopped at Pont, and kept there, and at St. Lis, a week more. I have, through mercy, had other prisoners' fare since I came in the Grand Chatelet here; but my money has been expended for some time, and a letter of credit which our friend John Davison ordered his correspondent at Antwerp to give me on a merchant at Lisle (for I had some thoughts of going that way) is in the hands of the Juge de la Police; neither if I have it can it be of any service at present, considering the circumstances of Lisle. If thou canst find out a friend to give me a little assistance for the present, it may be of service. The Lieutenant Criminel examined me strictly, with a great deal of civility, and after enlarged my prison, which at first was pretty strait and obscure; yet the Lord was good there also.

'I would be glad, if I should be continued here any time, to be somehow or other employed, toward subsistence, if possible. We are a great many prisoners of several nations and qualities. As I was brought chained to other prisoners, through the streets, I had to sound forth to the people, [in French] "Repent of your sins, O ye Parisians, and the good God will visit you with the saving knowledge of his truth, and will aid you in the time of adversity which will come upon all those who go on in their iniquities."

'The people were very free to give money, which when I refused, they gave to the other prisoners. I am civilly or kindly used by most or all of the better sort. I desire to hear from thee when this comes to hand; and that my dear love may be given to friends there, as if named, and at Rotterdam and Haarlem; and when thou writest to England, mind my dear love and brotherly respects to our dear friends there; especially to W. P. So, with salutations of true love to thee, with due respects to thy dear wife and children, I conclude thy poor obliged friend and fellow-traveller, who desires the prosperity of Zion,

C. MEIDEL.

John Field, also of London, who, before the death of Tomkins, was well known there, as the author of many short pieces, several of them controversial, next took up the work in which the latter had engaged, and, in 1711, produced a fourth volume, of upwards of eleven sheets, and having in it about fifty-four different narratives. This volume has a long preface by an anonymous writer, and also another, called an Introduction, by the compiler, Field.

The fifth volume came out in 1717, and this likewise is owing to the diligence of John Field. About fifty-seven deceased friends are commemorated by this volume; which is about a sheet larger than the fourth. It is ushered in by a preface of upwards of twenty small pages; which, like that of the former volume, contains exhortation apposite to the subject of the book. This preface is subscribed by Thomas Raylton, a printer, in George Yard, Lombard-street.

John Field, like his predecessor Tomkins, continued his attention to this means of stirring up the mind to seriousness and to virtue, almost to the period of his life, though it was protracted to an age far beyond that of Tomkins. For, after having published a third collection, forming the sixth volume, in order, from the beginning, he finally closed this service and his life, in the year 1723, at the age of seventy-five. He was therefore even far advanced beyond the age of Tomkins when he enlisted as his successor. This volume, though it consists of upwards of nine sheets, has accounts of only twenty-nine deceased friends; but some of them are longer than usual. Thomas Raylton again took up the pen as prefacer.

John Field had retired to Hammersmith, where he died; but he was buried at Bunhill-fields, London, and is described in the register of the quarterly meeting — of George-Yard, haberdasher. This was probably only descriptive of his company. I have heard that his trade was a woollen-draper. Thomas Raylton, of course, was his near neighbour, and probably his intimate friend. He too laid down the body in the same year, and his remains were interred in the same ground.

In the second edition of this sixth volume, in 1766, there is added an account of this friend. He was born in Yorkshire, in 1671, of parents not professing with friends; but was convinced when about fourteen. He suffered much for his steady adherence to what he esteemed his duty, his parents being severe; but at length was apprenticed to a blacksmith, in which service, though he laboured hard, yet, as his master and mistress were solid friends, he passed his time comfortably, and grew in religious attainment. When he was about twenty-four years of age, he came forth in public testimony, a service which he had long foreseen, and for which he seems to have been well prepared; though until the day in which he first thus broke silence, he had not seen his way clear for entering on that solemn work. After this he travelled much in the ministry, and at length settled in London, in the year 1705. The following year he married Tace Sowle, daughter of Andrew Sowle, who had been printer to the Society; and in 1718 was himself the printer. Tace Sowle Raylton was probably his daughter, who, and Luke Hinde, were afterwards printers, then Luke Hinde alone, and next his widow, Mary Hinde.

To these six parts or volumes, thus published by Tomkins and Field, no additional volume was printed until 1740, when John Bell, of Bromley, near Bow, Middlesex, compiled and published a seventh. It contains thirty-two narratives, with a long preface by the compiler, in about nine sheets. Among other names in this volume is that of his own wife, Deborah Bell, whom he survived upwards of twenty years, and of whom he thus winds up his account: — "In humble submission to His will, who gave and hath taken away, as knowing, though it is my loss, it is her everlasting gain, I rest; and can, in sincerity and truth, bless His name, who is worthy forever!"

John Bell was the son of Reynold Bell, of Gill, in Cumberland, and born in 1681. I have not learned when he came to London; but I find that in 1708 he was a member of the Savoy meeting, and had its certificate to visit Friends in Holland as a minister. Soon after his return he married Deborah Wynne, above mentioned, and settled with her at Bradford, in Yorkshire. In 1715 they removed to London, and lived a while in Clement's-lane; and, pursuant to the direction of the yearly meeting in 1723, 'that no person's name be entered in the morning-meeting's book as a minister till he or she produce a certificate from the monthly or quarterly meeting to which he or she shall belong,' they were both certified as ministers from the Bull and Mouth monthly meeting, together with the before-mentioned John Field, Thomas Raylton, and several others.

Both John Bell and his wife were much engaged in travelling in the ministry. Before her decease they had removed to Bromley, where, in 1738, Deborah departed, and John survived her until so late as the year 1761, aged about eighty.

The seven volumes already mentioned have all been printed by the Hindes: Volume I. 1759; Volume II. 1765; Volumes III. IV. and V. 1754; Volume VI. 1766; all by Luke Hinde; and Volume VII., 1771, by Mary Hinde; and are, I believe, sometimes to be met with, bound together in three volumes, duodecimo.

From the publication of the seventh volume, by John Bell, to the year 1774, this work remained stationary; but in that year, Thomas Wagstaffe, of London, added an eighth volume, differing from the others, in small octavo, of which it contains about fifteen sheets, and has about sixty-six accounts of deceased Friends. He has prefixed a short preface, and has added a short concluding address to the reader.

Eight volumes having thus been presented to Friends, and finding a ready demand, the work again became scarce. Accordingly, in 1789, John Kendall, of Colchester, published a revised edition of the whole, except one, namely, Hugh Stamper, in three volumes, twelves. He has written a preface, containing a large extract from that of Meidel, with reflections on the usefulness of the work. It is printed by James Phillips, successor to Mary Hinde, as printer to the Society; and has become the edition in general use.

In 1796, Thomas Wagstaffe again became the author of a volume, the ninth, which, in about seventeen small octavo sheets, contains sixty-six narratives, together with a short preface. It has undergone a second edition in twelves, which has been generally sold as a fourth volume of Kendall's collection.

Thomas Wagstaffe was born at Banbury, in Oxfordshire, in the year 1724. He passed the chief part of his life in London, where he long carried on the trade of a watchmaker; but in the decline of life retired to Stockwell, Surry, whence he dates his last preface. He, however, left that place when an old man, for Chipping Norton, in Oxfordshire, where he had relations, and died there in 1802. He was particularly addicted to inquiries into the transactions of ancient times, so far as they related to Friends; and had a memory stored with anecdote. His papers relating to such subjects having been mislaid since his death, it is probable that some pleasant if not valuable information is lost. In 1776, he prepared for the press, some account of the life and gospel-labours of William Reckitt, of Wainfleet, Lincolnshire; a little book well worth the perusal of such as love to read accounts of the travels of Friends devoted to the cause of truth.

Besides the publication and republication of most of these volumes, some selections from them have been printed; particularly one in 1781, by James Phillips, in twelves, forming a closely printed volume, entitled, "Brief memorials, &c., particularly of young persons, extracted from the eight volumes entitled Piety Promoted." William Rawes also, of Marnhull, in Dorsetshire, formed a similar, but smaller selection, under the title of "Examples for Youth." William Rawes was an acknowledged minister in good esteem, and very serviceable in the discipline, in the part where he resided. He died at Marnhull, in 1805, in his fifty-first year.

This work, deserving as it is to be made known wherever there is a genuine taste for serious, religious, Christian subjects, unmixed with superstitious forms, has not yet been much exhibited to foreigners by translation. Yet in the year 1770, Mary Hinde published a selection of seventy-two of the narratives, translated into French by Claude Gay, a native of France, but long a resident in this country. It forms a duodecimo volume of upwards of eleven sheets.

Claude Gay has translated all the accounts in the first volume of Tomkins. From each of the six succeeding volumes, he only takes an account of one man, and one woman; and he adds two accounts from manuscript, viz., of John Goodwin and Elizabeth Kendal; both which are in T. Wagstaffe's eighth volume. He has a short preface or introduction, giving some account of the work in general; in which he makes a useful remark to the following effect.

"I have no further hint to give thee, reader, than this; that if thou have received the truth in the love of it, and should perceive that some of the descendants of this people do not walk in the steps of their ancestors; and even that some having with Demas loved this present world, have wholly turned their back on the truth, be not discouraged, for truth descends not by inheritance. Neither be thou puffed up against them; but stand in the holy fear of God; and take the advice of the apostle Paul," (Rom. xi. 20—22.) [Well, they were broken off through unbelief, and thou standest by faith. Be not high-minded, but fear. For if God spared not the natural branches, take heed lest he also spare not thee.] "that, having finished thy course, and kept the faith, thou may receive the crown of righteousness, and enter into the joy of thy Lord." Next he inserts an exhortation extracted from the writings of William Penn, and then he gives an abridgement of the preface of Tomkins. In the accounts themselves, he simply translates the narrative; but he gives the expressions of the dying Friend in parallel columns of French and English.

Those who expect an elegant French style in Gay's translation will certainly be disappointed. He probably was not a man who had had the help of a liberal education; and he had imbibed much of an English idiom from his long residence in England. But though he was not an eloquent man, he was something better: he was an upright simple-hearted Christian. His birth-place was Lyons, in France, and his religion at first was that kind of Popery formerly current in France. But even the inspection of a popish version of the New Testament was a means sufficient to detach him from the superstition of Popery. On perusing Acts xvii. 24, &c., "God, that made the world, and all things therein, seeing he is Lord of heaven and earth, dwelleth not in temples made with hands, neither is he worshipped with men's hands," &c., the doctrine of transubstantiation (in which, as he told a friend, the Papists believe that the consecrated wafer is changed into the body, blood, soul and divinity of Christ,) appeared to be false; and the adoration of the host, idolatrous.

In fine, he forsook the Romish communion, and went to live at Jersey, in order to be among Protestants. Here he met with Barclay's Apology; and this book was the instrument to determine him to settle in the principles and profession of Friends. He suffered some persecution in Jersey, and was even at length banished, under pain of corporal punishment; but this was set aside by order of the king. He, nevertheless, took England for his home in the year 1745, and died at a very advanced age, at Barking, in Essex, in the year 1786. He translated, besides the work which has here introduced him to notice, the first part of William Penn's No Cross, No Crown. In private life, he was industrious, very unassuming, and harmless. In his public ministry, sound and fervent, but tender in spirit. He travelled at times in the exercise of his ministry, and often on foot; nor did he confine his labours to the country in which he dwelled; he extended them to Holland, Germany, and Switzerland. In a later visit, namely, to Guernsey and the other islands, he wrote and distributed a paper in French, of which the following is a translation, and which is worthy to be preserved.

It has already been said that he was a humble man, and consonant with this character, it may be observed that he was frequently engaged in prayer, in which it was usual to prefer his petitions in these appropriate terms, 'For the merits of Christ.' He was enabled to endure a lingering disease with great patience, and declared to those who conversed with him, that all fear of death was removed.

'To the People of Guernsey.

'My Friends of both Sexes,

'As I passed along your great street, one market day, I beheld your souls with the eye of faith, as part of the purchase made by the blood of Christ. My heart was affected, and deeply impressed, and softened, so that I shed tears. So I entreat you, in the name of this divine Saviour, do not defile these souls, which are so dear and precious, by any wilful sin. Among other things, do not take the name of God in vain: for he will not hold any one guiltless who takes his holy name in vain. God would save you. Why should any of you destroy yourselves? Abstain from drunkenness, and from all excess: and even from every appearance of evil. Love one another, as Jesus Christ loved you. Apply yourselves to the witness of God within you, whose holy manifestations and discoveries, as you submit and obey, will do much more for you than all you can hear from me, or from any one else.

'And though it is in the love of the gospel, that I invite you all to come and taste how good and merciful the Lord is toward all those who return to him with their whole heart; yet I am but a poor instrument, who have as much need for Him to preserve me in the hour of temptation, as any of you. But this witness of God is his word, even the Word of Life, which is able to save your souls. Amen!

'Claude Gay.

'Guernsey, 1st Seventh month, 1776.'

PIETY PROMOTED.

THE TENTH PART.

MARY EVENS, a young woman of seventeen, daughter of Benjamin and Elizabeth Evens, of Woodbridge in Suffolk, and eldest sister of Kezia Merryweather, mentioned in the Ninth part of Piety Promoted, was taken from the probations of time, on the 1st of the Eighth month, 1770: the following account of her close is but little altered from one penned by her pious and affectionate mother: for an account of whom, see page 220 of this volume.

She may be truly said, to have been an example of patience and resignation through the whole course of her affliction; and though (continues her mother) I was almost constantly with her, yet I never heard her in the least murmur or repine, though her pain was often very violent; but, she frequently said, that she was afraid she should not have patience enough.

On the last day which she lived, she lay pretty easy till towards noon, when she was seized with violent pain in her side. 'Dear mother,' said she 'lift me up, I cannot breathe.' The pain continued exceedingly sharp for three hours, during which time she was often concerned to beg for patience; and desired her father and me to pray for her, that she might have patience granted. 'Dear mother,' she said, 'thou canst not think what pain this is. This is pain indeed.'

In her greatest anguish, she broke forth in supplication to the Lord for a little ease, saying, 'I have received many comforts from thy hand, O Lord; more than I could expect or desire; and if thou art pleased to take me to thyself this afternoon, it will be the greatest comfort I ever received in my life.' After this, observing her to lie still, I asked if she should like to speak to her brothers and sisters [most of whom were younger than herself]. She said, 'Yes,' distinctly took leave of them all, and said at parting, 'All, mind and be good.' Seeing one of her sisters much concerned, she added, 'Don't fret for such a poor thing as I am.'

After this, it pleased the Lord to grant her request, and to give her ease. She gratefully acknowledged it, and had such sharp pain no more; but lay in a sweet frame of mind, but drawing her breath shorter and shorter, till the solemn moment arrived. A few moments before her close, she gave me one hand, and an intimate friend the other; thus quietly departing about six in the afternoon, as she had besought the Lord, and, I doubt not, is entered into the heavenly rest of the righteous.

SARAH EVENS.—An account has just been given of MARY, daughter of BENJAMIN and ELIZABETH EVENS, of Woodbridge. I come now to relate another deprivation which, in less than half a year after her death, these pious parents had to undergo in the loss of their daughter SARAH EVENS, who died at the age of nineteen, early in the year 1771. In this relation, the memorandums of her mother will be my principal guide; and I shall generally form my little narration in her own words.

But here, seeing I have still the pious close of another sister and of two brothers to relate, by which means Piety Promoted will probably contain accounts of two sons and of four daughters of the same family, it may not be improper, once for all, to mention that the parents were persons not only of exemplary conduct themselves, but very vigilant over that of their children. Being themselves imbued with a sense of the value of the restraints of the cross, they were careful to train up their dear offspring in such a manner as to prepare them for bearing it faithfully, when they had by degrees to act for themselves. Some of them, we see, were early delivered from the trials of the world, passing to final peace through a short path: others still survive, to bless the Christian care and love, and even the pious restraints, of their honourable parents.

On the 15th of the Twelfth month, 1770, SARAH EVENS had been down stairs for the last time; and was very much fatigued with getting up again. When a little recovered, she said, in an awful manner, 'Mother, I was afraid, some time ago, I should never get to heaven; but now am in hopes I shall: for I thought in my sleep, some days since, that there was only a little piece of something white that kept me; and I pulled it very hard to get it away; which I did, and then I got there.' Some days after, she said, 'I hope the time of my release will soon come.'

On the 24th, having had a very restless morning, between twelve and one she fell into a very comfortable sleep. When she awoke, she said, 'I have been asleep, for which I am thankful. It was what I prayed for: but I thought my prayers were not worth being regarded; but they have been mercifully granted.' After a little pause she said, 'What should I do now, if I was like some? May they be brought to a consideration of their ways.' Her mother replied, 'My dear, I hope thy mind is easy;' to which she answered, 'Yes, quite so. I have not any thing that makes it otherwise.'

Nevertheless, one day being very full of pain, and exceedingly low in her mind, she said to me, 'Dear mother, I am afraid now I shall not be safe at last.' I asked her if there was any thing that made her uneasy. She replied, 'No, but only fears.' I said, 'My dear, endeavour to keep thy mind still, and I hope thou wilt again be made easy.' On my going to her in the morning, and asking her how she did, she said, 'My body is no better; but I am favoured with an easy mind. I never knew such a day in all my life as yesterday. I am like another creature now, for now I witness peace.' She continued in patient resignation to the divine will, not once expressing a desire to live longer, but often saying it was better for her to go than to stay. Thus she grew gradually weaker; and on the last night of her sufferings she was exceedingly restless. On my requesting her to be as still as she could, she lay still for a few minutes, and then broke forth in supplication to the Lord, 'O! Father, be pleased to grant me a little ease before thou take me to thyself.' In a very short time her request was granted, and then she said, 'I was afraid my prayers were not worth being regarded; but they have entered, and I have rest.' She was often earnest to be released. A friend about this time asking her how she did, 'Thou seest,' said she, 'how I do. I am going, I hope, to heaven.'

She uttered many more expressions to the same import, continuing to draw her breath shorter and shorter, till between six and seven on the 16th of the First month, 'when,' continues her sorrowing, not repining mother, 'it pleased the Lord, who gave her to us, to take her from us; and I doubt not in the least, that she is entered into that rest which she so earnestly desired and prayed for.

'And, though it is a close trial to part, yet, as she expressed a little before her departure that she had not the least doubt that we should all meet again, several of her near relations being by her, the fervent breathing of my spirit is, that we may be enabled to follow her, and live for ever in realms of eternal bliss.

ROBERT EVENS, son of Benjamin and Elizabeth Evens, of Woodbridge, finished his short course of eighteen years the 29th of the Eleventh month, 1772. His decease was occasioned by a fall, in which the butt-end of a fork was forced with violence against the pit of his stomach. It did not prove immediately mortal, though he had more or less of constant pain, which he endured with great patience. His employment was at that time in agriculture, and he was able to go about his usual business, if he took care not to pursue it too eagerly; otherwise the ill effects of over-exertion would occasion a confinement of several days. He appeared to possess a firm mind, not easily to be moved; and a pleasant temper, exceeded by few.

As his ailments did not yield to the means made use of, but were rather growing worse, his employer thought it best for him to be under parental care; and he returned home about ten weeks before the period of his life. A rapid decline came on, accompanied with violent pain in the breast and stomach, and with an almost incessant cough.

In the forepart of his illness, he seemed to have some expectation that he should recover; but as his disorder advanced, he was wholly divested of all thoughts of that kind; and many times expressed to his parents the goodness of the Lord which he felt, and the comfortable seasons which were his portion. Being asked how he found his mind when looking to that awful period which might shortly approach, his answer was, 'Entirely easy;' and the last time a question of this sort was put to him, he added, 'but it looks as if I might have a lingering time, yet I hope to be preserved in patience.' Contrary, however, to his expectation, on the evening of the same day, his pain greatly increased, attended with great difficulty of breathing. No impatient expression escaped him; but, in the greatest extremity, he fervently prayed for patience; and, between nine and ten, he resigned his breath; and, saith his pious mother and careful attendant, arrived, I fully believe, at that mansion of rest, where he will sing high praises to Him who sits on the throne, and to the Lamb, forever more.

FRANCIS EVENS, son of Benjamin and Elizabeth Evens, so often mentioned in this volume, died when he had nearly attained the age of twenty-one, on the 25th of Tenth month, 1779. I take this account of him, as most of the others, from the memorandums of his mother, and I am inclined here to prefix the little introduction with which she has prefaced her account of this loss.

"My mind," says she, "hath often been humbled under the late trying dispensation, wherewith it hath pleased Infinite Wisdom again to try and prove us; and the fervent breathing of my spirit at seasons is, 'Though tried, O Lord, grant we may not be forsaken; and, though proved, let us not be forgotten of Thee, thou Fountain of all good, who, in the midst of judgment, remembereth mercy.'"

Francis underwent much conflict of mind before he was enabled to repose with confidence on the bosom of mercy. Many days and nights he was 'tossed with tempest,' lest he should not be 'favoured to obtain a habitation in the heavens.' But, after much labour, and fervent cries to Him who knows the integrity of the heart, the arm of everlasting mercy was extended, and he was enabled to acknowledge it, though he did not choose to enter into much conversation. He appeared from time to time broken and contrited, and would often say, 'No matter what becomes of the body, if the soul may but enter the glorious kingdom.' About two weeks before he died, his mother, perceiving him to be very low, asked him whether he had any expectation of recovery; 'No,' he replied; 'in a very short space I shall be at my everlasting habitation.'

His mother attended him constantly, and they had many

solemn seasons together, which, says she, were graciously owned by the incomes of the heavenly Father's love, to the tendering of our hearts. His fever, towards the last, affected his head; and, when he could not be distinctly heard, his mind seemed attracted upwards. Yet, probably from the degree of delirium which sometimes prevailed, he felt occasional disquietude; and once, looking steadfastly at his mother, who only was then with him, he said, 'I admire my mind should be so tossed; but not from an apprehension I shall not be received, for I have had a sure evidence of that.'

The last two days of his life his pains left him in a good degree, but the evening before he expired, he appeared to have a hard struggle for half an hour. The next morning his sister, passing the door of the chamber in which her dying brother lay, heard him loudly calling, Father. She thought her father had been in the room, but she found him below. He went up directly, and told the youth that his sister said he had called him. The youth looked attentively at his parent. 'I did not,' he replied, 'call for thee; but to my heavenly Father.' Then he lay still again a few minutes, and quietly breathed his last.

ANNA MARIA BOWMAN, wife of Henry Bowman, of Ringwood in Hampshire, and daughter of Benjamin and Elizabeth Evens, of Woodbridge in Suffolk, sister to the subjects of the four preceding memoirs, was carried off by a consumption in little more than a year after her marriage, and in the 27th year of her age, the 20th of the Twelfth month, 1793.

About a month before this, she had been confined to her chamber, from which time she gave up all expectation of recovery. About this time a message of love was delivered to her from Samuel Emlen, of Philadelphia, then in England. He said that a passage of Scripture had dwelt on his mind on her account, and that he should hardly do justice to his feelings if he withheld it. "In me shall the Gentiles trust, and their reign shall be glorious." This Friend was remarkable for his acquaintance with the Scriptures, and therefore I think there is some reason to suspect an error, either in the delivery of the message, or the recollection of it; for the text stands thus: "To it (viz., the root of Jesse) shall the Gentiles seek, and his rest shall be glorious." The languid, diffident, and humble young woman, wondered that he, an eminent and much beloved minister, should notice her so much as even to send his love to her; but she said that the sight which he had of her state was as balm to her mind.

The same evening she requested her husband not to grieve for her, but to give her up cheerfully. 'The more readily,' said she, 'thou resignest me, the greater will be thy peace. We have lived in love the little time we have been together; and, as I said before, the more readily thou givest me up, the greater will be thy peace.' Afterwards she repeated to an elder sister, who was attending her, the message of Samuel Emlen, and said to her, 'Well, I have great encouragement to look forward; and I desire patience, to continue to the end.' She desired her sister, who was writing to their parents, to give her duty to them, and request them not to grieve; and to tell them that she should be glad to see them once more, but that she desired to stand resigned.

The next afternoon she was convulsed to such a degree, as that those who were with her believed her to be near her close; but on being put to bed, toward evening she revived, and, after some inquiry respecting the attack from which she had just recovered, she said, 'It was a fit, and a warning of what is coming.'

To a young woman who visited her, she said, 'We have witnessed many seasons together, and some, I hope, to profit. I know thy situation is much exposed. Thou hast kept thy place, to thy credit, and the admiration of many. Stand open to the manifestations of truth. Give up, give up, to what thou knowest to be right, and thou wilt find thy account in it.'

On the first of the Twelfth month, John Merryweather, the husband of her sister Kezia, mentioned in the ninth part of this work, was telling of the satisfaction which he had in seeing her so easy and resigned; to which she replied, 'I stand ready, whenever the Lord is pleased to call.' Soon after, she desired to see her own brother, and, requesting him to take a chair, said thus: 'Dear brother, I cannot express what I have felt for thee this day. I know thy situation, and the difficulties thou labourest under; but let me impress the necessity of attending week-day meetings as much as thou canst. Thou wilt find thy reward. As to thy wife (who the reader should understand was not at this time a member of the Society), let her alone. She is a woman of tender feelings. Do not persuade her one way or another, as to religion. Be thou steady. The Lord loves thee. I am sure he loves thee.' She many times desired her relations not to fret; for that, she said, grieved her; and once she said to her husband, 'Look as cheerful as thou canst.'

The next day she was again faint and convulsed, but not so much as before; yet in the night her sister thought her worse, and inquired of her whether she were faint. After a while she replied, 'No. I felt as if I wanted for nothing just then. Be not frightened. I do not feel as if I was going. I think I shall have a clearer evidence at that time. I think I shall.' Her cough and shortness of breath were often very afflicting; but a sweetly composed frame of mind was the means of her daily support, and was an instructive lesson to those who attended her.

On the 7th, as she was undressing, in order to retire to rest, she said, 'I fear I shall not experience such a calm as I did last night. I have reasoned several times to-day whether the favour was not too great to be mentioned, for I felt as if I was in heaven, and saw the angels there.' She not unfrequently talked in her sleep, and once was heard to say very distinctly, 'When shall I drink of the water of that clear river?' This seemed to show that her sleeping, as well as waking thoughts, were fixed on the eternal 'recompense of reward.'

Her decline was rapid, and her patience did not fail; but she often begged that it might be continued to her. The day preceding her departure, her body was restless, she took but little food, and requested that not any might be offered to her. About one the following morning, she seemed inclined to sleep, and desired the family would also retire. At five, they were again called, and her husband going to her, she only said, 'My dear Henry,' and then fell asleep. In about half an hour her breath became greatly affected for a few seconds; but again recovering it, she laid her head on the pillow, and in her sleep, so quietly as scarcely to be perceived, she sweetly breathed her last.

ELIZABETH EVENS. — Though I have not to record many particular expressions of ELIZABTH EVENS of Woodbridge, wife of Benjamin Evens; yet as notice has been taken in this volume of so many of her children, who were conducted by the grace of their Redeemer to a peaceful close, some account of their pious mother seems an addition almost requisite.

She was the eldest daughter of Francis and Mary Lawrence of Norwich, and was deprived of both parents by the time she was about sixteen years of age; at which early period the care of four younger sisters devolved on her; and she performed her trust so well, that on her marrying, and removing to Woodbridge, they also came, and dwelt in a house adjoining to her residence.

About the twenty-eighth year of her age, she came forth in the work of the ministry, uttering in her own meeting at Woodbridge, these words; "Obedience is better than sacrifice, and to hearken to the voice of the Lord, than the fat of rams." This was in the year 1753. Rather more than three years afterwards, she set out on a visit to the meetings of Friends in Essex; after the accomplishment of which service, she had this testimony to bear; "I had renewed occasion to be thankful that it pleased my great Master, not only to move upon my mind to go forth in that service, but to go along with, and safely conduct me again to my habitation in peace. It is a cause of more joy than words can express."

Notwithstanding she had the care of a large family of children, and much affliction fell to her lot, by the decease of several of them when they were just entering, or had entered that time of life in which dutiful children become, in some respects, the companions, the friends, the support, and the solace of their parents; she continued freely given up to travel in the exercise of the gift which she had received, as the pointings of duty were manifested to her. The eastern counties, some of the northern and midland, with the cities of London and Bristol, were the principal parts to which her services were directed.

In the year 1782, she was much enfeebled by a paralytic stroke; nevertheless she continued a diligent attender of meetings when bodily ability admitted; and even sometimes, when many would think their weakness an almost insuperable bar. 'Do not give up,' said she on a particular occasion, 'the assembling with your friends, for it is many times strength in weakness; and the poor mind, being stayed upon Him who is the alone helper of the helpless, is sometimes, out of deep poverty, made in secret to bless the name of Israel's God.'

It was also after this debilitating disease had been permitted to enfeeble her frame, that she paid a religious visit to the meetings of London and some others in the neighbourhood; and after this she visited the families of Friends in Norwich, and most of the meetings in the county of Norfolk.

She was at length removed from this state of trial, in which she had so long endeavoured to fulfil the gracious design of her Lord, in visiting her with his love, the 13th of the Fourth month, 1796. She was not long confined to her chamber, and during this time, did not express much of her mental feelings; but there was a sweet composure on her countenance, which seemed to evince that her day's work was done; and that, with becoming patience and holy resignation, she was waiting for the period which, through his adorable mercy, should unalterably unite her to the beloved of souls.

BENJAMIN EVENS.—It has generally been esteemed particularly encouraging, to observe, in collections of this sort, the lively hope expressed by young persons, who have early felt the touches of redeeming love, have submitted to its purifying power in the dawn of their faculties, and have been early gathered into the garner of rest. But the survey of a long life, passed in almost uniform conformity to the law of the gospel, and closing in its peaceful spirit, even though it has not been marked with the performance of many signal and attractive acts of service in the church, holds out probably an instruction equally valuable, although of a species somewhat different. One prompts the youthful mind to enter with alacrity, and without reserve on the heavenly race; the other encourages the humble diffident mind, which aspires after the crown that is at the end, and has already made some progress, to persevere in it without fainting.

BENJAMIN EVENS, of Woodbridge, in Suffolk, who finished a course of about eighty years, the 27th of the Twelfth month, 1798, was considered by the Friends of that county, as a good example, and a very diligent attender of their meetings. In those for worship he at times bore a public testimony for truth, having long been an acknowledged, and approved minister; and, whilst his faculties retained their vigour, he was conspicuously useful in supporting the Christian discipline of the Society.

He did not travel much. There are not accounts of more than two journeys with a certificate. The first was to Friends in the counties of Lincoln, Cambridge, Huntingdon, and Norfolk; the other to those of London and its neighbourhood. At the time of this last visit he was already an old man, but humble and unassuming: which just tribute to his memory, the writer of this short memorial, who had then the privilege of having him for a guest, is desirous of adding to the testimony of his Suffolk friends.

A little incident occurred during this engagement which may not be improper to relate. In a meeting in which he had been largely engaged in testimony, he misquoted a passage of Scripture, and in a way that materially affected the sense. Finding out his error, he rose again towards the close of the meeting to acknowledge it to the congregation, to show how his variation implied a doctrine, differing from that of the text, and to testify his adherence to the latter. And in his walk from the meeting, his tears of sorrow flowed as he continued to expatiate on his mistake; and he appeared to claim and to need all the consolation which his attendant could afford him.

Some time before his decease, his faculties gave way; and his last illness was accompanied at times with violent pain; but he was preserved in love to all, and enabled to bear his sufferings with a comfortable degree of patience, and resignation to the will of God: to whom he frequently prayed, 'O thou fountain of all good, look down upon me if it be thy will, and ease me of my pain.' Once he expressed himself after this manner: 'My love is to all, but especially to the faithful. Let it be known, I die in peace with all men.' One night, before composing himself to rest, he exclaimed,

'Farewell, farewell. All is peace, peace, peace and joy.' These consoling words he again repeated, and then he fell asleep.

His prayer seemed mercifully granted during the two last weeks of his life, as he was generally much relieved from pain; and he at length departed, full of days, and full of peace.

JONATHAN RAINE, of Sunnyside, near Crawshay-booth, Lancashire, whither he had removed from Trawden, departed this life the 27th of the Eleventh month, 1773, aged about seventy-five years. His parents being members of the Society of Friends, educated him in the principles of our profession; but he seems to have neglected in great degree the circumspect way in which they had endeavoured to direct him; and to have been much infected with the spirit of the world, and the vanities of life. Thus he seems to have remained until his fortieth year, during which time he married, had three children, and was deprived of them all, and also of his wife. His residence was then in the county of Durham.

At length, as his friends relate in their testimony of him, it pleased the Lord to reveal his righteous judgments against the transgressing nature in him; when he stooped to the cross of Christ, and patiently endured the baptism of the Holy Spirit: thus becoming qualified for the work to which he was called. The reader may here truly anticipate, and conclude that the work in question was gospel ministry; but let him also be sure that by these means also, and only, qualification for other services, and for every service, in the Lord's house, must be obtained: and who is there that will not ultimately wish to be the Lord's servant, seeing that his undeceiving lips have declared, "Where I am, there shall my servant be."

In order to be more fully at liberty to follow the vocation with which this Friend perceived himself to be called, he left off business, into which he had engaged when young; for something of what has been termed 'true moderation' now bounded his desires. His first appearance as a minister was about the year 1740.

In the year 1746, he married Margaret Birtwistle, daughter of Henry and Mary Birtwistle, of Rossendale, Lancashire, and soon after came to reside at Trawden, within the compass of Marsden monthly meeting; where he was a diligent, zealous, and exemplary minister, and member of religious society. He travelled through various parts of Great Britain; and in the year 1760, was one of a committee appointed by the yearly meeting to visit the meetings of Friends in Ireland. He attained to a good old age, and had, in the winding up of his days, but a short allotment of illness.

About two hours before he breathed his last, having lain still for some time, he desired to be helped up, and, as nearly as can be remembered, spoke as follows: 'I want to tell you a little of what has appeared to the view of my mind, as I was lying and reflecting, that my time seemed to be near the conclusion. I earnestly breathed to the Great Informer, that he would be pleased to show me my own state, and how it was with me, and to forgive all my sins. And there was shown me some little stones, laid in regular order, and a path through the middle of them. The first heap, it was told me, were the sins of my youth; and they were all passed by and forgiven, for the sake of Christ: though my sins and backslidings were many. Yea, there was a time when my trouble and distress were such, I could have wished that man had died as the beast that perishes, and that there had been no rewards nor punishments after death. I could have been content to have been shut up in a dungeon, never to have seen the light again, if I thereby might have gained peace. In unutterable condescension it pleased the Lord to break in upon my soul, as the light of the sun after a long darkness; which so overcame me, that I believe if an account had been brought me that all I had in the world had been lost, it would have given me no concern. Oh, Friends, you that are young, my desires have been earnest for you, that you might seek after that which is better than any earthly enjoyment; and bend your necks to that which is able to yoke down every unruly passion, and every inordinate desire; that thereby you may obtain everlasting peace.

'The others that were showed me were all white stones. There was no dirt upon them. Though there had been many slips, and many omissions, yet they were all washed away and remitted. There remained only one, which was, that I had been sometimes too thoughtful that the people might have somewhat spoken to them; and as that sprung from a good intention, it was also remitted: and then, friends, the peace, the comfort, and sweetness that I felt was unspeakable.

'I was desirous to leave this as a legacy with you. Oh, you that are young, seek after it. Press after that divine help, which alone can make you possessors of that peace which the world cannot take away.'

A little while after this, he perceived his wife to be sorrowing, and said, 'Do not grieve for me, my dear. I am quite easy. I could not have believed a few days since, I could be so resigned, and willing to be dissolved. But, oh! the condescension of the Almighty, and the unutterable love which fills my heart!'

SARAH CLARE, was the daughter of Thomas and Hannah Clare, of Warrington, born there in the year 1759, and was removed the 31st of the Seventh month, 1781. She was an innocent young woman; but not noticed for anything particularly striking in her conduct, till she was visited by the illness which terminated her days. It was a consumption; and after it became the means of confining her, was only about ten weeks in performing its office. She had then entered her twenty-third year, and from the beginning of her illness she appeared to be resigned, and often bore testimony to the Lord's goodness, and to his tender dealing with her, in favouring her with his presence, and the lifting up of the light of his countenance upon her. In an affecting manner, she once said 'I am afraid I shall not be able to be thankful enough for the kindness and goodness of the Lord to me: and this latter part exceeds all. I cannot convey to another what I have felt, and the desirable prospect I have in view: nothing in this world to compare to it. If I might choose, I had rather die than live; but I do not wish to go before the right time; but to wait in patience.' Patience, indeed, seemed to be the covering of her mind.

On one occasion, she expressed her sorrow in observing, that so many of our youth were strangers to retirement; saying also, 'I love it, and the company of solid friends. 'But,' said she, 'if others want to come and see me, if it might instruct them, or cause them to consider their latter end, I should be glad. One knows not. It may be brought to their remembrance in future.'

At another time, she expressed herself thus: 'I feel quite easy. Death has no terror. It is a fine thing to have no will or choice of one's own, but to trust in the Lord. Though my cough seems troublesome, and matter hard to get up, yet hard things are made easy to me.' Indeed, such sweetness attended her mind, that she seemed as though she were in heaven whilst on earth.

About an hour before her gentle spirit departed, she took an affectionate leave of the family, who were present, thinking she was then about to enter into the rest of God. She was however again detained for a while, and said, with an audible voice, 'I have been at the door of heaven. It was open for me. I beheld the Almighty sitting on his throne.' She also said, that it was then intimated to her that there was something more for her to do. Then she embraced her sisters, and with great fervency of mind added, 'Do come and see how good he is. Oh, it is a sweet place. He gathers his lambs in his arms, and carries them in his bosom. Oh, I could invite all to come and see how good he is. He is not a hard master. Praises and glory be to him forever.'

She afterwards, when her voice faltered, was heard to utter the words Jacob and Israel; and appearing to be in what may be termed a triumphant melody, breathing shorter and shorter, she quietly passed away.

POTTO BROWN, son of John and Sarah Brown, of Earith in Huntingdonshire, was born there the 16th of Fifth month, 1765. He discovered, in early youth, a serious and religious turn of mind, which his tender parents were concerned to cherish; and as he grew up towards manhood, the seed of the kingdom sprung up in his heart, and gradually increased. He was a good example to the youth, in his words and actions; and was beloved by those who had any acquaintance with him, both friends and others. He left behind him a journal of his life; in which many minute particulars, and incidents relating to himself and others, are noted; and from which the following extracts are made:

In a letter addressed to a youth with whom he had formed an intimate acquaintance at school, he expresses himself after this manner:

'I hope, as we travel on through this transitory state, we shall be enabled to cast the cares of this world behind us, looking to the Author of all good: who will help all those who trust in Him. I believe, beyond all doubt, that all those who trust in Him will not lack the bread of life.'

On the 6th of Eleventh month, 1783, a remarkable occurrence fell to his lot, which take nearly in his own words:

'This morning, a little after four, I set off from Ely to

go to Ramsey, to attend the marriage of my cousin Joseph Brown Allen, and Ann Turner. When meeting was gathered, we sat in silence about half an hour; when Thomas Cox, of Earith, rose up; and having appeared in public testimony about half an hour, sat down: about a minute after which he was seized with an apoplectic fit, and expired immediately. This sudden and awful stroke threw the meeting into confusion. We gathered again in about a quarter of an hour, when Isaac Gray stood up and spoke. Soon after he had finished his testimony, cousin Joseph Brown Allen and Ann Turner were married, and the meeting broke up.

'In this meeting I was favoured with a vision as follows: I held down my head, and shut my eyes; when lo! to my inward view, I beheld our Saviour coming down in the clouds, in the dress of a country farmer, with a great coat on. He stretched forth his right hand toward a man who walked to him; and took hold of his hand. This man went with him; and he looked towards me with an eye of concern. I went as I thought towards him, and took hold of his hand; but he told me that I could not go till the briers and thorns were removed which lay betwixt him and me. This gave me a surprise, and all vanished away. I then held up my head, and saw Thomas Cox dying.

'The 9th of the same month Thomas Cox was buried at Earith, but I could not go, because my foot had been very much strained: so I lay in bed till dinner. The Lord then showed me, to my great comfort, that my dependency must be on him: so that I began to inquire how it stood with me and my God. Then was I humbled to cry, "Help me, O Lord, or I perish." The word was, "Draw nigh unto God, and he will draw nigh unto thee, indeed." Then began I to meditate on the Lord in the night season, and was greatly refreshed thereby. A voice passed through me, saying, "Thou must not have any conversation, but what may profit thy soul; for unto that man that ordereth his conversation aright, will I show my salvation. Thy mind must be set on heavenly things, and thy conversation on heaven."'

In a discourse he had shortly after with his cousin Ann King, on the subject of what he had seen in the meeting at Ramsey, she said to him, 'I see the interpretation is plain. The briers and thorns must be cut up before thou canst go to heaven. Keep to the exercises that are within thee;' 'for I had told her,' says he, 'how it had been with me ever since.' 'Thou hast read some books to thy hurt, which I advise thee in future to avoid.' 'These words,' said he, 'were spoke with such authority, that I knew full well she was empowered of the Lord. They ran through my heart like oil, and gave strength and comfort to my soul. Trust thou in the Lord, O my soul; for the Lord loveth holiness, and purity is his delight.'

The 29th of Eleventh month he wrote after this manner:

'For the last three days nothing material has occurred; but glory be to our God, for he hath dealt wonderfully with his servant. I cannot express the comfort I have felt in keeping to the operation of the word of life in my own heart. The Lord hath showed to me the pure state in which our primitive Friends stood; and also the fallen state of many amongst us at this day; which is to be mourned by me. I hear some American friends are landed, who will come and strengthen those, to whom it pleaseth the Lord to manifest his glorious work. He will not be mocked by men of low degree; who set their minds on earthly enjoyments, and think not on the name of the Lord. He has given every man ability to know that he is a just God, who dwelleth in the heavens; and those who will serve him must set their minds on heaven; whence they shall receive their help. Those who are heavenly shall declare his name to all generations, to the convincement of thousands, that the Lord is God! Blessed be his name! saith my soul, for taking me by the hand, and leading me out of the paths of vanity! May I be enabled to evince, by words and actions, that in conversation the Lord is to be praised; and honoured in stillness. I hope those who shall see my journal after my decease, may not think I have written this of myself. I can honestly say, that the Lord hath guided my hand and opened my mouth.

'The next day I went to Littleport meeting; where it pleased the Lord to open my mouth in a public manner, in which I had great satisfaction, in that I had been obedient to the divine will.'

In answer to a letter he received from his mother, in which she expresses her great concern for his welfare; he says, 'The Lord hath been pleased to pluck my feet out of the miry clay; and to open my mouth to make known his will amongst his people. I hope it will ever be my care to keep near him, as I have experienced a drawing near of the Lord to me; my heart is broken and contrited: blessed be his holy name! He hath showed me the way wherein I am to walk. O, entreat my brothers from me, to follow after the Lord in purity and holiness, and to wait for his counsel. O that I could express the hundredth part of what I feel in being renewed in his counsel; but I must leave them to the Lord.'

'The 2d of Twelfth month. This day a cloud covered me, and a temptation wounded my soul. I was drawn to consider how the Lord pardoned the thief on the cross, and to make it a cloak for trusting to a dying hour; but I felt the rod that chastised me, and heard a voice, saying, "How camest thou to take thought against thy God? He will not be slighted, but looked unto with a single heart, for all help."

'The 11th. I found that, during my late journey, while my mind was turned inward, then was his presence with me; I was preserved in the truth, to my inexpressible comfort. O may I always keep watch, lest the enemy draw my mind from being stayed on the Lord.

'The 17th. Many are the temptations which the enemy

lays to draw my mind from the Lord; but, look thou, O my soul, to the Lord with unfeigned sincerity, and with full purpose of heart, in the humility of that spirit which enlightens thee and strengthens thee against them all.

'The 4th of the First month, 1784. In the course of a visit I lately made to my parents, two of my relations opened their minds to me, concerning my public appearances, wishing I might be favoured to support the honour of the blessed truth; which was done in so affecting a manner, that it helped and strengthened me much. This day I went to Littleport meeting, where I spoke a few words. Oh, how I felt the Lord with me this day; blessed be his name! Many were the breathings of my soul at times, that the Lord would keep his fear always before my eyes, that I might not speak a word, but to his honour. Oh, that it was the case of all those who profess with us, that nothing might be done but to the glory of God: that we may say, "Thine is the kingdom, the power and the glory, for ever!" Then should we answer our high and holy calling.

'The 15th of the Second month. I never used to write concerning my spiritual welfare till I was in a right frame of mind, under the influence of the power of truth. From the 19th of last month I have known a going backwards, as from Jerusalem to Jericho; but the hand of God was not shortened: but he has made me know that I must be obedient to him.

'The 17th. This day, in my retired thoughts, I was made sensible how much we ought to keep ourselves in humble reverence to our God, under a consideration of his omniscience and our nothingness. Oh, if people would but behold their dependency on Him, they would be afraid of having their minds taken from under his protection; much more of doing any thing that would not tend to his glory; but, on the other hand, they would testify against every thing of a contrary tendency; knowing that God is jealous of his honour, and will be sought unto with fear and trembling.

David saith (Ps. lxxvi.), "Thou, even thou, art to be feared, and who may stand in thy sight when once thou art angry."

'The 19th. This day was a day of hard labour to me, because I was off my guard last night, by entering into a long and needless discourse, which drew my mind from the Lord; but he was good to me, and heard me when I cried, for my spirit was bowed down in humility before him, and heavenly joy abounded when I confessed my error to him. This is an evil which many of our Society fall into, even those who have been religiously inclined. (See Book of Extracts, on the head of Conduct and Conversation.)

'The 25th. I have this day oftentimes felt a refreshing power, with a secret promise that, if I kept under the guidance of the power of truth, I should not do any thing to dishonour it, for a fear arose in me that I did things that were not an honour to it. A voice was in me, "Humble thyself, and thou shalt be favoured." I have felt a service in keeping a journal, as it helped to keep me from going back; encouraged me in seeing how I was favoured before, and what progress I had made in the truth. What pleasure has it given me to write of my progress heavenwards! On the contrary, what lashes have I felt, when I was not in a frame to write! When I had walked obedient to his power, he always gave me a frame to write.

'The 27th. Last First-day, I wrote to a Friend concerning our serving burials, which I saw, in a clear light, was not consistent with us as a people; because, when we serve a burial, it is to gratify the pomp and vanity of the people of the world, which is a plain contradiction to that Spirit which we profess to be guided by.

'The 8th of Third month. This day I had a concern to speak to a Friend concerning gaping in meeting, and on another subject. He was very high in his expressions; but, finding that I spoke according to the Spirit, he was silent, for truth will always prevail.

'The 9th. This day, being alone, I read my journal over

to the Second month, which helped me to see how I followed after God, who called me to be more and more humbled. Oh, I felt his goodness to flow towards me!

'The 18th. I saw I could not be in such a humble state as I had been called to come into without I became as clay in the hands of the Great Potter. I saw that my body was to be the temple of the Holy Spirit, and that no defiling thought must lodge within me.

'The 21st. I went to our meeting at Ely, and many were the refreshings that my mind there felt. I saw that the Spirit of Christ was the only way that leads to celestial bliss, and that he teaches his followers to be humble as he was humble; that we must not barely believe that he came down amongst men, in a body prepared for him, but must also believe in his power, that leads to life eternal. Be still, O my soul, and thou wilt find his power made manifest in thee.

'The 16th of Fourth month. I find that the more I give up my mind to seek after the kingdom of God and his righteousness, the more I advance in the work; the more I keep in the power, the stronger I grow. My soul longeth for the living God; yea, my inward cry is raised for the bread of life, more than the natural man hungereth after natural food.'

Here ends the journal of this pious young man.

About this time his health began to decline, and some symptoms appeared that seemed to threaten a consumption; he was therefore removed from his master's to his father's house, that he might try his native air and the effects of medicines; but the disorder baffled both. In the latter part of his illness, he was remarkably patient under his bodily affliction, which was long and sharp; those who assisted in his illness, said they never saw any one bear so great pain with so much patience. A little before he was confined to his chamber, his mother, who was helping him to bed, found he grew weaker, and said to him, 'Potto, dost thou not think thou art grown weaker within these few days?' He answered with as much cheerfulness as if he had been in health, 'Yes, I know I am; but what matter? If the outward man grows weaker, the inward man grows stronger; I experience the strengthening of the new man every day.'

Another time, being very sick and in great pain, he said he could not bear too much, mentioning how much Christ bore for him; but his mother could not expressly remember his words. One day his father, sitting by his bed-side, and observing him appear dull, asked him if he was any way uneasy about his future state. He said, No; for he had many comfortable assurances it would be well with him. He then burst into tears, and said he was uneasy for his brothers, fearing they might be drawn from the truth. His father desired him not to make himself uneasy about them; for there was the same divine hand to guide them, which guided him; and if they adhered to it, it would do the same for them.

A few days before his departure, a friend from Ely came to see him, and asked him how he did. He said he was very ill, but did not wish to live, nor did he think it his place to pray for death. The night before his departure, he said to the woman that sat up with him, 'Go tell my mother that I am very bad, and think she would like to be here.' When she came to him, he told her he was a great deal worse; but he desired that she would not be troubled at his change, which he expected would be soon. He uttered many more sweet expressions, which cannot be remembered, and departed this life the 16th of Tenth month, 1784, aged nineteen years.

The following was found in his pocket-book, after his decease, giving an account how he spent his time, whilst ill at home.

Eighth month, 13th. 7 to 8, reading; 8 to 9, walking; 9 to 10, writing; 10 to 11, retirement; 11 to 12, walking; 12 to 1, dinner; 1 to 2, walking; 2 to 3, reading; 3 to 4, writing; 4 to 5, walking; 5 to 6, reading; 6 to 7, retirement.

TABITHA MARRIOT was the daughter of Richard and Susannah Ecroyd, of Marsden in Lancashire, and was born in the year 1724. She was enabled early to bend to the visitations of the grace of the Lord, and by this means had discernment and strength to avoid the vanities and dangers to which many appear prone. As she advanced in the path of righteousness, many deep baptisms and conflicts of spirit fell to her lot, which she endured with patience, until she was reduced to a resignation of will that resembled the clay passive in the hand of the potter. Thus she was prepared as a vessel meet for the Lord's service, in which, as a gospel minister, she first publicly engaged in the twenty-sixth year of her age. 'The Lord,' said she, in a week-day meeting, 'is good to his people; especially to those who are desirous above all things to be conformable to his will.' The declarations of our ministers are called testimonies. This appears to be truly a testimony. She bore witness of what she felt.

She was soon concerned to visit Friends in their meetings. Her first visit in this religious service was in Cumberland, in company with her beloved elder friend, both as a woman and a minister, Sarah Taylor of Manchester, of whom there is an account in the ninth part of this work. She continued frequently to be engaged in this service for about eight years, when, in the year 1758, she was married to Richard Marriot, of Mansfield in Nottinghamshire, and went to reside there. In about two years, however, they came and settled in the compass of Marsden monthly meeting. The confinement incident to an increasing family sometimes kept her at home; yet she still continued to travel in the service of truth, visited various parts of this nation, and was often engaged in visiting the families of Friends. She was esteemed a deeply baptised and powerful gospel minister; her deportment in the exercise of her gift was grave and comely, and her expression clear; and in supplication she appeared to be at times favoured with near access to the throne of grace.

In private life she was an example of meekness and lowliness of heart, and filled up its various relations with great propriety. Towards the close of her days she was tried with deep affliction; but she was enabled not only to support it with becoming resignation and fortitude, but at times so far to be borne above it, as even to be much enlarged in her gift of public ministry. She seemed to aspire after total resignation to the will of the Lord, in all the dispensations of his providence to her. She once said to a beloved friend, alluding to the probations of her latter life, 'The cup that is handed to me, shall I not drink it without repining?' and in her last public testimony, she had to declare of the goodness of her Lord.

About the beginning of the Sixth month, 1786, she became ill of a slow fever, and, on the 15th, she was found by a relation who visited her, so weak as scarcely to be able to speak audibly. Yet the same day she revived, and finding her children and some other relations together, after a time of silence, she addressed them to this import: 'I have felt so strong a desire for your good, that I must have been weak indeed, could I not have got down stairs to express it to you. I have been led to look at the state of our meeting; and as many of the elders are removed, I wish you weightily to consider what is in your power to do for the Lord. Oh! how ardent is the desire of my heart, that you may do nothing against the truth, but for the truth! My heart has been humbled in the recollection of the goodness of the Almighty to me, from my very early years, in that he gave me his good Spirit to check and reprove me when I had done amiss; and I am thankful that the Lord inclined my heart to turn at his reproofs, to receive his corrections, because I had sinned against him. I regret that I have not made this divine law my more frequent study; yet this I can say of a truth, I have loved it; and indeed it has been a lamp unto my feet, and a light unto my path. I have loved to meet the Lord, and to wait upon him, even in the way of his judgments; and may now say, though I know not how this weakness may end, I never before, in the course of my life, have been so continually favoured as of late; never before had such unclouded prospects of that holy habitation, where all sorrows and tears shall be wiped away.'

After this opportunity, in which more was uttered than is here set down, she continued in a feeble state for some weeks; and then seemed to gain a little strength; but her disorder returned about the 20th of the Eighth month, and was attended with considerable lethargy. Nevertheless, when awake, she was clear in her understanding, and aware of her approaching close. On the 4th of the Ninth month, as she was sitting up, she said, 'Oh that I had wings like a dove, that I might fly away and be at rest:' and after she was put in bed, she spoke to this effect: 'I resign myself, my children, and the church, into the hands of a merciful Creator, who is worthy of high hallelujahs, and eternal praise, both now and for evermore! Amen.'

Her last recorded expression was on the following day, a prayer for the church. 'O,' said she, 'most gracious Father, be thou pleased to look down with an eye of tender compassion upon thy poor afflicted seed.' Two days after, on the 7th, she quietly departed.

ANN NAISH, daughter of Joseph and Betty Naish, of Congersbury, a village in Somersetshire, about twelve miles from Bristol, was born about the Third month, 1773. From her childhood she was of a serious deportment, and of a calm and condescending temper, even in cases where her youthful inclination might be opposed: so that the salutary directions of her parents were readily obeyed. Her understanding appeared, at least to keep pace with her age, if not to surpass it; and her steady care to please those who had the charge of her education, endeared her to them; as her kind, affable, and obliging behaviour gained her the love of her associates.

This promising maid was called in her bloom from the vicissitudes of time. Whilst she was at boarding-school at Milverton, not very far advanced in her fifteenth year, she was taken ill. Her disorder, water in the head, soon affected the part with violent pain, and was not long in producing frequent delirium, and sometimes convulsions. She was, however, allowed many intermissions, and clear intervals of reason; in one of which, a friend asked her, whether she were willing to go. She replied, that she was willing to leave it to the Almighty; that at some times she could not desire any thing; but at others she had desired then to go.

It was a week before her affectionate father saw her; and he too availed himself of her undisturbed intervals to apprize her of the uncertainty of her recovery. She repeatedly expressed, in very satisfactory terms, her resignation and acquiescence with the will of the Almighty, often saying, 'I am not afraid to die.' At one time she spoke to her father thus: 'Dear father, thou hast been a tender, affectionate father to me. Have I not been a dutiful daughter to thee?' He answered fully in the affirmative; and she went on, 'Oh, I would not have been otherwise for all the world!' There was at that time some little article of her apparel, which by some means had been introduced, and which her father thought not consistent. He gently remarked it to her; and she freely acknowledged it was wrong; saying, that it proceeded from pride, and that those who kept near to the principle, [the Spirit of Truth,] would be preserved out of such things.

Her gratitude to those about her, especially to those who were more immediately employed in the various offices of assistance which her illness required, seemed to be almost unbounded: and her patience, her serenity, and the innocence and sweetness of her spirit, brought to mind the words of the Redeemer, "Of such is the kingdom of heaven." She departed, after two weeks' illness, the 4th of the Seventh month, 1787.

MARGARET GREENWOOD was the daughter of Thomas and Bridget Greenwood, of Greenwood-haugh in Dent, a district in Yorkshire, on the confines of Westmoreland and Lancashire. Her father occupied a small estate, which till lately was about the yearly value of eighteen pounds. On this small farm, which, together with knitting, was their sole means of subsistence, they brought up five children. These, when at home, as they generally were, and not engaged in the business of the farm, were employed in knitting, by which they could earn a little money. Margaret lived constantly with her parents; for she was afflicted at times from her youth, with an acute rheumatism, which rendered her incapable of much active exertion. This had a tendency to temper the natural vivacity of her disposition, and to render her the more susceptible of religious impressions. A few years before her death she was much devoted to the promotion of piety, and was often concerned to notice and to reprove what she saw to be reprehensible, either in those of her own, or any other society.

About her twenty-seventh year she came forth in the ministry; and her ministry, as well as her innocent life and conversation, was acceptable to Friends. A short time before her decease, she went to Dent Town, in order to warn a vicious and ferocious man of the consequence of his conduct. It was supposed that she would meet with insult, and rough usage; but he was softened, and even received her meekly; and she returned in peace.

She had been engaged in order for marriage, and the day was agreed to be the same on which her sister also was to be married. Each suitor had the name of John. One morning early, their father said to the two sisters, pleasantly, that he supposed they would not give up their Johns for any consideration whatever. Margaret replied, after a pause, that there was one thing, and but one, for which she would give up her John: a place in the kingdom of heaven.

She appeared at that time to be free from indisposition; but about ten in the forenoon, as she sat employed in her knitting, she breathed her last. The preceding day she had attended the general meeting at Dent Town, and had borne a lively and weighty testimony; and as a meeting was held at the same place six days afterward, on account of her burial, the minds of the people were impressed in an extraordinary manner. Her remarkable answer and decease were on the 22d of the Twelfth month, 1787.

JANE FRYER, of Warrington, Lancashire, daughter of Benjamin and Margaret Fryer, was born at Kendal, in Westmoreland, in the year 1761. From an early age she was religiously disposed. Her mother died when she was very young, in consequence of which a considerable care devolved upon her, who was the eldest child. She afterwards went to be an assistant in the family of a friend at Bristol, where she was much beloved for uprightness and integrity, and where she evinced much care and interest for the welfare and preservation of children. This benevolent and beneficial temper of mind was the means of inducing her to open a school at Warrington, to which town she had removed. Here, also, she was greatly esteemed by those who united with her in religious profession, as well as by others who entrusted her with the care of their children: an employment for which she seemed to be particularly well qualified. Nor did she teach by precept alone; her example, as a religious character, was salutary; and on both accounts her loss was much lamented.

Her great concern for the welfare of youth remained with

her in her declining state of bodily health. She said, 'If my being afflicted might but furnish instruction to our young women, I should be glad. I have been very desirous their minds might be weaned and brought from the exteriors that are about them. Oh, what vanity they will feel them when such a time as this comes. My mind has been exercised on their account as I have sat in our meetings. I have longed that they might experience the work of real religion; but things have felt so low, that something of an alarming nature must come to rouse them; and that language hath been sounded in mine ear, "Cry aloud, and spare not; lift up thy voice like a trumpet;" but, alas! who is sufficient for these things? I was but a child.'

At another time she signified that, being favoured with great calmness, and her mind covered with universal good will, she was induced to wonder at so general attachment in her fellow-mortals to sublunary things.

Once, when two friends were with her, she said, 'Oh, may I have patience to wait the Lord's time, without offending him in being over-anxious. Let us unite together in desiring I may be preserved in perfect resignation to his holy will.' After a short pause of silence, she was engaged in prayer, thus: 'O, dearest Lord, Almighty Saviour, if thou wilt, condescend to favour thy poor, unworthy, afflicted child with the lifting up of the light of thy countenance — who am deeply tried. But thou knowest best, O Father, what is best for us, and necessary that we should pass through, in order to fit us for thy glorious kingdom; where nothing that is impure or unholy can ever enter. Therefore, I beseech thee, dearest Lord, let not thine hand spare, nor thine eye pity, till thou hast made me perfect. Then I hope to be dissolved, poor dust and ashes, and clothed with angel's raiment. O, permit me to join them in praises and thanksgiving. My will, thou knowest, has been subservient to thine; and I have endeavoured, according to my small ability, even from a child, not to offend thee, O my God. Therefore, I beg of thee to permit the guardian angel of thy presence to conduct my poor soul to its everlasting rest: believing, if I offend thee not, there is one prepared for me, where I may forever ascribe praises to thy holy name.'

A little after, she desired her friends to pray for her, telling them it was a trying season, and that she was sometimes ready to say, 'Why am I thus prolonged?' adding, 'Thou, O Lord, knowest for what end, and thy time is ever best. Oh, that I may be favoured with thy divine presence! That will make up all.'

At another time she said, 'My mind enjoys great quietness. Oh, the kindness and condescension of the Almighty to me!' She said also to the friends mentioned above, 'I love you, and desire that our spirits may unite together in worshipping Him who can kill and make alive. I have had to-day sweetly to feel, like a foretaste of that peace which I humbly hope to partake of soon, without interruption.' One of her visitors remarking, that she believed all doubting would be done away before the final removal of Jane, the latter replied, 'I have thought so to-day;' and then she broke forth in praising her Redeemer. She also expressed her desire of a release, in the words of the Psalmist: "Oh, that I had wings like a dove! Then could I fly away, and be at rest." 'I lie lingering,' she added, 'just on the brink of eternity. What an awful situation! But as the clay to the potter, who dares say, What dost thou? When a child, I loved retirement — and such awfulness attended my mind, though I had no language to utter, nor knew what it meant; yet I durst not disobey these tender sensations; and I believe the Almighty owned these seasons, and opened my understanding in early years. I have been desirous not wilfully to offend him; and have had many hidden exercises, remembering it was said, "In the world ye shall have trouble; but in me peace:"* which brought great sweetness over my mind.

* This, thus placed, is commonly supposed to be a text of Scripture; but it is not one. The nearest to it, is the last verse of the

Blessed forever be his name!' Soon after, as she was lying in great composure and serenity of mind, she left the toils of mortality, in the twenty-seventh year of her age. Her decease was on the 22d of the Eighth month, 1788.

LYDIA HAWKSWORTH, of Bristol, was the daughter of Samuel and Deborah Waring, of Alton, in Hampshire, and born there about the year 1733. She departed this life in London, at the age of fifty-five. Her mind had been early visited with impressions of the love of God, and as she kept under its influence, she advanced in the just man's path, and was exemplary to others. Having thus by example been in degree a preacher of righteousness, she at length believed herself required to bear a verbal testimony to the Lord's cause.

In the spring of the year 1768, when she was about thirty-five years of age, she was married to Abraham Richard Hawksworth, of Bristol, a Friend who had lately become signal for a remarkable change in conduct; for having turned from the spirit and manners of the world, to bow to the yoke of Christ. But their union, so far as death can dissolve the tie, was of short duration. He died in the course of the same year. A meeting was held in Friends' meeting-house in Bristol, on the occasion of his interment; and his widow, standing up, and laying her hand on the coffin which contained the remains of her beloved partner, bore her first public testimony, with weight and clearness; and, there is reason to believe, with no small effect on the meeting. Having thus devoted herself to a service for which she had long been under preparation, she continued exercised in spirit, and humbly waiting for the renewals of power; by which, in

---

16th chapter of John, "These things have I spoken unto you, that in me ye might have peace. In the world ye shall have tribulation; but, be of good cheer, I have overcome the world."

time, she was made an able minister of the gospel. She was esteemed to be sound in doctrine, clear in spiritual judgment, and cautious not to be more in show than in substance. She was a lover of retirement, and in it often, through deep conflict of spirit, was enabled to grow in the root. At various times she visited the meetings of Friends in most of the counties of Great Britain, once those of Ireland, and was also a diligent attender of meetings for discipline.

Towards the close of her life she was tried with great affliction of body, by illness; and to all human apprehension, the lamp of life, as herself expressed it, was just extinguished. At this time she dictated to a friend some things which engaged the attention of her mind; among which were the following advice and observations.

'Let ministers be careful not to judge too highly of any of their services: for it is only when the breath of the Lord blows through the trumpet, that life and harmony are known, and the great truth is evinced, that it is only his own works that praise him, or benefit the churches: nothing that man can do. In most places, the elders want to stand deeper in Jordan. A more unreserved, total sacrifice of the world must be made, and even the accursed thing cast out of some of their tents, before they can stand as valiants for the Lord's cause upon earth. Every shekel of pure gold in the sanctuary ever had, and still must have, the signature of HOLINESS upon it: for what is of man is but man: the Lord bloweth upon it, and lo, it is nothing, however specious in the eyes of man.

'I see clearly that when the ancient simplicity and purity are known again amongst us, then the glory of the Lord will appear as in former years; and his praise sound forth through all the churches. Therefore, under the fresh flowings of gospel love, I salute my beloved friends everywhere, and bid them farewell in the Lord.'

Her last illness was long and painful; but she was enabled to support it with patience and resignation. She often experienced her cup to overflow with divine love; and often administered pertinently to the states of those who visited her. To a near relation, she expressed herself after this manner: 'Don't mourn for me. I have a comfortable hope that my heavenly Father will receive me into his kingdom.'

On the 17th of the Twelfth month, 1788, she departed, as has been said, in London, and her remains were deposited, where she first drew her breath, at Alton.

SARAH GRUBB, wife of Robert Grubb, of Clonmel in Ireland, was daughter of William and Elizabeth Tuke of York, and born there the 20th of the Sixth month, 1756. When she was very young she was deprived of her mother; but about the tenth year of her age she became the care of her father's second wife, Esther Tuke, of whom there is an account in this volume, whose tenderness, and whose solicitude for her increase in things which belong to salvation, she has frequently confessed. The care extended in her education had its natural effect: it was the means of preserving her from many dangers incident to youth. Nevertheless, the vivacity of her disposition, and her propensity to withstand that which was connected with self-denial, occasioned many a struggle, before she fully submitted to follow the Lord without reserve.

About the age of sixteen it was her lot occasionally to wait upon that eminent minister, John Woolman, in his last illness; and his example of resignation and faith made a deep impression on her mind. To her it was that he said (as mentioned in the 8th part of Piety Promoted,) 'My child, thou seems very kind to me, a poor creature. The Lord will reward thee for it.'

In the twenty-third year of her age, she first appeared as a minister; for which service she had undergone no small preparation, and had passed through deep conflict. Her first appearance was in prayer, and some of her attendant feelings she thus describes: After enduring, on a First-day morning, a state of agony till the meeting separated, she attended that in the afternoon like one deserted; yet, contrary to her expectation, the matter returned; and, assisted by a seasonable testimony from a ministering friend, 'I ventured,' says she, 'on my knees; and in a manner I believe scarcely intelligible, poured out a few petitions. Now I feel in such a state of humiliation and fear, as I never before experienced.'

There is something peculiarly touching to what I trust are the better feelings of the awakened mind, when we observe this dedication of the faculties in the prime of youth; when, as it were, the first fruits of the increase are offered to the Lord; and when, through the various stages of holy preparation, the soul is at length conducted to a public confession of his power and goodness. In the harmony of the divine economy, there is no place for emulation and envy; but I have often thought this period of open dedication in our visited and called youth, to be eminently sweet, and deserving of our admiration and love.

Sarah Grubb travelled much. She first accompanied her mother into Westmoreland and Cumberland; and in the same year joined another relation in a religious visit in Cheshire and Lancashire. Other services succeeded, during the time she remained single, and was a part of her father's family.

In the year 1782, she married Robert Grubb, who had sometime lived at York, and they settled at Foston, a village about ten miles from that city. Soon after her marriage, she visited Friends in Scotland and Cumberland, and some other places, in company with Mary Proud, then of Hull. From this time, she was frequently engaged in travelling in the exercise of her gift: particularly she accompanied Rebecca Jones, of Philadelphia, in a visit to Friends of Ireland. In 1787, she settled with her husband at Clonmel, in that nation. The following year, she joined several other friends in a visit to some parts of Holland, Germany, and France; and on her return from this journey, she was instrumental in establishing a boarding-school for girls, the children of friends, near Clonmel; of which, when at home, she had the superintendence.

I pass over her other services in these kingdoms, and hasten to relate her last undertaking, which was another visit to the continent. Her husband and George Dillwyn, of America, with the wife of the latter, were her companions in this journey, as they had been in the former one; and they left London soon after the yearly meeting, 1790. They sailed for Dunkirk, where at that time several Friends resided, and proceeded through Holland. At Amsterdam, she was tried by a separation from her husband, who thought himself obliged to return home, to assist his brother and partner, then considered to be near his end.

From Holland, the remaining company went by way of Munster, to Pyrmont, where several resided who appeared much separated from the common forms of worship, and were seeking after substance. Of this sort they found others at Rintelm and Minden. I shall trespass on my proposed brevity, to mention a blind woman, who walked to the latter place seventeen miles to meet them. She spun for a living, and her friends occasionally assisted her. The visitors asked her if she were not straitened in this respect. She replied, that she knew she was poor; but that when the question arose in her mind, "Lackest thou anything?" the acknowledgment always succeeded, "Nothing, Lord." O, that not any professor of the Christian name would ever fix his desires upon riches. Here we see it exemplified, that "Godliness with contentment is great gain, having the promise of the life that now is, and of that which is to come."

They next went to Buer, Osnaburgh, and Herwerden, (so much mentioned by William Penn,) and by Bielfeld, where they stayed some days, and through some other places, back to Munster; and were afterwards at Crevelt, Dusseldorf, and

Mulheim, a town near Cologne. Here Sarah drew up and signed a letter, addressed to Leopold, then having lately acquired the crown of Hungary, to which letter her companions added also their names. It is as follows:

To Leopold the Second, King of Hungary, Bohemia, &c.

Amongst the numerous congratulations awaiting thy accession to the imperial crown, accept, O king, our Christian good wishes, and solicitude for thy present and eternal well-being.

We are conscious that we have no claim to the liberty of addressing thee, but from a belief that the Lord Almighty, who ruleth in the kingdoms of men, and giveth them to whomsoever he will, hath inclined us to leave our habitations to visit some parts of this country, and now engages us, in gospel love, to express our secret and united prayer, that thou mayest be an instrument in his holy hand for the advancement of that glorious day, spoken of by the prophet, "when swords shall be beaten into ploughshares, and spears into pruning-hooks; when nation shall not lift up sword against nation, neither shall they learn war any more."

The great design of our universal Parent, in sending his beloved Son a light into the world, is for his own glory in the salvation of mankind; and for this gracious end, he hath given to all men a measure of his own eternal Spirit. To co-operate with him herein, dignifies human nature, and is particularly deserving the most scrupulous attention of princes. The smallest revelation of this heavenly gift in the believing soul, having a degree of omnipotence in it, brings into subjection the natural will and wisdom of man, and discovers to us the noble purposes of our creation. It diffuses that true benevolence which characterizes genuine Christianity, and renders dear to a prince the happiness of all, even the meanest of his subjects; imprinting upon his mind the superior value of an immortal soul, to all worldly acquisitions.

Through the neglect of a principle so pure and important, how hath the rational part of God's creation been sacrificed to the irregular passions of sovereigns, and many unprepared souls precipitated into an awful futurity! That the gospel dispensation is intended to remedy these evils, and promote the government of the Prince of Peace; that the Gentiles are to come to its light, and kings to the brightness of its arising, are truths to which the sacred records abundantly testify.

May this be thy happy experience, O king! that so the power thou art providentially entrusted with, being subservient to divine wisdom, thy example may influence the minds of other princes, who also beholding its excellency, may unite in encouraging their subjects to decline, in mutual charity and forbearance, whatever is contrary to the purity and simplicity of the religion of Jesus. And mayest thou be enriched with all spiritual blessings; that these, added to thy temporal ones, may not only perfect thy happiness, but perpetuate it beyond the narrow limits of time, and qualify thee, acceptably, to cast down thy crown at the feet of Him who is King of kings and Lord of lords; who liveth and reigns for ever and ever.

GEORGE AND SARAH DILLWYN,
Of Burlington, New Jersey, North America.

SARAH GRUBB, Clonmel, } Ireland.
JOSHUA BEALE, Cork, }

Members of the religious Society of Friends in those countries and Great Britain, commonly called Quakers.

Mulheim on the Rhine, 29th of 9th Mo., called September, 1790.

Soon after this she returned to England, visited her relations in the North, and reached her home at Clonmel the 12th of the Eleventh month, greatly exhausted in bodily strength.

Passing a night at Ackworth, on her way from York, with

a near and beloved relation, she thus expressed herself: 'O, my dear! I think sometimes that I shall soon be gone. It seems as if my day's work was nearly done, and on looking towards home, as if I might not be long there.'

On her way to Clonmel, she was at the national meeting of Friends in Ireland, held at Dublin. In a sitting of the meeting of ministers and elders, she gave some account of the journey from which she was then returning. In doing this, humility seemed to be the covering of her spirit. 'We have done little,' said she, 'but the Lord is doing much;' and her concluding words were an humble adoption of those of the Psalmist, "Return unto thy rest, O my soul, for the Lord hath dealt bountifully with thee." These are from Psalm cxvi., a psalm well worth the perusal of the mind conflicted, and yet hoping in the mercy of the Lord.

Soon after her return, she attended the quarterly meeting at Cork, where also she gave an humble account of her late journey. At the close of the meeting she was taken ill, and was confined at the house of Samuel Neale. In a message to a young woman who then presided at the school at Clonmel, she said, 'Salute her very affectionately: tell her I have been much favoured with quietness of mind from the first, though a stranger to how the present afflictions or trials may terminate; but the grain of faith and hope which is mercifully vouchsafed, I esteem preferable to all knowledge.'

Four days before her close, she dictated a letter to a particular friend, in which are the following expressions: 'My soul, though encompassed with the manifold infirmities of a very afflicted tabernacle, can feelingly worship, and rejoice in nothing more than this, that the Lamb immaculate is still redeeming, by his precious blood, out of every nation, kindred, tongue, and people, and making a glorious addition to the church triumphant, whose names will stand eternally recorded in the book of life. I express not these things from a redundancy of heavenly virtue, but from a soul-sustaining evidence, that, amidst all our weakness, and conflicts of flesh or spirit, an interest is mercifully granted in Him, who giveth victory over death, hell, and the grave.' Nearly the last words which she spoke, were those of that cheering passage of holy writ, where the Saviour of men thus addresses his disciples: "My peace I give unto you."

Thus, on the 8th of the Twelfth month, 1790, she finished a course comparatively short, but filled with deeds of dedication. Her natural turn of mind, as has been related, subjected her to deep baptisms and close conflicts; but grace had so fully effected the work of renovation, that the observer saw little in her but the unaffected, unassuming, simple, humble and resigned Christian.

JEREMIAH WARING, who died at the advanced age of seventy-five, at Thorpe, in Surry, had been for a long time well known in our religious Society, especially to such Friends as attended the yearly meeting, at which, for fifty years, he was nearly constant. He was the son of Samuel and Eleanor Waring, of Witney, Oxfordshire, and born there in the year 1716; but, his father removing to Alton, Hampshire, on his second marriage, he passed his childhood under the care of his grandfather, Jeremiah Waring, a valuable ministering Friend, of whom there is an account in the Seventh Part of this work, by John Bell. Of his father and mother-in-law, Samuel and Deborah Waring, there are accounts in Thomas Wagstaffe's Ninth Part.

Jeremiah, the subject of this memoir, appears to have been of exemplary conduct from a child. He was very assisting to his parents in bringing up a numerous family by the second marriage, and in the management of their trade; but, having a competence for his own limited desires, he never embarked in trade on his own account. He devoted his talents and time to the service of others, and particularly to that of the Society of Friends, and his leisure hours to reading and retirement. He took great delight in reading the Scriptures, in which, accordingly, he was very conversant; and he was accustomed, when a young man, after the avocations of the day, to walk out, like Isaac, into the fields, and 'meditate at eventide' in the law that he loved. He was hospitable to his friends, and compassionate to the poor; and his benevolence was not confined to merit. He used to say, 'Did we receive no more than we deserve, how little should we possess.'

He was twice married. His first wife was Barbara, the widow of Daniel Pack, of Alton; his second, Mary, widow of Daniel Weston, of Ratcliffe. On occasion of the latter marriage, he removed to reside at Wandsworth, in Surry; but their union was of short duration. Of Mary Waring, there is an account in Thomas Wagstaffe's Eighth Part. He continued to reside at Wandsworth until, in the wane of life, and as infirmities approached, he went to reside with his only daughter and child, the offspring of the former marriage, at Thorpe-Lee, in the same county, where his days were closed.

In the summer of 1790, after a journey to Ackworth, his constitution began to decline; and, though the decay was almost imperceptible to his constant attendants, it was firmly impressed on his own mind, that he should not be restored to his accustomed health. He would say, after taking a medicine, 'This will not do; and nothing will do long. I am persuaded this illness is intended for my end.' At other times he would say, 'I am tired of the doctors. Physicians can do me no good. There is but one Physician: the Physician of value.' Thus he gently declined for eight months; but then the advance of dissolution was accelerated, and for the succeeding three months his ailments made a rapid progress. His appetite and digestion failed, and he became weaker daily. He frequently took notice of these symptoms of decay, and would remark, 'It is a mercy that I can look on approaching dissolution without terror.' Yet it does not appear that he had then received that full assurance which his soul desired; for he said once, 'Could I have an evidence that I might be admitted to a place of rest, it would matter not how soon. Oh, what a glorious change would that be, from a state of pain and sickness!'

After various fruitless attempts to relieve him, he was, with reluctance, prevailed on to consult an additional physician; but he earnestly pressed the first who had attended him, to say whether he had any hope of his recovery. Perceiving a hesitation on the part of the medical man, he repeated his question, adding, 'Don't be afraid to tell me, doctor: I can bear it.' One day, after suffering considerable pain, he said, 'I am resigned, I think pretty much, as to life or death. Thy will be done.'

He had been, as has been hinted, particularly attentive to the concerns of our religious Society; but within a week of his close, he told an intimate friend, and some of his near relations, who were with him, that he feared he had not been so useful in the Society as he might have been; and, continued he, with tears, 'I have ever loved the cause; and I wish all those whom I love, to be more circumspect than I have been.' He used to converse pleasantly with his friends who visited him; but when he was alone with his daughter, he would frequently say, 'I want to be more inward.'

A few days before his death he said, 'I have, at times, a hope, He that has been my morning light will be my evening song.' Soon after saying this, he told a Friend who called to inquire how he did, that he 'thought he might then reasonably expect every day to be his last:' and he always spoke of his great change with perfect composure. The morning preceding his departure, he said, 'I have lived to see the light of this day, but I scarcely think I shall ever see another.' About seven, he sent for his daughter, and said to her, 'I believe I am going.' Seeing her distressed, he added, 'Nay, don't distress thyself. We must part; but I leave thee in the hands of a merciful Creator.' His daughter said that she had hoped the separation would not so soon have taken place; to which he replied, 'We know not what is best. Times and seasons are in the disposal of unerring wisdom. If he sees this the right time, it is so, and we must submit.'

Soon after, he was desirous of rising, and whilst he was assisted in dressing, he said, 'I long to be clothed with the white linen, the righteousness of saints.' In the evening, when retired to rest, he said, 'All my trust is in Infinite mercy.' Soon after, some of his relations being in his chamber, he took an affectionate leave of them, having first said, as nearly as can be remembered, thus: 'I am going where the wicked cease from troubling, and the weary are at rest. I feel that goodness and mercy which have been with me at times all my life long, to be near me now; and, though I have fallen into many frailties incident to my nature, have never entirely forsaken me: and I have a secret hope that all will be well. The Lamb and his followers shall have the victory: those who have come through many tribulations, and known their garments to be made white in the blood of the lamb, the immaculate Lamb. May the God, who, I trust I may say, has been mine, and my father's, and my grandfather's also, be the God of all present.'

Within a short time of his close, he desired to be left with his daughter only; to whom he gave directions respecting his interment, and some other matters; particularly, that he might be affectionately remembered to such of his relations as might incline to attend it. Soon after this, he said, 'I die in charity with all the world, and have now, I think, nothing more to wish for, but an easy passage.' This, at midnight, was allowed to him, when, finishing his course with the 2d of the Tenth month, 1791, he departed without a sigh.

FIDELITY HULL, of Uxbridge, Middlesex, was the daughter of Thomas and Elizabeth Stark, of Fordingbridge, in Hampshire. In her early years, she was in some degree inclined to indulge herself in a deviation from the simplicity of her religious profession, which deviation her more corrected judgment afterwards disapproved; yet not by any means in such a degree as is usually termed gay or extravagant. About the twentieth year of her age she was married to Samuel Hull, of Uxbridge, and became the mother of two children, whom, however, she did not live to educate: for she soon showed symptoms of a decline, that terminated in her dissolution.

Early in her illness, her heart became more and more disposed to seek for the knowledge of the Lord; and when her disease gained ground, she entertained much doubt of recovery; yet she said that she should not mind the leaving of this world, if she had an assurance of happiness hereafter.

She now saw the vanity of indulging in dress; also the pernicious tendency, to young people, of reading novels, and similar productions. Pernicious indeed is this practice. Simply considered, it is a waste of time. Relatively, it indisposes the mind for the serious concerns of real life; and for its truest, greatest concern, the preparation for a better, through the grace and redemption of Jesus Christ, our Lord. Her anxiety on this account was manifested by a letter which she wrote to a relation; in which she entreated her, that if she had any such books, they might be destroyed for the sake of her children. Similar advice she also left in writing, for such as might have committed to them the care of her own son and daughter.

A few months before her decease, a Friend called to visit her; and believed it right to address her with a few words of encouragement. She was, at that time, preserved in a good degree of resignation; though she had not yet that full assurance of happiness which she had longed for. Nevertheless, at the time, his words were particularly consoling;

and in a subsequent opportunity, he was made instrumental of more complete relief to her much tried mind. She broke out as it were in rapture, 'Why does the Lord deal thus bountifully with me, a poor sinful creature, undeserving the least of his mercies? What is this I feel? Thou hast healed me of all my maladies, both inwardly and outwardly. O my Lord, and my God, how sweet is thy presence! What shall I render unto thee, O my God? Oh! this is what I wanted. Now I am happy. I thank thee, O Lord: for thou indeed art good.'

She then paused; but soon she turned her eyes affectionately on her mother, saying, 'Thou hast no need to sorrow for me, for it will be well with me.' Nor was this merely a sudden perception of unexpected relief, and a transient effusion of joy. The next day she told some visitors of her favoured state, and expressed herself in a very tender manner. 'The Lord,' said she, 'is good. Yesterday was a memorable day to me. I think I shall never forget it. My bonds are unloosed. There is balm in Gilead. I feel more sweetness than I can express in words.' She also expressed her hope that her visiting friends could feel something of the same; and she entreated her husband to give her up freely.

But although her consolation was thus great, and at one time, as we have seen, so transcendent as to supersede her sense of bodily infirmity and pain; her disease advanced, and her consequent suffering was often felt and acknowledged, though not repined at. To her brother, once she said, 'My tribulation is great. Oh, how careful we had need to be, to make the Lord our friend! for if I did not feel him near, I could not support [myself] under this great affliction.' Nevertheless, she had a word of encouragement to most of those who visited her, and she often exclaimed that God is love; and that those who dwell in him, dwell in love.*

*I take this opportunity of observing that this, though true, and a very common saying, with many pious Friends, is a transposition

She had once an opportunity of conference with two Friends. I am not informed whether they were Friends in the ministry, though there is room to suppose it. They were encouraging her not to withhold any thing she might have to communicate to them. Making a pause, she replied to this effect: 'I cannot speak unless power is given to me. I have felt at this season much stripped, and expect to be tried with the buffetings of Satan. What can I say to the Lord's servants; but that they should hold on their way, and they will experience peace and joy for evermore.'

Various admonitory and encouraging remarks were written or uttered in the course of her illness. She told some of her relations by letter, that if they could feel the peace which she felt, they would leave all the transitory enjoyments of this world, to endeavour after it. She often earnestly desired those about her to keep near to the Almighty, and said that he would do great things for them. Once she said, 'It is clearly presented to my view, that the gates of heaven are open to receive me.' She frequently remarked, that the peace and comfort of her mind overbalanced her very great bodily afflictions and infirmities.

Once, when some of her relations returned from meeting, she addressed them thus: 'I hope you have had a comfortable opportunity together;' and she remarked, that though for some time she had been prevented from going to meeting, yet she was often comforted by the divine presence. At another time when some friends were present, she expressed herself after this manner, 'Thy will be done: not mine. It is better to go to the house of mourning than to the house of mirth. Oh, that we may be favoured to feel good from the tree of life! Perhaps we may see the sun arise in all

---

of the text of 1 John iv. 16, "God is love: and he that dwelleth in love, dwelleth in God, and God in him." This whole chapter is eminently worthy of serious and repeated attentive perusal. It is the effusion of love, through "the disciple whom Jesus loved." Read it; rivet in your recollection, ye tender and beloved youth.

his glory: which is glorious indeed, to those who view it in its spiritual appearance.' O Lord, be thou pleased to hear us, for we have great need of thy supporting presence. Give us to sing praises to thy great and glorious name for ever and for ever more. Amen!'

About three days before she departed, being so weak as scarcely to be able to speak, she sent for her husband's father, Thomas Hull, a valuable Friend, who lived in the town. Several others of her relations came with him, to see her; in which visit, after a solemn pause, she was raised in a wonderful manner in praises and prayer, to the Almighty; and gave such good admonitions to those around her, as were the means of greatly humbling and contriting their minds.

She departed at length in great peace, the 15th of the Third month, 1792, about the twenty-third year of her age. A large meeting was held at her interment, in which a ministering Friend, (Thomas Cash, of whom there is an account in this volume,) from a distant part of England, being present, mentioned in his testimony, the sweet, heavenly frame of mind in which he had found her, and the satisfaction which he had felt in being with her about eight hours before her decease.

DANIEL BOWLY, jun., son of Daniel and Sarah Bowly of Cirencester, Gloucestershire, was a young man possessed of a good understanding, and an amiable disposition; the pliability of which, together with an employment which frequently exposed him to temptation, promoted, though it did not sanction, a wide deviation in conduct from those religious principles in which he had been educated. Of this deviation he became fully sensible in the course of a long illness; which he often acknowledged to be a mercy from that divine Providence, whose fatherly care had many times preserved him from sudden death when unprepared.

In the commencement of the disorder, which proved a consumption, his mind appeared to be deeply affected with the danger of his situation, though he then expressed but little of his feelings. As his weakness increased, he remarked how exceedingly awful the prospect of the final change appeared; and he earnestly desired that he might know a fitness for eternity, and that when the time came, the divine presence might be near. His past conduct, he said, had been very erroneous; but that his supplication for forgiveness had, in his illness, been attended with such sweet refreshment, that he hoped it might be according to his desires. At other times, his sins appeared so great that he could hardly entertain a hope it would be well with him. 'What can be expected,' said he, 'from a death-bed repentance? That is a time when all would gladly be saved. There will not probably be an opportunity given me of proving my sincerity, by an amendment of life; so that men may doubt it; but the omniscient Being knoweth how far I am sincere, and I hope, if it really be so, it will be accepted by Him: yet there is nothing equal to a proper dedication of time in health.'

Another time, he said, 'I hope the Almighty will forgive my sins. It is mercy alone that can save me, who have devoted so much of my life to business, and the amusements of this world; pleasure, as it is generally called; but it is a strange sort of pleasure. It is pain, I feel it pain.'

In another opportunity, he said, 'What I have to deliver, is from a prospect of the awfulness of death, which in a short time will be my lot. Mankind in general are certainly under strong delusion; yet how kindly the Almighty condescends, from time to time, to give a degree of his light and help! But man may outlive this day of grace, which, through the merciful mediation of my dear Saviour, is now extended to me.'

At another season, appearing much distressed, he desired his sister to read a chapter in the Bible to him; after which he broke forth in earnest and pathetic exhortation to those present, to prepare whilst time and health were afforded; saying, that a little encouragement, during the reading, had been given for himself; and that he believed it was for some one present he had been so tried; adding, 'I long that my friends would begin the work of religion in the life of it, for if the first offers are slighted, oh! how does the visitation deaden on the mind! It appears to me as though my own redemption is now nearly completed, and that I may be detained here for the good of others; and I hope if there be anything to be done, the Almighty will enable me to do it.'

He also said, 'How comfortable would it be to meet my relations in that state of happiness, where I believe a residence to be preparing for my soul! I believe the Almighty detains me here as an example of his great mercy, and as a warning to some; but I earnestly entreat none will depend upon the same singular act of mercy. All the friendships of this world must be given up; and, if the mind be not illuminated with an immediate proof of the presence of our dear Saviour, yet it should be resigned, and prepare itself for the reception thereof, by a surrender of everything which does not appear consistent with a state of preparation.'

One time, speaking of trade, and that he seemed glad he had done with it, he said, 'I hope I am not hardened or insensible of my state. I have earnestly supplicated for repentance, and have sometimes experienced something like touching the hem of the garment; but not quite so neither, as that was fully efficacious; but this lasted only for a time, and I seemed again left. In the forepart of my illness, a few times I asked for recovery, if consistent with the divine will; with desires to be strengthened to lead a different life from my past; and to serve that good master whose doctrines I have, as it were, trampled under foot; but I have since seen the favour it may be to me to be taken from such a trial.'

He said also, 'What a favour it is to be members of our

Society! Its rules forbid nothing that is good for us. How earnestly do I wish my near connections, in particular, may keep to the truth! Though the path may appear hard at first, yet as they follow their Leader with a single eye, it will become more easy. There may be times of withdrawing of the divine presence, and then the enemy will seek to enter: but by earnest supplication, preservation will be granted, and at times a comforting foretaste of future happiness; and the prospect of getting every day nearer to such an incomprehensible reward, is a favour beyond expression.'

'How little satisfaction results from a life of pleasure, attending places of diversion, &c. Ah, the disappointments such meet with! I believe bitter portions are often their lot.' He observed how he had been struck, when at those places of amusement, with a conviction that he was far more blamable than his companions, who had not so guarded an education; that, however innocently some of them attended, it was not so with him.

Embracing one of his brothers with great tenderness, he desired him to attend to what he had said, which was not in his own will; but, he believed, through the Spirit of Christ, who in his unspeakable mercy had made of him such an example. He exhorted his brother and sister to endeavour to train up their children in the right way; as it is from the rising generation an advancement in society is to be expected. He remarked the many memorable instances in 'Piety Promoted,' of children from nine years old to fifteen and twenty, appearing in public testimony in meetings; and he said, he thought the care of children a great trust; but that the reward would be answerable, if rightly discharged. He recommended beginning with them as soon as their minds opened; and not plunging them into business at too early an age; and he remarked the great preference due to religion before earthly substance.

One morning, inquiring if it were not the meeting-day to morrow, and being answered in the affirmative, he said, 'I almost long to go. How pleasant is the thought of being retired there from the world, when the generality of the people are in the height of its engagements!' How foolish and unwise are men who are bartering their souls for gold, paltry gold! The too eager pursuit of it is a great hurt to some of our Society. If I were to recover, and found business stood in my way to peace of mind, I think I would give it up entirely; or do but little, and live accordingly. What signifies grandeur or curious food? The taste goes no farther than the mouth, then it is over. If some men heard me talk thus, they would think me foolish; but in this I am wise, and know what I say.'

He advised young men not to spend their time unnecessarily at inns, but rather to go to friends' houses, where he thought they would be welcome. He had, he said, thought otherwise; but that in the liberty he then felt, he could go to any friend's house.

'I believe,' said he, 'the hope which I have, will continue with me to the end; yet the enemy is very busy, and would persuade me I have nothing to do with the kingdom of rest; but that is his temptation, and I must pray for patience; for I think the prospects I have had from time to time cannot be delusion.'

A friend asking him how he did, he replied, 'I am very weak, but I hope I shall be willing to bear everything the Almighty may be pleased to lay upon me, so that I can but just get within the gates of peace.' At another time, he said, 'I wish I had served my dear Saviour in my health. Oh he is a kind master. How much time have I lost! how distressing must be the situation of those who are sleeping the sleep of death, until the last trumpet be sounded in their ears!'

Several friends being in his chamber, one evening, he spoke of that wonderful gift dispensed to all, even that Holy Spirit which manifests our duty; and he recommended an immediate compliance with its discoveries; 'For since,' said he 'these illuminations are not at our command, it is very unsafe to trifle with them, by giving way to the suggestions of the enemy; but rather resign whatever may be called for;' adding, 'Can we not return a part to Him who gave the whole? What if it deprive us of a few luxuries? We can have but food and raiment; which only differ a little in kind between rich and poor.'

He recommended, that after being at meeting, and having been favoured there with tender impressions of good, as he sometimes had been, great care should be taken not to lose them, by too soon entering into conversation, concerns of business, or attention to anything of a contrary nature, whereby the mind might be deprived of the benefit intended.

'Our profession,' said he, 'is a very exalted one; and if we keep to it, would make us as lights in the world. Our religion teacheth us to believe in immediate communication with God, through his beloved Son; which is an unspeakable privilege to all who attend to it: and, wonderful condescension! that he who is Lord of all, should thus notice poor man; and, time after time, be visiting with the offers of his mercy to insure our happiness; visitations we should be very careful not to reject, as being a common favour, and think we will accept them at some future time. For, though the Almighty is long-forbearing and delighteth in mercy, we know not when may be the last offer of his grace to assist us in the work of salvation. What a dreadful thing would it be to withstand the last!'

Speaking of the evidence he had of his future peace, he said, 'I have a clear view that I shall be received into the kingdom of rest and peace. I see the gates of heaven standing open to receive me, and thousands of the just waiting to embrace me. I desire but just to get within the pales of safety, to be in the presence of the Lord, and to behold his glorious countenance. "O! death, where is thy sting? O! grave, where is thy victory?" Christ taketh away the sting of death. My dear Saviour is reconciled to me. I know he is. His mercy is very great. I cannot speak enough of his mercy.'

Some one remarking how exceedingly quick the last three weeks had apparently passed away, he replied, 'Yes, and perhaps there are some who have not done anything in the time, which is a serious consideration: for in one week a man may be taken sick and die; and if we do not close in with the visitations of God in time, we shall be lost forever.'

At another time, 'Let us be earnest in making ready for the glorious kingdom of rest and peace, where, Oh, that we may enter! And all may, if they will. Let us endeavour to do a little every day; let none be discouraged, though their progress in religion may be slow; yet let them keep on in their little way: for I believe our kind Saviour may, at times, withdraw his sensible presence from us to try how our faith will continue; yet if we hold on, our reward, at last, will be great, and as much as those who feel a present one.'

On the 9th of the Eighth month, his sisters, who lived at a distance, came; at which he much rejoiced, having often expressed a desire to see them again. The next morning he affectionately addressed them, desiring they would be particularly careful of the cultivation of their children's minds; and not make business the first object for their sons; a very little being sufficient, and that great portions were by no means desirable. In much weighty advice to those present, he wished them to make an offering of all they had. Particularizing one of his sisters, he also said, 'What thy conscience tells thee, that mind; and what is told thee to put on, that wear; and what is told thee to give up, give. Fear not the great or rich, but be alike to all.

'Be religious, and then you will have our Saviour's arm to lean upon. Oh, he is a merciful Saviour! I have found him such; an easy master, a kind friend. Ah! how I regret that I neglected serving him some years. Think what a superior education we have had, to most; what a nice institution is ours—the peculiar institution of God; and I believe it is not to die away, although some of our Society have gone from it, for whom I am sorry.

'I believe great advantage may arise from frequently comparing time with eternity, an awful eternity. It appears to me exceedingly awful. Heaven and hell are placed before us. We have now our choice; and we know what wretches hell is composed of; foul minds, full of remorse for ever; for their worm never dieth. On the other hand, in heaven there is great harmony. Oh, I have had beautiful prospects! I have seen the innumerable company of angels, and the spirits of good men! But how is it? We are ashamed of not complying with man, and not ashamed of doing so to God. We can apologize to man and say, we are sorry we did not do so, or so, and we can directly go, commit neglect before God, and feel no sorrow for it. Oh, what mercy there is! In great wisdom and unspeakable kindness is the good Mediator given to reconcile us, and work redemption in us. Do not let us fear man. What is he? Look upon me, and see a poor weak thing who can hardly speak.'

After this earnest exhortation to those, for whose eternal happiness he was so affectionately and deeply solicitous, he was much exhausted, and, desiring to be put to bed, uttered the following short ejaculation; 'Oh, Lord God Almighty, be thou pleased to look down upon, and be with us!' With some difficulty he got to bed; and for several hours his cough and other symptoms were very alarming, and were thought to indicate approaching dissolution; but after having slept some time, he took some refreshment, and said he must now endeavour to say a few words more, as he might not have another opportunity. Most of his near relations being present, he called particularly to one of his sisters, requesting her to sit near him, that she might hear what he had to deliver; and he was wonderfully strengthened to testify with power to the truth; beautifully setting forth the means of salvation appointed for all.

Some of his relations standing by his bed-side one evening, he remarked how contemptible the world appeared; and speaking of its wickedness, he added, 'I would not be understood to despise the world itself. No; it is the creation of God; and we are placed there to enjoy all things with temperance. If it were as it ought to be, it would be a sort of paradise; it would be a happy pilgrimage to eternity; it is the depravity of man that makes it so detestable.'

He cautioned some of his friends to beware of the fatigues and incumbrances of business, saying, 'It will not do for those who have been all the week in the hurry of business to go to meetings, and appear before the Lord in form only. A man whose time is wholly engrossed in business in common, if he goes to meetings pretty constantly, and sits there two hours, yet it is to be feared his thoughts will be engaged on that which takes up the greater part of his time; and if it be so, it is great mockery of God. Neither will it do to go on in an outward show of dress or address, if not true worshippers of the Lord, in spirit and in truth. They must daily give up their minds to him, daily retire to worship him. I know a man ought to provide for his family, and carry on a proper business, which I believe to be right; but it should by no means be the first object, for riches will be nothing in the end. What would I give now for all the world? Why nothing at all.

'I don't regard what the natural man may advance in opposition to this doctrine of giving up all for the sake of religion. I am now upon the brink of death to the body, but opening into the life of the spirit. I am going to live forever, and I am certain nothing will do but giving up every earthly obstruction for the cause of God. Make him a sacrifice; offer up all you have; offer up your lives to him, as Christ did his for your sakes and mine. Perhaps some may, from the strength of health and abilities, be ready to conclude what I say proceeds from weakness. I know it does not, but that it is the truth, and you will all find it so; and that man who trusts to the strength of his own mind, or natural understanding, will be wrong, for nothing will do without God. Now, remember this; think of it upon your death-bed, and you will feel it is true. So farewell in Christ.'

The 12th of the Eighth month, addressing one of his sisters, he said, 'Sister, how many times have I been preserved from death, times more than I can remember! Ah, how often, sister, have some of us been raised, as it were, from death! We should often think of it, and how we have answered the kind intention. It may not be so again. The next may be the last time. Then do let us begin to prepare and do every thing that is required of us. I believe plainness of dress is. We are indeed a chosen people, and what may not be wrong in others is so in us. Plainness of dress is as a hedge about us. The world is not then seeking our company. Do remember what our Saviour said, "Whosoever denieth me before men, him will I also deny before my Father who is in heaven." '

At another time he said, 'I should be distracted if, on this death-bed, with all this pain and weakness of body, I had my sins before me. What horror should I feel!'

A Friend expressing a desire to help him, he replied, 'None can help me essentially but my dear Saviour: he can release me, if it be his blessed will.'

He advised one of his relations to bring up her children in a plain way; knowing, from experience, what a disagreeable situation those were in who accommodated themselves to their company. 'This,' said he, 'will not do.' He believed the easy way chosen by many of our Society had as little religion in it as any, or less, and was highly displeasing to the Almighty. He also recommended a single line of conduct. He often spoke of the benefit of retirement, and said that other things must be given up to gain it. He wished not to be interrupted during meeting time; for, although not able to go, he loved to compose himself, when the nature of his complaints would admit of it, and was often favoured with great stillness at those times.

He impressively said, 'The enemy is still very busy with his insinuations, and would persuade me that all is done, and so lead to neglect; but I must watch and pray to the end, and be very earnest with the Almighty to continue his favours, and that he will support through all.'

For some time he was much proved with poverty of spirit, added to great bodily weakness; but his desires were for patience, saying, 'It is very trying to bear such great lowness and sinking of body and mind. What can I do, but endeavour patiently to bear it, looking constantly to the Almighty?' Some one asking him how he was, he answered, 'I am very low, but I keep mine eye upon God.'

His sister, having sat up with him, remarking how comfortable a night he had passed, he said, with much sweetness, 'Yes, I prayed for a little respite, and it has been granted me.' About this time his strength recruited so much, for a few days, that the possibility of a recovery was hinted to him. This at first seemed almost more than he could bear; but after a pause he said, 'In this also I will endeavour to seek after resignation, and keep mine eye to my Saviour; who, I ardently hope, will now take me, having in kind mercy so prepared me for my change. Can it be, after the near prospect that I have had, that I shall enter life again? I must endeavour, earnestly endeavour, after patience.'

Some hours after, being asked how he did, his reply was, 'I feel myself quite resigned. I have supplicated for patience, and I hope I shall be contented to live, if it be the Lord's will. I know he can preserve and keep me. Indeed I have experienced such resignation, that I think I could feel a pleasure in living, that I might bear my cross in the world.' He was indeed preserved in a very patient, waiting, frame of mind, and expressed but little for several days; but his company was truly pleasant, and his deportment evinced where his mind was centred; though he said the enemy was so busy, tempting him to doubt, that he had hard struggles at times to keep his faith.

The effort of nature, upon which the intimation of recovery was grounded, again subsided; his cough became more troublesome, and increasing weakness was evident. He remarked, 'I believe I was too anxious to go, a little time since; but now I feel willing to wait the Lord's time for the end. I have reason to hope my disorder is making its progress.'

He was naturally of a compassionate disposition; and, during his illness, often spoke feelingly of the poor, recommending liberality to them; which, he said, he had seen to be a Christian duty; and how much greater satisfaction would result from relieving their wants, than from unnecessarily accumulating wealth.

About the end of the Eighth month, he was strongly impressed with a belief that some one of his relations would be removed before him; and in a day or two after, an account came that one of his aunts, who had been for a long time in a poor state of health, was very unexpectedly deceased. When this was mentioned to him, referring to the above intimation, he said he thought he should now be soon released.

On the 1st of Ninth month, he said, 'The state that I expect to enter is that of calmness and peace: divine peace, the purest spirituality. When I have spoken of gates or doors, I wished to imply an entrance into this state; for I believe my ideas of future happiness are not gross. I hope to live in the presence of God, and to feel constant support from him; and I do not wish to know more.'

The next day he was very weak, and reluctantly left his chamber. Some hours after, he was seized with a violent fit of coughing, so that the hour of separation seemed, both to himself and friends, fast approaching; and, in a short respite from the cough, he expressed triumphantly, 'I am happy, I am happy! If I never speak more, give my dear love in Christ Jesus to all my friends.' After being relieved, by bringing up the phlegm, he was put to bed, and some time after remarked, 'Death is awful! very awful! but I have full faith in my foundation.'

At another time he said, 'I believe my dear Saviour is ready to receive me, figuratively speaking, into his arms; that is into purity; and I believe that is what all good minds desire to enter into.' He desired he might not be disturbed when he was thought to be going; and hoped he should have an easy passage, and that he might go off in a sweet sleep. 'He said, 'I have earnestly prayed for you. Do you pray for me.' Shortly after, observing his friends affected, he said, 'It is not from a callous disposition or hardness of heart, that I appear unmoved at parting with all my near, dear, and beloved relations. It is the advantage I shall reap myself, that is my support; and knowing there is a powerful visitation extended to you, so that you may all gain an admittance, and soon be in the same place with me.'

In the evening some one remarking how exceedingly hard it rained, he said, 'I like to hear it; the sound of it is solemn, being the work of the Almighty. The withdrawing of the sun, and darkness, is like what good souls experience in the work of redemption; when divine light is withdrawn from them, and the damps of melancholy felt. In these seasons what strange ideas is the mind tried with; such as are very apt to cast down timid minds; but there is a secret support sustains, though at such times not sensibly felt.'

On the 3d he expressed an earnest desire for an easy passage, making solemn supplication, as follows, 'O, Lord God Almighty! have pity upon me. It was thou who created both soul and body.' Some time after, to a near friend, he said, 'I believe the enemy has now almost done with me.'

On the 4th he was very weak, but still and composed. He said, he was going to the Father and the Son; and, looking on his friends, bade them farewell. A short time after, he remarked that he felt such an entire resignation that, if it were the Lord's will, he was willing, even now, to recover or die; and how comfortable it was to be thus favoured to the end. About twelve o'clock he took an endearing leave of two of his cousins who had tenderly waited upon him; soon after which, a considerable alteration was apparent, and his voice was become so weak that little could be understood; but he continued in a heavenly frame of mind, full of love.

The last connected sentence which was distinctly heard, was as a seal to the foregoing truths, being this: 'I have the satisfaction to say, I have been washed in Jordan.'

Not long after this, he appeared to be retiring to sleep; but the fact was, that he was quietly departing; which he did in the manner for which he had so often prayed, without a groan, or even a sigh.

His corpse was interred on the 11th of the Ninth month, 1793, in Friends' grave-yard at Cirencester. Aged twenty-five years and eight months.

ELIZABETH RATHBONE, daughter of William and Rachel Rathbone, of Liverpool, was born the 15th of the Fourth month, 1756, and was removed by a decline the 30th of the Ninth month, 1793. Her mother died when she was little more than four years of age. Her father, on whose own education not much pains had been bestowed, was so sensible of his loss, that he determined to give his own children as good a one as could be obtained, within the limitations which should always bound a religious parent in his conduct to his children. Desirable accomplishments may be purchased at too dear a rate; and when the acquisition of them really interferes with the more important learning—the learning of him who is meek and lowly of heart—it is time for the Christian parent, at least, to be closely on his watch. Thus limited, her father saw the advantage of mental acquirements; and his paternal care was repaid by the acuteness and diligence of his daughter.

She quickly imbibed instruction, and was so fond of being taught, that she was often held up as an example by those who instructed her. Her disposition was lively and volatile; yet she was not observed to make any wide deviation from the simplicity of her profession. This, however, was rather owing to the watchful care of her pious father, than to her own self-restraint. Without that, there is reason to fear that she would have wandered far astray. For, notwithstanding her youth was so carefully guarded, she admitted many things to a share of her regard, which, when she was fully awakened to a sense of her spiritual state, she found it her duty to resign. One of her great amusements was reading, and her reading was far from being confined to profitable books. In the choice, too, of her associates, she sometimes loved to be among such as rather led her away from the path of self-denial, than assisted her to enter and pursue it: and it is probable that in such company she was a welcome visitor. A good understanding, well informed, added to the vivacity of youth, and to a temper desirous of pleasing, is generally received with applause; but there are few who possess these accomplishments, in whom the consciousness of talent, and the praise of others, do not occasion a secret self-approbation, bordering on pride.

About her seventeenth year, her mind became impressed with serious thought; and she found that a narrower way than that in which she had been accustomed to indulge, was the path to peace. She said to her much beloved sister one day, after having been in some gay company, 'This kind of visiting I must resign. I do not know how it may be with thee, but at such times I exert all my powers in such a manner, to accommodate myself, to appear agreeable, that when I return and reflect, I find I have given all out, but I take nothing in.' Her father, of course, would express his disapprobation of time thus spent, and said that he saw in it a snare. She acknowledged that he was right, and soon began to alter her course. She yielded to one impression of duty after another, until in a few years she became a very religious character; and, as the influence she had with many of the younger class was great, a very useful one. The sequel will show that she had learned to say, I am an unprofitable servant.

She remained for about twenty years a much esteemed member of our religious Society, but often endured great depression, and even conflict of spirit; not only from the sense, with which her mind was touched, of the state, the low state of the church; but from frequent apprehensions that she might be called to minister to its wants by a public testimony. Her last illness was lingering. It afforded ample time for retrospect, and for application of heart to Him who can supply every want of his humble and dependent children; and she was mercifully enabled to avail herself of the opportunity.

In the forepart of her confinement she was deeply tried with the desertion of that good in which she had delighted, and with painful apprehensions that her day's work, when weighed in the balance of the sanctuary, would be found wanting. Her conflicts were great; she dwelt much in retirement, and was very cautious of relating to others what her soul was passing through. But about three months before her decease, she found freedom to open her mind to her sister, her most intimate friend. She confessed that if she had erred, it had not been for want of knowledge; but that a full portion of divine light had been granted to her. 'I now see,' said she, 'it is an awful thing to be found carefully acting in conformity to it. By this light, in my early years, my understanding hath been often opened, not only to see clearly into my own state, but also into the states of others; some of whom I seem clear of; and this I count a favour. My bodily weakness is such, from complicated causes, that

I should find it difficult, if now required of me, to obtain relief.'

Speaking of some of her social duties, she said, 'Ah! had I served my Maker with as much faithfulness and dedication as I have performed these, I might have looked forward, in this awful time, with confidence. Yet, I think I dare tell thee, I feel my faith so strong, and so indubitably fixed in the merits and intercession of a crucified Saviour, that my mind is wonderfully supported and stayed in quiet composure, having an evidence mercifully vouchsafed that some of my transgressions are blotted out from the Lamb's book, but that this is granted of his own free mercy. If I had not the most unshaken belief in the gracious Mediator, I know not what I should do now; but yet I feel I have still to pass, as through the river of judgment. I have laboured to cast all my care upon Him, through that help which he has administered.'

On a certain occasion she was sending a message to her brother's wife, and delivered it nearly thus: 'Thou mayest give my love to my sister, and tell her I should be glad to see her, as soon as her condition will render it prudent. And thou mayest also tell her that my mind is so centred in deep, inward quiet, that I feel resigned and weaned. Oh, that I could give her an idea of what I now enjoy in this state! Were ten thousand worlds offered, I would not accept them in exchange for it, nor change this bed of sickness for the most prosperous condition that could be placed in my view. No human help that could be administered would be adequate to what I now feel. All is made up in this deep inward quiet.'

Some weeks after this, when she had been conversing with her sister respecting her secret conflicts of later years, and expressing her faith that her multiplied transgressions were washed away, she added, 'I think I have seen, more particularly of late, that the state of the church triumphant is not more glorified than the members of the church militant would be, at seasons, if they had faith to believe, and in the exercise of this faith, carefully occupied, in deep abasement, with their several gifts. How precious would be their fellowship! How would they participate with purified spirits in union and communion! Oh, how I long that those in the ministry would keep their places! Then indeed, I do believe, they and all the living members of the mystical body would know, in a much larger degree than they do, a partaking together of the glorified state. But then,' she faintly and movingly added, 'I know it is difficult to believe this possible, whilst engaged in conflict and dismay; especially when we remember the manifold infirmities which encompass us, during our continuance in these shackles of mortality.'

On the 24th of the Ninth month, which did not precede her departure one week, she made an effort to clasp in her arms her sister, who was then sitting by her; and she said, in a very moving manner, and with a flood of tears, 'O, my sister, how have I desired that thy mind and mine may be strengthened in the hour that is approaching!' In this she alluded to her dissolution. 'If I durst have asked for it, for thy sake my language would have been, "If it be possible, let this cup pass from me;" but I dare not: for how do I know, if my life was given at my request, what might afterwards follow; what flaw, or what stain I might contract.'

The following day, when her sister, who had sat up with her a part of the night, was about to take her leave, Elizabeth, looking at her tenderly, said, 'O, my dear sister, thy distress moves me, though it appears very endearing. But let my confidence be thy stay, because the arm that is underneath is worthy to be trusted in. It is worthy, for it will be found sufficient. I feel that I dare lean upon it. It hath been my support; and be thou satisfied that this dispensation is all in wisdom. I have seen it clearly; and if the help which has hitherto been mercifully afforded do but continue, I trust I shall be able to take the cup with resignation, and keep in patience to the end. But, if ever, through the pain of the body, I should let drop an impatient expression, do thou deal faithfully with me, and be sure to tell me of it; for on this head I have many fears.'

She was much distressed with difficulty of breathing; and on one occasion, when her sister, who had been endeavouring to give her some assistance, said to her, 'What shall I do for thee? I do not know how thou supportest these sore nights;' she replied, with great sweetness, but very emphatically, 'Oh, they are mixed with constant goodness—constant goodness.'

In the morning of the 27th, she said divers things respecting the children of her brother and sister Benson, and respecting the close and intimate union which she and her sister had been favoured with. 'Oh,' said she, 'how I wish that thy dear Abigail and Rachel may be thus united! Press it upon their minds. It is a point of importance for children of the same parents, to cultivate a tender regard and sympathy with each other. It is difficult for the best chosen friends to enter so intimately into the varied circumstances and difficulties that attend our allotments in life, as two sisters who seek to have the divine cement, to strengthen the natural bond of union. My early friendships were carried too far, and on this account a weight of condemnation ensued; for I found that I had been planting heavens of my own, and earths of my own; and when the day of the Lord came, which burns like an oven, I saw all these pleasant pictures were to be destroyed.'

To her sister's husband, she said thus: 'As to the intimations of encouragement which I have received from man, that my spirit was already a pure spirit, I have never been permitted to build upon, or draw consolation from them; but in the deepest and darkest plunges I have had, unworthy, totally unworthy as I have felt myself, and all I had to hope for was divine mercy, my faith has not failed, that he who said to the leper, "I will, be thou clean," was able to render me meet to associate with saints and angels, and the spirits of the just already made perfect. I can now freely mention, that if I had been perfectly obedient to the vocation wherewith I was called, I was intended to have filled up a different station in the church, from what I have done. Whether my life might thereby have been prolonged or not, is hid from me; but if in this I have erred, I hope it is washed away. Though I have sometimes looked at the separation of the spirit from the body with fear and apprehension; yet it is now wholly taken away. My last two nights have been sweet nights. Death has lost all its terrors, and I feel the grave will have no victory over me.'

A few nights previous to her departure, she often spoke of her father, as she had frequently done before, in very affecting terms. She said that she was satisfied that his spirit was sweetly centred in celestial regions; that she had often been permitted to hold sweet communion with it; and added, 'Ah! I feel he is gathered.'

About eleven o'clock on Seventh-day morning, the 28th, she was seized with a very strong spasm; and believing herself about to depart, she desired that her sister and her husband might be called. After they came to her, the convulsive affection abated, and she desired to be placed in a chair. Being there, she said, 'Indeed, my dear sister, my sufferings are very great. Let me request thee to endeavour to reconcile thy mind,' to her sufferings doubtless she meant, 'and don't ask me to get into bed any more.' This request was of course readily granted; and from this time commenced the more apparent symptoms of approaching dissolution.

In the afternoon she asked for two of her sister's children, and spoke to them beautifully, adapting very remarkably her discourse to their understanding. When they were leaving her, she made signs for their return; and, kissing them, as she had done before, she burst into tears, and said, 'My dear children, may the Lord bless you!' She had also desired that, if she lived till morning, she might see her own brother and his children. She also desired her sister's husband to read that passage in the Revelation, where it is said, "Blessed are the dead who die in the Lord;" and when he took the

Bible, she said, 'Thou mayest read the whole chapter.' This being done, a solemn pause ensued.

Her own brother was now also with her; and with great calmness, and very distinctly, she thus expressed herself: 'I have been thinking much this day of the passages which have now been read; but I did not recollect they were uttered through so much distressing experience. I am convinced that a submission to the crucifying power must be witnessed —a submission to that which alone can make a separation between joints and marrow, between the precious and the vile; all must be crucified, before they can be profitably understood, or opened to our understandings. But as the unfolding of them is patiently waited for, in child-like simplicity, these mysteries will be revealed to us: especially, as we become redeemed from the wisdom of the world, and all its pollutions, and follow the Lamb immaculate in perfect simplicity—follow him whithersoever he is pleased to lead us, without grasping at too much, being assured that sufficient hath been, and will hereafter be, revealed to us. As we are thus content to follow him in all his manifestations, we shall experience a measure of the new birth, or of the new life unto righteousness, to be so formed in us, that whether he may lead, or put us forth into service, or we may be led in a way incomprehensible to our fellow-pilgrims, it will be enough. For in this total surrender of our wills to the Divine will, in which we are enabled to say, Work with me, as it seemeth good unto thee, the great name will be equally glorified. For his glory consists in our doing his will; but this requires the total surrender of all our faculties; of all we have, and of all we are, to him: and however deeply we may be tried, whatever we may have to pass through in this life, or in death, it will be our support. The evidence of it hath been to me as the shadow of a mighty rock in a weary land.

I have been much tried with poverty, and [have] passed through many sore conflicts, even during this sickness; but my trust and confidence remain unshaken, that as we are stayed upon his name, which is his power, though we may be brought to the balance of the sanctuary, and [it] may appear poised, as to the weight of a hair, and we, not being permitted to see how it preponderates, or how it may turn with us, may be surrounded with deep dismay; yet as we have been willing to surrender ourselves wholly unto him, he will make up every apparent deficiency. In this purified state, we shall have to behold Zion a safe hiding-place, and Jerusalem a quiet habitation; so secure, that not one of her stakes can be removed, nor one of her cords be broken!

'Had not my confidence been in prospects and convictions like these, I know not what I should have done in this trying hour. It is all I have to lean upon, and I feel its support.' After a pause, she added, 'And now, my beloved brothers and sisters, do you remember this my dying testimony.'

Her attending relations were apprehensive, from the struggle which this exertion had occasioned, that the conflict would have ended in her speedy dissolution; but she again revived, and passed Seventh-day night and First-day in more ease than was expected. About twelve, on First-day night, she had a return of the spasm with great violence, which was succeeded by a slight delirium. Towards morning she became much troubled, expressed a fear that her sufferings were prolonged in displeasure, and said she was sensible of being held on some account; but that on examining herself, she could not see the cause. Then she looked on her sister in a very moving manner, and said, 'O my sister, I fear thou canst not give me up. It seems as if I felt thy resistance; and my captive spirit wants to be set free.' Her sister replied, that she did all in her power to submit; did not dare to call in question the dispensation; was mercifully permitted to feel calm; and thought she could venture to say, 'I have resigned thee.' 'Ah,' said Elizabeth, 'but hast thou made a cheerful surrender of me? for that only will be acceptable from thee.' Her sister again replied, hoping that she could make some allowance for her weakness; and would feel that some would also be made by Him who condescends to compassionate our infirmities; that her dear sister knew the loss would be very great; yet, sensible of Elizabeth's sufferings, and beyond all doubt of her fitness to enter the mansions of undisturbed rest, she had laboured against all selfishness.

A short time after this, Elizabeth, looking with unutterable sweetness, took her sister in her arms, and kissing her, said, 'I am afraid I have afflicted thee. I do, my dear sister, feel for thee, for thou art to be felt for; but do give me up. I must go. May the Lord support thee. I am free to tell thee now, and I have not had liberty before to do it, My work is done, and I am ready. I do not feel the weight of a hair. And now, after a conviction like this, if I should turn to thee, and again feel the tender bonds which of myself I could not resign, thou canst not wonder if I long to be dissolved. I have seen it is in wisdom and mercy that my sufferings have been thus prolonged. Had I been taken in the forepart of my illness, I fear there was so much dross to be purged away, that I should not have been found in acceptance; but I have been mercifully dealt with every way. And now, all being removed that hath appeared as obstruction, I have nothing to cope with but the conflicts of the body.'

After this, some medicine was given to her; and as she took the cup in her hand, she was heard to say, 'O Lord, if it be thy will, grant that this may be the last draught of this kind; but, O Lord, preserve me in patience.'

About six, on Second-day morning, the 30th, her sister went to her, and said, 'I think I have now strength to say, I do freely resign thee. I humbly hope thy request will be granted, as I verily believe the Lord has heard it; and that his arm will be round about thee to the end.' Elizabeth replied, 'I am thankful to hear thee say so.' She continued to the close perfectly clear and sensible, said, in a sweet frame of mind, something further testifying her love for her sister, and in about half an hour, without the least apparent emotion, passed quietly away.

24 *

ESTHER TUKE, of York, long known and beloved in the Society of Friends, who died the 13th of the Twelfth month, 1794, was daughter of Timothy and Ann Maud, and born at Westcoals, near Halifax, in the year 1727. Her parents afterwards removed into the neighbourhood of Bingley, where her father died when she was about twenty-five years of age. In the early part of her life, she was captivated with some of the vanities to which youth is liable; but the loss of her father, and a concurrence of some other trying events, tended to humble her, and to prepare her for the reception of a divine visitation which, about this time, was powerfully extended to her. To this gracious influence she bowed in filial submission. She was willing to bear the cross, and to despise the shame; and chose rather to suffer affliction with the people of God, than to enjoy the pleasures of sin for a season.

At this time of her life she was very distantly situated from the particular and monthly meetings to which she belonged; yet she was a diligent attender of both. Many were the exercises which she had to experience; but as she abode in patience under the operations of the holy Hand, she became a vessel sanctified, and prepared for the Master's use. About the thirty-fourth year of her age, she gave way to an apprehension of duty, which had long been in her view; and appeared in public as a minister, with these few words; "The just shall live by faith." From this beginning, apparently small, she was enabled to increase; and as she grew in years she was thought also to grow in faithfulness and dedication; and truly attained to the state of a mother in Israel. About four years after this more public espousal of the cause of righteousness, she entered into the marriage state with William Tuke, of York, then a widower, with several children. In this station her discretion as a mother, and the impartiality of her affection towards her own children, and those of the former marriage, were such as are too seldom found, and afforded an instructive example.

As to her travels in the service of truth, they were extensive. She paid a general visit to the meetings of Friends in Ireland, was several times in Scotland, and Friends in most parts of this nation were partakers of her religious labours. But it is rather the weight than the extensiveness of her service which those who knew her best have been desirous to commemorate. She not only deeply lamented the obvious departure of many amongst us from our various testimonies; but the state of such as are engrossed with the cares of this life; for she knew that, though such may have been in past time awakened, and may yet retain a specious appearance; yet, their affections being centred in the earth, they lose the qualification for religious service, and often obstruct it, even when they appear to be its advocates.

She was particularly solicitous for the right education of youth; and such was her concern on this subject, that she united with a few other Friends in establishing a school at York for girls; and, at their request, took the superintendence of it. In the execution of this charge, she appeared to gain the general good will of the children; but she had greatly to lament the neglect of parents, to bring into due subjection the tempers and wills of their offspring. This neglect increases the difficulty of education, causes the cross occurrences of life to be more painfully felt, and renders it harder for the youthful mind to submit to the necessary restraints of the Christian life.

In the middle stages of life, she was much tried by bodily indisposition. This increased with advancing years; but did not prevent her exertions when duty called her into religious service; and she often travelled under difficulties that few would have encountered. Still, she looked beyond these afflicting dispensations; and frequently expressed her desire gratefully to number the blessings with which she was favoured.

Thus, as the course of her life was instructive, not less so were her closing days: they were strongly marked with the humility of a disciple of Jesus. She had often mentioned her apprehension that her last illness would be short, and would not afford much opportunity for verbal expression of her feelings; and in the view of her final change, she often testified much satisfaction and peacefulness. Her last illness accordingly only continued about a week. Great, at that time, was the sweetness, and deep the solemnity, frequently felt by her attending relations and friends. In the self-abasement, already mentioned, she once did express herself to this purpose: That notwithstanding she felt herself as one of the lowest of beings, yet, as she had been favoured to administer what might be only like a cup of cold water, in the name of a disciple, she fully believed that it was not the divine intention that she should lose her reward; and that, though she should continue as in the depth of poverty, this belief was sufficient. And well might she thus say: Her confidence was in the promise of her Lord, whose words are yea and amen forever! "Blessed are the poor in spirit, for theirs is the kingdom of heaven!"

WILLIAM PRIDEAUX.—In the ninth part of this work, published by Thomas Wagstaffe, in 1795, there is an account of Mary Prideaux, a Friend, of Cornwall. It is a pleasing portraiture of a dedicated and happy mind. She was the wife of WILLIAM PRIDEAUX, the subject of the present memoir; and it appears that they were united in a relation even more than conjugal. The married state is generally allowed, by the virtuous, to afford the most complete specimen of human happiness: but when, to the ordinary requisites for producing this happiness, is added a unity of religious feeling, and a joint and harmonious endeavour to serve the Lord, then, the state has attained the summit of the felicity of which it admits.

WILLIAM PRIDEAUX, of Kingsbridge, in Devonshire,

was born about the year 1716; and in the early part of his life did not profess the tenets of the Society of Friends; but being convinced about the thirty-third year of his age, he became a lively and useful member of it. He was long in the stations of an elder and overseer, and was a man peculiarly qualified for sympathizing with the afflicted either in body or mind.

He lived to a very advanced age, surviving his pious wife nearly twenty-three years; but the various lively expressions that fell from him during the illness which terminated his lengthened course, demonstrate that in mind he resembled the prophetic description of the Psalmist, speaking of the righteous, "They shall still bring forth fruit in old age; they shall be fat and flourishing."

A few days after he was taken ill, he said, 'It is a mercy, that I feel ability to say, "Thy will be done." 'Tis not in man's power to say so; but I feel the power which enables me, and am thankful for it. There is no terror in looking forward.' Then he broke out, 'O my soul;' but seemed too full for further utterance, otherwise than in sounds which bespoke the melody of his heart. After this, by means of some medical assistance, he appeared to recruit; but a symptom succeeded which appeared to portend, unless removed, a speedy dissolution; and he received pleasure when he discovered it.

One day subsequent to this, on taking leave of a relation, he said, 'I have always loved the truth, and now it doth not fail me. What I have always desired, I now experience. I have nothing but peace in looking forward or backward.' Soon after he said, he loved to see his friends, but loved better to feel them: twice exclaiming, 'All is well:' and the same evening he said, 'I have nothing to do now. What a great favour! we who have loved the truth in our health, to experience its support on a dying bed!'

The next day he remarked, 'It is not enough to call God Father by creation only; but we must know him to be so by regeneration also.' On being asked if he were pretty comfortable, 'Yes,' said he, 'I don't know when I was otherwise. How should I be otherwise? My Lord God Almighty is with me, my dear Redeemer, whom I wish thee and all to honour, even in the little concerns of life. He hath done for me far beyond what I could ask or think.'

Thus he continued a few days, evincing from time to time his resignation, his gratitude, and his hope; and on the evening before his departure, on an ineffectual attempt to relieve him by a surgical operation, the calmness of his mind did not appear to be interrupted. He had, however, suffered much fatigue from the attempt, and complied with the request of his medical attendant, in taking an anodyne medicine; but between four and five in the morning, he distinctly said, 'I am going;' and his breathing soon becoming more difficult, it ceased in a short time, and he passed away without a sigh, in the eighty-third year of his age. During his illness it had been evident that death was his desire; but it is not recollected that he ever complained that his sufferings were tedious: and the true resignation which through grace he had been enabled to attain, was to be discerned in the serenity of his countenance.

SOPHIA POPE, daughter of Robert and Margaret Pope, of Staines, in Middlesex, departed this life the 10th of the Fourth month, 1799, in the twenty-second year of her age. She was a young woman of a lively disposition, and had not been remarkable for peculiar attention to religious duties, and the concerns of a future state, until about the last year of her life. About the time that she began to show symptoms of increasing care on these subjects, her youngest sister Harriet was removed by a consumption, at the age of nearly 18 years. Harriet had been infirm from her infancy. A paralytic affection, which occurred before she was one month old, had disabled her right side. She, too, closed her days awake to the true interest of life; and Sophia, the more immediate object of this memoir, now also alive to similar feelings, penned the following short memorandum respecting her departed sister.

'My dear sister, a few days before her decease, mentioned how uncomfortable the state of those must be, who delayed repentance till an hour when nature seemed scarcely able to support the weakness under which a debilitated frame laboured. And, though she was not conscious of having committed any great error; nevertheless, being too unguarded, her disposition had, she feared, betrayed her into an unbecoming quickness of speech; but having felt deep remorse whenever that was the case, she hoped she had met forgiveness: for a sick-bed was not a place to recount past faults: the mind, at such a time, had enough to do to preserve perfect stillness. And, as she thought she should soon leave us, she wished that we, who remained, would be comfortable; and added, that had she lived to a more advanced period, she might not live in the manner she wished.' Her decease was the 25th of the Sixth month, 1798.

Sophia's good impressions continued with her; and beside the language of conduct, are also evinced by some notes which relate to the end of this year, and the opening of the new one, and were copied from her pocket-book. On the former of these occasions she says, 'Another year of my life passed! Ah, could I but improve every one of my remainder! And though health hath forsaken me for the present, still, if it should please him in whose hands the determination of things pass, to restore me to health, I hope a greater attention to the truly needful will be my case.' Her new year's meditations ran in the language of prayer: and here I would warn the critical reader, that in such expressions, he must neither expect perfect accuracy of language, nor be offended when he perceives it to be wanting. The mind may be too intensely fixed upon the thing, to advert to the mode.

'Teach me,' says she, 'thou great Author of all events below, to bear thy dispensations with patience becoming me, who am entirely dependent on thee. And although health hath left me, and I seem gently following a current that leads to my final end, be pleased to make the passage through the valley of the shadow of death easy: easy, I say, for O, that the sting might pass first. Hard it is to the natural part to leave kind parents and friends; but, with thy aid, may they with fortitude support their minds, hoping that the change may be for a more worthy inheritance than I could have attained below.'

By these remarks we see that disease had already seized and impaired her frame. The same lingering but sure conductor of many a blooming youth to the tomb, which had cut short her sister's days, was now preparing to do the like to hers. She did not see a third of the advancing year; but for the most part was preserved in resignation, and in near affection to her parents and relations. About three days before her departure, she prayed thus: 'O Father, although I have not walked before thee so circumspectly as I ought, yet thou hast been pleased, at seasons unknown to any but thyself, in my retirement, to enable me alone to worship thee. Thou hast many times comforted me. Support and preserve my dear friends under their trial. Thou hast been pleased to take my dear sister, I trust, to thyself. I pray thee that my spirit may mingle with hers.' After a little pause, she remarked that long life was not desirable, on account of the many temptations to which we are liable here: and at another time she said, that she hoped her lamp was trimmed.

SARAH CRAWLEY was born at Hitchin, in Hertfordshire, in the year 1717. Her mother, who, like herself, lived to a great age, was, I think, the daughter of John Field, the compiler of the third, fourth, and fifth parts of Piety Promoted, and was so ancient as to remember William Penn, in whose company she had been. This, her daughter, came forth in the ministry when very young, and found it her concern, in early life, to visit the meetings in different parts of Great Britain and Ireland. After this, she travelled little for many years, having, as she said, no concern for such engagement. She continued, nevertheless, in the frequent exercise of her gift, at home in her own meeting, manifesting her constant dedication, and demonstrating the liveliness of her spirit. During this long recess from travelling, she kept a small shop, in the business of a confectioner, in her native town, and had a long while for an inmate her aged mother.

At length, in the decline of life, she apprehended herself again called forth to travel in the work of the ministry; and she accordingly travelled into many parts of England, and once more into Ireland, sometimes under great weakness of body, yet evidently borne up in spirit.

One of her later visits had been to London, and at length she believed it her duty to come and reside there. She accordingly removed into the limits of the Peel monthly meeting, where she continued the last four years of her life. In this new situation she was not idle, but frequently visited the meetings of Friends: until a hurt which she received from a fall in her apartment, was the means of confining her to her bed-chamber, and mostly to her bed, during the remainder of her time. She was admirably supported under this trial, and said, that all was made up to her by the precious communion which at seasons her spirit was favoured to feel. She several times remarked, that her coming so late in life to London might seem strange to others, as it often had done to herself: nevertheless, she continued to believe she had been right in taking that step, and said that she had not repented of it, even in her most proving seasons.

When circumstances which used to give her pleasure were

mentioned to her, she remarked that she seemed to have done with things relating to time; and that when she was capable of thinking clearly, all her thoughts centred on eternity. At one time she said, that her mind was particularly struck by that passage of Scripture, "I have refined thee; but not with silver. I have chosen thee in the furnace of affliction." She also remarked that she had a firm hope that all would be well with her; for she thought she had been favoured to see, as it were, the gate of heaven open; into which, in an humble manner, she expressed her trust that in a short time she should be admitted. Once, also, when a Friend, returning from the Peel meeting, not far from which Sarah's lodging was situated, called on her in her chamber, she remarked, that although she was then prevented from meeting with her friends, she had that morning been meeting with the 'General assembly and church of the first born which are written in heaven.'

She was a woman of a cheerful disposition, which did not forsake her when she was finally confined for many months to her bed; in which, nevertheless, from the nature of the injury she had received, she was unable to take the repose of a recumbent posture; but constantly, sleeping and waking, night and day, sat up; having some contrivance to lean on before her, when she went to sleep. I several times called on her in this state, and scarcely ever left her without having been witness to her cheerful turn of mind.

She died the 5th of the Second month, 1799, aged about eighty-one, having been a minister about sixty years.

MARY BASS, was the eldest daughter of Henry and Elizabeth Bass, of Ramsey, in Huntingdonshire, and was born about the year 1775. She was considered an exemplary young woman; and as she was bereft of her pious mother at a very early age, the care of a large family soon devolved on her. Her mother was daughter of Isaac and Barbara Gray, of Hitchin; and on the decease of Henry Bass, which took place in the year 1796, his three daughters settled in that town.

In the year 1799, she showed symptoms of that disease which was the means of terminating her earthly course. It was thought to be that afflicting ailment known by the descriptive name of water in the head. The pain which it occasioned was at times very intense; and did not always occur without inducing a temporary delirium.

She did not at first appear to believe that her disease was mortal, as will further appear; and she suffered a long train of deep bodily suffering with great resignation.

Taking leave once of a brother, she advised him to be diligent, saying, 'I am sure there is need of it, for it is a hard thing to have anything to do on a sick bed. What a comfortable thing it is that I have nothing to do! But I believe I shall get better.' Her brothers (for it seems more than one were present) appearing affected, she added, 'You need not grieve, for if I die, I shall go to heaven.' Something similar to this she said to one of her sisters. 'If I die, it is hid from me, and no doubt wisely so. It is often the case. I do not wish to be presumptuous about it; but I do not think I shall. If I do, you have had a greater loss.' Here she referred to that of their parents.

After having passed a few days in comparative ease, her pain returned with great violence: on which she remarked, 'How trying it is to pass through the fire a second time!' On another occasion, being in great suffering, she signified her apprehension that she should be soon laid low. To an aunt she once said, 'I do not wish to be selfish; but I think I had rather die than live.'

She once desired a sister to be called up in the night, for she had felt herself so much exhausted by the pain, that she seemed to believe her end to be approaching. When her sister arrived she addressed her thus: 'Let me kiss thee, my dear sister;' then pausing, added, 'Canst thou give me up?' Her sister expressed her hope of submitting to the will of Providence; and Mary replied, 'But thou should do it cheerfully.' On First-day evening, after a day of great suffering, she said, 'I am now only waiting the will of the Lord;' but a sense of her close was not yet given to her, for after a pause she added, 'I do not know but I shall get better yet.'

The Third-day following, she was very quiet and composed, and she desired to have some of the Scripture read. This had not been done for some weeks, though it had been her own daily practice, when in health. After this had been done, she remarked that it seemed to her like First-day. 'Indeed,' said she, 'it has been to me a Sabbath, a holy day of rest.' In the evening she said, 'When the pain has been sometimes so great, as to make me sweat to a great degree, then I have thought my sufferings, though great, were nothing in comparison of sweating great drops of blood, through agony of mind.'

At another time she observed one of her brothers to weep, and said to him, 'Don't grieve.' Her brother then expressed his sympathy, and his hope that she might be favoured with a little ease: to which she answered, 'It is very kind. If it had not been for the presence of the Lord, my sufferings would have been tenfold; but he has been exceedingly good to me all through my illness.'

Once, on a First-day in the afternoon, after having been very ill, she broke forth in supplication, saying, 'O Lord God Almighty, permit me this once to supplicate thy holy name on behalf of my dear brothers and sisters, both present and absent. Be pleased, O Lord, to multiply their blessings. Feed them with food convenient for them. Make them as pillars in thine house. And my dear sister ——, be pleased to sanctify her afflictions unto her. Grant her patience, O Lord. Thou canst do all things according to thy might. And if it be thy will, receive my soul, and grant me an easy passage into thy heavenly kingdom. Thou knowest I love to serve thee above all things: and if I have withheld any thing that is right, it has not been through disobedience, but for fear of being too forward.' After some time, she added, 'I am glad I am thought worthy to be taken from the troubles to come: for they will be great, and I hope Friends will stand fast.'

The same evening she was assisted to get out of bed, when she addressed several of her relations, who were standing by, after this manner: 'You cannot think how easy this illness has been made to me. The Lord has been so good to me, that I have not even thought the time long. I can't see my way clear to heaven yet; but I do not know that any thing is in my way.' A relation remarking that she hoped there was nothing in the way but time, Mary replied, 'I hope not. If there was, I hope the Lord would make it manifest, for he has been so kind to me.' After sitting awhile in great composure of mind, she said, 'The land mourns, because of great bloodshed. Lord, forgive them, for they know not what they do.'

About this time one of her brothers, not having been lately present, came to see her: with which visit, though then she was very ill, she appeared to be much pleased; and after expressing her gladness, she advised him not to look at others for example, but to follow the dictates [of truth] in his own mind. A wish for her recovery having been mentioned by one of the company, she replied, 'The Lord is as able to raise me up now as at the beginning, if it be his will. If not, I hope he will soon release me.'

She continued about three weeks after this, in great quietness of mind, and several times signified she was only waiting to be released; being perfectly resigned to the will of Providence, which ever way her disorder might terminate.

Thus, being favoured to close her days in great peace, on the 20th of the Twelfth month, 1799, and about the twenty-fourth year of her age, she expired without a sigh.

SAMUEL EMLEN, of Philadelphia, a frequent and much-loved visitor of Friends in this country, who died in that, his native city, the 30th of the Twelfth month, 1799, was the descendant of one of the early settlers in Pennsylvania, and born the 15th of the Third month, 1729–30. He had the advantage of probably the best education which Philadelphia then afforded; and his own genius, aided by a memory uncommonly retentive, enabled him to improve himself in learning as he advanced in life. He served a mercantile apprenticeship with James Pemberton (also mentioned in the present volume), but never himself engaged in trade. He was religiously disposed from early youth; and, having the prospect of competency, he devoted his maturer age, and indeed his whole life, to pursuits and services of a religious nature.

In the year 1756, Samuel Fothergill, Catharine Peyton, and Mary Peisley (of whom there is some account in this volume), were returning from religious visits in North America. Samuel Emlen bore them company in a vessel bound to Dublin; and, falling in with Abraham Farrington, a ministering friend also from America, became his companion in a religious visit to friends in some parts of Ireland. On this journey, at a meeting at Carlow, Samuel Emlen first appeared as a minister. He passed the winter chiefly at Warrington with his friend Samuel Fothergill, a man well adapted to please and instruct him; and, after continuing some years in England, he embarked for South Carolina with John Storer of Nottingham, and accompanied him in his religious visit to that province, and some other southern parts of North America.

In 1764 he married Elizabeth Mode of Philadelphia, and as the health of both himself and his wife was infirm, they came to England, and resided some years at Bristol, in order to be near the Hot well. Here he had two children born, but his wife was taken from him, departing in the First month, 1767. He then returned to Philadelphia; but came again to England the next year, to conduct to America his two sons.

In 1772 he came again to England on a religious visit. He crossed the sea with John Woolman. They arrived in time for the yearly meeting, and Samuel, shortly after, had to attend the burial of his beloved friend Samuel Fothergill; whom, in his last journey to England, he had joined in visiting the families of one or two monthly meetings in London. In the course of his visit he went to Holland, with William Hunt and Thomas Thornborough, two American friends, also travelling on religious service. It is remarkable that his friend and ship-mate John Woolman, and this his later companion, William Hunt, were both removed by the small-pox in England in this year: as his former companion Abraham Farrington had been, but not by that disorder, in 1758. Of the two former, there are accounts in the eighth part or volume of Piety Promoted; and of the latter there is one in the Collection of Testimonies concerning public friends deceased, published in 1760. Samuel Emlen, whose talent did not appear to lie so much in general travelling, as in visiting friends in cities, and places where he could readily go from house to house, returned to Philadelphia, if my information be correct, in the following year.

In the year 1784 he came to England again on a religious visit, in company with four other ministering friends, namely, Thomas Ross, George Dillwyn, Rebecca Jones, and Mehetabel Jenkins. They landed in time for the yearly meeting, and soon after, Samuel Emlen went with George Dillwyn, and John Kendall, of Colchester, to visit the few friends then resident in Holland. Previously to his departure from America, he had entered again into the married state, with a friend of Philadelphia; and he returned to his family in the autumn of 1785.

His next visit to England was in 1792. He then crossed the Atlantic with Sarah Harrison, a ministering friend coming to visit England, and Mary Ridgway and Jane

Watson of Ireland, returning from a like visit in America. He returned, in 1794, with John Wigham and Martha Routh, two friends going on religious visits from this country, and landed at Boston.

He was a man of a feeble frame of body, and was afflicted with a disorder which rendered travelling peculiarly harassing to him; and which probably was some means of preventing him from coming to London in his seventh and last visit to these nations. He arrived at Liverpool in the summer of 1796, accompanied by Deborah Darby and Rebecca Young, on their return from visiting friends in America; and by William Savery, a fellow-minister of his own monthly meeting, that for the Northern District of Philadelphia. The services of Samuel Emlen were chiefly confined to Lancashire, and some parts of Ireland. His absence from home was about eighteen months, an interval shorter than is often taken up in these religious services; but during this absence he became again a widower.

Samuel Emlen passed so much of his time in some parts of England, that we have little need of other information, than that which recollection affords, to describe his character; and, generally speaking, it is by comparing the life, and the approach of death; the path which has been trodden, and the prospects which open on its close; that instruction and encouragement are derived from narratives like these. To say little of his cheerful temper, and the store of his memory, which made his company pleasant to those who loved to contemplate religion under its brighter forms; and of course especially so to well-disposed young people, in whose society he took great delight, I think I may venture to say, he was a man fearing God, and hating covetousness. His mind, though often at liberty for lively conversation on outward matters, seemed to be constantly revolving on the more important things which pertain to life and salvation. Thus, few were so ready with a word in season on religious topics; particularly in addressing with pertinence the various persons to whom from time to time he thought himself required to minister.

He was well read in the Scriptures, and eminently versed in some of the prophetical writings: and in later life, when by a residence with him under the same roof, I had the most opportunity of observing him, he used to have the Bible read to him after he had retired for rest. In his public service he was very fervent, particularly in endeavouring to arouse the careless professors of a religion which does not allow all the indulgences which they seem to think themselves at liberty to use. With all this, and crowning all this, he was a humble man. He ascribed all he had, and all he was, to the favour of his Lord. I was considerably struck, once when he was sick in London, to hear him say, 'Thanks be to the Lord, for the hope I have in his mercy.' It then seemed a less strong expression of confidence than, probably, through inexperience, I should have expected from a man whose whole life seemed devoted to God. I have since lived to see that it contained everything which the self-abased Christian can desire: and such a Christian was he.

His constitution, as has been hinted, was naturally infirm; and in the latter years of his life, had been further impaired from the frequent recurrence of the pain to which his disorder subjected him. In the autumn of 1798, after a long walk in a cold wind, he was attacked by new symptoms of disease, which his physicians supposed to be those of the gout. His wrist was affected with violent pain, which immediately spread up his arm, and seemed to affect the region of the heart. Such attacks seldom lasted more than fifteen or twenty minutes; and seldom confined him to the house more than two or three hours, until within a short time before his decease.

In the Eighth month, the following year, whilst residing with his son at Westhill, near Burlington, on account of the prevalence of the yellow fever in Philadelphia, he thought himself sensible of a slight paralytic affection; but on his return to the city in the Tenth month, his health seemed to be improved, and he experienced little interruption in his accustomed employment of calling on his friends and of visiting the abodes of affliction. This latter was a practice to which a considerable portion of his time had long been devoted. He considered it a religious duty, and it was congenial to his benevolence. In the Twelfth month his gouty spasms returned with increased violence, and on the 15th of that month, being at meeting, and having delivered a lively testimony, he found himself ill; and leaning, through weakness, on the rail of the ministers' gallery, he repeated pathetically those well-known lines of Addison,

"My life, if thou preserv'st my life,
 Thy sacrifice shall be;
And death, if death should be my doom,
 Shall join my soul to thee."

On this, the meeting was broken up; he was assisted to go into an adjoining dwelling; and, after he recovered a little, was conveyed home; but the next morning he was well enough to attend the usual meeting of ministers and elders, and his own meeting on Third-day. In this last, he was large in testimony to the excellency of that faith which had been his shield: commenting on the text, "This is the victory that overcometh the world, even our faith."

In the latter part of this week, his spasms returned so frequently, that his physician urged him to confine himself to his house; and he went out no more. But during the succeeding week, he received the visits of his friends in his parlour; and conversed cheerfully with them, and with his family. Once, while two of his fellow-labourers in the ministry were with him, he was attacked by a fit of acute pain: during the extremity of which he manifested the trust of his mind, by saying, 'I have a comfortable hope that my spirit will be reposed in the bosom of Jesus:' and when his suffering abated, he addressed them in a very lively manner, with this language, 'Remember, "Ye have not chosen me; but I have chosen you, and ordained you, that ye should go, and bring forth fruit, and that your fruit should remain."' When he was alluding to the care taken of him by those about him, he said, 'I deem their sympathy and affectionate attendance on me, as a blessing from heaven; for which God will bless them.'

During his wakeful hours, the attributes of the Almighty were almost his perpetual theme. He frequently acknowledged the rich consolation with which he was favoured; and he often repeated these words: "Their sins and their iniquities will I remember no more; and I will cast all their sins behind my back." At one time he exclaimed, 'Ye shall have a song, as in the night, when a holy solemnity is kept: and gladness of heart, as when one goeth with a pipe, to come in to the mountain of the Lord. Oh, the tears of holy joy, which flow down my cheeks! Sing praises, high praises to my God. I feel nothing in my way. Although my conduct through life has not been in every respect as guarded as it might have been; yet the main bent of my mind has been to serve thee, O God: who art glorious in holiness, and fearful in praises. I am sure I have loved godliness and hated iniquity.'

The day before his decease was the only one in which he was confined to his chamber. He was on that day visited by several Friends, with whom he still conversed pleasantly. One of them remarked, that the frame of his mind seemed as serene and peaceful, as could be conceived of a spirit on the verge of a happy immortality. At the accustomed time he went to bed easier than usual; but he was awakened before midnight by a violent return of pain; and when the common means of alleviation had been unsuccessfully tried, he desired that nothing more might be done: saying, 'All I want is heaven. Lord, receive my spirit.' He requested those about him to pray for his preservation in patience, himself adding, 'My pain is great. My God, grant me patience: humble, depending patience.' Presently afterwards he repeated this passage: "Call upon me in the day of trouble. I will deliver thee; and thou shalt glorify me." Then with great fervency he said a considerable part of that called the Lord's prayer, subjoining, 'Oh, how precious a thing it is, to feel the spirit itself bearing "witness with our spirits that we are his."'

Soon after this he said, 'Oh, the soul is an awful thing. I feel it so. You who hear me, mind. It is an awful thing to die. The invisible world, how awful!' As he was apprehensive of the near approach of dissolution, he entreated that nothing might be done to him but what he might request, 'that my mind,' said he, 'may not be diverted — that my whole mind may be centred in aspirations to the throne of grace.' About three o'clock in the morning, which was the 30th, he inquired the time; and when he was told it, he said 'The conflict will be over before five.' Shortly after, he prayed for deliverance, saying, 'Almighty Father, come quickly, if it be thy blessed will, and receive my spirit.'

He then lay quiet a while, and seemed released; but, as if he felt again the clog of humanity, he said, in a low voice, 'I thought I was gone;' adding, '"Lord Jesus receive my spirit."' These worthy words were the last which this Christian uttered, and about half-past four, he gave up the spirit.

HANNAH WILSON, a Friend, who attained to an advanced period in life, and who appears, from the testimony of her monthly meeting, to have been green in old age, was born at Simgill, in Grayrig, Westmoreland, the 20th of the Seventh month, 1717. Her parents were John and Margaret Blamier, who are said to have given her a religious education. Being favoured when young with the visitation of divine love, and receiving and adhering to it, she found it a stay to her mind, and the means of preservation from the dangers incident to youth. She was frequent in seeking for seasons of retirement, and solitary places, wherein to wait upon the Lord for the renewal of her strength. Thus, in her conversation and conduct, she became circumspect herself, and a good example to others.

About the fortieth year of her age, and a few years after her marriage with George Wilson of High Wray, near Hawkshead in Lancashire, she came forth in public testimony; to the comfort of her friends, who judged her ministry to flow from the fresh influence of Divine Life. In this service, she visited some of the counties near that of her birth; and was esteemed to be well qualified in the useful, but delicate employment of religious visits to families. For she was clothed with the spirit of love, by which means she had much place in the minds of those, who seemed to dwell at a distance from due subjection of conduct. She was a very diligent attender of religious meetings, even when suffering under much weakness of body; and often, when she came to them with considerable difficulty, she had to minister, in a lively manner, for the encouragement of others, to wait steadily and patiently for the help of the Lord: and He, who had been her morning light, became evidently and remarkably her evening song.

During a long and painful illness, she was favoured with much peace of mind; and at various times said, with clearness and animation, 'It is sealed to my mind that the day's work is done; and when this painful conflict is over, there is a place of happiness prepared for me. Lord Jesus come. Thy servant is ready.' A few hours only before her departure, she exclaimed with an audible voice, 'Thanksgiving and glory!'

She departed the 7th of the Third month, 1800, in remarkable stillness, having been sensible to the last.

BENJAMIN KIDD.—Those who have endeavoured to travel on, in the path which leads to the heavenly Canaan, the region of rest, have more or less, at times, found it beset with difficulties; notwithstanding its just and sole claim to the title of a way of pleasantness, and a path of peace. They have in a degree partaken of the experience, "Without are fightings, within are fears." To such, it is pleasant to see these difficulties all surmounted at the close of a long life, through the love of the Redeemer: who, saith the writer to the Hebrews, is a high priest touched with a feeling of our infirmities.

Thus closed, at the age of seventy-five, the life of BENJAMIN KIDD, of Godalming. He was a man of a meek and quiet spirit, humane and charitable, and conscientiously upright in his dealings amongst men; and he was enabled to assert in the decline of life, that 'his care had been great, that he might do nothing to offend his God.'

He was an acceptable minister, but was not engaged to travel much, or to a great distance; yet he once visited, namely, in 1785, the meetings of London; and also travelled into some counties westward of his habitation.

But, though his conduct was exemplary, and seemed to hold out to others an invitation to follow him, as he followed Christ; yet, during his last and long illness, he was at times assailed with doubts, under the apparent desertion, or withdrawing of that support, that divine good, which his soul loved, and longed for above all things. But this solace was again mercifully extended; his doubts were removed; and, as he told a near relation, 'a sweet assurance was granted him, of an admission into eternal rest.' He added, that 'he never before had had so bright a prospect;' and he enjoined her not to grieve, 'for,' said he, 'it will be well with me.' After this he spoke but little that could be understood; though he frequently appeared to be engaged in prayer to be released; yet that he might be enabled patiently to wait the the Lord's time.

He departed the 15th of the Third month, 1800, having been forty-three years a minister.

SARAH BLAND, of Norwich, was the daughter of Francis and Mary Lawrence of that place, and born the 27th of the Fifth month, 1732. The testimony given by the monthly meeting of Norwich, imports that she was early visited by the power of truth; though her youthful inclinations induced her to deviate, in some degree, from the narrow path, in which its followers find it their safety, as well as duty, to walk. But it was at length her happy experience to know her unregenerate will subdued; and, having passed through various exercises, and baptisms in spirit, she became able to testify to others what her own eyes had seen, and her hands had handled; and received a gift in the ministry about the twenty-second year of her age.

This account which I am now about to prepare, will probably differ in two respects from the greater part of those which compose this volume. Of dying expressions, properly so called, it will contain but few; and as for a long series of years I was acquainted with Sarah Bland, and knew something of her worth, I may take the liberty of deviating the more from the province of compiler, and of speaking from knowledge. Her first husband was my maternal uncle; her second, my friend from my childhood.

She was married in or about the year 1755, to Samuel Gurney, of Norwich, son of Joseph Gurney, of whom there is an account in the Collection of Testimonies, published in 1760. To him she was a faithful companion during about fifteen years, which they lived together. Previous to their marriage, a paralytic disease, which afterwards increased so as to render him incapable of moving any limb, had begun to affect him; but when at length it had attained its extreme of disability, his exemplary patience made his company instructive; and his knowledge and good humour rendered it pleasant, even to the active and the young. He departed this course of patient suffering in the early part of the year 1770.

In 1775, she married Thomas Bland, of Norwich, with whom she passed the remaining part of her life, except occasional journeys; one of which, in the year 1786, was a visit to Friends in Lincolnshire, and several counties, as far as Westmoreland, with the concurrence of her monthly meeting. She was also concerned to visit some meetings in the counties bordering on that of her residence; but her travels in the work of the ministry were not extensive.

A general view of her religious life may be had from a paper, in the form of an address to the Lord, in acknowledgement of his mercies, which she wrote about the year 1788. A part of it is as follows:

——'How hath mine heart been led to meditate in thy law, and to adore thy boundless mercies towards me, from my early infancy to this day! Thy hand, which fashioned me, hath pointed out my path; and in unutterable condescension hast thou, as a tender father, checked me when straying from it; and, like a shepherd carrying his lambs in his arms, brought me back! Oh! adorable mercy! let me never forget thy kindness in my youth. And when past the days of childhood and of youth, how bountifully didst thou provide for me, granting me not only the dew of heaven, but the fatness of the earth! a south land, and springs of water! And when, in thy wisdom, thou hast seen good to dispense the bitter cups, the wormwood, and the gall, thy hand bore up my head; yea, thy right hand was my support. Thou made my bed in my afflictions, and gave me a song of praise in my troubles.'

She was in some respects of a tender constitution; and as she advanced in age, had frequent interruptions of health, which prevented her from the usual engagements of social life, and from the constant attendance of religious meetings.

On one of these occasions, at a date subsequent to that of the paper from which the foregoing thanksgiving is extracted, she committed to writing a memorandum of some further retrospections and meditations, of which the following is a specimen:

'Having, from want of health, had much leisure to look back and trace the footsteps of my life, from the early visitations of divine love to my poor soul unto the present day, my mind has been often bowed under a humble sense of the great mercy, and unutterable kindness of Providence, in granting his protecting and preserving grace. I feel at this time, as at many others, an ardent desire that I may experience the same near to me, through the remaining days of my life; and be permitted, at the solemn close, to die the death of the righteous, that my last end may be like theirs.'

These two extracts were inserted in the testimony issued by the monthly meeting respecting her; but she had added to the latter, some hints of her experience on the subject of those written memorials which the yearly meeting annually receives, and in some degree requires, respecting deceased ministers. 'My mind,' says she, 'has been often impressed, on hearing the testimonies read, of divers ministering friends deceased; and I have felt, that whenever it shall please Him in whose hand is the breath of all the living, to call me from this field of painful labour, if then my friends have ground for a hope that I have kept the true and living faith, and unity with my brethren, it is all I desire, and should rather nothing more might be said: being sensible it is through the abounding mercy of the Most High, we are preserved.'

The foregoing extracts may serve to show the tenor of her life, and that humility was a principal ingredient in her character: consonant to which disposition I believe it may be remarked, that in the exercise of her talent as a minister, she was remarkable for being often engaged in prayer.

She lived to the age of sixty-eight, and departed in peace

in the year 1800. Her last address to some of her relations was finished with these words: 'You see how a Christian can die; in hope, and humble confidence in her God.'

MARY LUDGATER, of Coggeshall, in Essex, was the daughter of Richard and Mary Bradshaw, of Goswell-street, London, and born about the year 1770. Of her childhood and youth, not much is remembered; but during a residence at Poplar for some years, between her twentieth and thirtieth, she was considered a serious young woman, and evidently improving in best things.

It is not always from the most conspicuous on the scene of action, that we hear the most triumphant expressions of hope and praise, at the approach of death. The same baptisms which are the means of qualification for eminent service, sometimes induce a fear, a depression, a sense of unworthiness in the instrument, which makes it slow in believing that the Lord vouchsafes to regard it, and that he will finally crown it with eternal blessings; though it may often have had to hold forth his unfailing loving kindness, for the encouragement of others.

Toward the latter end of the year 1800, Mary Bradshaw was married to Thomas Ludgater, of Coggeshall, in Essex; and the following year gave birth to a daughter. In a few days she became so ill as to render her recovery very dubious; but her mind was preserved above the fear of death. She said to a friend whom she had for some time desired to see, 'Dear friend, how I have longed to see thee! I wanted to have some conversation with thee; but I am so weak, I cannot now say much. I believe I shall be happy. I have not buoyed myself up with hope,' (of recovering, probably she meant;) 'but oh! the goodness of my heavenly Father! Thou wouldst admire, if I was to tell thee what I have passed through since I came to this place. I have often rebelled, but my heavenly Father has not forsaken me; for strong convictions have followed, and I hope of late I have been more careful. Oh! how often I have wished that I might become as a piece of blank paper, and that all might be begun afresh. When I have been humbled and obedient, all has gone on so comfortably; even family concerns, and everything, has gone on pleasantly: and when I have gone to meetings, and sat, as it were, at the threshold, oh! what comfortable meetings have I had!'

At another time, after a sweet pause of silence, she remarked, 'How sweet it is to feel humility, and not high-mindedness:' and several times, when her pain was violent, she appeared to be craving help to bear her sufferings with patience, saying, 'O, my heavenly Father.' Her sister was once expressing her belief that He would help her, and making some reference to her innocent life. 'Oh,' replied she, 'when once the book of reckoning is opened, no fig-leaf covering will do.' The same evening, she appeared to be sinking fast away from the trials of time; but she revived, and said, 'I thought I was going. I have been with my Beloved. He held me so fast, I thought I should not have returned;' and she added, 'He will hold me, and not let me go. Oh! the sweet fruits I have seen and tasted of! And, if the foretaste is so sweet, what must the possession be!' After this, she told her husband that she never expected to see him again, in mutability; she took some nourishment, at her own request; asked for her infant, and kissed it, and said it was a sweet baby; but more than once said she had quite resigned it to her heavenly Father's will.

As she seemed so much to revive, her medical attendant asked her whether she would be willing to return to her friends. 'Yes, to be sure,' she replied, 'if it is the divine will;' and she added that she thought she had been enabled to say, "Not my will, but thine be done." Yet she observed that the Almighty, who could command the winds and the waves, that they should come so far, and no farther, might also permit the disorder to go so far only, if it pleased Him.

After this, however, her disorder increased; and she besought her heavenly Father that he would grant that her affliction might soon come to its height; and that he would be pleased to give her an easy passage. On the morning of the 23d of the Ninth month, she told her husband that she had had rather a trying night; but that when she thought of her Redeemer, it stilled her. To her husband and her sister, the day before her decease, she said, 'Don't hold me. I think you do; but give me up freely, for I am going to rest and peace.' Early the next morning, the 26th, she expired.

THOMAS RUTTER, of Bristol, departed this life in a lively hope of the mercy of Christ, the 2d of the Ninth month, 1803, aged 59. He had been a minister from his youth, having first come forth in obedience to what he regarded as a requiring of the Lord for that service, when he was about eighteen years of age. Previously to this, in his very boyish time, he had suffered the follies of youth to degenerate into vice; and at length into infidelity, and a contempt of serious things and serious persons. However, to please his father, he still continued to go to meetings, in one of which his attention was caught by a preacher whose subject was the passage from 1 Pet. iv. 18. "If the righteous scarcely be saved, where shall the ungodly and the sinner appear." Immediately he was filled with awe, and with a light which discovered to him clearly his sinful condition; and he was broken into many tears. Nevertheless, he soon attempted to shake off these impressions; but in vain: he sunk under the contest, and then was tempted to despair. He confessed however in his mind, that he had been divinely visited; and being sensible that nothing short of the arm of Omnipotence could save him from being lost, he sought it earnestly with humble supplication. He read the Scriptures, he often sought retirement, and was very diligent in public worship; but his soul was long detained in a mournful state.

At length his mind was gradually enlarged, and his first comforts arose in meditation, though they were but faint. The ministry also of two certain friends was useful to him; and he made them a visit, supposing that they would feel for his state, and would comfort and instruct him. But he was disappointed, and led to cry, 'Lord, if thou help me not, I perish; for vain is the help of man.' But when, after this gradual preparation, it pleased Infinite Kindness to afford him a sense of favour, the current of love was so strong, that he knew not how to forbear calling on every creature to join him in the song of praise. For a time he felt no evil, had an almost continual sense of the Lord's presence, and hastily concluded that his regeneration was complete. But temptations again beset him, and he soon felt the further necessity of daily watchfulness and prayer. Religion appeared to be a very deep work; but he was supported in the path of patience by some portions of comfort, and by the secret presence of the Almighty.

It was not long after he was brought into this watchful state, that he felt his mind strongly impressed to speak by way of exhortation to others. From this service he was very averse; and endeavoured, with contrition and tears, to examine his call, and, like Gideon, to try the fleece. The more he examined, the more the evidence was confirmed, till after various baptisms, he gave up his soul to obey, should further requirings be manifested. This was not, however, speedily the case. He underwent a further trial of apparent desertion, which he humbly received as a chastisement for his delay; but at length a more full resignation was the means of reproducing peace, and he found an engagement to come forth with these words: 'Christ's sheep hear his voice. Let us wait, to hear the voice of Christ.' After this also, he sunk very low in his mind, but was gradually enlarged, and soon became a zealous, reaching, and acceptable minister.

He travelled in most parts of England and Wales, where there are Friends, and was twice in Ireland; but to particularize his journeys would be foreign to the purpose of this compilation. He was twice married: first to Ruth, daughter of Samuel and Deborah Waring of Alton, Hants, who was removed in 1778, after a union of about ten years; and next, to Hester Farley, of Bristol, who survived him.

During his last illness, which was painful, and borne with Christian fortitude, he uttered many expressions, showing his faith, and his resignation; and he bemoaned the situation of such as defer to the time of sickness, the important concerns of their souls' well being. 'The pains of the body,' said he, 'are enough to struggle with.' Speaking of himself, he said, 'I have nothing to glory in but my infirmities. I have known something of that law of grace, whereby boasting is excluded. No merit in me! All of grace! All of the pardon and power which are in Christ! O! that I had the tongue of an archangel, to sound forth this glorious truth, that it is "not by works of righteousness, which we have done; but according to his mercy he saved us, by the washing of regeneration, and renewing of the Holy Ghost." Consonant to this also, he frequently said, 'I never was more deeply sensible of my own unworthiness; and that all is of mercy, mere mercy!' A little before his departure he signified his assurance of an admittance into the kingdom of eternal rest; and at his close was mercifully favoured with an easy release from the pains of mortality.

JOSHUA WHEELER, of Hitchin, in Hertfordshire, was the son of Rudd and Fidelity Wheeler, of the same place, and born about the year 1756. His childhood, according to his own account, partook of the wildness sometimes observable at that age. Nevertheless, he early discovered a disposition to sobriety, which paternal care tended to cherish; and it ripened at length into a degree of stability which had its influence upon others. His mother was removed by death when he was about fourteen, and then a boy at school; but he had learned to estimate her worth, and his grief was proportionally pungent; and when he came home to his father's family, and entered into his employment in his trade, he still more sensibly felt her loss, in the domestic circle in which she now no longer occupied a place. It is believed that the serious impressions which about this time he received, were signally blessed to him; and that he became, by his steady conduct, able to co-operate with the religious exercise of his father's mind, for the preservation of the younger part of the family.

He was used thankfully to call to mind, and to mention the preservations he had witnessed in early life, when he was sent out on business to distant markets, and sometimes among very rough and unprofitably company. He recounted the care which he found necessary to keep near to the principles of truth, and to act according to its dictates; the comfort or the grief which he had found on looking over the transactions of the day, as his conduct had been steady or deviating; and the consequent encouragement or caution which it held out to him for the future.

About the twenty-fifth year of his age, he married Elizabeth, daughter of William Brown, of Ampthill; and they set out in life with many pleasant prospects before them But in the course of one year, the health of his wife became so much impaired, as to prove a trying dispensation to both of them, during the remaining years which they passed together. But it nevertheless appears to have been a dispensation of mercy. It prepared her for a better inheritance; and proved to him a season of refinement, and of detachment from earthly gratifications; still further fitting him for usefulness to others. His wife died in the Fifth month, 1793, after they had been married about twelve years.

Soon after this event, about the thirty-eighth year of his age, he gave up to an apprehension of duty, which he had some time entertained, and came forth publicly as a minister. His testimony was acceptable to his friends, and he was very solicitous to be preserved from moving without their unity. Once, in particular, in a religious meeting, with great diffidence, he expressed his desire to stand open to the feelings of the least babe who was alive in the truth; and the belief which his brethren entertained, that he was generally careful, not only to begin, but to close with the life, confirmed his testimony to their minds and judgment. A paper, of which the following is a copy, and dated in the Ninth month, 1793, will show the reverence with which his mind was clothed, when he entered on the service. It is entitled, 'The opening of Isaiah's ministry.'

'First, he was favoured with a sight of the majesty and glory of God; and heard the seraphim declare the Lord's holiness, and that the earth was full of glory; and with such power and authority, that the very posts of the door moved, and the house [was] filled with smoke. Then, as a natural consequence, he was filled with a feeling sense of his own unworthiness and sinful state, and under the weight thereof breaks out, Wo is me, for I am undone, because I am a man of unclean lips, and dwell among a people of unclean lips, for mine eyes have seen the king, the Lord of hosts. In this humble state was the seraph sent unto him with the live coal taken from the altar, which having laid on his mouth, he comforts him. Lo, this hath touched thy lips, and thine iniquity is taken away, and thy sin purged. Then did he hear the voice of the Lord, saying, "Whom shall I send, and who will go for us?" Being thus previously prepared, in a grateful sense of the Lord's mercy, and with a willing mind, he was enabled to offer himself. Here am I, send me.

'Thus, O Lord, be pleased to favour me with a sense of

thy Almighty goodness; or such a sense thereof as my feeble state may be able to bear; and that in thy light I may see my sinful state, and, with one formerly, abhor myself as in dust and ashes. And oh! when sufficiently humbled under a sense thereof, that I may witness the effects of the live coal, and hear those gracious words, Thine iniquity is taken away, and thy sin purged: and under [a] deep sense thereof, that I may surrender body, soul, and spirit, into thy gracious direction.'

Towards the latter end of the year 1795, he entered again into a married state, with Elizabeth, daughter of William Tuke, of York. It did not appear to be his lot to travel much from home in the exercise of his gift; yet, with the consent of his monthly meeting, he travelled, in the year 1797, in some neighbouring counties; in 1798, he extended a western journey as far as Plymouth; and in the following year he went northward as far as York. In all these journeys, though not without an engagement of mind arising from an apprehension of duty on his own account, he travelled generally in company with others.

After his last journey, his life was almost one continued series of bodily indisposition; yet he continued anxiously concerned for the cause of Truth. As private opportunities occurred, he still laboured for the good of other individuals, in a spiritual sense; and one thing which frequently excited his fears was, lest the gracious purpose of the Lord towards his visited children should, by one means or other, be frustrated. For about four months before his last illness, he enjoyed rather an improved state of health; yet he did not form great expectations of its continuance; but rather apprehended that his enfeebled frame would yield to the rigours of the winter then approaching. Accordingly, on the last day of the year 1802, he was seized with an increase of his distemper. In rather more than two weeks he took to his chamber, and as his disorder was attended with a distressing degree of nervous irritability, it proved at times a close trial to his faith.

Once when thus oppressed, he exclaimed, 'Oh, this irritability! When I try to close my eyes,' for after a disturbed night he had been endeavouring to procure a little repose, 'I seem given up to the powers of darkness and confusion; but I hope this is not the state my spirit will be centred in.' His wife saying that she believed not, he added, 'No. I believe my change will be an entrance into peace, through that mercy in which I can confide; not in any works of my own.' Some further consolatory conversation passed between them. He was then sitting up in his chamber; but about nine o'clock he was helped to bed by two assistants, and he had some refreshing sleep. Soon, however, the cold sweat of death pervaded him generally; and on the appearance of this alarming symptom, at his own desire, his father was sent for. When Joshua was informed that his father was arrived, he rather hastily, and as if he feared his articulation would fail him, uttered a few short, but sweet sentences to some around him, concluding with 'Farewell. May the Lord bless and preserve you all.'

This benediction was the last sentence which he attempted to utter; though it was not till about an hour afterwards, and at half an hour past midnight, that he breathed his last so quietly, that the exact moment when he fully put off mortality, was scarcely to be ascertained. His departure was on the 21st of the First month, 1803.

SARAH STEPHENSON.—It is scarcely needful here to give a copious account of SARAH STEPHENSON, of Melksham, in Wiltshire, who died at Philadelphia, whilst on a religious visit, the 25th of the Fourth month, 1802. The reader who desires further information, is referred to Memoirs of her Life and Travels in the service of the Gospel, published in 1807.

She was the daughter of Daniel and Sarah Stephenson, and born at Whitehaven in Cumberland, in the year 1738. In her youth she was not without her temptations to the gratifications of a vain mind; but was inwardly restrained from giving way to them in a great degree; and, by various exercises and conflicts, was at length brought to take up her cross to them. When very young, indeed almost in childhood, she had felt the love of Christian virtue; and when reading the lives and happy conclusion of the faithful, had often paused, and craved of her heavenly Father, (in whose power she then appears to have firmly believed), 'Be thou pleased to make me like these thy servants, whatever my sufferings in this life may be. "If thou wilt be with me in the way that I go, give me bread to eat, and raiment to put on; thou shalt be my God, and I will serve thee."'

She first came forth in the ministry about the twenty-seventh year of her age, and not very long after went to reside in Wiltshire. After this, the greater part of her life was taken up in upright endeavours to discharge her duty, as it was opened on her dedicated mind. Great at times were her conflicts; but transcendently great were her consolations, and she had often to acknowledge the sweetness of the sustenance with which her gracious Lord supports the strength of his humble disciples. She was particularly concerned in the awful service of visiting Friends in their families, in many, if not in most places where she travelled: and she travelled in most parts of Great Britain where there are Friends, in several repeatedly, and in Ireland twice.

At length, about the sixty-second year of her age, with a body enfeebled by her past labours, but with a mind strengthened by the long and habitual exercise of faith, she prepared to set out on a visit to America; a concern which for many years had attended her mind. In this journey, Mary Jefferys, of Melksham, who had been her companion on several former ones, found herself also bound to attend her.

They landed at New York the 31st of the Eighth month, 1801, attended several meetings there, on the Main, and in Long Island; and then proceeding towards Philadelphia, reached it the 8th of the Second month, 1802. After some rest, they attended the meetings of Friends in that city as they came in course, and on the 9th of the Third month, entered on a visit to the families of one of the monthly meetings; but Sarah was so weak, that she was scarcely equal to bear the fatigue of three visits in one day. The engagement was therefore soon suspended; but she said that the making of the attempt had afforded her satisfaction; whether she lived to move further in it or not. After various means, ineffectually used to relieve her ailments, on the 9th of the Fourth month she was confined to her bed, and in about three weeks breathed her last. Her disorder seemed of the pulmonary kind, and the consequent and violent coughing and expectoration rapidly fatigued and reduced her.

During her illness, her exercise of mind on account of others, was for the most part taken from her. She said she had done what she could in time of health: and she confirmed the testimony of a minister who had visited her some days before, namely, that there was nothing in her way. To one who was affected at observing her increasing weakness, she said, 'Don't be at all uneasy. I have been sweetly comforted by my good Master's presence.' A friend remarking to her that "Her bed had been made in her sickness," 'Yes,' said she, 'wonderfully so.' Being asked how she felt as to recovery, she replied, 'I have no prospect of it. I believe I have finished the work. I have no care, but on account of my dear child:' by which term she meant her companion, Mary Jefferys. The latter, after this, expressed her entire satisfaction at having come with her, and said that she thought it a favour to be with her, even though she should be left so far from her native land: at which Sarah seemed almost overcome with joy, and said, 'Now, how glad I am, that thou hast told me! Now I hope that my good Master will soon take me to rest, and thou wilt be supported and rewarded. There is little here but trials, disappointments and conflicts. Now don't hold me, my dear.' Then she seemed as if she would sink away; but was heard to say, in a low, but melodious voice, 'Glory! glory!'

One day, after a fit of violent coughing, which left her much spent, she said, 'It will be right, let it be which way it may; and that is better than all the world. It seems as if it must be nearly over now, I have so little strength left.' A little after, she seemed to be uttering praises, saying, 'How good! how good!' and seemed engaged in sweet supplication. A friend asking her how she did, she replied, after a pause, 'I cannot say much; but my king reigns.' She uttered but few more expressions; but towards evening, finding herself to sink fast, she saluted those around her with her dying lips, and said, 'Farewell, farewell:' and before seven, she ceased to breathe.

This account being abridged from a larger one in the Memoirs, I subjoin the concluding exhortation. 'Here, reader, pause. Dwell on the closing scene, and taste the blessedness of the death of those who die in the Lord!'

JOSEPH BROWN.—In the present day, when it may at least be said, that liberality of sentiment, and mutual allowance for difference of judgment, on religious matters, prevail in a degree unknown in the times when our pious forefathers first engaged the attention, and drew upon themselves the abuse of their countrymen, it is rare to find any one suffering imprisonment for ecclesiastical causes. But as in the life of JOSEPH BROWN, we have an instance, and not a solitary one, of such being the case, a concise sketch of the attendant circumstances may not be improperly introduced in this place.

JOSEPH BROWN, was an inhabitant of that retired part of the West Riding, of Yorkshire, called Lothersdale, where he endeavoured to maintain a wife and a large family of children,* by the laborious trade of constructing dry stone fences, so common in that and other rocky parts of England. He also occupied a small quantity of land; but with all his efforts, was but little, or scarcely above want. He was a man generally respected, and about his thirty-first year had come forth in the ministry, with the acceptance of his friends. Notwithstanding his poverty, he was nearly a constant attender of his monthly and quarterly meetings, generally performing the journey on foot. He twice attended the yearly meeting in London, where I remember to have observed with pleasure the simplicity of his manners and appearance.

In or about the year 1781, he, with several other Friends, was summoned, at the suit of the Vicar of Carlton, in which parish he lived, for not having paid his small tithes, which amounted, as appeared by a subsequent inquiry, to about thirty-four shillings annually, and were consequently far within the limits of the power of a warrant from a justice. The magistrates before whom he appeared, judging the alleged demand exorbitant, recommended a more moderate claim; but the prosecutor refused to abate, and commenced an Exchequer process. This, after long delays, produced a decree which determined the average amount of nine years' tithe to be nearly as above stated. The costs were above half as much more. For not complying with this decree, in the Fifth month, 1795, he was committed to York Castle, together with seven others, his neighbours, and partners in the defence of the suit, and at length in imprisonment. The names of his fellow-prisoners are, John Wormall, John Stansfield, Henry Wormall, Henry King, John Wilkinson,

* At the time of his commitment he had ten children; but they were not all dependent on him for support.

William Hartley, and James Walton; most of them in low circumstances, and all of them dependent on their own industry for support: the withdrawing of which, threw the families of some of them upon the charity of some of their friends for relief.

How long they would have remained prisoners is hard to say. I do not recollect that any attempt was made to sequester their property; and had this been attempted, it is probable that the property of some of them would not have been sufficient for the demand, costs, and expenses. At length, however, in consequence of a representation to the king, stating the suffering case of several of his peaceable subjects, and the continued delay of the plaintiff, a clause was inserted in an act of Parliament, empowering certain magistrates to terminate this oppressive case; by which means (except John Wilkinson, who had died in the jail) they were liberated after something less than two years' confinement; and distraints were made on their property, to the satisfaction of the examining magistrates. It may be proper to add, that they were kindly treated in the castle and generally pitied by most that heard the case.

The friends of the quarterly meeting of Yorkshire, in their testimony concerning this friend, observe that, though he was much afflicted with infirmity of body (for he laboured under a pulmonary complaint), and various deep exercises of mind, both before, during, and after his imprisonment; yet he was enabled through all to evince much patience and resignation of spirit. In the course of his religious labours, say they, he had frequently to encourage others to a like dependence on the arm of everlasting help, as well as to strengthen friends in the support of their various testimonies, particularly that for which he had so deeply suffered. He departed this life the 28th of the Sixth month, 1803, aged about fifty-two years, having been a minister about twenty-one years.

A few days before his departure, some friends called on

him, previously to setting out for the quarterly meeting. He told them that he had also thought of attending it; 'but,' added he, 'we are short-sighted creatures.' He desired his dear love to friends, and remarked that he never felt more love to them than at that time; and that he was easy, and resigned to the will of Providence, who had been wonderful in goodness, and had supported him through many difficulties, to his own admiration: so that he had to rejoice, even in tribulation. He added, that whether it should please the Lord to take him at that time, or to restore him again, he was easy as to the event.

Thus it appears that peace and love attended his close; and where peace and love take up their abode, it would not be an irreverent strain of expression to say, that heaven is begun.

Oh! that every awakened soul would daily seek after the sweet influences of gospel love! It sweetens society; it begets its likeness in others; it excites gratitude; and even if bestowed on the ungrateful (as saith our dear Redeemer, love's holy and exhaustless fountain, the rain falls on the just and on the unjust), it brings its own sweet reward with it: for it attracts the approbation of God. Where then will be contempt? where the indulgence of evil surmisings, and hard thoughts? where either studied or careless detraction? where even the needless disclosure of real failings? where the least place for any enmity?

These hurtful practices, and pride, the promoter of many of such practices, will fall before the prevalence of pure Christian love; and surely, when these are exterminated from the heart, is it not so far prepared for its best and most sacred purpose, to be a temple of the holy Spirit? Amen!

RICHARD BAKER, of Dover, was born at Sandwich in Kent, the 26th of the Eleventh month, 1734. His parents, who were of the Presbyterian persuasion, were anxious for the religious education of their children, in which, so far as relates to their son Richard, they probably were successful. About the eighteenth year of his age his mind was closely exercised respecting the concerns of his soul's well-being; and in this state he joined the society called Methodists, among whom he was held in great esteem, particularly as a person who was endued with an extraordinary gift in prayer. During his continuance in this connection, he was preserved in great humility, and was earnest to press forward to the true rest. Thus he became weaned from all dependence on external help, experienced something of the true silence of all flesh, and was gradually drawn into the simplicity of truth.

He joined friends about the twenty-third year of his age, and was an exemplary member of our Society. He was careful not to exceed the limitations of truth in his trade and outward concerns, and was solicitous that his moderation should appear to others. Living in a town where there are often advantageous contracts to be had from government, and orders for the use of its establishments in that quarter, he believed it best to decline one of which he might have partaken, lest he should seem to weaken his testimony against war, by seeking the profits arising from it. Indeed, his mind was filled with hopes superior to those of gain; and the animation of his very countenance, when engaged in religious service, demonstrated his genuine devotion to the Lord's cause. Nevertheless, he conducted a considerable business in most of the various articles necessary to the furnishing of a house, and conducted it with reputation.

He was much bound to support the discipline of the Society, and was a very frequent attender of the yearly meeting in London. Being of a tender constitution, he was at various times much reduced in body, and appeared as on the brink of the grave. In particular, during the time of that meeting in 1779, he became so enfeebled by a disease which appeared of the consumptive kind, that he was obliged to leave the town, and to retire to a village on the south side of it. While he was at this place, our late friend Esther Tuke, of York, (already mentioned in this volume) then in London, paid him a visit; but the current of verbal consolation chiefly flowed from him to her, and to two young people who bore her company; so that Esther, who had been long a minister in much esteem and acceptance, had to remark that, as in the temple of old, the glory of the Lord so filled the house, that there was no room for the priest to minister.* At this time Richard Baker had not come forth with a public testimony in our meetings for worship.

To another visitor he spoke thus: 'Although I might mention severe pains of body, yet I have felt more peace and comfort, and have had more clear openings into that which unlooses the seals, than ever I had in time of health. I have endeavoured to be fully resigned to the divine disposal, and may say, with the truest sincerity, that in that season I have desired more that my feet might be turned into, and preserved in, the path of the righteous, than to experience the joys of the kingdom it leads to. Although I have formerly wondered at the necessity of loving one's neighbour as one's self; yet I have now thought if there was one person in the world who had more disregard for me than another, that my love has gone out the strongest to that person.

'As to my present indisposition, I feel a resignation therein,

---

* See 2 Chron. v. 13, 14. "It came even to pass that as the trumpeters and singers were as one; to make one sound to be heard in praising and thanking the Lord; and when they lifted up their voice with the trumpets and cymbals, and instruments of music, and praised the Lord, saying, For he is good, for his mercy endureth for ever, that then the house was filled with a cloud, even the house of the Lord: so that the priests could not stand to minister by reason of the cloud; for the glory of the Lord had filled the house of God."—See also 1 Kings, viii. 10, 11.

which is productive of a peace and comfort that is inexpressible; and believe if it pleases the Lord to restore me to health, it will be for the sake of others; but that I leave. I have seen the state of leaving children to the Lord's care, and that the widows should trust in him. If any thing has lain with more weight than another, during my indisposition, wherein I have been led to trace back the steps of my life to my very childhood, it is the not having earlier experienced this state of resignation, and love to my neighbour, in its full extent. Although it has been, and is thus with me, it may yet be otherwise; and this may be preparative to a trying dispensation I may have to pass through; for, "Whom the Lord loveth he chasteneth, and scourgeth every son whom he receiveth." All care and concern respecting my outward affairs are taken away; and as to my going or staying here, I leave to my friends, who can judge best for me.'

On his arrival at home, he thus wrote to one of the young people who had accompanied Esther in the before-mentioned visit; and though his words are certainly not Dying Sayings, yet, as they show the state of his mind when death seemed at hand, they are perfectly congenial to the design of this compilation.

'The great decrease,' says he, 'of those disorders which were lately so prevalent upon me, and the daily increase of strength which I have been favoured with, for four or five successive days, give great cause to expect it may seem meet [to] Divine Providence to answer those fervent desires my friends have expressed for my recovery: although I must confess the prospect thereof does not give me any pleasure; not expecting I shall ever see a time wherein my spirit will be more subject to the Divine will, nor [more] united and leavened into that power which is out of the reach of all the united powers of darkness to molest, or death itself to separate from, than favoured to witness in the late illness. However, being still mercifully preserved in a sense that every dispensation of Providence to us is ordered in unerring wisdom, I feel my mind stayed in a good degree of resignation, and willing to be brought yet again to be a companion with the tribulated flock of Jesus. I have only a desire to be preserved in the lowly minded, watchful state, where [the] ear is preserved open to hear the voice of the true Shepherd, and ability to follow in that which is manifest is witnessed: that so his great and sacred name may yet be glorified, who over all is worthy, saith my soul. A sense remaining of the many mercies I am favoured with, both spiritually and temporally, makes every thing so easy, that I scarcely dare to call my indisposition an affliction.'

About the year 1780, and the forty-sixth year of his age, he came forth in the work of the ministry; in which service he seemed clothed with universal love; and as his deep experience was the means of enabling him to say, with the beloved disciple, "That which we have seen and heard, declare we unto you," his labours were often consolatory to the spiritual traveller. His service was chiefly confined to the limits of his own quarterly meeting, and the neighbouring ones, except one visit to Friends in the west, and one in the north of England, also two journeys into Wales.

His decease at length was occasioned by an injury received by a fall. He lived in that part of Dover which is built near the foot of the Cliff; which seems almost to overhang the street, and suggests the idea of ruin, should any considerable part give way. On this cliff, accessible by numerous steps, his garden was formed; and as he was on the stairs leading to it, on the last day of the year 1803, a part of the chalky cliff fell, with a quantity of earth and some timber, hurrying him along with them, and overwhelming him. It seems wonderful that he was not immediately killed; but he received an injury irremediable by human art. The bladder was hurt, and a paralysis also ensued from the bruises occasioned by the tremendous fall; but the mind was unimpaired; and its faculties, calmed by resignation, and brightened by love, were still employed in thanksgiving and praise.

On the evening of the fall, he expressed the quietness of his mind; and, inquiring for a Bible, desired that the 32d Psalm might be read to him: repeating the 2d verse, "Blessed is the man unto whom the Lord imputeth no iniquity, and in whose spirit there is no guile." The whole of that and the following one being read, he said, "This poor man cried, and the Lord heard him, and saved him out of all his troubles." The 34th being also read, he said, with great tenderness, 'I have felt much refreshed from some of these passages. I have neither fear nor terror. I feel quite easy respecting my situation. My mind is centred in God. I ask for patience and resignation under this trial. Surely mercy and goodness have followed me all the days of my life.'

The next morning, First-day, and the first of the year 1804, being asked if he lay comfortably, 'My body,' said he, 'is as comfortable as you can make it; and my mind is comforted in a well-grounded confidence in the mercy of God in Christ Jesus.' In the evening he said to his daughter, 'Mary, where is that passage, "Many shall hear and fear, and trust in the Lord?" Wonderful deliverance; marvellous indeed!' In this it is probable that he alluded to his escape from immediate death, under the fallen fragments of the cliff. 'It may be,' he continued, 'to prove an encouragement to some poor mind to trust in this preserving power, that I am on this sick-bed.' Being told that the passage was in the 40th Psalm, the whole was read to him; and he was particularly affected with the verses from the 8th to the 12th, inclusive; "I delight to do thy will, O my God: yea, thy law is within mine heart. I have preached righteousness in the great congregation: lo, I have not refrained my lips, O Lord, thou knowest. I have not hid thy righteousness within my heart: I have declared thy faithfulness and thy salvation. I have not concealed thy loving-kindness and thy truth from the great congregation. Withhold not thou thy tender mercies from me, O Lord; let thy loving-kindness and thy truth continually preserve me." After this he said, 'I have yesterday and to-day been looking over Friends in several places, and think I never felt greater love than at the present time. I wish they may be preserved in the truth; and I have earnestly desired, whatever I suffer, I may not dishonour the great name. My mind is carried above outward things. I desire not to boast; but at present I feel no cloud in the way. It is a great favour to be so comfortable, and feel the divine presence. When that is withdrawn, then am I troubled.' Several times he exclaimed, 'I rejoice in tribulation.'

On Second-day morning, under sensations of great weakness of body, his mind seemed so strengthened, enlarged, and centred in divine life, that like the good scribe, he brought out of his treasury things new and old. He expressed again his entire resignation to the dispensation allotted to him. 'I am persuaded,' said he, 'there was a divine hand in it, and that he could have prevented it; but his ways are mysterious. What an inexpressible favour, to feel no dread of death!'—'What poor creatures we are. I know I am a poor creature to do anything; but through Christ strengthening me, I can do all things. My sufferings are great; but what are they compared to Job's; and what did the dear Saviour suffer!' In the latter part of this day he said, 'How sweet it is to feel that charity that thinketh no evil, but putteth the best construction upon all things. I look over friends with much sweetness and love; never more so. I feel the greatest confirmation that "God is love," and that they that dwell in him dwell in love.'

After he had been up to have the bed made, his married daughter, who was standing by him, inquired how he felt. He answered, 'I am more easy now; but such a severe struggle of pain I had, when sitting in the chair, as was hard to bear: but I have much to be thankful for. We must labour after resignation, not knowing how the event may terminate. Labour to be resigned; often feel after that which will support in the day of trouble, and the Lord will bless thee. Ah, the fading enjoyments of this world! They cannot afford comfort in a trying day. If it is the will of God, I had much rather die than live.'

When this daughter, who lived at some little distance in the town, took her leave of him for the night, he said, 'Farewell, dear child. Don't fret thyself about me, nor be too anxious; but endeavour to be resigned, and give up cheerfully. If thou grievest, the dear babe will suffer.'

The next morning, he appeared so much more ill that his wife, his son-in-law, and his two daughters, were with him at an early hour. To these, or some of them, he said, 'I know you all, and I love you all. I have nothing to communicate that ought to be otherwise. I am perfectly satisfied.' Then he addressed his son and daughter, saying, 'Be watchful, and the Lord will bless you. Beware of the world, and its delusions. It often promises what it cannot impart. I have nearly passed through life; and I have found no refuge like that of turning in to God, and placing my confidence in his never-failing arm of power.'

'Now, Lord,' he added, in the voice of supplication, 'if it be thy will, receive me into a mansion of glory.' More he said, which was not distinctly heard, after which he desired to be removed a little, and said, 'I want attendance now; but I shall not want it long, if it is the will of the Supreme Being. Whilst the hand of Providence is with us, we need not sink. That has been my support, a never-failing support —to turn to God.' Then he seemed afresh engaged in supplication; but as it was evident that he was in a suffering state, his daughter inquired of him whether he was in pain. 'Yes,' he replied, 'not so much now; but I have not been free all night. No, no. They do best that seek after happiness within. I have found it so in the depth of trials. There has been no refuge, like that of turning in to God.' After a little pause, he added, 'I lay down my head in peace. God is magnified. Religion is glorified.'

About this time, his medical attendant was sent for; and to him also Richard expressed his resignation and composure of mind. 'Doctor,' said he, 'I would not have thee make any extraordinary effort to keep me alive. I had much rather die, than continue in this world. My outward affairs are settled. I have no concern about anything. My mind is wholly redeemed from this present world, in a greater degree than I ever could have expected. I die in peace with all men. I am at variance with no man; and I die in the hope that when this tabernacle of clay is dissolved, there is a mansion laid up for me in a better world.' A Friend who dwelled in the town coming to see him at his request, after imparting salutary advice, and testifying his love, he went on, 'I see the hand of Providence in my present situation. Some may say one thing, and some another: but it matters not. I am perfectly satisfied with the will of God. I looked for no other than immediate death; but it pleased Infinite Wisdom to spare my life a few hours, that I might speak to my relations and friends, and prove an encouragement to some present (several were in the room), and I have a hope it will be a means of bringing glory to his name. Many will hear, and fear and trust in his name.' After some other matter, he added, 'I have often thought of late on the words of the apostle, "I beheld, and lo, a great multitude, which no man could number, of all nations, and kindreds, and people, and tongues, stand before the throne." You,' addressing some present, 'are likely to be the support of this little meeting. Be faithful, and your labours of love will be blessed.'

Divers other comfortable and encouraging sentences fell from him in the course of this day, among which was a message to an absent, though intimate Friend, to whom his daughter was writing a letter. 'Perhaps,' said he, 'it may be an encouragement to tell him, to hold on in well doing. The prize is sure to them that hold out to the end. Tell him I am carried above all trouble; out of the reach of that which is troubled about a future state.' He desired one of his daughters to pray for his release; and he said to his children standing by, 'I have done what I could for you; and my prayers have been heard. I have watched over you with a fatherly care. My blessing is with you. It is pleasant to see tenderness prevail. I love to see you all about me, my sweet family.'

But though this dedicated servant of the Lord had thus so far triumphed over the fear of death, and as it were exulted at the prospect beyond the grave; it seemed meet to infinite, unerring, and unsearchable wisdom, to permit him one conflict more. About four on Fourth-day morning, notwithstanding he had reposed in some degree of comparative ease, his pains returned, and seemed to increase as the day drew nigh. His patience and his faith were tried as it were to a hair's breadth. He often exclaimed, 'Dearest goodness;' but in this season of deep probation, the spirit of supplication did not seem with him as at other times. In his anguish he said, 'If I could but discern the face of death, if at ever so great a distance, it would afford a glimpse of hope.' This, however, shows that still it was not death nor futurity that he feared; but he added, 'But this seems hid from me.' Then turning his soul to his long-accustomed source of support, he uttered this petition. 'Most gracious God! Suffer me not to lose my confidence in thee. Be thou my support in this trying season.' About seven he appeared desirous to know the medical attendant's opinion, and being informed that there was a probability of his release before long, he exclaimed with great energy, 'And is there such a prospect? then am I comforted. Does the doctor say so? then am I thankful.' From this time his mind seemed much relieved; but his pain for a while continuing great, he said, 'My sufferings are very great, but it is my heavenly Father's will that it should be so.'

His close, however, was not immediately at hand. Towards noon fomentations were applied, which gave him so much relief, that his fond wife was induced to tell him that she began to have some hopes; but he replied, 'I am sorry for that. I want to go home.' He afterwards said, 'Be tender to travelling friends. They have their dippings; and if they did not sometimes meet with kind friends by the way, their difficulties would be great indeed. I have known the difference in my passing along.' And he also added, after a little pause, alluding to that encouraging passage of Matt. x. 42, "No one [who] handeth a cup of cold water to a disciple, from the love they feel to the cause, will go without reward."

In the afternoon he said, 'No ease, no intermission now;' then with hands clasped together, 'O my God, be thou my helper, as thou hast been my helper. Grant me patience to endure this suffering. I have been accustomed to live by faith from day to day, but now it seems reduced to so short a space, that I cannot see from hour to hour.'

In the evening his pains seemed a little alleviated; and his daughter expressing a hope that he would pass quietly away, he replied, 'If it may be so, it will be a mercy. A few minutes' ease, what a favour!' His strength now failed very fast, and though his bodily afflictions did not appear much to abate, yet his mind seemed to continue centred in that holy power which enabled him to bear them with great composure; and early on Sixth day morning, the 6th of the First month, 1804, without a struggle, a groan, or even a sigh, he gently passed away.

HANNAH STEPHENSON, daughter of Daniel and Sarah Stephenson, and younger sister of Sarah, who died in Philadelphia, as already related, was born at Whitehaven the 15th of the Seventh month, 1745, but removed with her parents to the Isle of Man, about the seventh year of her age. There was not any meeting of friends on that island, nor any member of the Society besides those in her father's family. Yet, though in this remote situation she was exposed to many temptations, her mind was secretly touched with the visitations of divine love; and as she gave up to them, after many conflicts, was favoured and enriched with the incomes of peace.

About the year 1762, her father died, at which time she was far from having forsaken the gaiety of the world; but it is more than probable that the influence of her more devoted sister, who had resided at home with her parents for some time before that event, had a beneficial effect on her mind: and after the decease of her father it became evident. The following year she went to live as a servant at Birmingham. Afterwards she removed to Stebbing, in Essex, and lived with a woman friend who kept a shop in that place; and next she became an inmate in the family of Sarah Beck, a valuable friend, and a minister, who then lived at Witham, in the same county. It was during her residence in Essex, that Hannah Stephenson first came forth as a minister, about the twenty-second year of her age, in a meeting at the neighbouring town of Kelvedon. This public act of dedication was performed in much brokenness of spirit; and as she abode in humility, and was attentive to the clear discoveries of manifested duty, she became an acceptable and lively minister.

After some residence in Essex, in the year 1778 she again removed, and settled in London with her younger brother; but after a residence of about four years, she finally removed to Bristol, to live with her aged mother. This last change was in the year 1782.

Previously to her leaving Essex, she had sometimes found it her concern to travel in the exercise of her gift. In 1771 she visited London, Kent, and Buckinghamshire, in company with Sarah Beck. After this she was much at her home for nearly seven years; but not without performing divers services, particularly visiting the families of some meetings in Essex; but in 1788, she joined Esther Marshall, of Leeds, in a visit to the meetings of Surry, Sussex, and Kent; and also to those of Essex, Suffolk, and Norfolk, and to the families of Friends of Norwich. The same year she accompanied Deborah Townsend of London, in visiting the meetings round the metropolis; and in 1781, the families of that of Tottenham. After her removal to Bristol, she was also engaged with the same Friend in several religious services; first, in the counties of Somerset and Wilts, in 1782; next, in visiting families in the northern parts of Somersetshire, and the southern parts of Gloucestershire, in 1783; and lastly, namely, in 1785, in a visit to meetings in the counties of Dorset, Devon, and Cornwall.

In the next year she joined Ann Jessup, a Friend in the ministry, from Carolina, in a long northern journey, which extended as far as Glasgow.

In 1787 and 1788, she was united in gospel labour with Mary Davis, of Milverton; with whom, in the former year, she visited Wales, and in the latter, the families of Friends in Somersetshire; and in 1789 she again joined her former companion and very intimate friend, Deborah Townsend, in Northamptonshire, Lincolnshire, Cambridgeshire, and Hertfordshire.

In 1792, she was one of several Friends who undertook the important service of visiting Friends' families at Bristol: and the next year she once more engaged in service with her beloved friend Deborah Townsend, in the counties of Gloucester, Worcester, and Warwick. After this, she was much confined with her mother until the year 1800, in the Seventh month of which year, this dear object of her filial duty and of her tender solicitude, departed, in the ninety-third year of her age.

The remaining services of Hannah Stephenson were chiefly in what, in a large sense, may be termed the neighbourhood of Bristol; except that in 1801, joined by an aged ministering Friend, Ann Byrd, of Uffcolme, in Devonshire, she visited the families of Friends of Liverpool, having also religious service in their way. Her last illness was lingering. In the Tenth month, 1803, it was my lot to see her, both at the house of Joseph Naish, of Congersbury, Somerset, whither she had retired for the benefit of country air, and at that of John Waring, in Bristol; whence I think she never again departed till she left the probations of mortality. She seemed to me like one who was (as I once heard our ancient friend, Isaac Sharpless, say of himself in the yearly meeting) retiring with her penny.* In this family she had sometime resided; here she was often visited by Friends who knew her worth, and loved her; and here therefore she had frequent opportunities of demonstrating that her attachment to her Lord, and to his cause, remained in undiminished strength.

One evening in the Eleventh month, some of her near friends were standing round her bed. A calming solemnity spread gradually over their minds, and they were gathered into stillness. She soon expressed her perception of it, though in a feeble voice. She said she was thankful her lot was cast with those who knew how to prize this precious feeling; and that she had felt the assistance of their spirits, in gathering into this quiet habitation; desiring that they might often seek after it, and remarking that Jerusalem was to be a quiet habitation: and after a little pause, with a strengthened voice, she addressed each of the friends with particular exhortation. She then sweetly expressed her thankfulness for the refreshment which had been granted, and said it made her sick bed like a bed of roses.

It would exceed the limits which I generally propose to this work, to insert all the comfortable and instructive expressions, of which an account now lies before me. She once desired a young woman, who was her usual attendant, to say if she did not think her weaker than at any time before. The young woman assented, and Hannah replied, 'My getting weaker is not grievous to me, but joyous;' and then

* See the parable of the labourers in the vineyard.

she signified her longing to be finally released. At another time, being in much pain, she said, 'I am a poor creature, hastening towards the silent grave;' but reviving, she added, 'When I am favoured with intervals of ease, all my pain seems swallowed up of sweetness.' Speaking once of her bodily sufferings, 'Why,' said she, 'should any of us mind being tried, when the beloved Son himself had a crown of thorns put on his head, and was crucified between two thieves.' 'May I,' she added, after some pause, 'quietly pass away, without bringing the least shade on that precious cause which has been dear to my life. It has been my meat and my drink to do my heavenly Father's will, as far as I knew it; but all through his help: nothing of myself. To me "belongs blushing, and confusion of face."'

After she had been some weeks confined, addressing herself to a friend, she said, 'It has unexpectedly occurred to my mind, my dear, that expression of our Lord's, "Strive to enter in at the strait gate, for many shall seek to enter and shall not be able." I believe, my dear child, thy mind is at times thus engaged. O then maintain the strife: for, though the way may be narrow to flesh and blood, yet it will be found wide enough to those who are rightly concerned to walk in it; and to be a way of pleasantness; and its paths, paths of peace. "Strive" then "to enter at the strait gate, for many shall seek to enter, and shall not be able."'

She was one day speaking to some Friends of her gratitude for her allotment in the family, where she was an afflicted inmate. She said that it was the kindness of her good Master, and his love, that had influenced their hearts to render their house a comfortable home to her. 'Oh,' said she, 'the precious influence of this love! How does it open the heart to feel for, and to be helpful one to another! And how would it thus do for many more, if enough cherished! It would lead others in tender sympathy, to acts of this kind, for we are not designed by our great Creator to live to ourselves, but to be helpful one to another. Oh! the sweetness I have felt, on this bed, in retrospecting my attention to intimations in this way. Many times have I gone to persons in distress, and in proportion to it, of my little, imparted to their wants. And oh, how acceptable has it proved! Even a few shillings, in addition to their few, have produced the tears of thankfulness, and I have returned abundantly recompensed by sweet satisfaction in having contributed to the relief of such. And there are some not in a very abject situation, yet at times in very straitened circumstances; hard to bear, and hard to them to make known by asking help.' Such she thought should be sought out by those who were of ability; and she particularly desired that the affluent would view themselves but as stewards, accountable stewards.

One of her near friends taking a final farewell, her mind at the time was tenderly affected in a renewed feeling of her heavenly Father's love, and she broke out in the language of thanksgiving, 'Oh! what shall I render, what shall I render unto thee for all thy favours?' She continued, saying, 'How repeatedly, by this bed-side, has the cordial of sweet consolation been administered to my poor mind, through servants and handmaids, all corroborating the same thing, tending to strengthen my supporting hope, which I trust has had its origin from the sure word of promise, which I esteem the greatest of all favours: and may now express, I believe without boasting, that a comfortable assurance has been given me, in language strong and clear to the ear of my soul, and that more than once: I will crown thee with glory and honour. I will crown thee with glory and honour.' In the afternoon of the same day she pleasantly related a dream which she had a few nights before. She seemed to be with her sister in a garden, where her sister, standing on the steps of a summer-house, appeared to be putting a garment on her.

Not long after this, when the children of the family, among others, were with her, she sweetly addressed them, and observed, that though some of them might not then understand all that was said, yet that it might be as bread cast upon the waters. She desired the eldest to be an example to her sisters, importing her belief that it was her heavenly Father's will that it should be so; and expressing her hope that the children would remember what she had said, as the words of a dying friend.

Her bodily ailments were great. She suffered much from cough, much from great debility, and at times from the soreness occasioned by long continuance in bed. One time, after having prayed for help, and having taken something which seemed to nourish and relieve her, she remarked what a favour it was to have such things, at such a time. One present observed that she had been thinking how some must suffer, for want of such accommodations. To this Hannah replied, 'Providence can make it up to them in some way or other. He can shorten the conflict. The Almighty is just and equal in all his ways.'

In the evening of the 6th of the Second month, 1804, she told a friend that she had that day seen her end, with greater light and clearness than she had ever done before, and that she believed it was not very distant. She remained only about five days longer. The day before her departure was a trying one, in which she had little sleep or rest, and took but little nourishment. Towards evening, a gentle slumber afforded some respite; but afterwards her cough returned, her breathing became increasingly difficult, and her bodily conflict was great. Some of her friends who had retired, came again to her chamber. She appeared glad to see them, and with earnestness said, "Rejoice evermore, and in everything give thanks." Thankfulness, no doubt, reigned in her soul, in the expectation of a speedy relief from the oppressive state of her enfeebled frame. But this she yet was permitted to endure for a time. 'This,' she said, 'is a hard conflict. This is a long conflict. How shall I endure? Lord help. Send a little help from thy holy sanctuary, if it be thy holy will, I pray thee;' adding soon, 'Lord, shorten the conflict, I pray thee.'

This, her last audible petition, seemed to be fully answered. A gradual abatement of suffering took place; and though the power of articulation failed, her mind seemed to be sweetly composed, and she frequently appeared to be engaged in mental supplication. There is reason to believe that to the last she retained her understanding; and at last, as she had often expressed her desire that it might be the case, she quietly passed away.

ELIZABETH MILLIS, of Southwark, was born in that place, about the year 1742. Her father dying early in life, left a widow and two daughters, with but slender means of support. He had however been a watchmaker, and this his daughter had so well learned one part of that business, as to be able to maintain herself with reputation, if her health had been equal to support a life so sedentary. In process of time she accepted a kind invitation from some relations at Hartford, to come, and be a resident in their family; in which her conduct was exemplary, and she became very useful.

She was religiously inclined from her childhood; and is said to have been very early at times, exercised in mind with a prospect that it would be required of her to espouse the cause of truth, by public ministry. But she was naturally of a diffident disposition; and it is thought that so far from being duly helped and encouraged, by such as should have been as fathers, that she even had her own diffidence increased, by perceiving that she was not alone in her backwardness to be engaged in that solemn work. It was not until about the forty-second year of her age that she came forth as a public minister. Her appearances in the ministry were not frequent; but her friends thought them acceptable and lively; and being of a weakly frame, bodily affliction frequently prevented her attendance of meetings.

After the decease of her relation at Hartford, she again settled in Southwark.

In her last illness, she had been speaking of her sense of the state of the Society in the monthly meeting to which she belonged, in a manner which evinced her steady and continuing concern for its prosperity. A Friend, who had been inclined to pay her a visit, being present, expressed her wish that she might be like Elizabeth at such a time as that: in which Elizabeth was contemplating the near approach of her closing day. 'Oh!' replied she, 'I do not wish any to be like me; for I am far, very far short of what I ought to have been. Had I been faithful to knowledge, I might have been more useful, and escaped many and great afflictions. But none know all my difficulties, and all my sufferings. It is of mercy indeed, that I have not been cast quite away, for disobedience: so that none need be discouraged. I want to press all to faithfulness, that they may not have to look back as I have done, and bemoan themselves for past omissions; but of late I have felt a degree of quietude, which I had no cause to expect I desire to bear all that may be permitted, to fit and prepare me for the close. I hope to be patient, and not too anxious.' After some time, she added thus: 'I am favoured with calmness; and though this is by no means a time of feasting, there have been seasons when I seemed as if I could have called on the whole creation to join me in praise! This is not often the case; but I desire to be content and thankful.'

She departed the 31st of the Fifth month, 1804.

A short sketch of the engagement of mind of Elizabeth Millis, referred to in the foregoing account.

She earnestly exhorted two women Friends who were with her (one of whom is since departed, surviving E. M. about four years), to stand firm. 'You,' said she, 'whom the great Master hath given to see and feel how things are, had need stand firm. I never was more sensible of the necessity of your standing firm, than of late; because there are so many who are not concerned to maintain the conflict, and to be exercised in an inward labour; but are busied about trifles, things of little moment in comparison of the inward work. They are too busy in the outer court; but be you firm. So will you be enabled to stand, and not sink.' One of these women-visitants replied, 'We want faithful brethren to help us.' Elizabeth answered, 'That indeed is too much the case; but be you faithful. Who knows but you may be strengthened, to help them? If you do the part allotted you, they may in time be aroused to a sense of their condition; and become more concerned for themselves, and for the cause' sake, which seems ready to fall for want of right support.'

She then paused, but soon added, 'Oh! how I feel for our young men! I wish for their preservation: but they must look to Him only, who can preserve; and not be discouraged by the prevalence of example. There are but few in the present day; but few to lead the younger ones forward.' Her exercise of mind on account of her desire that the men Friends might be more closely bound to the service of truth, had indeed been long to this effect. 'Oh! that our men Friends were more concerned at heart, and more sensible of the situation of things! What can be done to arouse them?'

These feelings and these remarks, though thus originally applied to one monthly meeting, will probably find an appropriate application in many more.

WILLIAM SAVERY.—In a collection of this kind, published in Great Britain, it will, probably, be particularly acceptable to many readers to find an account of WILLIAM SAVERY, of Philadelphia; because he attracted general regard in the parts of this nation, where in the course of a religious visit, his lot was cast. Those who long had espoused the cause of truth, valued him for his love to it, his zeal, and his soundness of principle. To the visited youth, he was endeared by the lively interest he took in their religious welfare; and there were few to whom he did not recommend himself by his cheerful temper and frankness of character. Indeed, he was a man beloved both abroad and at home; but he was removed from the society of his friends, at, comparatively, an early period; departing in his native city the 19th of the Sixth month, 1804, in the fifty-fourth year of his age.

He had served an apprenticeship to a Friend in the country, who carried on the business of a tanner; and served it with the reputation of a young man preserved in a good degree of innocence; but on his return to the city when his term was expired, his social and lively disposition led him into hurtful company. He associated with some who were themselves the votaries of vanity and folly; and they encouraged him in a deviation from the simplicity of truth. In this state, however, after some years, he was deeply affected with conviction, at a meeting held after a burial. The impressive occasion, and some testimonies then publicly delivered, were the means of awakening his mind to the infinite concerns of the life to come, and the impressions which he then received were permanent. This was in 1778, about seven years after his return to the city, and in the twenty-eighth year of his age.

The submission of youth to the secret touches of the grace of Christ is lovely; and though we have often to mourn that so many, for want of it, are carried away in the stream of vanity, still, thanks to the Redeemer of men, these instances of early dedication are not unfrequent. But it is not so often that we see this blessed subjection take place, when, on one hand the manly character is fully assumed and established; and when, on the other, the decay of future years is seldom the subject of contemplation. Such, however, seems to have been the case of this our departed brother. If he did not offer to his Lord the beginning of his strength, it is probable that at length he was induced to bring all his accumulation of strength, and his knowledge and power of mind, and lay them at the feet of his Saviour.

In the autumn of the same year, having been married, he settled in the compass of the monthly meeting for the Northern District of Philadelphia. He experienced various conflicts, forsook his former gay companions, and passed much of his time in retirement. About the thirtieth year of his age, he came forth in a public testimony for the truth; and endeavouring to dwell inward with the gift with which he was endowed, he became an able advocate for the holy cause which he had espoused. And it is believed that his labours were blessed, and made conducive to the benefit of numbers: especially of the youth, to whom, say his fellow-citizens, he was an eminent instrument of good. In Pennsylvania, also, there are many inhabitants who ordinarily speak the German language, their families having originally come from Germany; and to many of these William Savery was serviceable in a religious sense, as he had acquired a knowledge of their vernacular dialect.

He was much engaged to travel in the work of the ministry; and in process of time, believed himself to be so much required to give up his time to that service, that from the year 1789 to 1795 inclusive, he was several months in each year absent from home, on these gospel errands. In 1796, with the full unity of his friends, he embarked for these European parts. He landed at Liverpool, and soon proceeded to London: after a short stay in that city, and some other services, he went into Germany, and visited those who profess with Friends at Pyrmont, Minden, and other places. He had for a companion David Sands, a ministering Friend from the State of New York; and they extended their travels as far as Berlin. After this they bent their course to the south of France, where, not very distant from the city of Nismes, there was a small number of persons also professing with us, scattered in several towns of that district: which service being performed, they returned through France and Holland, in time for the yearly meeting of 1797.

When thus again returned into the bosom of a society which he loved, he continued diligent in the exercise of his talent and gift. He visited Friends in many of the principal towns and cities of England, Scotland, and Ireland; and often had more public and large meetings, with persons not members of our Society. A truly catholic and Christian sentiment, with the expression of which he concluded his testimony in a very large meeting, convened in London, I think, for young people, has so much remained on my mind, and is so fully descriptive of the expanded benevolence of his heart, then additionally glowing with the fervour of a faithful servant in the performance of duty, that I am desirous of placing it here. It is a hint at a state of universal good-will: which, however apparently distant, is worthy the contemplation of those who love to trace their blessed religion to its utmost earthly limits; a state, said he, 'When every country shall be our country, and every man our brother.'

Having, by these labours of love, discharged himself of his apprehensions of duty in these nations, he returned to his family in the Ninth month, 1798. Thus, in the occupation of the talent committed to him, he was prompt and diligent; nor when at liberty from religious service was he less so in his outward concerns, in which also he laboured with assiduity, not only for the support of his family, but that he might have somewhat to spare for the necessitous and afflicted; to whom, according to his ability, he was a liberal benefactor.

In 1802, that part of the city in which he lived was visited by a pestilential disease, which carried off many of his neighbours, after a short illness. As, at this juncture, he was so circumstanced as not to be able properly to quit the sad scene and the city, he gave himself up to be useful in it.

He visited the sufferers, as well among other religious societies, as his own; he relieved their wants by the distribution of alms committed to his care for that purpose; and he often was enabled to impart counsel, in the love of the gospel, to the consolation of many of the afflicted. The following year the same calamity returned, and our Friend found himself again engaged in like manner to be an instrument of succour to the distressed; devoting himself to the service both night and day.

At length, in 1804, symptoms of a dropsy came on. He had been of a full and rather corpulent habit; but his face and the upper parts of his body assumed an emaciated appearance, while his legs became swollen. In this state, however, he did not remit in the necessary attention to his business; and he continued, as he had long been, a very diligent attender of meetings. In some of these he expressed his belief that his abode in this state would not be long; but animated with the view of a blessed immortality, he signified the little concern that this belief occasioned, provided that blessing were attained.

As to his continued attention to business, he told a visitor that it was necessary to look to our outward affairs, seeing there had been so many reproachful failures: and at this time, when probably his disease had increased, he seemed desirous once more to go to meeting, that he might warn some of the elderly part of the Society, who, he said, had got into the earth, and some of the youth, who had got into the air. 'I thought,' said he, 'I was strong for the work; but now, I am a child, brought back to my horn-book; and have nothing to trust to but the mercy of God, through Christ my Saviour.' Thus, reverently depending, he was to the last preserved in great resignation and composure; and the last words which he is recollected to have said, were, with uplifted hands, 'Glory to God.'

MARY TATE, wife of John Tate, of East Cottingwith, in Yorkshire, was daughter of Richard and Ellen Shaw, of Newton in Bolland, in the same county, both members of our religious society. From her youth she was of an orderly conduct; but as she grew in years, her serious concern for her most important interest, the well-being of her soul, and her acceptance with the Lord, increased also. At length it led her into a lively exercise for the support of our religious testimonies, and for the welfare of others; and she gave up to the apprehended requirings of duty, to appear in public ministry, about the thirty-fifth year of her age. In the course of about eighteen years more, she finished a life of trial: for as her constitution was peculiarly feeble, she was often subject to illness; and she bore such allotments with Christian patience. In that which proved to be her last, she uttered several expressions which indicated the resignation and hope of her mind.

At one time, she had been speaking respecting some outward things, to a person who had expressed a hope that Mary would live to enjoy them herself. She replied, 'I have neither hope nor fear; but am quite easy which way it may be.' At another time, her husband expressing his fear that she was going to leave him, she said, 'If it be so, I shall go to a better place.' About two days before her decease, she broke out in the words of those mentioned in the Revelations: "Great and marvellous are thy works. Just and true are all thy ways, thou King of saints." * Adding more of similar import.

---

* This holy song, and the circumstances of it, may be worth recalling to the reader's view. "And I saw as it were a sea of glass mingled with fire, and those who had gotten the victory over the beast, and over his image, and over his mark, and over the number of his name, standing upon the sea of glass, having the harps of God. And they sing the song of Moses, the servant of God, and the song of the Lamb, saying, Great and marvellous are thy works, Lord God Almighty! Just and true are thy ways, thou King of saints! Who

'Thus,' say the Friends of her monthly meeting, in their testimony, 'was the spirit of this our exercised Friend released from a very afflicted tabernacle; and we trust is gathered to the just of all generations, where sorrow and pain shall be no more.'

Her departure occurred the eleventh of the Eighth month, 1804.

EDWARD MAY, of Henley, in Oxfordshire, departed from the vicissitudes of time, at Ampthill, in the county of Bedford, the 19th of the First month, 1805. At Henley, he had passed the greater part of his time, where he long carried on the trade of a clock-maker. He was a reputable member of our religious society, and having, towards the middle part of life, apprehended it his duty to come forth as a public minister, he endeavoured to be faithful in that important and solemn service. With the concurrence of Friends, at different times, he visited many parts of this nation in the love of the gospel: in some of which visits he travelled for a great part on foot.

In the latter part of life he resided a while at Alton, in Hampshire, but at length removed to Ampthill, in which town one of his sons had some time resided. Here he evinced his continued concern for the cause of truth, by his diligence in attending meetings in the place, and others not very distant; and his private conduct was weighty and exemplary, so that he was thought to "show out of a good conversation, his works with meekness of wisdom."

While writing this, which is chiefly copied from the testimony of his monthly meeting, I am somewhat impressed with a caution, that we should not suffer ourselves, in briefly

---

shall not fear thee, O Lord, and glorify thy name? for thou only art holy; for all nations shall come and worship before thee: for thy judgments are made manifest."—Rev. xv.

reviewing the good conduct of our departed friends, to degenerate into the habit of mere eulogium. I do not say this with any particular reference to this Friend, but as a general remark now occurring: and as it is applicable to every case, so probably to none more applicable, than to relations concerning those whom we term the most eminent. As the disciple is to let his light shine, that it may glorify the heavenly Father, so the truly Christian observer will behold it, with a due and ready reference to the giver of the endowment.

At his first confinement to his chamber, he did not apprehend his close to be very near; yet he examined himself, as to his spiritual state, from his youth up; and he had the privilege to find that the great work was done, his sins were forgiven, and all was peace. He was often engaged in vocal prayer, and his earnest desire was, as we have seen it hath been that of many humble souls, inhabiting afflicted bodies, that he might be preserved in patience. And he was preserved in patience, and a quiet, peaceful frame of mind, throughout his illness, which was a fever; but he also had an ailment of a very painful nature.

The day before that in which his course in mortality was terminated, some Friends called to see him. His disorder had then advanced so far, as that he could scarcely articulate. Nevertheless, with an audible voice, he was enabled to bear his last vocal testimony to that Divine Power which can support the mind under the most afflicting circumstances of time. He added, with righteous Job, "All the days of my appointed time will I wait, till my change come."

SAMUEL CLOTHIER BRYAN.—In the life of SAMUEL CLOTHIER BRYAN, of Glastonbury, Somersetshire, who attained to the advanced age of ninety-two, we have an instance of long, protracted, steady perseverance in the path of the just. His native place was Shepton-Mallet, in the same county, where he lived upwards of sixty years; after which, and on the decease of his wife, he removed to Glastonbury.

His education was not what is usually termed liberal; and he fell into many of the hurtful modes of conduct incident to youth: so that when it pleased the Lord in mercy to show him his dangerous state, and to open to him the way of life and salvation, he found that his evil habits had rooted themselves so deeply, that the cross of Christ was, in his view, hard to be borne.

But the goodness of the Lord still followed him; and convinced him that it was the only means of overcoming sin. Thus he bowed to the revelation of its power, and as he continued in faithfulness, he experienced deliverance from evil, and an increase in the favour of God. Such also was his sense of the favour thus conferred on him, that he felt himself constrained in a public meeting, to acknowledge the abundant goodness of the Lord, adding, 'May we never be forgetful of his mercies.' At this time he did not expect to be ever alike engaged in future; but being further instructed in the school of experience, and believing it his duty to testify from time to time, of what he had seen and felt of the things which accompany peace and salvation, he became an acceptable minister, and so continued nearly to the close of his pilgrimage.

His ministry was plain, edifying, and Scriptural. He seemed not to seek applause, but simply to do his duty, and not to desire to attempt more. His services were chiefly confined within the compass of his own quarterly meeting: in which, when of bodily ability, he often walked to the neighbouring or other meetings; and was exemplary in the diligent attendance of his own. Nor was his talent at instruction confined to public meetings only; his visitors were often instructed by the pertinent remarks which he had unexpectedly to convey.

In early life he had met with difficulties, and had laboured hard to provide for his wants; but as he was of a humble mind, mean things satisfied him, and he could spare to others whom he thought to be in greater need. His manners were homely, and he took so little care for the accommodation of the body that he was thought to neglect it; yet he possessed a mind independent, save on what he esteemed the law of the Lord.

The infirmities of age, as they increased upon him, did not appear much to impair his mental vigour. He often expressed his willingness to depart, if it were consistent with the will of the Lord; but he also manifested great resignation and patience, and full assurance that a rest was prepared for him. 'It is the greatest of all favours,' said he, 'to be released from an old decayed tabernacle, and to have an evidence of being for ever united to the spirits of just men made perfect, and to God, the Judge of all, and to Jesus the Mediator. I feel no unity with bad spirits, and believe my portion will not be with them.'

On the 23d of the First month, 1805, after a short confinement to his bed, he peaceably breathed his last.

SUSANNA MOORE was the daughter of Benjamin and Susanna Grubb, of Clonmel, in the county of Tipperary, Ireland, where she was born in the Third month, 1770. She was a woman of an innocent and humble mind, and circumspect in life and conversation. When she was about twenty-one years of age, she was married to James Moore, of Clonmel, with whom she lived about fourteen years; and when she had arrived to her thirty-sixth year, a period at which the important and endearing characters of wife and mother are fully developed, she was taken from her husband,

and left him with six daughters; for the religious education of whom, in her life-time, she had been uprightly careful.

Her health began to decline in the latter part of the year 1804, and much indisposition was her allotment for several months. She continued, however, until the Eighth month, 1805, and rode out for the last time the day but one preceding her decease. She could scarcely support the exercise, and returned without benefit. In this crisis, when attempts to relieve a much enfeebled frame were made in vain, it was her privilege to have those about her who knew how to estimate the value of spiritual relief to the mind. It was her greater privilege to know where to seek it for herself.

When she was in bed, her brother, standing by, remarked to her, that he was sensible God was near, and that he hoped her dependence would be there. She replied, 'I am very glad. There is nothing else to look to now.' Nevertheless, the night was a distressing one to her, through bodily suffering, and in the morning a conflict of the mental kind was permitted to assail her. It has been hinted that she was of a diffident and humble mind; and now, perceiving the apparent symptoms of her close, she imagined that if ever she became prepared to enter into rest, it must be by the means of great inward suffering: and, with this view, for a short time her depression was very great.

At this juncture her brother's wife was engaged in solemn supplication, praying that the effective word, which had once gone forth in the season of storm, when no human effort could be of any avail, and which pronounced, "Peace, be still," so that there was a great calm, might now be mercifully pronounced, to the calming of the troubled waves. Thus was her sister enabled to petition; and before the noon of that day, Susanna was given to believe that the work of final redemption and purification, which she had seen to be so great, was not now to do. This peacefully ending conflict calls to mind the words of the evangelical prophet, who spoke so clearly of the latter times. "I will bring the blind by a way that they knew not: I will lead them in paths that they have not known. I will make darkness light before them, and crooked things straight. These things will I do unto them, and not forsake them."

In the evening, having first had an opportunity of conversing with her husband alone, she was desirous of speaking to her sisters. They accordingly stood around her; and, after a short pause, with great composure, she addressed them nearly thus: 'What I wanted to say is, that it is a great comfort to me that the children have such aunts. I hope you will take care of them, and endeavour to keep them from doing wrong, and keep them plain. It is what I always wished, and what I intended. It is what their father wishes. I did not think it was now that I was to be taken. I thought I should have gone on to the end of my time (to her delivery), and that it would be then; but when I heard of E—— M——'s death, it came into my mind that as she was taken from her children, why might not I? But I did not think it possible I could be brought to be so well satisfied and resigned as I am. I thought there must be something horrible on my mind if I was going to die: and it was that which put me in the way I was this morning, because I could not feel any thing like it.* I feel no weight.'

Having thus spoken concerning herself and her children, she afterwards was enabled, though in much affliction of her bodily frame, to take leave of them, as they were standing about her. 'I wanted,' said she, 'to tell you, if anything happens to me, to be good and love one another. Don't fall out with each other; but be kind and loving. Mind what your father and aunts say to you; and as Susanna is the eldest, mind what she says, and I hope she will be a good

---

* Her meaning, clear, no doubt, to the by-standers, is scarcely so on paper. She had let in a notion that very deep exercise of mind must prepare her for eternal rest; and not feeling herself thus deeply exercised, she was alarmed, and thought herself about to go unprepared.

example to you.' Then to Susanna, who was about fourteen years of age, she added, 'Mind what I have said; and take care of thy poor father, and of his things.' She also during her illness cautioned Susanna against the reading of hurtful books. She said that such had been offered to her when she was young; but that she had refused to read them; and that she now found the advantage of such an abstinence. There are some truths that young people can scarcely know, but by the testimony of the experience of their elders: and I am willing to assure them, that vain and defiling things impressed on the memory in youth, will often turn up in more advanced life, at times when the awakened mind, knowing their polluting tendencies, would gladly cast them away. In her more private conference with her husband, among many other things, she desired him not to have her children taught to draw; and not to permit them to go much from home on visits.

When she was looking round her, not long before her close, her husband inquired whether she wanted anything. She replied, 'No; but I like to look about me on those I love.' When her sufferings of body became almost too great to be expressed, her brother's wife signified her belief that the arms of her heavenly Father were ready to receive her; adding, that her relations all gave her up, for a happier state of being; and that therefore she hoped the time would not be much prolonged. The dying friend replied, 'That is a comfort to me in my distress. I am satisfied. The sooner the better.' She was heard to be in supplication, when her voice so faltered that much of what she said could not be distinguished; but when she was almost in the very article of death, one word was distinctly heard, and that word was, Thankful.

This account, with more, I have from her brother; who nearly thus remarks on the whole:

'These things are not noted down to exalt the creature; but to the praise of the great name of him, whose power was so wonderfully displayed, in one who thought herself less than the least in his family: and that others may be encouraged to look to the same source of help and strength; and in that alone to confide.'

Susanna Moore departed the ninth of the Eighth month, 1805.

JACOB BELL, son of Jacob and Sarah Bell, was born at Plaistow, in Essex, the 18th of the Eighth month, 1783. He was remarkable during his childhood for his amiable manners.

When he was in his thirteenth year, his father took him as an attendant on a journey; on which occasion his innocent and engaging, but manly behaviour, attracted the notice of many friends: especially his solid deportment at meeting, which was often attended with many tears. This seemed to show that, in those early years, his mind was endowed with the principle of grace and truth which comes by Jesus Christ.

When he was about sixteen years of age, he was bound apprentice to his brother, John Bell, chemist, in Oxford-street. He served his apprenticeship with much diligence, and at the expiration of it, engaged himself as an assistant to his brother. In about six months, however, he had contracted a pulmonary complaint, and in the Fourth month, 1805, he came to his father's house at Plaistow, for the benefit of the air. He seemed at first to mend; but as his amendment was of little duration, he was recommended to try the air of the vicinity of Southampton.

The disposition of his mind, at this time, may be seen by the following extract of a letter to his brother, written not long after his arrival in the neighbourhood of Southampton.

'Rose Hill, 23d, Sixth month, 1805.

'My dear Brother,

'Reflecting on the varied [various] dispensations allotted to mankind by a merciful Creator, I cannot but at times be thankful for the one allotted me, though apparently afflicted, whether I should recover or not: at the same time feeling for the anxiety of my dear relations. How many are called from this scene of action without many days' warning. When we take into consideration the many trying baptisms those have to pass through who are devoted to the best of causes; if allowed the choice, it seems as though the shorter time might be preferred, by those who enjoy a hope of mercy; yet at the same time not doubting that they meet with their reward, manifold here, as well as hereafter. Sometimes, looking forward towards the possession of health and strength, I am ready to fear my weakness in taking up the cross. At times, petitions are put up for an increase of stability, and willingness to attend to the inward monitor.

After remaining seven weeks near Southampton, and finding an increase of disease, it was concluded to try the Hot-well water, and accordingly he set out for Bristol; but at Bath his parents were much alarmed by the breaking of an ulcer in his lungs. This enfeebled him much; but he thus expressed himself to his mother: 'You have done what you can. Make yourselves easy. I shall do well.' He used the Hot-well water freely, but unavailingly; and as he did not appear to amend after a stay of five weeks, the physician recommended his return home, where he arrived the 14th of the Ninth month.

While at the Hot-wells, he wrote a letter to a friend, of which the following is an extract.

'Bristol Hot-wells, 28th Eighth month.

'Dear Friend,

'Seeing the Almighty sees meet in wisdom and mercy to visit his created beings with afflictions of various kinds, it is

30 *

no doubt our duty to endeavour to bear them with cheerfulness, and as much fortitude as we are capable of; knowing they are for some good purpose. Instead of repining at my lot, I have great cause to be humbly thankful; for how many are called from this transitory scene, as it were at a moment's warning: which has not been my case.

'I think I may say I have been favoured in a good degree with that serenity of mind, which thou hast been so solicitous I might enjoy. By placing our whole dependence on the Almighty holy arm of power, we shall be blessed with resignation and patience, that will uphold us through every difficulty, or season of trial. Though at times I have been favoured to feel great satisfaction and comfort, in respect to the termination of my disorder, should it prove contrary to the desires of my friends; yet it is necessary for me to keep on the watch, and attend to our inward instructor: knowing our unwearied adversary is ready to rush in at every weak corner.'

After he came home, notwithstanding the continuance of medical advice, and of the most unremitted maternal care, he grew worse, and had an additional ailment, the thrush, which occasioned great difficulty in taking either food or medicine; but he bore it with Christian fortitude, desiring to be favoured with patience, and was wonderfully supported.

On the Fifth day before his decease, his parents only being with him, he said nearly as follows: 'Being brought into a state of suffering, how different things appear to what they have done. If it please Providence to remove me, I may escape many trials which we are liable to.' His mother said she hoped that he felt his mind comfortable under his present situation. He replied, that 'at times he did, although,' said he, 'we are liable to many slips;' adding, that he should have wished to see his way with greater clearness. 'O, father,' said he, 'is there any hope for me?' His father replied, 'Yes, in a future life;' and made some other remarks to comfort him in this trying state. On taking leave of his sister, who afterwards had come into the room, he said, he hoped she never would be afflicted as he was; desired her to mind the inward teacher, the Spirit of truth, and to wait upon it in meetings, and not to think of idle subjects, which had been cause of uneasiness to him; and he requested she would be attentive to what Providence pointed out to her.

On the Seventh day, a visible alteration took place in him. On parting with his brother, Sheppard Bell, he said, 'Give my dear love to Betsey,' (wife to S. Bell;) 'I suppose I shall never see her again. Farewell, dear Sheppard. My time is now short, very short. I hope you will be patterns in the Society. Farewell, dear Sheppard.'

After this, his mind was much stayed upon the Lord. He prayed very fervently, at one time audibly, as follows: 'O, Almighty Father, if it please thee, shorten my sufferings, and that my patience may hold out.' He also desired his father to pray for him; and, after a weighty pause, supplication was put up to the Almighty, that he would be pleased to be with him to the end, and grant him a place in his kingdom, among those who are already sanctified.

He was quietly removed, departing without a struggle, on First-day morning; and there is cause to believe he was favoured with increased clearness, and that his petitions were granted. He was upwards of twenty two years of age when he was thus removed. His decease was the 27th of the Tenth month, 1805.

It may be truly said that his life was a life of innocence. He had a great regard for the Scriptures of truth. He particularly desired that his Bible might be given to a young man of his acquaintance, who had lately opened a boarding-school.

LOUISA CONRAN was the daughter of Samuel and Anne Strangman, of Mount Mellick, Ireland. At an early age she manifestly showed the tokens of a Divine visitation to her soul; and, as she bowed in obedience to the leadings of truth, she became an example of humility and self-denial to the youth; while her stability and solid conduct recommended her to those more advanced.

In the year 1783 she removed, with her husband, John Conran, into the compass of the monthly meeting of Lisburne, in the north of Ireland; where also, as she had previously been, she was diligent in attending meetings for worship and discipline, and exemplary in her deportment in them. She was endowed with clear discernment in matters relating to the discipline, and was active in the promotion of it. She seldom missed attending the yearly meeting at Dublin, and several times attended that of London. Nevertheless in her last illness, she was tried with poverty of spirit. "Blessed," indeed, said the lip of truth, "are the poor in spirit: for theirs is the kingdom of heaven." Yet this state, like some others which, through adorable mercy, are preparatory for the reception of "the true riches," is often, for the time, deeply proving to the creature. She was accordingly frequent in fervent supplication that her sins might be forgiven, and that her dross, and tin, and reprobate silver, might be done away. Yea, even her former "works of righteousness appeared to her but as filthy rags." She acknowledged that she was nothing; but that Christ was all. In an emphatic tone, she declared her unshaken belief in him; that he was the Christ, the Son of God; and that her hopes of salvation were through him.

With respect to the testimonies which friends have to bear, she said, she had been concerned to keep them from her youth up: and her belief was, that they were the testimonies of truth. She took an affectionate farewell of her female servants, and recommended them to let truth and honesty be the governing principle of their lives. She desired her love to be remembered to several friends, and concluded with saying, 'I love all.'

At length, after a fit of great debility, in which she had dozed for several hours, her husband, who was sitting beside her, was surprised to hear her speak: and the last words which she is recollected to have spoken, and those she spoke distinctly, were the following. 'Who,' said she, 'is this great enemy that surrounds me? Christ will overcome him.' It was thought that she then perceived the approach of her dissolution. After this she appeared sensible, though silent; and having accepted some liquid which was given to her, she quietly expired without a sigh.

She departed the 4th of the Twelfth month, 1805, aged fifty years.

ANN PUMPHREY.—Of Ann Pumphrey, wife of Stanley Pumphrey, of Worcester, a memorial was drawn up by her husband, of which the following is a copy, somewhat abridged, but very little otherwise altered; and that only verbally, and principally, if not wholly, in the narrative parts.

On reflecting upon the edifying tendency which the expressions of my dear wife, during the few days of her illness, may have upon her surviving friends, I have been induced to engage in the task of selecting a few of those expressions. As they show in an indubitable manner the advantages of religion, at a period when every other source of consolation would be inadequate, they may operate as a stimulus to those who are suffered to remain yet a little longer combatants on this stage of probation. And, oh! that we who were eye and ear witnesses of this triumph of religion, may, in an especial manner, evince by our conduct that it has been sanctified to us.

Ann Pumphrey was the daughter of Samuel and Elizabeth Baker, of Birmingham. Her mother died during her infancy, but her father marrying again, the loss was very much repaired by the care of her mother-in-law, of whose watchful attention and parental restraint she has frequently spoken with affection and gratitude; having witnessed the advantages which accrue from submission to those whose judgments are qualified to give counsel in the slippery paths of youth. She was in early life, as appears from some of her own memorandums, prone to vanity, and much inclined to follow the fashions and customs of a degenerate world; but, being followed by the reproofs of instruction which remain to be "the way of life," she was favoured to bow to them; and sweet was the reward of obedience. After patiently abiding under the preparing hand, she appeared in public ministry in the year 1790; and she was favoured to labour in the exercise of her gift to the edification of the church, not only at home, but abroad. Having, with the sanction and unity of her monthly meeting, travelled on a religious visit to Friends in Wales, in 1798 she accompanied her friend Sarah Lynes through the Midland and Northern counties of England; in the course of which journey much arduous and self-denying service was required and performed.

In the summer of 1800, she removed, on her marriage, to Worcester, where her conduct and conversation endeared her to Friends. She was a constant attender of meetings, except when indisposition, or the indispensable duties attached to a young family, prevented her. She was low in her own estimation, and charitable in judging of others; and gratitude for favours received was a prominent trait in her character. Of her journey through Wales, she has left an interesting narrative; and many fragments, found since her decease, are strongly characteristic of a mind seeking after durable riches.

Her last illness was an inflammation of the bowels, immediately following a lying-in, which was on the Sixth-day, 13th of Twelfth month, 1805. On the First and Second day following, her pain was very acute. She did not say much, but appeared in inward exercise of mind. On Third-day she began to consider her recovery as doubtful, and said to me, as I sat by her bedside, that she had anticipated peculiar pleasure in nursing this dear babe; and had, on mine and the dear children's account, been very desirous of being restored, if it had been the will of Providence. 'Neither was I,' continued she, 'without a prospect of further service in the Lord's cause, but I now believe the work will be cut short in righteousness. I found it hard work to get to a state of resignation; and to say, as I think I now can sincerely, "thy will be done." I feel very much for thee, my dear; I know thy loss will be very great; but seek after the resignation of pious Job, who, having witnessed great deprivations, was strengthened to say, "The Lord gave, and the Lord has taken away, blessed be the name of the Lord." I have no doubt but if I am taken from you, thou and the dear children will be abundantly cared for by the Father of mercies, if thou abidest in his fear. Should I recover, this will show what serious impressions a sick bed makes upon the mind. If I do not recover, it will be a consolation to my friends to know that I have nothing to do but to die: having an undoubted evidence of an admission into those regions of bliss, where the wicked cease from troubling, and where the weary are at rest.'

She remarked, that she had been thinking much of the description her dear Sarah (Grubb, late Lynes) had given her of the removal of her sister Moore, of whom there is an account in this volume; and thought she could adopt it as her own experience; that though she had found it very hard at first to leave her dear connexions, she was now favoured with that degree of resignation; and that she could give her directions as though she was setting out on a pleasant journey. And she did leave instructions, how she would have some things disposed of, with entire composure.

On Third-day night the fever ran high, and her sufferings were very great; but her head was preserved clear, and remained so to the last, and her faculties were not the least impaired.

On Fourth-day morning, the 18th, she signified a wish to see some of her near relations; and messengers were despatched to Birmingham and Alcester, with information of the alarming state in which she lay. In the course of the evening, her father and her brother James came. During this day she manifested great resignation to the divine will, and was often advocating the cause of truth. To her nurse, a person not of our religious society, for whom she had a great regard, she said, 'God is no respecter of persons; for all those that fear him and work righteousness, will be accepted of him, let their profession to religion be what it may. I am no bigot, but am fully of the belief that the faithful of all denominations will be accepted.' She expressed full satisfaction in all her nurse had done for her, and added that, though some things might not be quite palatable, she was sensible the fault was in her own taste, not in the cook; or words to that import.

Divers of her relations coming to see her, she expressed the sense she had of their kindness, and addressed several of them in a very edifying manner. She said that she was desirous that Friends of the place, when gathered in their religious meetings, would wait upon the Lord for the renewal of their strength; upon the Minister of ministers; who can restore judges as at the first, and counsellors as at the beginning; that He can qualify others to fill up the places of those whom he sees meet to take unto himself; and that He will do it, if there is but faithfulness to every manifestation of his will. She desired me to remember her affectionately to several, not of our religious Society, adding, 'I am no bigot. Pure religion is a very simple religion, and leads into great purity of conduct and conversation. Every one has an internal guide to eternal life, if they will but attend to it.' And on sending a similar message to some of her poor neighbours, she subjoined, "High and low, rich and poor, our heavenly Father made us all."

About twelve o'clock on Fourth-day night, we thought we observed an alarming alteration, and were very apprehensive her close was near at hand; but, contrary to our expectation, she revived, conversed pleasantly with a young Friend who sat up with her, and appeared tolerably free from pain. I had hitherto had but little rest since my dear wife's first attack, and yielded to the solicitations of my friends to go to bed; but was called up before day-light on Fifth-day, another alteration for the worse having taken place. The same morning, my father, Thomas Pumphrey, arrived from Alcester, and continued with us to the last, as also did Samuel Baker, his wife, and son.

This, and the day following, which was that immediately preceding the night of her dissolution, her mind seemed particularly engaged for the promotion of truth; and she was led to admonish and comfort many of her relations and friends who came to see her. She addressed her own aged father in the most affectionate terms, believing that he might adopt the language of the Psalmist, and say, "The Lord is my shepherd, I shall not want." She encouraged him to continue to trust in the Lord, who had been his shield through many trying dispensations; who had seen meet to comfort him with his rod and his staff; who had blessed him many ways, and would continue to bless him; that he had been the stay of his youth, and was now the staff of his old age. To her mother in law, she expressed how much she was obliged to her for the care exercised over her in her youth, adding, 'I believe the restraint that religious parents have over their children is often a great preservation from the many snares of life. I have reason to believe it was a great blessing to me that I was early restrained by my parents, my disposition being too much prone to vanity.'

Seeing her father, Pumphrey, in the room, she observed that she did not know he was there, but thought the same expressions of the Psalmist she had quoted to her own father were applicable to him. At another time, seeing him enter her chamber, she said, 'Dear man, he is one who loves the truth. Oh, what love I feel for all those who love and keep in the truth! Indeed, I feel nothing but love in my heart towards all men.'

Her nurse lying down upon the bed by her, she thought it had been her husband's sister, Ann, and was going to speak to her; but turning round, saw her mistake, and exclaimed, 'Ah, dear Mary, it is thee, is it?' and throwing her arm around her neck, with the utmost affection, she added, 'Thou hast been very kind indeed. I am abundantly obliged to thee. I am afraid I shall wear out your patience. She desired her sister Ann to give her dear love to her absent sisters, with desires for their preservation; adding, 'I delegate my precious boys, Samuel and Thomas, to your care. They have been much with you already. I am fully satisfied, and can leave them comfortably under your management. Give my love also to brother John; I wish he may follow those things that make for peace.'

I was at this time sitting behind, and supporting her, when she thus addressed me. 'Ah! my dear Stanley, didst thou think I forgot thee? No, though last mentioned, thou art my most beloved. I feel much for thee. I know thy loss will be very great; but the lenient hand of time will blunt the edge of grief, and thou wilt have many things to divert thy attention from the mournful subject. As I mentioned to thee before, I would have thee endeavour after the resignation of poor, pious, patient Job; who, when stripped of all, could say, the Lord gave, and the Lord has taken away; blessed be his name. It was he who brought us together, and it is a consolation that he has enabled us to keep our covenant. I hope he will be thy support; and he will, if thou art concerned to live in his fear.'

Speaking of the resigned state of her own mind, she said, 'Had I not attained this state of resignation, and been made willing to leave my dear husband and sweet babes; and my days had been lengthened out, but not in mercy, what an afflicting state would that have been; but I am enabled to resign all, and say, thy will be done in all things. "O death," she ejaculated, "where is thy sting? O grave, where is thy victory?" Death has no sting for me; neither has the grave any victory.' Again; "Many are the afflictions of the righteous; but the Lord will deliver them out of all their troubles."

Her disorder had now assumed a most serious aspect; and the surgeons (for a consulting surgeon had been called in) informed us of the great danger they apprehended. One time, when they had left the house, she asked what they thought; whether they did not conceive her case to be dangerous? Not receiving an immediate answer, she added, 'You need not be afraid to tell me: I am prepared.' The faculty are too apt to show what I consider an improper backwardness in making patients acquainted with their real state. I will tell you once for all, and then you will judge whether I have not great reason to be prepared. On Second day my mind was powerfully impressed with the message sent to king Hezekiah, "Set thy house in order, for thou shalt die, and not live." It naturally affected me; but I did hope for the sake of my dear husband and children, that, as the term was lengthened out to him, the like favour might have been mercifully vouchsafed to me. However, on Third-day the language intelligibly was, thou shalt not live, thou shalt surely die. So you see,' she repeated, 'I have great cause to be prepared.'

To a near and dear relation, who had been generally with her during her illness, she said, 'Thou hast been, my dear cousin, a kind attendant. Thy kindness hath soothed and comforted me, many times, under my great bodily affliction. I feel something pleasant whenever thou comest near me;

and I believe, my dear, thou wilt be rewarded both here and hereafter. I have often esteemed it a favour that I have been connected to such kind relations; and have many times been consoled by it.'

To a Friend of the meeting, who came to her, she spoke in very encouraging terms: 'I have sympathized with thee,' said she, 'and at times have felt the conflicts of thy poor mind, have been enabled to stand up, as I apprehend, for thy encouragement; and have craved that a double portion of the spirit of Elijah, may rest upon the Elishas. Oh, may you all be faithful to manifested duty; the way of truth is a very simple, plain way.' She expressed herself in an affectionate manner to the surgeon, and said she felt very grateful for the great attention he had shown, and was well satisfied with what he had done; that she hoped he would be rewarded, both in time and eternity. She also encouraged him to trust in the Almighty, who was no respecter of persons; but would reward all, according to their works.

Fifth-day night was a night of great bodily conflict. She was tried for the last day or two, with violent fits of coughing, which exhausted her so much, that we several times thought nature must yield. She would frequently say after such exertions, 'Oh, how thankful should I be for one hour's quiet before I go.' But many times when we conceived the conflict was nearly over, she would revive to admiration; and perhaps seeing a fresh face, or feeling her mind impressed with fresh instruction to those about her, would speak with the animation and perspicuity of one in full health and vigour. She sometimes said that she hoped she should not hurt herself; but when she felt any thing upon her mind, she could not refrain; 'For,' added she, 'I have but a short time to finish my work in.'

On one of these occasions two of her cousins came, whom she had previously expressed a desire to see, and whom she had not seen during her illness; but she was so ill, that at first it was judged improper to introduce them. Nevertheless, as her dissolution was, to all appearance, very near at hand, they were admitted to the foot of the bed; with no other view than that they might witness the last, sad, solemn scene. However, she revived again, and seeing them there, called them to her by name; and after addressing them in an edifying, affectionate manner, concluded with, 'Farewell, farewell; but remember, the way to farewell is to do well.' On my telling her she had contributed largely to our consolation under such affliction, and that it might perhaps be comfortable to her to hear the testimony which her father had just been giving of her, namely, 'that she had never, that he recollected, in the whole course of her life, in any one instance, wilfully offended him:' she replied, 'I always wished to be a dutiful child.'

She often expressed her gratitude for the care we took of her, so that she did not want for any thing, and was nicely waited upon. 'The kind attention,' she said, 'of my relations and friends on this occasion, has been great, and has tended to sweeten the bitter cup allotted me.' She requested her brother James to send to her friend Sarah Grubb the intelligence of her case; to give her dear love to her, and to her husband, and his relations; to inform her that the precious cement of affection and regard towards her remained unchanged; that she frequently recurred to the seasons of divine refreshment they had experienced together; and although she had had to drink many bitter cups, and to pass through deep baptisms with her: some of which had been as hard to the fleshly part, as the sacrifice of her natural life, (alluding to their exposure and service in the public markets;) yet she had never felt any opposition to it in her own mind, and believed it was in the line of required duty. She also often expressed her fears that her attendants would be overdone, and was anxious that they should take care of themselves, when they were manifesting attention to her.

On Sixth-day evening, the doctors called, and concluded

she could not live through the night. One of them called also the next morning. She was then very feeble, and her breathing extremely difficult; but in a state of entire composure and resignation. Indeed, during the whole course of her illness, she was not heard to utter a murmuring word; and said she had not even a murmuring thought. The whole of Sixth-day she was evidently in a dying state, and in the evening it was thought by all present that in a few more minutes the scene would close. Her relations were standing round the bed in solemn silence, and with mournful anxiety awaiting her last expiring breath. With a view to render respiration less difficult, two of us were affording her what air we could, by the help of fans; when, to our admiration, she revived, and said she should like to see her dear son Samuel, once more. This was at first rather discouraged, lest it should tend to discompose her: but she said, she thought she could bear it; and would endeavour not to distress the child. He was accordingly brought, and the interview astonished every one. Although we had been expecting every minute to be her last, she turned round, put on a smiling countenance to meet the child, kissed him, showed him one of the fans, observed how fine it was; she had not, she said, seen so fine a one many a day; told him to be a good boy, to give mother's love to his brother Thomas, and tell him to be a good boy; kissed him again, and bade him farewell. The child was no sooner gone than she exclaimed, "Great and marvellous are thy works, Lord God Almighty; just and true are all thy ways, thou King of saints!" 'It is the Lord's doing, and it is marvellous in my eyes. It must be his doing; for the more I consider how I am supported, the more I am surprised at it!'

She gradually grew weaker and weaker, till about one o'clock on Seventh-day morning, the 21st of the Twelfth month, 1805, when she quietly breathed her last, in the thirty-ninth year of her age, departing from the vicissitudes of time, to the unchanging happiness of eternity.

Thus did this amiable pattern of filial, conjugal, and parental affection, and of Christian patience and holy resignation, finish a comparatively short, but well spent life; leaving a memorable example of the enlivening, heart-consoling effects of religion upon the mind, at the awful period of dissolution. Oh, may the thoughtless be aroused to more reflection; and, impressed with a sense of the uncertainty of time, attend to the divine injunction, "Be ye also ready."

ANN TAYLOR, a young woman who died at Manchester, the 7th of the Fourth month, 1806, was the daughter of John and Ann Taylor, of that town, and born in the year 1788. She received the greater part of her education at home, and much of the latter part of the time, was usually employed in the acquirement of useful accomplishments, under the care of her father's second and surviving wife, Jane Taylor, formerly Jane Ellwood.

The following narrative of the happy temper of mind displayed by this pious maid in the course of her final illness, will show that the care extended to her had not been in vain. It will be related for the most part in the person, and in the words, of her affectionate mother-in-law.

On Fourth-day, the 25th of the Ninth month, 1805, she was much affected whilst in meeting, during the ministry of a Friend, who, among other things, had said, 'Day after day, week succeeding week, and year after year passeth away; and what preparation is made for our latter end?' The consideration, 'Am I ready for the awful change?' impressed the mind of Ann. Attending, after meeting, a corpse to the grave-yard, though then apparently in good health, she had a strong belief that her own interment would be soon. On the Seventh-day following she was taken ill with a spitting of blood, confined to bed for several days, and expressed some fear, lest she should be removed when unprepared: however, in about two weeks she was so far recovered as to be able to go about the house.

A short time after this partial amendment, the disease returned, and she appeared in great distress of mind, saying, 'I don't yet feel sufficiently prepared.' I asked her whether any particular thing stood in the way. She replied, 'I don't know of anything but a want of attention; not having my thoughts turned inward whilst in meetings; which I now see has been a great loss to me. By suffering my mind to ramble, I have wasted much precious time: surely it is playing the hypocrite. Seeing this to be the case, I resolved, when last at meeting, that, if permitted to go there again, I would be more careful and diligent; but [I] now believe I shall never go more.'

On my remarking it was a favour that our eyes were opened to see where we had omitted or committed anything, contrary to known duty, she replied, 'Yes, mother; and I hope to be very careful every way, the little time allotted me here; for all things are possible with him who knows what is best for us.'

She frequently took a retrospect of her life, and strictly scrutinized her conduct. 'I never, knowingly,' said she, 'told a falsehood, which now affords me great peace.' She often expressed a concern for several young Friends, who belonged to the same meeting, saying, 'I believe if some of them were laid upon a sick bed, as I am, they would see the folly of pursuing anything, but that which is most likely to fit them for an inheritance in the kingdom of heaven. But oh! how pure must all be, that enter in there! There are too few, when young, and in health, who think deeply enough of their latter end.'

She had many returns of her complaint; and she was favoured in a particular manner with patience and resignation. 'It is the Lord's doing,' said she, 'let him do what he will. I know it is for my refinement, and if I had a greater evidence of going well, I could leave all earthly things with joy; for it will be but a little time before those I leave behind me must go; yet I hope my great-Master will favour me with patience and resignation to wait his time.' I said, that I believed she would be favoured with greater assurance before leaving us. She answered, 'Then I want nothing more, but shall be happy.' One evening she said, 'I fear I have not loved my Maker so much as I ought; which may be the cause of his presence being so long withdrawn now in my affliction.' I observed to her, that the patience and resignation with which she was favoured, in so extraordinary a manner, came not from man. She answered, 'I hope to be preserved from murmuring, for that would be unwise on my part; and I give myself up entirely into my Maker's hands, to do with me as he sees best.'

She several times testified great compassion for her fellow-creatures, whose situation excluded them from even the common necessaries of life. 'How much,' said she, 'have I to be thankful for, being provided with every needful thing to relieve my bodily sufferings, and [also with] affectionate attention! There seems very little ground to hope for my recovery, yet it is not impossible; and if I should be restored to health, the rest of my days shall be spent to the honour of a merciful Creator; but I have little prospect of ever getting much better.'

One day she appeared very thoughtful, and expressed her great fear, that she was not yet enough prepared to meet the awful event. The next day she was visited by two Friends, one of whom said that the sweet, innocent state of Ann Taylor's mind, felt very precious to her. When they were gone, Ann said, 'I love the company of these friends, and would have such to come and see me:' and she several times desired that those who went into her room, would not converse about the common occurrences of the day; for her mind was much weaned from earthly things. A relation, who once came to see her, remarked her exemplary patience; and said, that when his time was so near a close, he should think it a great favour to experience the same degree of resignation. After he had left her, she said, 'I cannot expect to be rewarded like him. He has given up much; but what have I done to look for any reward? What crosses have I taken up for Christ's sake?' It was observed that she had denied herself of many gratifications, which some were indulging in, and such as many deem innocent and allowable. She replied, 'Yes, because I considered myself only a steward over everything I possessed; and believed it wrong to indulge in anything that would take up too much of my time, or fill my mind with what was unprofitable: and though I never felt uneasy with any part of my dress, yet I now believe it right to make clothing in a manner that will take up the least time. Convenience and cleanliness should be the only things looked to in apparel; for it is vanity to dress [adorn she probably meant] these poor bodies that are but dust.'

As her breathing became more difficult, her change seemed approaching fast; but she said, she felt very comfortable in herself. One evening, a woman-friend visiting her, mentioned her belief respecting the future well-being of Ann, and that her heavenly Father's arms were open to receive her. After this visitor was gone, she saw me shed tears, and said with an earnest tone of voice, 'Don't shed tears for me. I am going well.' This she expressed several times over. When we were by ourselves, she said, 'Mother, how can it be that the friend had to say that she wished her evidence might be as certain that she should enter into rest, as it was that I shall? What have I given up, compared with her?' After some little further conversation, she remarked, 'Thou knowest it is said, "In my Father's house there are many mansions:" and if I get to one of the very lowest, I shall be content.' She desired a friend in the room not to be so affected, for that she should soon be happy; and on my confirming this, with the expression of my belief, she said, with an overflow of affection, and a melody that can only be felt,

'Yes mother, yes; I shall be happy; and I hope thou and I shall meet there together.'

When her breathing became still more difficult, she continued patient; but she frequently prayed that she might have a little relief. When [thinking her end close at hand] I called up the family, she inquired whether I thought her going. I said, I believe so. 'Then,' said she, 'take leave of me, and give my love to Friends, and to every body.' Lying still a little, and feeling herself easier, she raised her voice, and addressed her sister in a distinct manner, as follows: 'Be kind to thy mother, and when poorly, wait on her, and do everything she wishes thee to do. Make a good use of thy money. Mind to give a great deal to the poor. Thou knowest that a short time since we were four; now three; and will soon be only two; then one; and so we pass away. Turning to me, she requested I would distribute some money to three poor widows, and mentioned the relieving of others in distress.

After this she laid down her head, and feeling herself better, said, 'Mother, I think thou may be mistaken. I am not going yet.' I told her that I believed she soon would, and her affection seemed again to overflow, and tendered every one around her. She bade each individual farewell, and in a distinct manner cried out, 'And now, O Father, if it be thy will, take me quickly.' Then having paused a little, she mentioned two young women, our servants. Being told they were in the room, she looked up, and again said, 'Farewell.' She then breathed shorter and shorter, till about seven o'clock in the morning, when, without a struggle, she breathed her last. She departed at the age of eighteen, on the 7th of the Fourth month, 1806.

ANN KNIGHT, daughter of Edward and Martha Knight, of Great Bardfield, in Essex, was removed from the trials and temptations of time, the 20th of the Fourth month, 1806, not having accomplished her sixteenth year. She was the eldest child of a numerous family, to which, as she was early addicted to piety, she was an excellent example. In early youth she preferred the company of those more advanced in years, to the amusements which commonly engage children: and was indeed herself of a riper understanding than is common.

It was her practice, when she retired for rest, to examine the transactions of the day; and when occasion of regret had occurred, she was not satisfied to sleep, until she felt that peace of mind which ensues from repentance. As one instance, her mother going to the bed-side, found her in tears. On being questioned as to the cause, she replied, 'On looking over the day, I find I was out of temper, and too cross to my little sister. I cannot go to sleep till I find forgiveness; and, dear mother, I hope thou wilt forgive me also; and then I can go to rest, and sleep sweetly!' It should, nevertheless, be remarked, that few children showed less of temper towards their younger brothers and sisters; few were more loving; and few endeavoured more to compose and settle their little differences: so that she had early her share in the blessed character of the peace-maker.

In our religious Society, in which vanity in dress is certainly more discouraged than in most others, which mingle in the common concerns of life, the restraints which prudent parents find necessary to impose on the disposition which is endeavouring to indulge it, are often irksome to the inexperienced and youthful mind. It appears that this pious maid had not been without her temptations this way; but disease had probably been the means of abating her desire to adorn a body, of the frailty of which it had warned her. The 26th of the Second month, she had returned in ill health from the house of a relation; and the following day she told her father that she once had thought that she should like to dress like others; 'But now,' said she, 'it is all done away. I have no desire for it at all:' and she added, that what would please her parents would please her; and that she was very sorry to see some of her relations run out in dress, and deviate from the plain language, and from their profession. 'They will find,' said she, 'that will not bring peace of mind.'

In a few days she was confined to bed, and said to her parents, 'I thought I should like to have stopped a little longer with you, if it had been the Lord's will. It is hard parting with you, but I hope I shall be resigned. You are very near and dear to me; but the Lord can make hard things easy.' It was remarked to her that He had done that for her many times; to which, with a raised voice, she replied, 'That he has, and I feel easy. I feel nothing to burden my mind, and that is a favour; but I hope I shall see my way clearer before I go:' and this, there is full reason to believe, she was favoured to do.

Between two and three weeks before she died, two of her brothers came home from school to see her. She told them that she was glad to see them once more in this world; and after pausing a little while, she exhorted them to fear the Lord, and to keep to plainness, in language and dress: saying, 'If you do not, it will bring a burden on your minds. I do not accuse you; but I know the enemy is very busy to draw away the mind, if you do not keep a watch.' Addressing also her parents, she said, 'I hope you will give me up to the Almighty's will. He is not a hard master; but a tender Father to his children that obey him. I have felt him underneath many times to keep me, when the enemy has been endeavouring to draw me aside from my watch, both when in meetings as well as out. But, blessed, be his holy name, he has preserved me; and he will also preserve you, if you obey him.'

She mourned, as has been already mentioned, over some of her relations, whom she apprehended to indulge too much in dress; an indulgence from which she had some years felt herself restrained: and she desired her father to write down her feelings, that he might not forget to tell them how much it had grieved her, that they should spend in it so much of their precious time. 'They will find,' said she, 'it will not bring peace of mind at such a time as this; and they know not how soon they may be brought as weak as I am.' She several times mentioned a first cousin, Ann Taylor, who had been at her father's house, in blooming health, the summer before she died (and whose happy exit has been just related); she compared her strength at that time with her present weakness; and said, 'I had a sense given me, I believe it was a divine intimation, that I should not see her again. I do not know which will go first.' They died within about thirteen days of each other.

At another time she lamented the vanity and luxury of the world; she remarked how the bountiful Giver had provided food and clothing for all, if it were rightly used; and she in particular lamented the vanity of dress, in such as frequent balls, and the like assemblies. 'Oh,' said she, 'what vanity! This is a world of trouble, and I am freely given up to leave it this night, if it be his will; as freely as I can sit by that fire-side. Eternity is awful, to be sure; but I hope and believe I shall be happy.'

Toward the close of her time she had violent pain in the bowels and limbs, which induced her to say, 'I hope patience will hold out. Dear father and mother, pray for me, that patience hold out.' She begged to be released, if it were the Lord's will: but she said, 'I hope I shall not be too anxious to be gone: I think I shall not.' After one of her fits of great pain, she lay still for a considerable time; and then said to her father, 'Dear father, how the Lord has been with me when I lay still. I was so comfortable, I thought I was in heaven; I was so happy, happy. Praised be his name for evermore! I cannot praise him enough, he has been so gracious. I was in hopes I was going. Pray do not hold me. I fear you hold me. If my pain come again, I know not what I shall do, lest I should murmur, and that would be a sad thing. Now I am happy. I hope patience will hold out.'

She exhorted a young man, an inmate in the family, to beware of unprofitable company, and of suffering his temper to arise. She reminded him that he might soon be brought as low as she was; and that then he would find it enough to struggle with the pains of the body.

A few days before her departure, early in the morning, after having lain very composedly for some hours, she called to her mother and said, 'My dearly beloved mother, I have something to tell thee. This has been a blessed night to me. I have seen heaven, and they are all happy, happy, there. The Almighty has been so near me. I thought he bid me take leave of all the world: which I can freely do, to possess that peace and happiness which I have seen; yea, for the lowest place in heaven; as the things of this world signify nothing to me; no, not in the least. No matter what becomes of this bit of clay, when the spirit is gone to heaven. Do not put yourselves to much expense in burying me.' After this, reviving after a convulsion fit, she said, 'I thought I had been going; but I could not go, without once more praising the Lord. Where are the dear children? Bid them fear the Lord, and love the Lord Jesus.'

The day before she died, inquiring the day of the week, and being informed, she said, 'It is Seventh-day again, and I am here yet. I want to be gone, but hope I shall have patience to wait the Lord's time. That is the best time.' The day of her release, she desired her parents to pray to the Lord for her, that she might have an easy passage. This petition appeared to be granted. She fell asleep for a few minutes, and, without one sigh, expired.

HANNAH MARIA MILES, daughter of Robert and Hannah Miles, of Melbury Abbotts, near Shaftsbury, Dorsetshire, was born in the early part of the year 1787. Her parents joined the Society of Friends by convincement, about the year 1796, when their daughter was a child of nine years of age. From her childhood she was serious, and orderly in her conduct.

When she had attained the state of a young woman, she was seized with a pulmonary consumption, which gradually brought on her dissolution. In the early stage of her illness, she was sensible that she should not recover, and she expressed herself on this wise: 'I am very unwell, and believe I shall not recover, but shall have a lingering illness. I should not mind it if I had spent my time better; for I have seen enough of this world, not to wish to live any longer in it, if I had true peace of mind. I have given way to many hurtful things, such as dress, not so consistent as it ought to have been; likewise reading improper books, which, if it have no other bad tendency, takes up that time which may be better employed. I sincerely hope, that our family may be careful to avoid those hurtful and hindering things; and not put off the great work until sickness come. I have had many good meetings and precious visitations, but too soon forgot them.' She also said, 'It is some satisfaction to me that I have been preserved from talking much when in company; but I have nothing to boast.'

Her distress continued for some time; but once, being asked whether she felt her mind more composed, she replied, 'I hope it will be better, but must not expect it at once.' Some weeks afterwards, on a First-day, she became much more indisposed; when no one was present with her but her mother. After a season of quiet she said, 'Dear mother, I have heard, as it were, a voice sounding in my ear, "Watch and pray, lest ye enter into temptation."' Her mother advising her to attend to it, as to a loud call, she replied, 'I hope I shall, for I think I cannot be with you long.' The mother observing, that the parting with her would be a bitter cup, Maria answered, 'I hope, my dear mother, thou wilt be resigned, and give me up; for thou hast many others left, if I should be taken. Yet I think it will be a great trial to thee; but the Lord gave, and it will be the Lord that taketh away.'

For some weeks she did not say much by way of religious communication; but she often seemed in deep retirement. Having at one time been left alone, she was afterwards found in tears, and the cause being inquired, 'I have reason,' said she, 'to be thankful that I was not taken away suddenly: if I had, it would, I fear, have been bad for me.' Some time after this, two friends paid her a visit, which seemed to be very helpful and strengthening to her mind, for she appeared generally calm and composed. Reading the Scriptures was her daily practice and delight; and there is reason to believe they were much, and profitably opened to her understanding. When it was thought advisable to employ a physician, she remarked that it was the last trial; and that if it would be any satisfaction to her relations she was content, but that she did not think it would be of use to herself. Her mother once expressing a hope that some means might prove helpful to her recovery; 'No,' said she, 'I do not expect it; for I believe more good will be done by my death than if I was to recover.'

About the time the physician was employed, she was again visited by a ministering friend, whose testimony seemed to be the means of setting her at liberty, and making way for her to declare her own exercises, and to impart advice to those about her. Soon after this visit, a violent bleeding at the nose came on, which rendered her so weak, that she lay in a sort of stupor for some days. At length she revived, and expressed herself thus: 'I thought I should have gone before now, but I seem a little recovered for the present, but it will not be long.' Seeing her sister much affected, she said, 'Dear sister, do not grieve too much; for though we love one another dearly, and I know thou wilt miss me, yet we must part some time or other, and why not now?' adding solemnly, after a pause, 'Yes, it will be now.'

To her two eldest brothers she said, 'O brothers, I hope you will seek the Lord in time of health, for it is a great blessing. I have a great love for you, and I may be taken away suddenly, but [I] hope you will remember what I have said to you.' Her aunt, Charlotte Matilda Burt, coming into the room, she said, 'Dear aunt, thou dost not shun a sick house; but it may be best for thee: for it is better to go to the house of mourning than to the house of feasting. Seek the Lord, for it is not such a very hard thing. Seek ye him, and he will be found of you.'

Some days after, her grandfather, John Miles of Cann, near Shaftsbury, came to see her. She was then very weak, and her breathing difficult; but on his coming into the room, she addressed him thus: 'O, dear grandfather, do thou seek the Lord God, for he is merciful. Thou art an old man, and ought to be prepared; for there are so many sudden deaths, that we know not how soon we may be taken. Do thou, dear grandfather, prepare to meet me in heaven. I have great love for thee and my dear grandmother. Seek ye him, that he may be found of you.' She then sat still a while, after which, assisted by her sister, she kneeled down and prayed for her grandfather, and all her dear relations. On rising from her knees, she seemed much refreshed, and even her breathing became easier than it had been before this religious exercise.

Awaking one evening from an uneasy slumber, she exclaimed, 'What have I to do with thee? Get thee behind me, Satan;' and then she fervently prayed, 'O Lord, do thou protect me, and support me under the afflictions of the body. O Lord, thou knowest thou art dear to me, and if it be thy blessed will, take me to thyself, from the various pains and tribulations of this life: yet not my will, but thine be done, O Lord.'

Her parents remarking that they had great reason to be thankful, on her account: though their loss would be great, it would be her gain; and therefore they hoped to be resigned, believing that she was; she replied 'Yes. I have given you all up: for "they that love father or mother more than me, are not worthy of me." Yet I have had a hard struggle with myself to give up such near and dear relations.' Being asked if she would be content to be restored again, if it were the Divine will, she said, 'I hope I should; but I had rather go now;' adding, 'Not my will be done, but thine, O Lord.' She then desired to see all her little brothers, and her sister Emma. She took an affectionate leave of them, after praying fervently for their true preservation in this life, and more not recollected. As her cough was now very troublesome, and she found increased weakness, she did not at this time expect to live over the night; but requested the company of her parents and the elder part of their family. To each of these she spoke in great tenderness, and gave them individually memorable advice.

Continuing to apprehend that her close was at hand, she again was engaged in supplication, on this wise. 'O Lord, do thou be pleased to take me this night, if it be thy will; and grant me an easy passage out of this world to the next. O Lord, I pray thee, take me to thyself whilst my lamp is burning, that I may not be like the foolish ones, who, when the bridegroom came, their lamps were gone out.' After this she took, with great composure, an affectionate leave of each one present. 'Give my dear love,' she added, 'to my sister Betsy, and tell her to remember what I said to her when she was at home, and then all will be well.' After this she again uttered the language of supplication, 'O Lord, do thou be pleased to give me an easy passage out of this world to the realms of bliss.'

A pause of stillness ensued, but in a short time she broke forth as in ecstacy: 'Oh! it seems to me I see the angels walk in white robes! O death, where is thy sting? O grave, where is thy victory? What hath Jesus done for poor sinners? He bled and died for us! Oh, what sweetness have I felt in my affliction: that peace which nothing in this world can give or take away! Some time since I thought I felt something like peace, but it was not the true rest, for I was then in a doubting state; but when I came to believe, no tongue can describe the sweetness I then felt!'

When morning was approaching, she said, 'I did not think to see the light of another day; but I believe I have something to say to some one not present;' and she inquired whether any one were expected that day. Being answered 'No,' she replied, 'I think there is.' The sequel proved her apprehension to be just; for her uncle, John Miles, of Gillingham, who had not visited her before during her illness, came that day to see her; to whom she freely imparted what was on her mind for him.

For two weeks after this, she was much employed in speaking to several of her relations in a powerful and affecting manner, by which her bodily strength appeared to be further impaired. The last person who saw her, those of the family excepted, was her maternal grandfather, Thomas Burt, also of Gillingham. To him she had much to communicate, and she also prayed fervently for him, and for her absent grandmother. The week following, her debility increased, and she appeared thankful that her exercise of mind for her relations was over. She expressed her hope that she had not spoken in her own strength; and on being cautioned against exerting herself too much, she cheerfully replied, 'Never mind the poor body.' She often continued to pray for patience to endure the oppressive weakness of her frame, and to hold out to the end. At one time she said to her father, 'I do sincerely wish, if it is the Lord's will, I may be taken to-night; and buried at the monthly meeting, as there may be a large gathering of Friends, that if any thing is said, it may be for the benefit of my dear relations.'

Two days before her decease, she became at times delirious, through weakness. She observed it herself, saying, 'My poor head is not quite right;' and she testified her thankfulness that she had been favoured with her reason so long. Once she said, 'Pray for me, for my weakness is so great, that I fear I shall not be able to pray for myself.' She was desired to turn her mind inward, and it was hinted to her that words mattered not. She answered, 'No,' and was afterwards often observed as in supplication. About this time she said, 'Oh, the enemy will be busy, but I hope my patience will hold out to the end;' adding, 'My trust is in the Lord.'

Her cough had now left her, and her breathing was become more difficult; so that though she often spoke, the whole of what she said could not be distinctly understood. Thus she once began, 'The Lord is my staff;' the remainder was not clearly comprehended. On the last evening of her life, she spoke thus to her sister: 'O Fanny, when thou art in the situation thou seest me in, do bear it with patience and Christian fortitude: and I believe thou wilt, as his grace is sufficient for thee.' Then she prayed again: 'O Lord, if it be thy will, take me this night out of this pain and affliction of body.'

At length the approach of death still further impaired her speech; but she desired to be turned on one side, and having taken a small quantity of wine and water, with an expressive look she said, 'No more.' Her parents were sitting by her, when with great composure and sweetness she took both their hands, and for a considerable time held them in her own, then cold with departing life. The scene was affecting, and she requested all present to be very still; but in a while remarked, that her breathing was so laborious, that she could not be so still as she could wish. After this, however, she did lie more still for some time, and her breathing seemed less difficult for a few minutes: when, reposing her head on one hand, whilst her mother held the other, she softly drew her last breath, as the infant drops into the slumber of repose.

JACOB BELL was born the 17th of the Fourth month, 1737, Old Style, in London; and departed at Plaistow, in Essex, the 19th of the Twelfth month, 1806. His parents were Jacob and Margaret Bell, of London. He resided the chief part of his life in the city of London, afterwards in Wapping, then for a short time at Ilford in Essex, and lastly at Plaistow.

According to his own account, his mind was sweetly impressed with the love of God at an early age; but not sufficiently abiding under its holy influence, he too much yielded to his natural inclinations, particularly in vanity of dress; though in this, it is probable, his subsequent humility, and the consciousness of motive, overrated his juvenile vanity. Nevertheless, to continue his own relation, the Almighty so followed him, by the Spirit of his Son, Christ Jesus, that he was preserved from gross evils; and at length, by means of some close trials, he was brought to serious reflection, and witnessed "repentance to salvation not to be repented of."

He married, in 1771, Sarah, daughter of James and Anna Sheppard, of Wapping; and of ten children who were born from this marriage, four only survived their father: so that he was no stranger to that great domestic affliction, which arises from being bereft of children. Of one of these, an account is given in order of date in the present volume.

His first appearance in public testimony was in the year 1774, when he was about thirty-seven years of age. This engagement was not only entered on, but continued in, very much in a cross to his own will, and at first with great difficulty. Through life he was a man that avoided public notice; yet, persevering steadily through the difficulties incident to his peculiar turn of mind, and careful to endeavour after due evidence of the requiring, he became an acceptable and lively minister.

At different times during the latter part of his life, in which he had laid aside the engagements of trade, he visited with certificate a great part of the meetings of friends in

Great Britain, with the Isles of Wight, Guernsey, and Jersey; and also sometimes appointed meetings among persons of other religious professions. His last journey of this kind was entered on, under the pressure of recent afflictions from the loss of children: one of them the youth already hinted at. He was then in his sixty-ninth year; and it fell to my lot to be a witness to his conflict; when, on one hand, life was fast ebbing from a beloved and hopeful son; and, on the other, the time for setting out on his mission was fast approaching. Death, that death I trust which is the entrance to life, even the death of the righteous—death decided the question: he followed the remains of his son to the grave, and as it were, consecrated his sorrows in the service of his Lord. When he came back from this journey, which was to Guernsey, Jersey, &c., and returned his certificate to the monthly meeting, he bore his testimony, in much tenderness of spirit, to the goodness of the Lord, in sustaining him through this engagement: peculiarly arduous to him at that time.

He was a man humble in spirit, and a great lover of retirement, very diligent and exemplary in the attendance of religious meetings, and careful over his own family.

The state of his mind in the near prospect of his approaching dissolution, may appear from a passage in some notes of his, dated a few weeks before his departure, and left in his own handwriting. After remarking that he had great consolation in looking back, having been preserved solely by the arm of Divine strength, from many dangers in the progress of life, he adds, 'Thanks be to God; I trust, through his mercy, I am yet in the road to that city, whose walls are salvation, and whose gates are praise; and do feel, according to my measure, that quiet and resignation under my present indisposition, that I am made easy as to the event; desiring that the Lord would favour with his continued protection through the varied dispensations of his providence. Then, I have to believe, I trust from a well-grounded hope, that all will be well.'

HANNAH BOWLY was the daughter of Daniel and Sarah Bowly, of Cirencester, in which place she was born, in the year 1763. In the early part of her life, and as she was advancing to her twentieth year, she seemed much inclined to reject the simple attire of a Friend; and having about this time a visit to Bristol in prospect, she provided herself with gayer apparel than she had been accustomed to wear. But in Bristol her career of vanity received a check, and her mind was favoured with religious impressions, by means of the ministry of Robert Valentine of Pennsylvania. Her gay attire was soon laid aside, and she became a consistent and conspicuous example in her father's family. She remained at home during the lives of both her parents; but soon after the decease of her mother and surviving parent, she resided a while with a brother; and afterwards with a niece, who jointly with another friend, kept a school for girls in Cirencester. After some time, the school was given up, but she still remained on the spot, till, on the decease of her brother, before mentioned, (whom she tenderly and closely attended in his illness,) she at length finally settled, for the short remainder of her life, in the habitation from which death had removed him.

Before a survey is taken of the closing days of this Friend, it will be useful further to remark, that by nature her temper was high and inflexible. Of the effects of Divine grace it is not, probably, for man to say which is the greatest. His limited capacity should make him cautious in judging. But it may possibly be said without presumption, the redemption generally appears to have a brightness, proportioned to the previous bondage. Nor is this confession of what she was in her nature, derogatory to her character; since she willingly yielded herself up to follow a meek and humble Saviour, when she perceived upon her mind the attractions of his love. It may also convey encouragement to others, who think they feel their own complexions and tempers, unfavourable to the growth of that true Christian humility, which their enlightened judgment approves and desires, if the triumph of grace be here more fully set forth, by the knowledge of what it had to overcome.

Hannah Bowly was taken ill on the last day of the year 1806, with a sudden and very considerable discharge of blood; supposed to arise from the rupture of some vessels in the lungs. She was almost immediately confined to her bed, which she kept for the most part during three months. Towards, however, the latter part of this time, symptoms of amendment appeared, and she was able to remain up some hours of each day; till at length one forenoon, as she was preparing to sit up, another violent discharge of blood took place, which seemed to suffocate her, and she expired. Her decease was in her forty-fourth year, on the 21st of the Third month, 1807.

The retired state of her mind during the intervening time was very instructive; and bespoke her reliance on the same Divine power that had visited her in more early life. But she was at times much tried for want of that assurance, for which she earnestly waited; and in attaining which, she was in mercy enabled to say, 'I can now call God, Father.' It was under great depression that once she said, 'My mind seems to partake with my body in weakness;' and that she repeated those awful words, "My God, my God, why hast thou forsaken me?" 'This,' said she, 'was the language of the Saviour; and I suppose this deprivation is needful to complete the cup here.'

She contessed to a relation, that she had to regret the not having attended to some manifestations of duty. 'These omissions,' said she, 'have lain heavy upon me; but now they seem removed. By resisting secret apprehended calls publicly to espouse and exalt the cause in meetings, I have sometimes involved myself in unspeakable gloom, and incurred weakness many ways. I might not now have been in this situation, if I had given up in simple obedience. I may possibly recover, which if I do, and feel an impulse in the same way, I hope I should be faithful, but never forward. My heart seems now remarkably bound to the willing in Israel. I hope impressions received at this time will be so indelibly fixed, as to produce submission to any service that may be pointed out as duty, should my life be lengthened; for which I have no desire, but to evince myself more zealously bound, in heart and mind, with those who are pursuing the right way. But I know not how far I might withstand the besetments, snares, and trials of time. I believe I should have as much need of the prayers of my friends in life, as in death. Perhaps some may think I am taken away because more enveloped in the gratifications of time; but they have not been such to me; for of late, in particular, surrounding things have been more burdensome than pleasant. It now affords me comfort, that I am conscious of not intending to make a show with the addition to my income, or spending it for self-gratification: but I designed applying it to useful purposes, that would yield solid satisfaction. If I were to live longer, and enjoy all the comforts of this life, I might not be more fit to go than now. I look back on all the accommodations of it, without any regret in leaving them.'

At another time, she said, 'Yesterday, I anticipated, not with pleasure, a lengthened illness; but the exertion of leaving my bed, to have it made, in the evening, convinced me of such increased weakness, that I need not fear a long continuance. I am very comfortable. How thankful I ought to be, for the sweet support I feel! I trust death is now robbed of its terrors; but not of its awfulness.'

Mentioning once the opportunities of speaking to divers of her friends, which she had had during her illness, she said, 'I hope what I have expressed will not do any harm, and have not been words without knowledge; neither have I spoken from premeditation, but simply from fresh arisings. If I could do anything to help those philosophers, who believe, or try to believe, in the sufficiency of reason for the guide of conduct, I should rejoice to do it; but such are not easily reached, even by what is uttered from dying lips: having fortified themselves against such communications.' A friend present asked her whether she did not think examples of consistent Christian conduct to be the most convincing to such sort of people. She replied, that she believed they were.

At another time she observed, that the Holy Scriptures were an invaluable treasure. 'They have many times,' said she, 'afforded me great comfort, and I regret not having read them more. What beautiful, instructive passages they contain! I once had a sweet opening, that was given me, I thought, chiefly for encouraging instruction to myself; and that, if I yielded entire obedience to divine requirings, swords should be beaten into plough-shares, and spears into pruning-hooks: those strong powers and dispositions of the mind, comparable to hurtful weapons, instead of being destructive, should be so sanctified, as to be turned into usefulness in the vineyard.'

As her strength decreased, she was favoured with great tranquillity of mind. Several times she said, 'I feel peaceful poverty.' At other times she abounded, by the prevalence of a lively faith, which gave her ability to say, 'I feel unmoved confidence, supporting me, and opening my prospects to brighter scenes.' Once she added, 'I believe, however gloomy and discouraging the appearance of things relating to the state of our Society may be, that some will see brighter days; and that its testimonies will continue to be maintained by some, in their purity: and a succession of those [will be] prepared, who will support the ministry. I think the solicitude I now feel on account of others, is not so much on account of individuals, near connections, or families; but that the real right may increase and prevail amongst Friends generally: true, right, ancient simplicity.'

She one night asked a Friend, who was sitting up with her, whether she thought that there would be, in a future state, a knowledge of each other; and remarked that some were of that opinion. But Hannah confessed the question to be above her comprehension. She said there was something pleasing and gratifying in it; yet that she thought looking that way was looking short of one great object of eternal enjoyment and adoration. She thought that not to be the best aspiration of soul which desired any felicity but that which proceeds from the Divine presence.

Once, when very low in body, she was also much contrited in mind, and said, 'I feel as unworthy to approach the throne of grace as it is possible for any poor mortal to feel. So abased am I to dust and ashes, [that] the reduction, the nothingness, I am brought into, is not to be described or conceived. It may partly be occasioned by the connection of the mind with the body. It is very trying and proving to bear: but may contribute to the work of preparation for a triumphant end. Though I have no cause to presume mine will be evidently so, yet I am favoured with a consoling, supporting hope, that, through adorable mercy, I shall sing of victory hereafter.'

She mentioned one day the saying of Richard Hubberthorne,* one of our early Friends, in his illness: 'Out of this straitness, I must go; for I am wound up into largeness; and am to be lifted up on high, far above all.' 'With humble admiration,' said she, 'for all boasting is excluded, it has seemed to me that I can now adopt this expression.'

The last instance which it may be necessary to give of her mind being fixed on the Lord, may be that of her adopting the words of a still more ancient servant, in his day; and whose writings the spiritual traveller still feels fraught with

* R. Hubberthorne died in Newgate in the year 1662, whither he had been committed, after some personal abuse, by a persecuting alderman, in consequence of being taken up at the Bull-and-Mouth meeting. The prison was then crowded with Friends, and the noisome confinement probably occasioned not only this Friend's death, but that of his fellow prisoner, Edward Burrough. See Sewell's History — Anno. 1662.

consolation, when permitted not merely to read, but to feel their energy. Her mind seemed tenderly affected with the incomes of the love of her God, and she said that she had been thinking of some comfortable expressions of David. Then in a sweet manner she repeated several. "Bless the Lord, O my soul, and forget not all his benefits: who forgiveth all thine iniquities, who healeth all thy diseases, who redeemeth thy life from destruction, who crowneth thee with loving kindness and tender mercies."

HANNAH HALL.—It often happens, and it is cause of reverent thankfulness that it is so, that tedious sickness is allowed to be the means of refinement and preparation for the great change. Happy also is it for such as have "their loins girded, and their lamps burning," and are ready at a short notice to meet the bridegroom. This seems to have been the case of HANNAH HALL, of Little Broughton, near Cockermouth, in Cumberland.

She was the daughter of William and Rachel Wigham, of Cornwood, in Northumberland, and was born in the year 1747. A few years after her marriage with John Hall, of Broughton, and about the twenty-seventh year of her age, she came forth in a public testimony in meetings, and her services were acceptable to Friends.

She did not travel much, but had a large family to watch over, which she brought up in an exemplary manner, and was herself a pattern of economy and industry. Nevertheless, in 1783, she visited meetings in Lancashire and Cheshire, in company with her mother, a valuable minister; and about ten years afterwards, paid a religious visit, in company with some other Friends, to the inhabitants of the Isle of Man. In this visit her short and lively offerings seemed often to open the way to larger communications of her companions. In 1801, she visited the meetings in Scotland;

and afterward the families in the greatest part of her own monthly meeting of Pardshaw: where she was herself a diligent attender of meetings, and esteemed as a woman of a meek and quiet spirit.

She often proclaimed the uncertainty of life, and was strenuous in exhorting all to make timely preparation for their solemn and final change; and in both these respects was herself an example, for she was removed, at about the age of sixty, by a violent disorder, in twenty-four hours. She expressed an unshaken confidence that a place of rest would be her allotment, when the pains and conflicts of time should pass away. Her decease was on the 29th of the Fourth month, 1807, and her last moments, so far as an indistinct articulation could be understood, were employed in solemn supplication.

JOB THOMAS. — In adding to the accounts, prepared for this volume, of the happy departure of many faithful servants of the Lord, that of the triumphant conclusion of JOB THOMAS, I feel an inclination to avow that I consider it as no light employment. He appears to have been favoured with a more immediate manifestation of the glorious state which was about to crown his suffering life, than is commonly allowed to spirits yet clothed with mortality. The veil seemed to be withdrawn: the beatific vision to be displayed. He spoke of what he saw, and was on the point of possessing; and if it be lawful to publish an account of condescension so transcendent, of mysteries so sacred, of glories so infinite, I can hardly believe that admiration is the only feeling that should be excited by the perusal. There is a holy awe, a reverential dread, that seems to be due from the awakened mind, on being thus, as it were, a witness of a frail mortal putting on a glorious immortality. And when we almost see the omnipotent and righteous Judge dispensing his reward with his own holy hand; and placing on the Christian the crown of righteousness; surely deep self-abasement should possess the creature, and the heart of every reader should bow before him, who holds these infinite and inestimable treasures at his will: and, as a part of that holy will, has made known that, through the redeeming virtue of his beloved Son, they are accessible to the broken and contrite spirit.

But before we survey the conclusion, let us advert to the path, through which, this, our departed Friend, was led to blessedness, so far as it is known.

His youth, probably, had been tinctured with some of the vanities incident to that stage of life: for he has been frequently heard to lament that he had not been more obedient to the Lord's requirings in early life. But he was scarcely known to his surviving friends in any other capacity than that of a diligent attender of meetings for worship and discipline, an approved minister, sound in doctrine, and holding fast without wavering the profession of the Christian faith. Gospel love enlarged his heart, and he had an universal desire for the salvation of his fellow-creatures. He was bold in delivering plain truths, and in the Welch, his native tongue, he was persuasive, clear, and fluent. His religious visits, however, were much confined to Wales; the meetings of Friends in which principality he visited several times; and, in the compass of the monthly meeting to which he belonged, he frequently had more public meetings with those of other societies.

He once attended, as a representative, the Yearly Meeting in London; and when in this great city, his heart yearned towards his numerous countrymen, dispersed within its circuit. He wished to have a meeting with them, but as he had not, on leaving home, asked for a certificate of his monthly meeting's approbation of his then travelling in the ministry, it was judged irregular to convene one: and his disability of body not long after supervening, an opportunity did not again occur.

In the estimation of the world he would have been accounted a poor man; and his habitation was certainly mean. It was a small farm house in Caermathenshire: such as, on this side the Severn, would be called a cottage; retired and sequestered, but not far distant from the public road; and nearly midway between Llandovery and Llandilo. Yet here he was hospitable, and gladly received his friends; of which hospitality I can testify from experience. His means of support arose not only from the trade of a shoemaker, but from the occupancy of a small farm.

About the year 1797, near his own dwelling, he was thrown from a young horse, and received so great an injury on the spine, as at length to occasion the deprivation of voluntary motion in every limb. His head, only, remained subject to his will. This he could still turn, whilst he was beholden to personal assistance for his removal from his bed to his chair, for any slight alteration of position in it, and in short, for almost every common function of the body: the free performance of which, though it is scarcely observed by the healthy and vigorous, constitutes much of the comfort of animal life. But his body, thus deprived of motion, was still sensible to pain: and much, very much, of this positive affliction was added to the negative one of total helplessness. He used to be fastened, rather than to sit, in a chair, and his body and legs were nearly in one strait and stiff line; with his useless arms lying before him, and his bowels, or some other of the interior parts, often grievously affected with violent pain: to which his worn and pallid countenance gave ample testimony. Yet his mind seems to have been unimpaired. He received much comfort from the visits of his friends, especially of such as he esteemed alive in the truth; he kept up religious meetings in his house, and often laboured in them in doctrine, for the edification of those who were assembled with him; and he dictated some epistles.

It was my lot to see him three times during this trying confinement. The first time was in 1802, in company with several others, and among the rest a ministering Friend, on her way to embark at Milford, for a religious visit in Ireland. As I remember, he was at that time very lively in his spirit, and imparted much encouragement to the travelling minister; but I am not quite sure whether it was at this, or at a succeeding visit that I was particularly struck, if not edified, with observing how steadfastly his mind seemed to be anchored in Christ; and hearing how clearly and fully he spoke of that confidence.

Thus suffering, and thus supported, he continued about ten years. At length, towards the beginning of the Eighth month, 1807, his symptoms of disease increased, and on the 15th of that month, being considerably more indisposed in bodily health, he called his wife and son to his bed-side; and, with a pleasant countenance, spoke to them, in the Welsh language, nearly as follows.

He inquired of them, whether they had any thing to say to him; 'for,' said he, 'the blessed hours are approaching; yea; and before this night I shall have escaped in safety, where neither trials nor troubles shall come. Be content, and do not grieve after me; for I am setting off to endless joy, to praise him who has brought me patiently through the whole of my troubles, and inexpressible afflictions. Support me, O Lord, for these few minutes; for I am nearly come beyond the boundary of time, to a boundless eternity. I am now near giving you the last farewell; but take warning, and be daily on your watch, for, in the hour you do not suspect, death, namely, the king of terrors, will come to meet you, who will make no difference between one or the other. But in the strength and love of Jehovah, you will not fear death; if you seek him whilst he is to be found, and serve him with a willing mind and an obedient heart; for his paths are paths of peace, and his ways are ways of pleasantness. O, pray continually to the Lord, to draw your desires and affections from off earthly things, and to establish them upon things heavenly and everlasting.

'My hope is in the mercy of him, who has washed me in the fountain set open for the house of David, and the inhabitants of Jerusalem. Not through my own merits, but through the merits of the crucified Immanuel, who died for the sins of all mankind. And you who have to remain a little after me, give the praise, the reverence, and the honour to him; and supplicate day and night before his throne, until you have certain knowledge that you have been baptized with the baptism of the Holy Spirit; which was sealed by the blood of the everlasting covenant. Remember, it is not an outward baptism that will serve; which is but the practising the old shadows. Know also, that it is not the profession of religion that will do; but one that is pure and undefiled before God. This will conduct you in safety to the everlasting habitations.

'Now the time of my dissolution draws nigh; for me to go to the place where I have been these two nights. The Lord himself came to meet me; and took me with him to the height of heaven; among myriads of his holy angels; where his saints were before him, and will be forever.

'Behold, now I give up the spirit: and lo! my comely companions, coming to hold my head above the waves of Jordan. Behold! the gates of heaven open, and the Lord himself with arms stretched out to receive me to his mercy. I hope that you, who are behind will follow me thither. Success to the gospel from sea to sea, and from the river to the end of the earth: also to my dear brethren; that they may persevere in their faith to the end of their days, and then their rest will be with the Lamb, where no pain or affliction will come.

'Behold, the blessed time is come, for me to depart in peace with every one, with good desires for every one, and forgiving every one. Receive my last farewell, and the Lord bless you with the blessings of Mount Zion.'

Having uttered these expressions, he soon quietly breathed his last. The end of this man was peace!

MARY STANSFIELD, wife of John Stansfield, of Lothersdale, in the West Riding of Yorkshire, was daughter of John Slater, of the same place, and grand-daughter of Mary Slater, mentioned in the Eighth part of Piety Promoted. She was, when an infant, deprived of the benefit of a mother's care, the decease of her own falling out soon after her birth; but she grew up in stability of conduct, so as not only to be able to attend to her father's domestic concerns; but as, for a considerable time before his decease, he was much disabled from attending to his trade, she had the management of that also: and after she lost this surviving parent, she continued it till her marriage with John Stansfield, also of Lothersdale.

It has been already mentioned, in this volume, in the memoir concerning Joseph Brown, that seven persons were, with him, committed to the county jail of York Castle, on an exchequer process for non-payment of small tithes. One of these was John Stansfield, the husband of Mary; but the suit had been commenced, and had been long carried on, even after her marriage, in the name of Mary Slater. This induced her to believe that, in the long-expected issue of the prosecution, her own person would be the victim of the asperity with which it was conducted; and she endeavoured to reconcile her mind to it, and to prepare for it, by weaning an infant at the breast. Nor was her resignation to suffer, and her preparation of mind, lost on her, when it was determined that her husband should be the imprisoned person: she bore the separation, and his absence, with becoming fortitude; and was chiefly desirous that the testimony which they believed themselves required to bear, might not be weakened by any improper conduct on their part.

When the prosecution at length issued, as has been already related, in distraints of the goods and property of the prisoners, her only care seemed to be lest she should not have one good bed left, for the accommodation of travelling Friends; as the house had long been a free and hospitable place of entertainment for such visitors. She was not, however, tried to so great a degree as this; and indeed, not only during the whole of this trying business, but in other parts of her conduct, she seems to have been a preacher of righteousness. She was a woman much beloved, and her decease was felt as a general loss in her neighbourhood, both by Friends and others; for her disposition to perform the duties of social life, by rendering assistance to those who were in need of it, was considered as fully equal to the ability which she possessed.

Having thus endeavoured to be upright in her day, she was further enabled to support the character of a pious woman, during a long and painful illness. In the early part of this suffering dispensation, she committed to writing some of the feelings of her mind, and the following brief extract is taken from that memorial: 'Having of late felt my mind much tendered at times, through the Lord's unspeakable goodness to a poor unworthy creature, I trust, if I be removed, it will be in mercy: and from my feelings at this time, [I] think I can say, The Lord's will be done.'

After this, however, she passed through some deep baptisms. She often said that her pains of body were permitted for good, being intended for her further refinement; and that she believed it would be well with her when her sufferings were over. Though these were great indeed, 'they were light,' said she, 'in comparison of those experienced by our blessed Saviour; who, although without sin, sweat as it were great drops of blood; and when athirst, and in the agonies of death, had vinegar and gall offered him to drink; while I,' she continued, 'have everything I can take.'

Much weighty advice did she impart, particularly to her

husband and children, whom she often exhorted to trust in the Lord; 'and then,' said she, 'you will have nothing to fear.' She reminded them of the Psalmist's language, "I have been young, and now am old; yet have I not seen the righteous forsaken, nor his seed begging bread." To her husband she added, 'O, my dear, thou must endeavour to look to the Lord for help; and then, never fear, never fear. I can say from experience he has been very good to me, even in the midst of affliction, now as well as formerly; for I was left, having nothing but him to trust in; and have found him a merciful helper and preserver.' To her mother-in-law, probably her husband's mother, she said, 'I have never experienced real satisfaction or consolation in anything short of Divine goodness. In my greatest trials and exercises, he hath comforted me the most.'

On one occasion she said, 'Pray for me, ye that can pray. I am desirous to be released, and you all seem to hold me back. Do not hold me. You see I cannot live. Pray for me, that the silver cord may be loosed.' Then she prayed herself with fervour. 'O Lord, cut short thy work in righteousness; yet not my will, but thine be done. It is an awful thing,' said she, 'to live, and I find it a serious thing to die; yet can with thankfulness acknowledge, I am not afraid of it. But this I could not obtain in my own strength. Oh, no. It is the unspeakable goodness of the Lord to a poor unworthy creature.' About a week before she died, some return of appetite occasioned, in an observer, a hope of recovery; but Mary said, 'I much dread going into the world again. The Lord knoweth it. I had rather depart, fearing I may not be [again] so well prepared.'

One time she had all the children called to her, and in a lively manner expressed her wish that they might experience preservation from evil; adding, that she had prayed to the Almighty on their account, to whose care she committed them. She said she had never desired much of this world's substance for them, and that her principal concern was for the good of their immortal souls. At another time, to her husband, she said, 'O, my dear, how have I prayed for thee, that thou mayest be preserved from the inordinate love of the world! Oh, this world, this world! If not minded, it will be apt to steal away the mind from a right relish of that which is good. Remember that one soul is of more value than all the world. If we have food and raiment, we ought to be therewith content.

A little before she died, she said, 'What a blessing it is,' alluding to the quiet which she enjoyed; 'and Divine goodness favours me so, that I feel no want of anything, either in body or mind.' After this she grew gradually weaker; and at the age of about forty-three, on the 21st of the Second month, 1808, she quietly departed.

THOMAS FAYLE, a much esteemed Friend, of Dublin, who died in that city, the 21st of the Fifth month, 1808, was born in the King's county, in 1742. He was placed as an apprentice with a friend in Dublin, which afterwards was his place of settlement and residence. He was of a sober and thoughtful disposition in early life; and from his youth up, continued to evince the effects of the preserving influence of truth. As his years increased, he advanced in usefulness in our religious Society. He was much concerned that its Christian discipline should be well supported; and much engaged himself in the administration of it. He was a man of plainness, sincerity, and firmness. He spoke his sentiments honestly, whether in meetings for discipline or to individuals; and he encouraged others to speak the truth, every man to his brother: he was also many times engaged in visiting Friends in their families.

Nor was his usefulness confined to precept alone: he acted as he recommended others to act. He was an elder who endeavoured to rule his own house well; being very solicitous that his children might walk in the path of simplicity, consistency, and safety. The preservation of them was one of the objects nearest to his heart. He encouraged the appearances of good in them; he warned them of that which had a contrary tendency; and, when he saw it needful, he added restraint to admonition. Thus, by endeavouring to check every wrong thing at its beginning, and to prevent its growth before it had gained strength, he was a blessing to his family. This wise, provident, and one may almost say politic concern, of a man who had at heart the preservation of youth, remained with him almost to the last: for, not long before his departure, in a large committee of the yearly meeting of Dublin, he addressed the parents on the subject of their deficiency in restraining their children, particularly in dress. He expressed his apprehension that some parents making a plain appearance themselves, even led their children into this deviation, by dressing them while very young in a way conformable to the fashions of the times.

He was a constant attender of his religious meetings, where his countenance and demeanour bespoke the humility and reverence of his mind, and he was several times at the yearly meeting of London. In his own dealings with other men he was upright and punctual; and he was very desirous that Friends might not pursue their trade so as to encumber their minds, prevent their growth in the truth, or interfere with their religious service: here also he was an example.

With apparently a strong constitution of body, he had been allowed the privilege of almost uninterrupted health, till the 15th of the Fifth month, 1808. It was First-day; and though he then appeared to be somewhat unwell, he attended both the meetings. In the evening he desired the Bible might be read; and after a time of silence, which was usual when the Scriptures had been read in his family, he made some observations on the instructive parable of the sower. The two following days he continued to be indisposed, but was not so ill as to alarm his family until the next day; and even then he walked out to a considerable distance. But on Fifth-day he kept his bed; the physicians seemed to have but little hope of his recovery, and he desired to be suffered to remain quiet and undisturbed. He spoke also of the probability that his end would be the result of his illness, adding nearly thus: 'There seems no sting. I never made much show; but what I did, I endeavoured to do it honestly. I have a hope to be admitted within the pearl-gates.'

After this his strength declined rapidly; yet he did not appear to suffer much, if any pain. On Seventh-day he was confirmed in the opinion that he should not recover, and said, 'I am favoured with great quietness. A short time after, in an humble, thankful frame of mind, and deeply feeling the favour of which he was partaking, he said, 'What a strange sight it is for me to see!' Being asked what he meant, he replied, 'For me to be called away, and to be quite ready!' Thus, with quick gradation, yet gently, he sunk away; and about midnight quietly breathed his last.

ABIGAIL FAYLE.—Though the decease of ABIGAIL FAYLE was more than two years before that of her husband, I am induced here to place the record of it, that the instruction of their exemplary lives, and the encouragement of their peaceful retreat, may continue together to shed a salutary influence on the mind of the traveller to the holy city.

She was the daughter of James and Susannah Malone, of the county of Carlow; and born in the year 1745. In her youth she was of an orderly conduct, religiously disposed, plain in her attire, and studious to be consistent. When she was about twenty-eight years of age, she was married to the subject of the preceding memoir, Thomas Fayle, of Dublin. To him she proved an affectionate and sympathizing wife. She was not only desirous to do what she herself thought to be right, but to encourage him to fulfil every duty to which he believed himself called: even though it might lead him into service at a distance, and deprive her of his company and encouragement at home. She was also, on her part, very anxious for the preservation of their children; solicitous to keep them out of hurtful company: and consonant with this caution, she was also desirous to restrain them from hurtful books. This is an insidious evil, and probably requires in many families a more vigilant care than it obtains. The advancing state of modern education will sometimes leave the child to peruse writings of which the parent may have little knowledge; but it is probable that an upright, awakened parent will generally have discernment sufficient to detect error and to observe a snare; and to such it will be but a poor excuse, that the children are deluded into sin by their ignorance and want of vigilance.

In her domestic economy she was desirous to avoid superfluity, particularly in furniture; and she united with her worthy husband, according to apostolic injunction, in a readiness to entertain strangers, especially such as were travelling in the service of Truth. This is a kind of hospitality often repaid by the benefit accruing to the younger branches of the hospitable family.

The health of this Friend had been in an impaired state for several years; and in the spring of 1805, she became evidently much more indisposed, and suffered much pain: in which condition she earnestly desired that the Lord would grant her patience to bear what it might be his will that she should suffer. To one of her sons, she spoke to the following effect: 'Seek first the kingdom of heaven, and all things will be added. All things necessary will be added. Do not suffer the honours or profits of this world to draw thy attention from that which is alone necessary. The riches of this world should be considered as dross and dung, that so we may win Christ. My pain is great. What a long illness I have had, now nearly two years! I believe it is for my good. I am not murmuring. I hope I am not murmuring at the long illness I have been favoured with. How thankful I ought to be for the many favours and blessings I have experienced!'

On the 12th of the Fourth month she had been down stairs; the next day she was increasingly ill; on the 14th she was manifestly declining, and the following day she quietly departed.

LUCY BARTON, daughter of Benjamin and Martha Jesup, of Woodbridge, in Suffolk, was born in the year 1781. In very early life, her mind appeared to be favoured with serious impressions, which were considerably strengthened by a delicate state of health; and her conduct and conversation were uniformly such as endeared her to her friends and relations.

In the twenty-sixth year of her age she was married to Bernard Barton, also of Woodbridge; and during the short period which intervened between their marriage and her decease, her mind was seriously exercised that she might attain a more solid establishment in the Truth than is the result of mere education or tradition. The following lines, found after her decease, among some memorandums, are thought worthy of preservation: they were written, it is supposed, not long before that event took place: 'This morning, being more than usually unwell, I was led seriously to reflect on my unfitness to exchange a mortal for an immortal state of existence. Religion is with me, I am afraid, little more than theory; yet I should not do justice to the great Author of it, did I not acknowledge that, if my unrestrained inclination did more frequently yield to my judgment, I should, in a much greater degree, possess the practical part of it. This, I am sensible, can alone render me an object of approbation in the sight of Him "who is of purer eyes than to behold iniquity."

'How often do I feel compunction for not cordially embracing those marks of Divine mercy and condescension which are, from time to time, offered me. Oh! may I not withstand the day of heavenly visitation to my soul! but rather may I endure all that human nature is capable of supporting, though it may amount to a deprivation of every earthly enjoyment, if that sense of the Divine presence, which I am now sometimes favoured to enjoy, might from time to time be renewed. This would fully compensate for all that could befall me in this fading and transient state of existence. I am so well aware of my own utter inability, in my own strength, to resist those suggestions which are congenial to my natural inclination, that I am often ready to despair of ever attaining to that degree of advancement in Christian experience, which, in some moments of deep humiliation, I have believed it was intended I should.'

With a mind thus exercised, it may be supposed she was in degree prepared to receive the awful summons, though it might come unexpectedly; which was the case. On the 20th of the Sixth month, 1808, she was confined by the birth of a daughter; and, for two days after that event, no unfavourable symptoms appeared; but on Fifth-day, the 23d, she complained of considerable pain, which increased on Sixth-day morning, but rather abated towards evening. On Seventh-day morning, unfavourable symptoms so much increased as greatly to alarm those about her, and induced her relations to wish for further medical advice. A physician was called in, who informed them that he could give very little hope of her recovery, or of her long continuance.

Her aunt, Mary Alexander, who had been with her through the day, was desirous of knowing how far she was aware of her own situation, but had avoided intimating any thing like an apprehension of danger; hoping a suitable opportunity might offer on her mother's arrival, who, with her father, had been absent. After Lucy had seen her parents, and her aunt was alone with her, without any previous remark, she said, 'Aunt, does the doctor think me in danger?' Mary replied, 'He does, my dear, consider thee in a precarious situation.' To this, after a solemn pause, Lucy observed, 'Well! I have been looking at it for a day or two; and I believe I can say I feel both faith and hope in the goodness of a merciful Redeemer; but it has sometimes felt hard to part with Bernard and the dear baby; for, though I have no doubt but she will be cared for, yet nothing can be quite like a mother! But I am resigned. I feel no fear; and humbly hope the close may be soon, rather than remaining long in present suffering.'

About two o'clock on First-day morning, she complained much of a blister which had been applied to her stomach, and wished it might be removed. The apothecary was sent to for his advice; but before he could get to her, she called her aunt to her bed-side, and said, 'Aunt, I would not have thee be alarmed, but I do not know but I am going. I feel so great a release from extreme suffering to no pain at all; and a coldness which began at my feet, and runs through my whole frame.' When the apothecary came, he did not suppose this event so near as she herself apprehended; but he was much affected to hear her speak of the prospect of so sudden a change, with the Christian firmness which her composed remarks on the subject plainly evinced.

Her husband and mother came to her immediately; and after a short time she requested her father might be sent for, and also the apothecary's wife, who had been a very kind assistant during her confinement. After they both came in, and all were sitting round the bed, she took leave of them individually, in a manner which tendered the hearts of all present; and then requested the child might be brought to her. She held it in her arms, kissed it most affectionately, and after that time took but little notice of it. About this time she likewise spoke of some of her absent relations, several of whom she mentioned by name, requesting her love might be presented to them; particularly some on her husband's side, who were distantly situated; and she expressed the satisfaction it would have given her to see them again.

Her brother, Alexander Jesup, had been with her the evening before; and in the course of the night she said it would have been pleasant to see her brother and sister Maw, but she supposed it was now too late. They came, however, a short time afterwards, and she was then much revived; and remarked to her aunt that she had thought herself going, but now it seemed hidden from her how it would terminate: adding, 'but whichever way it may be, to feel so relieved from suffering is cause of humble thankfulness.' When the physician came on First-day morning, he was much surprised to find her so revived, though she was thought to be still in great danger. She dropped many interesting expressions in the course of the day, several times repeating how great a favour it was to be freed from suffering; and that so much ease was more than she had expected, before she departed.

While some part of the family were at dinner, she sent for her husband, wishing to see him alone. During her conversation with him, amongst other observations, she expressed her fervent wish that, in case of her removal, he might be enabled to support the trial with becoming resignation. On her being afterwards asked whether she had any directions to give respecting the infant, she replied, with great composure, 'Then I suppose my situation is decided.' She was informed it was not entirely decided, yet there was great reason to apprehend how it might terminate. She said, 'Well; as to the dear babe, I wish to leave it to those who know better than myself; I believe it is not right for me to encumber my mind about it.' But she afterwards informed her sister, that many of the infant's clothes were left unmade; and she expressed a wish, that if her sister had the care of them, she would let them be made plain and simple.

On First-day evening she appeared fast declining; and her mother sitting on one side of the bed, and her aunt on the other, she put out a hand to each, and said, 'Oh! how I love you all, you are all more near and dear to me than ever.' About this time she said, 'I should like to have seen Jeremiah (meaning her brother) but he no doubt will come to the interment.' She now declined so rapidly, that it was not expected she would have continued through the night; but she again revived, and in the course of a short time, there appeared a wonderful amendment. So great was the change, that her medical attendants gave her relations some reason to hope that she might recover; but though she continued rather improving for two days, nature gave way to the remaining disease, and about 7 o'clock on Fourth-day morning, the 29th of the Sixth month, 1808, after having entertained some expectation of being again restored to health, she quietly and resignedly closed this life; evincing her willingness to leave all below, by her last words, 'Providence knows best.'

GEORGE GIBSON, of Saffron Walden, in Essex, was the son of Francis and Mary Gibson, of Royston, in Hertfordshire, where he was born the 15th of the Twelfth month, 1731, according to the old style. He settled within the compass of Thaxted monthly meeting, when he was in his thirty-second year, and came forth in the ministry in his forty-first. He was a man of great moderation and integrity, appearing to be much redeemed from the spirit of the world; and a very diligent attender of meetings for worship and discipline; in which not only his public ministry, at times, but the reverence of his spirit in silent waiting, was instructive and encouraging. In his solemn approaches to God in supplication, he seemed to be clothed with the genuine spirit of prayer; and in latter life, as he drew near to the confines of the world to come, he seemed to have the more frequent access to the great object of the saints' faith. He attained to the advanced age of seventy-six, when, in full assurance of peace, he was gathered on the 23d of the Seventh month, 1808.

Several months before his departure, his health declined; and he would frequently express his apprehension that his continuance in time would not be long; but he spoke of his close, as of the consummation of his desires; and of his change, as unspeakably glorious. It had been his practice for several years, to note down in writing, occasionally, the feelings of his mind: of which memorandums, a short, but sweet collection remains. In one of these, dated more than three months before his decease, he says, 'I am sensible of an increase of such bodily pains, as indicate the dissolution of this tabernacle; but think I can say, I feel no alarm at it. Yet it looks awful. O Lord, I humbly pray thee, be near me, and strengthen me to look to thee, in the time of conflict: O, thou that hast been my rock and my refuge, my deliverer, and my hope of eternal salvation.'

He was enabled to bear his ailments with great resignation; and, as we find many other pious Christians do at such times, he prayed that he might not fall into impatience. Thus we see, that to the last, the creature has neither store-house nor barn. Every good gift, and every perfect gift, must still come down from the Father of lights; until complete and accomplished redemption crowns the whole, and inseparably unites it with him forever.

The seat of the disease which gradually broke the bond of mortality, was the stomach; and this organ at length failed in its functions, so as to resist all food, and to occasion great nausea and pain.

When in health, he read much in the Scriptures; and when he was too weak to be able to read, he continued to derive comfort in hearing them read. The thirteenth chapter of the first epistle to the Corinthians, in particular, had so much place in his mind, that at his request, during his illness, it was read to him by four different persons, at four separate times. This is the memorable chapter where the apostle enumerates the transcendent nature of love. Our translators have somewhat debased it, by rendering this word by charity; and I have often wished every reader, in perusing it, to substitute in his mind, as he goes along, the genuine word, love. A very few days before his close, he had the following passage from Isaiah read to him: "Comfort ye, comfort ye, my people, saith your God. Speak ye comfortably to Jerusalem, and cry unto her, that her warfare is accomplished, that her iniquity is pardoned, for she hath received of the Lord's hand, double for all her sins."

He remarked, during his illness, that the company of such friends was pleasant to him, as his spirit had been, and was, bound to in the everlasting covenant, which would not be dissolved with time. 'Rejoice with me,' once he said, 'that I shall soon put off these shackles of mortality;' or to that import. At another time, he said that the expressions of Job Scott were much in his remembrance and experience; 'for,' said he, 'I never saw a time before, when all things not criminal were so nearly alike to me, in point of any disturbance to the mind.' The following also, spoken at different times, demonstrate the object of his thoughts and hopes. 'I have a glorious prospect in view, and that is more than words. The enemy is busy; but not able to shake my confidence in the everlasting arm. The great Master himself experienced temptation and suffering; and how can his poor servants expect to escape them? Dear Lord, when wilt thou say, it is enough? The Lord is progressively doing his work; and, I believe, taking me home to a glorious inheritance.'

He frequently uttered, with great solemnity, the genuine filial address, 'My Father, my Father!' and sometimes added, 'My heavenly Father.' Thus he seemed to exemplify the declaration of the apostle, "Because ye are sons, God hath sent forth the Spirit of his Son into your hearts, crying Abba."

Two days before his close, though he was not then confined to his bed, and there appeared a probability that he would continue some time, he sent for a person not a member of our Society, and took leave of him with great composure and firmness; intimating that it would be the last time he would see him; and adding, 'If my neighbours inquire after me, tell them that I die in peace with all men; and with my God.'

The next day he was chiefly confined to bed, and in the fore part of it, he requested that he might not be disturbed, as he thought his end to be near. Afterwards he expressed himself in these words: 'I have been partaking of the pure stream, that flows from the throne of God.' In the afternoon he had a fainting fit; but recovered, and passed the night composed, and clear in his faculties. The following day, he suffered great bodily pain, and difficulty of breathing; but was also clear in his intellects, and was preserved in great patience. In the afternoon the fainting returned, and between three and four, the conflict ended.

THOMAS CASH.—Respecting Thomas Cash, of Morley, Cheshire, a man generally esteemed and beloved in our religious Society, I have not to record many of what are commonly considered dying sayings; yet as he died in great peace, after having lived in great dedication, a short survey of his rise, his course, and his decline, will, I believe, be encouraging to the Christian traveller.

It appears by the testimony which the friends of his own meeting have given of him, that he was born at Alderly, the 13th of the Eleventh month, Old Style, 1739. His parents were members of the Society of Friends; and he was a great comfort to them, by his industry and filial affection; but he does not seem to have been remarkable for any particular attention to the concerns of religion, until his twenty-fourth year. About that time, however, he was powerfully and effectually visited with "the day-spring from on high;" his mind became much humbled; and he often sought solitary places, in which to pour forth his cries to the Author of all good, for reconciliation and acceptance with him. He was made willing to submit to the baptisms which Infinite Wisdom allotted for his purification; and he gradually became conspicuous for the fruits of holiness; particularly meekness, humility, piety towards God, and good will to men. From this time he was remarkably diligent in his attendance of meetings, and made his temporal concerns give way to his religious duties.

In the thirty-second year of his age, and after many deep preparatory exercises, he came forth in the ministry. For several years his testimonies were short, and delivered in great simplicity. Indeed, simplicity was his characteristic through life. He was not one who would be commonly esteemed a man of five talents; but he occupied honestly and wisely, with those with which he was endowed; and as he steadily pursued his course, love and esteem followed him. By degrees, he was much enlarged; and most parts of the Society in these kingdoms were witnesses of his gospel labours. These, however, were far from being restricted to the Society alone; he was eminent for appointing meetings for the inhabitants in general of the places in which, in his religious travels, his lot was cast. His meek deportment and circumspect conduct adorned the doctrine which he preached; and in domestic life, he was kind to all around him. During the time he was in a business which occasionally introduced him into the converse and hurry of the world, it was his frequent practice to break off and retire, to seek for a renewal of strength from Him whom he desired to acknowledge in all his ways; but about fourteen years before his decease, having obtained a competency, he declined further business, that he might be fully at liberty for religious service.

He had been for many years almost a constant attender of the yearly meeting; and he came to that in 1808, in a state of health so weak, as to be unable to attend all the sittings; yet he had then in prospect a visit to several of the western counties. This, though with considerable bodily suffering, he performed; and having been nearly five months from home, he returned about the middle of the Ninth month, with his bodily strength much exhausted, but with a mind fraught with thankfulness and praise.

The following letter, written a short time after his return from this visit, is interesting, and shows the humble, grateful state of his mind, viz.:

'Morley, 18th of 10th month, 1808.

'Dear Friend, John Waring:

'I have been at home rather more than a month. I was on my journey about five months, and not well one day in all that time. But I think I may with thankfulness say, that I had not even a murmuring thought, either by day or night, the whole of the time. The Almighty, in tender mercy and abundant compassion, was very gracious to me, from one step to another, [during] the whole of it; and my friends' kindness very great in every place. The remembrance of such kindness often causes my eyes to overflow with tears of thankfulness; and I do not recollect one instance of shyness, either among the rich or those in lower circumstances, whilst I was out; and the Almighty, in unspeakable loving kindness, was strength in weakness, riches in poverty, and a present help in every needful time, to whom alone belongs all praise, world without end. Amen.'

In the few meetings which he attended after his return, and especially in his own particular meeting, he was more than commonly enabled to evince the continuance of the concern for the cause of truth and righteousness, which, for the last thirty-five years of his life, he had been so zealously endeavouring to promote.

Nearly a month after his return, and before he was confined to his house, I had an opportunity of paying him a visit, and it was a memorable one. He was then labouring under the disease which was the means of loosening the bonds of mortality, which was, I believe, a dropsy in the chest, so that his breathing was affected by the little exertions he made to accommodate his visitors. He spoke to us of his late journey, during which he said he had not had one day's health. In some of the latter stages of it, particularly when he was in the vicinity of Bristol, his nightly sleep had been much broken. He was often waked by the great difficulty of his breathing; but on these occasions he said he felt the goodness of the Almighty so near him, that it was no trouble to him to remain awake. An impaired memory prevents me from relating or recollecting much of his conversation; but, to use the term of our translators,* in their rendering of Philippians, iii. 20, it seemed to have been much "in heaven;" and I may say, without any strain of expression, that I have seldom paid any one so sweet a visit.

Soon after this, as we learn from the testimony of Morley monthly meeting, from which I have extracted most of the foregoing narrative, he was confined to the house, and, during the whole course of his illness, was preserved in much patience and resignation, those general attendants on the closing steps of the path of the just.

He often said that the goodness of the Almighty was great to him, comforting and supporting him under his bodily suf-

* I say the 'term' of our translators, because the word which they translate 'conversation,' they should have translated 'citizenship.' This passage has its parallel in Eph. ii. 19. "Now then, ye are no more strangers and pilgrims; but fellow-citizens with the saints, and of the household of God."

ferings. That appellation of the Supreme Being was one which he most commonly used, in speaking of the dealings of the Lord with his soul; and it is an appellation in which the creature, humbled under a sense of its own infirmity, will always have reason to delight. The gratitude which he expressed for all the little services which were done to him, and the peaceful serenity which evidently covered his mind, were comfortable and instructive to such as visited him. Thus his outward man gradually decayed, until the 16th of the First month, 1809, when, with an understanding unclouded by the frailty of his frame, and with the power of utterance continued to the close, he quietly breathed his last.

Having been somewhat struck, or rather agreeably affected, with some concluding expressions, which the Friends of Morley monthly meeting have subjoined to their testimony concerning Thomas Cash, I think them worthy also to be preserved in this place. 'We feel,' say they, 'our loss in these parts, where the labourers are few; but we know,' and happy, may we not all say, for those who do know, 'the Rock remains, the Foundation standeth sure. May we pray the Lord of the harvest, that he will send forth labourers into his harvest!'

SAMUEL DYER, of Bristol, was born in that city, the 10th of the Seventh month, 1747. He was strictly educated in the profession of the church of England, which was that of his parents. It appears, from some account left by himself, that at the early age of seven or eight, he had strong religious impressions. They were the means of exciting in him fervent desires for deliverance from the propensities of fallen nature; which seemed to overcome his best resolutions, and involved him in distress. When he was about thirteen years of age, he was further aroused to a sense of his condition, by means of a fit of sickness. He beheld the dreadful consequence of sin, and was enabled to pray for redemption from its bondage. 'In my distress,' says he, 'I cried unto the Lord; and he heard me, and was pleased, in degree, to lift up the light of his countenance upon me.' The effects, however, of this visitation do not appear to have been long perceptible to himself; and his good resolutions, he says, 'vanished like a morning cloud.' Nevertheless, it is probable, that the good seed sown in his childhood and youth, was never suffered to perish.

His friends, in their testimony, relate, that he went on under many deep exercises and trials, and when he was about seventeen years of age, felt himself inclined to attend the meetings of Friends, in Bristol. He was tired, as he himself remarks, of the forms and ceremonies in which he had been educated, and of a ministry which did not relieve his distressed mind. In his attendance of our meetings, although he found it difficult to keep his mind in sufficient stillness, probably from the bias of his education, as well as from the inherent propensity of the mind to be in action; he, nevertheless, felt much satisfaction; and at length joined the Society. About this time, he makes this acknowledgment in his memorandums: 'As to the Divine life, I have this remark to make, that I should grow more in it, was I but more in the stillness; even until the whole birth of the Son of God was brought forth in my soul. Be still, therefore, O, all that is within me; and know the Lord's strength and power to arise.'

To this power, about the time of his becoming of age, he apprehended it his duty to appear in public testimony; and endeavouring to continue in the faithful discharge of that duty, he was enlarged in his gift, and often exercised in it, in the city and vicinity of Bristol. He afterwards, at different times, found himself engaged to visit Friends in their meetings in various counties, and, in some places, in their families. A visit of this sort in London was among some of his later gospel-labours.

In domestic life he was an affectionate husband and a tender father; but the limits of his family did not bound his fatherly care. The youth in general were objects of it; and some of them have had cause to bless the Lord on his account.

He was long subject to a disease of the asthmatic kind, which often occasioned him to be confined at home; and he had been laid up with it during the family visit in London. His final illness seemed at first only a fit of his accustomed complaint; but it increased at length so as to confine him to his chamber, and, after about ten days of this increased state of ailment, was the means of conducting him to his close.

He suffered much pain in his body; but resignation composed and supported his soul. Previously to this juncture, he had often remarked the comfortable state in which his own mind was; and when his family were setting off for meeting, from which bodily weakness was detaining him, he used to observe, that when he was young he was a diligent attender. 'Go,' he would say, 'and I hope the Lord will be with you, and give you a good meeting.'

While disease was thus accelerating the hour of his release, he was at different times much engaged in prayer. At one time he prayed for his native city: 'The Lord bless and preserve this city and its inhabitants; and draw unto himself thousands and tens of thousands.' To a young man who attended on him, he said, 'There is a reality in religion, and I find it so: nor have I followed cunningly-devised fables.'

The day before his departure, he expressed himself to this effect: 'I believe it right to tell you my faith. I have been a sinner, and have gone into many follies in my childhood; but, by the love of God in Christ Jesus, I have been enabled to come, as a poor trembling penitent, to Him, who is the friend of sinners; and by thus coming, and abiding under the power and operation of his Spirit upon my soul, trusting in him, and not in my own righteousness, I am what I am. And [I] am persuaded, that neither death nor life, nor angels, nor principalities, nor powers, nor height, nor depth, nor any other creature, shall be able to separate me from the love of God, which is in Christ Jesus our Lord.'

The day on which he died, taking leave of a friend, he said, 'I find I have enough to do to bear the pains of the body. It is well for me that I have done my work; and I have a full assurance that all is well. Farewell. Give my love to Friends.' A few minutes before his close, he was again engaged in supplication, after which, at the age of about sixty-two, on the 30th of the First month, 1809, he quietly resigned his spirit

---

JAMES PEMBERTON, of Philadelphia, died there in his eighty-sixth year, the 9th of the Second month, 1809. He had employed a long life in various occupations of usefulness, and of active benevolence. To the service of the Society of Friends he devoted a large portion of his time; and his love for the cause of truth, his unusual assiduity in what he undertook, and his long experience, all exercised and used in the fear of his Creator, contributed to make him eminent. Nor was he circumscribed by the limits of our Society. More public objects of service to his fellow men also engaged his attention, and had his assistance in their promotion: particularly, he was a strenuous promoter of the measures taken for the abolition of the Slave Trade, and the relief of the black people. He was president of the Philadelphia society for improving their condition, in which station he succeeded the well-known Franklin, who had presided at its rise. In more early life, before the Revolution had introduced a new system of government, he had long been a member of the colonial assembly of Pennsylvania, as representative for his native city. In short, he seems to have walked usefully and honourably through life; and to have descended calmly to the borders of the grave; and yet, in surveying the unknown region which lay beyond it, he dared not to trust, for a peaceful establishment in it, on any of his former works of righteousness. All his dependence was on his Saviour: and that he found to be an anchor to his soul.

As he felt himself gradually declining, he looked back to the number of years which he had passed. Compared with the boundless existence before him, they appeared but as a moment; but yet he perceived them to have been marked with so many preservations, that his gratitude was afresh excited to his Almighty Benefactor and Preserver.

Within somewhat less than a month before his end, he had a fainting fit. After he was come to himself, he remarked, how awful it was to be on the verge of eternity. 'But,' continued he, 'we have a Mediator, an Intercessor. My mind has, for some time past, been unusually impressed with the vast importance of the Redeemer's mediation. I have never before seen it with the same clearness. I am free from pain of body or mind. The prospect of my change is awful; but, after all, I have nothing to trust to, but the merits of my Redeemer.'

The next day he said to Thomas Scattergood, (a Friend well known and much beloved in this country,) 'I am thankful that, through divine mercy, I feel an evidence within me, that I am not cast off. It has been the great desire of my life, that at the solemn close I might be favoured to feel that evidence. It was all that I wished. It seems to me that I cannot continue long, but I desire to wait patiently, and to labour after a perfect resignation to the Divine will. The longer I live, I see more clearly that it is not moral righteousness that will do for man. Nothing but the righteousness of Christ will avail us. We can claim nothing from our own merits. We owe all to Divine mercy.'

Nearly two weeks after this, he said to a friend who came in, and asked him how he was, 'I am on the confines of eternity, and find nothing in my way; but all is mercy, mercy!' Two days after this, after an interval of silence, he exclaimed, 'Oh, the blessing of an easy mind! who can describe it? It is all owing to Divine mercy, to nothing else: and this, I hope, I enjoy.' In the same day he addressed a grandson, who was with him, in a pathetic manner, as follows: 'I have often been thinking that whenever any suitable opportunity should offer, I would unburden my mind to thee. And it has now arisen in me to address thee with the words of king David to his son formerly. "Solomon, my son, know thou the God of thy fathers. Serve him with a perfect heart, and with a willing mind. If thou seek him he will be found of thee; but if thou forsake him, he will cast thee off for ever." And what a dismal state is this: to be cast off from the presence of that Being, who is the greatest friend of mankind. Nothing can be more dreadful. These expressions, I remember when young, were addressed to me by a very worthy friend, John Evans, of North Wales,* in a letter he wrote to me on the death of my father. I wish thee to impress them deeply on thy mind, and thou wilt find them useful after I am gone. It is impossible to estimate the advantage of living under Divine protection. His mercy and goodness are incalculable.'

In the evening of the same day, which was First-day, when his children and grandchildren were around him, he addressed them in an instructive manner, and on several subjects, some of which it may be useful to introduce here, in a form somewhat abridged. After recommending his family to live in harmony, 'My dear Father,'† said he, 'was a very

* That is, a part of Pennsylvania, so called, or in the language of the Welsh Friends who settled there, Gwynedd. Of John Evans, there is an account in the American Collection of Memorials.

† Israel Pemberton, mentioned in the American Collection of Memoirs.

upright man. As occasion offered, he gave advice to us, his children; and one of his most frequent admonitions, and which made very great impression on me in early life, was, To live in the fear of the Lord. It is the beginning of wisdom. It is indeed wisdom, and it is founded on love: as those [whom] we love, we must fear to offend. If this principle is attended to through life, you will not fear when the solemn period shall come. All will be peace.'

'David, speaking of Almighty Providence, says, that "His mercy endureth for ever." His mercy has indeed no end—no end! His goodness has followed me; and I have been favoured in my present indisposition much more than I had any reason to expect, and much more than I had deserved. I recommend to you the diligent perusal of the Holy Scriptures. Make yourselves acquainted with them. In them you will find an abundant source of instruction and edification. Reading the lives of pious men of former ages, and observing how they were supported under their trials by the Divine arm, tend very powerfully to place our dependence on Him, from whom comes all our support—all our benefits: and to whom it is impossible to make a sufficient return for his inestimable goodness. My parents took great pains with me, and I received very great advantages from the constant and unwearied care of a most affectionate mother.'*

The following day he said to a Friend, 'It is a great consolation to be free from a guilty conscience at such an hour as this: and that, I believe, I am. We have all fallen short, far short, of the glory of God; but we are under his mercy who careth for us. There is one thing which is not enough inculcated in our meetings—the mediatorship of the Son, our Lord and Saviour Jesus Christ: and I have never seen this so manifested as in my present indisposition.' He then adduced some texts of Scripture relating to this subject, with remarks on them, as: "No man cometh to the Father

* Rachel Pemberton. See the same Collection.

but by me." 'It is a great mercy,' said he, 'that God in his wisdom has appointed such wonderful means for the redemption of mankind. "We have a high-priest, touched with the feeling of our infirmities." Not,' he observed, 'such a high-priest as is ordained by man; but a high-priest who is really touched with a feeling of our infirmities. This mediation of the Son, with the Father, is a great mystery.'

The following day, in the evening, on being assisted to get into bed, he exclaimed, 'How many hundreds and thousands there are now sick in the world, and have nobody to assist them: and I have so many! How am I loaded with blessings!' This was on the last day of the First month. The succeeding day, this was his confession. 'Never was I more convinced of the goodness of redeeming love!'

In another week, his close approached with perceptible steps. He had mentioned his doubt of surviving the night of the 7th of the Second month; but on the 8th, about noon, after some refreshing sleep, his countenance brightened up, and he thus expressed himself to his only surviving child. 'As I draw nearer my close, I find the tormenting fear of death taken away, through the intercession of the great Mediator between God and man. I am very low, but not so low but I can yet commemorate the incomprehensible mercies of an all-gracious God.' To a particular friend that day, he said, 'Oh, that I had strength; that I had the strength of an angel, that I might declare the goodness of the Lord to me; but eternity is too short to utter all his praise.'

He continued, 'The Redeemer has said, "I am the way, the truth, and the life. No man cometh to the Father but by me." And he told his disciples, before he suffered, not to be troubled. "Ye have believed in my Father: believe also in me. In my Father's house are many mansions. If it were not so, I would have told you." He is, indeed, the

Alpha and the Omega, the beginning and the end, the first and the last. What a blessed company are already gone there before me! I feel the time of my own departure draws nigh.' As he was holding the hand of this visitor, on taking his leave, he said, 'I love thee, and all them that love the Lord Jesus in sincerity. Farewell.' These were the last words which he spoke on a religious subject. The next day he put off mortality.

APPENDIX,

CONTAINING SOME ACCOUNT OF DECEASED FRIENDS, OF AN EARLIER DATE THAN THE PRECEDING.

JOSHUA MIDDLETON.—At the distance of nearly ninety years, I am disposed to commemorate, with a short narrative, my maternal great grandfather, Joshua Middleton, of Newcastle, who died there the 27th of the Eleventh month, 1720. In doing this, and in looking over the few papers relating to this ancient Friend, which are in my possession, I am confirmed in the truth of a common remark of pious persons, 'That the memory of the just is precious. It is encouraging to observe, that the general trials, deliverances, habits, and sources of hope, are the same at every period of time.

Joshua Middleton was born at Darlington, in the county of Durham, in the year 1647. His parents were of the Presbyterian profession, strict in their way, and careful to educate their son in the principles of religion which they professed. He often acknowledged that their care had been of much service to him, in keeping him out of the vanities of life; and often, with much tenderness, would recommend to parents, to nurture their children in the fear of the Lord, and in the diligent reading of the Scriptures.

In his youth, after some years of communion with the Presbyterians, he was convinced of the principles held by Friends, and joined their Society. He underwent with this people divers sufferings and imprisonments, which he supported with patience. Not long after he joined the Society, he believed it his duty to come forth in the work of the ministry, and in this service he travelled in many parts of England, and in Scotland. His brethren of the quarterly meeting of Durham, in their testimony, say of him, that as he increased in years, the greater was his care of the churches; and that he exhibited a good example to Friends, by his constant attendance of monthly and quarterly meetings, though often under much weakness. His testimony was plain and intelligible. He was a man of a meek and peaceable spirit, and much beloved among all sorts of people; and his endeavours to compose differences were very prevalent. He was also liberal to the poor, and a great promoter of such liberality.

I am not informed at what period of his life he came to reside at Newcastle. He had first lived at Raby, a village near Staindrop, in Durham. I have a letter from him to his daughter Hannah, the wife of Joseph Gurney, of Norwich, (of whom there is an account in the collection of testimonies concerning public Friends deceased,) written about four months before his death. It shows the temper of his mind at that time; and, if the partiality of a descendant do not deceive me, is worth preserving.

'Newcastle, 16th Seventh Month, 1720.

'Dear Hannah,

'I had thine, whereby understanding of your health, am glad: and though I could like well more often to know of your state, yet, as I receive information thereof from ——, with whom we have now a frequent correspondence, I do not take offence at thy writing seldom: nor must you expect many letters from my hand, it being now a [great] trouble to write. So as Providence has placed us at such a bodily distance, we must endeavour to converse in spirit, remembering one another, and praying for one another, that we may be preserved out of the evils of this world, and over all the temptations and besetments that we may be attended with in this time of our pilgrimage therein; and willing and resigned unto the good pleasure of our God, when he shall call us out of it.

'This is what I am labouring for as on my own behalf: so would have you use like endeavour, that we may not sorrow immoderately, or be surprised; but waiting all the days of our appointed time, till any of our changes come. So with remembrance of my true love, with my wife's, to thee and thy husband, and your little ones, and to brother Gurney and his family, and all the rest of relations, I conclude this with my fervent prayer to the Lord for his blessing on you all: not forgetting —— and her children.

'I say, as the Lord hath favoured all of you with competent increase in the things of this life, my desire and prayer is, that your portion may not be in them; but that you may be blessed with spiritual blessings in heavenly places in Christ Jesus. Such are the fruits of his blessed Spirit: wherein that you may increase and abound, is the prayer of thy loving father.

'JOSHUA MIDDLETON.'

His last illness seems to have been a painful one; for his son, in a letter to another of his daughters, settled at Norwich, dated one week before the departure of their father, thus relates of him: he had been relieved from his pain and retchings by a removal of the stricture; 'but,' says his son, 'he has taken nothing these two or three days, and grows weaker and weaker; but continues sensible, and many living expressions drop from him. I doubt not but God has heard his prayer, and sweetened his bitter cup, which he said he had to drink. Soon after he had so said, he broke out into these expressions: "Blessed be the name of the Lord! He has sweetened my cup. I am refreshed." As we were sitting one night about him, he bid us go to bed, and let him go, and commit him to the Lord; and he should be received to mercy.'

CHRISTIANA PENN was the wife of William Penn, a grandson of the memorable William Penn, founder of Pennsylvania. Her parents were Alexander and Jane Forbes, of London. Jane Forbes was the youngest daughter of Robert Barclay, the apologist, and of Christiana his wife, (an account of whose close is to be found in Dying Sayings, Part Eighth.) Christiana Penn died the 1st of the Ninth month, 1733; but as there is not, that I know of, any printed account of her, I am induced to abridge an ancient manuscript, one which may, at least, be interesting to such as like to trace the descendants of men who have been eminent for virtue; and will tend, like the rest of this collection, to promote piety, by showing its blessed consequences at the close of mortality.

After a longer term of previous suffering than often occurs, her first child, a daughter,* was born. Her husband and friends then began to hope; but she had a view of her approaching dissolution, and endeavoured to be prepared for it. She was fervent and frequent in prayer, and earnest with her mother† to join her in it. She had a firm confidence that it would be well with her, often declaring that she did not wish to live. She mentioned with affection her near connexions in life; yet said, that so great was her comfort in the prospect and assurance of future bliss, she could freely part with them all.

She said the Lord had been so gracious as to forgive her sins, alluding to the follies of her youth, which she then esteemed to have been vanities, and therefore she earnestly desired, if it were his will, that she might be removed; for she was then ready, and certain of eternal happiness; but she feared that it might not be so well if she should live

* Who died a widow, 1803, named Gaskell.

† She was one of Robert Barclay's children, of whom John Gratton says: 'As they grew in years, they grew also in the knowledge of the blessed Truth;' which he much attributes to the care of their mother.

longer. 'Hast thou not given me up?' said she to her mother. 'I desire thou wilt give me up freely, and not endeavour to hold me, or interrupt me, but let me go; I am ready, and have nothing to do but to die.' At another time, her father inquired of her whether she would be willing to live, if it pleased the Lord. She answered, 'God forbid, but that if he have any service for me, I should be willing; but if not, I desire to die; for now I am ready, and have nothing to do but to die. My joy is full.'

She expressed a tender and affectionate regard for her friends, but most for her husband. She declared that she had great satisfaction in her marriage, and that she loved him with all her heart; and that her concern for him, and desires for his good, were very great and strong. Her patience in her illness, and her fear of offending her Maker by complaining, were remarkable: careful of her words, that she might not offend with her tongue. One time being in great pain, and finding herself thirsty, she said, 'Now my tongue wants cooling, but soon I shall be in Abraham's bosom, where all my sorrows will be at an end, and I shall rest forever. I have nothing to do but to die.' This was frequently her expression. She would continue in supplication sometimes for hours together. The sweet, heavenly disposition she was in the latter part of her time, even surprised those who visited her. She was so filled with a sense of the favour and goodness of God, and with firm faith in her future happiness, that she declared her eternal joy was begun.

She was allowed her understanding perfect to the last. She often inquired the hour of the day; was glad when she thought the last was approaching; firmly and quietly took her final leave; and, without a groan, or the least uneasy sign, at the age of eighteen years and a quarter, she ceased to breathe.

MARY NEALE was the daughter of Peter and Rachel Peisley, and born at Ballymore, in the county of Kildare in Ireland, in 1717. Her education was among Friends: but an indulgence, too little restrained, in the company of such as have not the cross of Christ in esteem, led her into deviations in behaviour from the simplicity of her profession; which at length occasioned a deep remorse. During several years she thus in some degree gave way to hurtful propensities. She was not at times without secret reproofs; but a fall from a horse, by which she considered herself to have been in danger of a dislocation of the neck, and of a sudden death, seems to have been an incitement to permanent reformation. Not long after, she was much struck in observing the awful, reverent frame of mind, in which two travelling Friends appeared to sit, waiting upon the Lord; and a fervent inquiry was raised in her mind after the revelation of the Father, through the Son. To this exercise, in her own experience, she was then much a stranger; but as she persevered, and by the operation of grace in her seeking heart, she attained the object of her search, and was satisfied.

About her twenty-seventh year, she came forth in the work of the ministry, and about the same time she fell into some outward trials and distresses; and she became either a teacher, or otherwise a servant, in the family of a Friend, of whose daughter she had the care. After a while she quitted this employ, in order to be more at liberty to fulfil her duty as a minister; and she visited in that service, in company with another Friend, the meetings of Friends in Ireland in a very general manner.

In 1748, she entered on a similar visit to Friends in England, in which she employed more than two years. In 1751, she accompanied Catharine Payton, of Dudley, Worcestershire, then on a religious visit in Ireland, in a visit to Friends in Munster and Ulster. In this journey, probably, was laid the foundation of that close religious fellowship, which rendered them sympathizing companions in further and more extensive services. In such service they engaged in the year 1753, and were nearly three years employed in visiting Friends on the continent of North America, returning in the summer of 1756.

It is not within the plan of this compilation to give even cursory accounts of such journeys; but an extract from a letter which she wrote from Bradford, in Yorkshire, in the first year of her travels in England, is particularly thought worthy of preservation. She seems, previously, to have been tried by means of much deprivation of that heavenly comfort and support, which she loved and sought.

'As I quietly rode along,' says she, 'the Lord was pleased in mercy to break in upon my mind by his living presence and power, and it became the language of my soul, Speak, Lord, and thy servant will hear. After which, many things were divinely opened to me; wherein I greatly rejoiced, and was thankful to the Lord my God. I then found a sudden but gentle rebuke; and heard, as it were, a voice that said, in the secret of my soul, The dispensations thou most delightest in are least pleasing to me; and not so beneficial to thy soul as that pure poverty of spirit, brokenness and contrition of heart, which brings into humility of mind. And the reason why this is so little desired, and so unpleasant to the creature is, that it can have no part therein; but is wholly excluded and set at naught; can discover no beauty or excellency in it. And for this cause it is that I will in no wise despise the offering of a broken and contrite spirit, as it is most pure, and without any mixture of the creature. For whether there be prophecies, divine openings or revelation, consolations, joying or rejoicing in the Holy Ghost, gifts of healing, or tongue of utterance; in all these self can rejoice, and have a share, being obvious to it, and bringing it honour. Then, said I, Lord dispense to me what is most pleasing to thee, and best for my soul, so long as my weak faith and patience can endure; and when I am ready to faint, give me a little of the wine well refined on the lees, that my soul may rejoice in thee, the God of my salvation.'

On the 17th of the Third month, 1757, she was married to Samuel Neale, a valuable minister then residing within the compass of Edenderry monthly meeting; and in the evening of that day, in an opportunity of religious retirement, her mind was impressed with a sense of the holy sabbath of rest. She remarked, that when the Almighty had finished his six days' work in the creation, he appointed a sabbath and sanctified it; she observed that, in the time of the law, the people were forbidden to do any manner of work on the sabbath day; and she said that there were some present who should, in a short time, cease from their labours, and enjoy a sabbath in which they should have no work to do.

The next two days were passed in receiving visits from her friends, and in sweet fellowship with her newly-acquired partner; but very early in the morning of the 20th, she was seized with a disease which was, probably, an inflammation of the bowels; and about three in the afternoon she expired. During this short illness, she sometimes raised her voice in a melodious manner, though she did not always express herself in words. She longed to be dissolved, and entreated the Lord to give her a release; and when, about half an hour before her decease, her pain ceased, she then said, 'I praise thy name, O my God, for this favour.'

JONAS BINNS, a boy in his fifteenth year, son of Jonathan Binns, of Crawshawbooth, in Lancashire, departed this life the 23d of the Ninth month, 1760. His surviving father gave a testimony concerning him, which I nearly copy.

He had great delight in reading the Holy Scriptures when very young. He said he preferred learning before money. He was often alone when others were at their play. He read much, and was often much affected, being observed, sometimes, to make a stop in his reading, and plentifully scatter his tears. And not only in reading, but when solidly set in meetings, tears did run down his face: which was affecting to the well-minded, and evidenced that he met with something worth waiting for; which, when but nine or ten years of age, he confessed. He was then very desirous to go to meetings, and being asked the reason, he was very still for a time, and then broke out into tears, and signified that he met with something in them, which sweetened his mind. He was steady in his conduct, and careful in his words, and often reproved others who were not so. He was remarkably patient under disappointments, and content with such things as he had. He was dutiful to his parents, and his behaviour and conversation were truly edifying.

In the thirteenth year of his age he fell into a decline; and in the last six months of his life he was under great bodily affliction, which he bore with great patience and fortitude. He was never heard in the least to repine, but seemed wholly given up to the Divine will. Thus far his father. A few of his expressions are preserved, confirming this paternal testimony.

Lying in a weak state, he said, 'The Lord hath been very gracious to me all along, and followed me with the extendings of his love. Praised be his name.' To his brother and other relations present he said, 'Grieve not for me. It will, I believe, be well with me.' He desired those present to take care of their company and their behaviour, adding, 'The Lord hath been good to me, and I think I would rather go than stay in this world, where there are troubles enough for every day. You have done all you could. Don't sorrow for me. I am going to eternity—a blessed eternity, where we shall meet again, if we live as we ought.'

JANE CORNOCK, daughter of Thomas Cornock, of Haverford-west, in Pembrokeshire, and of my paternal aunt Elizabeth, daughter of Silvanus Bevan, of Swansea, was removed from time on the 17th of the Eleventh month, 1768, by means of a rapid consumption, at the house of Elizabeth Bevan, of Swansea, widow of Paul Bevan, her mother's brother.

I saw her in London, in the spring of the same year, lively and gay; though not extravagant, according to the usual acceptation of that word. In South Wales, the country of her birth and residence, there was not among the youth in general, of her own rank in life (though that was by no means high) much, if any, suitable acquaintance; and she too freely indulged herself in the company of those who were much strangers to the restraints of Truth; and therefore more likely to encourage than to check the propensity to gaiety which she felt. She was smart in her dress; deviated from the simple mode of speech used by Friends, and was admired for singing. Yet I believe she loved upright Friends, and she had long been particularly attached to that valuable relation at whose house she breathed her last, and who, I believe, saw her expire. This Elizabeth Bevan was a minister; and I have heard Jane speak of her in that capacity with evident marks of approbation, mentioning the weight of spirit which she used to perceive over her aunt, previous to the appearances of the latter in this service

The last time I saw her, as before hinted, was about six months before her death. She was then what is called the life of the youthful parties who attended her aunt in excursions, common in the vicinity of London; but I have reason to believe that even then the world had begun to fade in her view. But I was then a boy, in my sixteenth year; I partook of the enjoyment which her company afforded; and though now I can sometimes rejoice in the reflection that many of those connected with me by consanguinity have been reached, when wandering, by the crook of the heavenly

Shepherd, and can wish, if not pray, for the collection of many more of them into the fold of safety, yea, of salvation, I was certainly then neither a religious character, nor a judge of it: though then, I believe, like her, a lover of good men.

At length, says another relation, it was the merciful favour of her gracious Redeemer to give her a sight of her errors, and a true penitent heart for every folly; also to enable her to hold forth a powerful exhortation to her intimate acquaintance to shun the pleasing snares and vanities of life.

Being thus redeemed, she had no desire for recovery. She dropt, before her close, many comfortable expressions; saying, that though the Lord was pleased to afflict her body, her mind was not afflicted; that she had sweet assurance, and that at times she seemed already in heaven.

END OF THE TENTH PART.

PIETY PROMOTED,

IN BRIEF BIOGRAPHICAL MEMORIALS

OF SOME OF THE RELIGIOUS SOCIETY OF

FRIENDS,

COMMONLY CALLED QUAKERS.

THE ELEVENTH PART.

BY JOSIAH FORSTER.

PREFACE.

In preparing the following biographical memorials, it has been my endeavour to exhibit the power of religion on the respective characters of those whose lives are here briefly described; many of whom, from a personal acquaintance with them, I highly esteemed and loved. If in some instances it may be considered, that human infirmities are but slightly, or not at all, adverted to, let it not be supposed that this has arisen from a desire to eulogize the dead, or from a forgetfulness that such infirmities have existed. It is, however, highly important to us who survive, that we should not, from the remembrance of these, be less concerned in regard to our own easily-besetting sins. To him that knoweth to do good, and doeth it not, to him it is sin. And it is a solemn truth, of which we may often need to be reminded, that it is to the Lord, the righteous judge of all men, that we must individually stand or fall.

My principal wish has been, in proceeding with the work, to show the transforming power of Divine grace, and to furnish the reader with additional instances of the efficacy of that grace, to make wise unto salvation all who receive it and obey it; desiring that others may be thereby animated to pursue that course of obedience and self-denial, in which those who are taken from us have endeavoured to walk.

Whilst thus performing the office of an editor, I have often found it no light undertaking, and that it was indeed a serious employment, to attempt to pourtray the feelings of those who were about to enter the invisible world. At the same time, in contemplating the lives of our departed friends, my faith has been confirmed in the soundness of that part of the Christian profession of our Society, which includes a belief in the inward manifestation of the will of God to the soul of man.

In examining the materials which were brought under notice for this work, it was found needful to make a selection; but it is by no means to be inferred, that those who are not brought forward, were not examples of piety and Christian virtues. It is, on the contrary, a pleasing and animating reflection, that through the power of the Holy Spirit, many others who were acceptable ministers amongst us, or who were less conspicuous in our Society, have run their spiritual race in faith, and finished their course with joy.

In some of these memorials, there is more frequent mention of the Lord Jesus than in others. Many who have entertained a sincere faith in the essential doctrines of the Gospel, doctrines which have been uniformly believed in and upheld by our religious Society, have, I apprehend, often avoided conversing upon them, from a fear, lest by such discourse they should imperceptibly weaken their reverence for these sacred subjects, and their sense of those inestimable blessings conferred on us by the coming of the Son of God in the flesh. Faith in the benefits of the propitiatory sacrifice of Christ, and in the guidance and help of his blessed Spirit, are indispensable articles in the belief of a Christian. But it is not the mere profession of these important truths which constitutes the true disciple. It must be the earnest endeavour of all who desire to bear that name, to be delivered from the bondage and guilt of sin, by the power of a living, operative faith; and to walk humbly before God, keeping his holy commandments.

May we then be daily pressing after these things, in watchfulness and prayer, looking unto the Lord Jesus, and confiding in Him, as a true and unfailing Shepherd. Then shall we experience Him to be unto us both "wisdom and righteousness;" and then may we entertain the humble hope, that He will finally "be made unto us sanctification and redemption."

J. F.

TOTTENHAM, 9th of 2d Mo., 1829.

*** In transcribing extracts from letters, or other documents, which were about to be inserted in this volume, it has been found necessary sometimes to supply a word or two; but care has been studiously taken, not to introduce any thing which should affect the meaning of the sentence.

PIETY PROMOTED.

THE ELEVENTH PART.

JOSEPH HARWOOD.—The life of JOSEPH HARWOOD, of Manchester, affords a striking instance of the efficacy of the grace of God, inwardly revealed to the soul, when it is faithfully and unreservedly obeyed.

He was born in the year 1712, at Bolton in Lancashire, where his parents lived in good repute. His father was a conscientious member of the church of England, a man of integrity; one who professed and knew that religion is an inward work. He died when his son was not more than twelve or fourteen years of age; but his piety and instruction had made a deep and lasting impression on the tender mind of his child, who, as he advanced in years, was more and more introduced into those conflicts which attend the Christian warfare.

He was often, ere he arrived at maturity, involved in sorrow of heart, when reflecting on those things which appertain to the life that is to come. In this state, and from a wish to be more at liberty to attend to the duties of religion, a very unusual motive for such a step, he entered the army, in the year 1731; but in so doing, he found himself greatly disappointed. His companions seeing his anxiety and distress, and being strangers to the real cause, formed various conjectures concerning him; but such were his sobriety, docility, and readiness to serve others, that he gained the esteem and confidence of his officers, and was mostly employed in their particular services.

He continued in the army about fifteen years, beloved and esteemed in his station, and acquitted himself with credit and fidelity. But that good and gracious Being, who had visited him early in life, continued to follow him in mercy and in judgment; and in the course of the latter years of his military service, was pleased to show him with indubitable clearness, the utter inconsistency of all wars and fightings with the Gospel of life and salvation, and to require him to bear a faithful testimony to the same. Through the gradual operation of the Holy Spirit, this conscientious man was made willing, in conformity with the example and doctrine of Him who came not to destroy men's lives but to save them, to refuse to bear arms any longer, and to submit to whatever might ensue, although he knew that a punishment no less than the loss of his natural life was impending. He was tried by a court-martial, and treated with great moderation and civility; some who had been his fiercest opposers becoming his advocates. The remarks which he made on his own behalf, produced great seriousness. The court forwarded a candid representation of his case to king George the Second, who, on the intercession of some friends, honourably gave him his discharge, after about six months' imprisonment.

Not long after his release, having joined our religions Society, he took up his abode at Manchester. In the course of a few years he was brought under a religious exercise of mind to speak as a minister of the Gospel, to which he yielded, about the fortieth year of his age. Being faithful in the use of the talent received, he increased in religious experience; and though his public testimonies were not long, he was often baptized into a sense of the condition of the meeting, being reverently concerned to feel the renewal of power from on high, ere he stood up to minister to others.

He visited the meetings of Friends in Ireland, and several times, those in Scotland; and also travelled in other parts of this nation. He was frequently engaged, in gospel love, to visit Friends in his own meeting and neighbourhood, to see how it fared with them in the best things; when, from easy, innocent conversation, he was often drawn into solemn silence; and therein his heart was replenished as with the dew of heaven, under the lively influence whereof, he offered seasonable exhortation and counsel.

He was careful not to entangle himself with the cares of this life, seeking to have his treasure in heaven. Though naturally cheerful, and very agreeable in company, his words were frequently seasoned with the salt of the covenant, evidently ministering grace to the hearers. As his heart was thus warmed with love towards his brethren, so was he also greatly beloved by them. Being a man of meek and inoffensive deportment, and much devoted to the promotion of peace and good will amongst men, his company and conversation were acceptable to most who knew him, of various religious professions.

Some years before his death he became very infirm, being afflicted with an asthmatic complaint; yet he constantly attended his own meeting, fervently labouring therein for the arising of Divine life, and often speaking as a minister, greatly to the comfort of his friends. After a short illness, he died on the 12th of the First month, 1776, at the age of sixty-four.

TABITHA MIDDLETON.—In the lives of many dedicated and humble servants of the Lord, it not unfrequently happens, that but few incidents are met with, from which a biographical sketch can be compiled; whilst their faithful endeavours to serve the Lord in the way of his requirings, may have exhibited a bright example to those around them. Such appears to have been the case with TABITHA MIDDLETON, of Wellingborough in Northamptonshire, who was the daughter of John and Sarah Hoyland, of Sheffield.

In a letter to an intimate friend, she thus describes her sense of the goodness of the Almighty in her youth.

"On looking over years that are past, I find abundant reason to acknowledge the mercies of Providence, in extending his heavenly visitation in the very early part of life, which raised strong desires to walk acceptably before Him. I well remember the exemplary care of my dear mother, at that time, whose conduct and advices made lasting impressions on my mind; though, as I advanced in years, 'the lust of the eye and the pride of life,' too much influenced the judgment, and weakened my good resolutions, which made even life a burden. But how have I admired to be in this state allured to prefer Jerusalem before my chief joy; concluding, that whatever I parted with or suffered, was not to be compared with the enjoyment of Divine good."

When about fourteen years of age, she was deprived of her mother. By this loss, and other events which succeeded, her mind appeared to be increasingly turned to seek for the consolations of religion. She resided at that time at Sheffield, and manifested a pious care and solicitude for the younger branches of her father's family: she was much beloved by her young friends generally, to whom she was also a good example, in a humble and circumspect deportment.

In the year 1783, she was married to Benjamin Middleton, of Wellingborough, when her religious usefulness became more extensive, in an enlarged sphere of relative duties; in the faithful discharge of which, the meek equanimity of her conduct presented an instructive lesson to many.

After a time of much thoughtfulness, she had, when about twenty-five years of age, yielded to a belief that it was required of her to appear as a minister. Her communications in this character were acceptable to her friends, and delivered in great clearness and simplicity; and she was, for several years, at times, diligently employed in various parts of this nation, in visiting the meetings of her fellow-professors. She was much concerned for the right exercise of our Christian discipline, in the spirit of love and meekness; and, being clothed with true charity, administered counsel, and sometimes close admonition, in a way that often appeared to be not only well received, but to be attended with a blessing, particularly to those in early life. She was indeed a mother in Israel, an experienced and judicious counsellor, a firm and sympathizing friend.

She attended her own and a neighbouring quarterly meeting, in the autumn of 1809, and was soon afterwards taken ill. The symptoms were not alarming until the day preceding her death; but the awful messenger was not to her a king of terrors. In the course of this illness she remarked: "I have been permitted to live until I am not afraid to die; nor am I anxious to live, except on account of my husband and children. If I should be taken away, it may be said I am released from all my labours." She died in peace, on the 18th of the Tenth month, 1809, at the age of fifty-nine.

MARY ALEXANDER, of Needham-market, in Suffolk, was, at a very early age, tenderly affected with the visitation of Divine love, which inclined her mind to piety. Before she had attained her seventeenth year, she was impressed with a strong apprehension that, if faithful to the manifestations of the Holy Spirit, she should, at a future day, be called to the work of the ministry; yet, notwithstanding this gracious condescension of the Almighty, for want of steadily abiding under the operation of his power, she deviated from the simplicity of her guarded education, and gave way to youthful propensities averse to religious restriction and seriousness. Yet mercy and truth followed her; her heart was often made sad, under a sense of disobedience; and she sorrowfully felt that there was much which required to be slain by "the sword of the Lord" before she could be brought into a state of acceptance. Thus humbled and contrited before Him, she became at length effectually awakened to a search after enduring happiness, often and earnestly imploring that all within her might be brought into subjection to his holy will.

She now found much consolation in the perusal of the Holy Scriptures, and deeply lamented having spent any of her time in reading plays, and writings of a similar description; being sensible, that nothing she had ever been in the practice of, had so much alienated her mind from the fear and love of God; and she often wished she could warn all, and especially the youth of her own religious Society, of the pernicious tendency of such writings.

About the year 1786, she lost her surviving parent; from which time, to the year 1789, she sustained, from various causes, many deep conflicts of spirit. Many, also, were the baptisms of her soul, from a nearer view of the prospect she had long had of a call to the ministry, which now came weightily upon her, and on which service, in much humility and fear, she entered in the course of the same year, being the thirtieth of her age.

The general tenor of her subsequent conduct gave evidence to others that she loved "the habitation of the Lord's house, and the place where his honour dwelleth." She was given up in much devotedness, to leave her own comfortable dwelling, and to advocate the cause of Christ, both among her own friends, and in more distant parts; and was frequently constrained to manifest her interest in the spiritual welfare of her fellow-members, by paying religious visits to the families of friends; a duty for which she appeared eminently qualified; and there is reason to believe that her faithful labours were often productive of solid benefit, both in and out of our Society, and that they yielded to her own mind the peaceable fruits of righteousness.

In the discharge of her more private duties, she gave proof of possessing a heart expanded by benevolence; and to sympathize with others, and render assistance to them in times of difficulty or affliction, was a conspicuous part of her character.

Her last Christian efforts in advocating the gospel, were comprised in a visit to the families of friends in the city of Worcester, and parts adjacent, and in holding some public meetings, in conjunction with a friend under similar concern. The last meeting which she attended was held at Alcester, on the 13th of the Eleventh month, 1809, and was one to which the inhabitants of the town were invited; it was very large, and was considered to be remarkably solemn. In this meeting she was engaged in fervent, vocal supplication. She had been unwell for several days, and soon after the conclusion of this engagement, it appeared that she had taken the small-pox. The disorder did not assume an alarming aspect until after the usual crisis, when the symptoms were such as to dispel the hopes that had been entertained of her recovery. Through the whole of her deeply-trying illness, she discovered much patience and resignation, and her mind seemed to be divested of every burden. Speaking of her late visit, she said she had been favoured with a precious evidence, that she had been there in better wisdom than her own. Articulation being often difficult, she did not express much; and, from the extremity of her sufferings, was sometimes anxious to be released, and thought her spirit long in departing, yet carefully avoided, either in word or manner, murmuring at the conflict. She was preserved, with little intermission, sensible to the last; and during the final efforts of nature, several times held up her hands as in the attitude of prayer. She quietly expired on the fourth of the Twelfth month, 1809, in the fiftieth year of her age.

The friends of Worcester monthly meeting, in taking a retrospect of her labours among them, observe: "We may weep over her as a friend, or as a relation; we may mourn the loss which the church has sustained, of one of its upright pillars; but on her account there appears no cause for sorrow. She was, we believe, favoured to finish all she had in commission; showing herself therein a good and faithful servant, and we doubt not she has entered into the joy of her Lord.'

DEBORAH DARBY was the daughter of John and Hannah Barnard, and was born at Upperthorp, near Sheffield, in the Eighth month, 1754, and died the 14th of the Second month, 1810.

She was naturally of a sweet and amiable temper, and, in her youth, of a lively, active disposition. In early life, she frequently experienced the contriting visitations of Divine love, and in opportunities of retirement was humbled before God. Her example, in thus withdrawing from the pursuits of time, and cultivating a watchful state of mind, and her reverence for the truths of religion, combined with a kind and cheerful demeanour, had an attractive and beneficial effect on some of the friends of her youth. Her care to retire to wait upon the Lord in secret, continued through life; and having known this habit, at an early period, to contribute to temper her own vivacity, she was often engaged to recommend the practice to others, especially to her younger friends.

In the year 1776, she was married to Samuel Darby; and they lived for a while in London, but afterwards settled at Coalbrookdale, in Shropshire, which was the place of her residence until the time of her death.

Having submitted to the convictions of the Spirit of Truth, she learned from experience, that, whether in prosperity or adversity, there is no joy comparable to that which results from a conformity with the Divine will. She was thus prepared to yield to an apprehension of duty to become a minister of the Gospel, and first came forth in that character in the year 1779. Being concerned to keep low and watchful before the Lord, she advanced from stature to stature in this sacred office, and her services were truly acceptable to her friends. In the year 1781, she first travelled with a certificate of the unity of her monthly meeting; and from that period, through a course of near thirty years, she was a diligent labourer in the Gospel of Christ, at home and abroad, amongst those of her own religious Society, and other professors of the Christian name. She repeatedly travelled through most parts of this nation, was several times in Ireland, and was absent from her native land nearly three years on similar religious service in America, in company with her endeared fellow-labourer, Rebecca Young, now Rebecca Byrd.

On landing at New York, the 8th of the Tenth month, 1793, she made the following memorandum: 'On waking this morning, we found ourselves in the harbour of New York, and had a beautiful view of the town. We went to the house of our friend John Murray, who, with his wife, received us affectionately; which impressed our minds with gratitude to the Author of Mercies, both ancient and new, who had thus brought us safely over the mighty ocean. May He so preserve us, as to bring us at last into that port and haven of rest, at the end of time, where the morning stars sing together, and the sons of God shout for joy!' Having endeavoured to know and to do the will of Him in whose service she had gone forth, she wrote the following short acknowledgment of his all-sufficient help, on the day on which she embarked for her native land: "We attended a public meeting at Newcastle.* After dining with about one hundred and fifty Friends, we had a solemn parting opportunity, in which much encouragement was handed, and prayer put up for mutual preservation, under the influence of humbling Goodness, that had, we trust, put us forth, gone before us, and now condescended to be our reward."

In the course of this journey, she often felt her mind

* A town on the western bank of the Delaware, below Philadelphia.

warmed with Christian love and compassion for the native Africans and their descendants, so numerously settled in the United States; and in the larger cities, religious meetings were specially held with this degraded and injured class of our fellow-men. In passing along, both in England and America, she at times visited those confined in prison, some when under sentence of death, fervently labouring to turn their attention to the Saviour of the world—to Him, who, as he is applied unto in sincerity and in truth, will still be found to be the Friend of sinners.

The character of this diligent labourer, when employed in the service of her Lord, is thus delineated by one who was long and intimately acquainted with her: "I can say of her, that in and under all our conflicts, and the severest of her particular trials, I never met with one whose conduct evinced a stronger confidence in God, or whose faith was firmer in the appointed means of salvation. Thus supported, even when the waves of affliction rose high, she was enabled to centre in resignation, and to follow on in the line of her religious duty. Loving the light, she manifested her love by simple and unreserved obedience, without consulting ease to the flesh, or present gratification. I think her humility was conspicuous, rendering her a good example to her fellow-servants; to whom, even to the least, she was ever ready to to give way, when sensible that the anointing was poured forth upon them. Her fervent zeal for the welfare and preservation of the youth, in that path of self-denial which Truth leads unto, cannot be forgotten. Wherever I travelled with her on its account, I was witness to her pious and arduous labours with that class of society. Seldom could her devoted heart feel satisfied to leave Friends' families without gathering the children; and many, I believe, there are in different parts, who have cause to bless the Lord for having made her an instrument of good to them."

The dispositions which have been noticed as obvious in early life, matured by years, and sanctified by the power of religion, rendering her an endeared and instructive companion; one who was ever attentive to the right discharge of her relative and social duties. She was solicitous for the help of the poor, and concerned that a due proportion of her outward substance should be expended to promote their comfort. She was not apt to take offence, and cautious not to give it; and exemplified in her conduct, even under the pressure of heavy affliction, the excellency of that Gospel which she was commissioned to preach.

In the spring of 1808, Deborah Darby left home on a visit to Friends in the southern and eastern counties. In the autumn of the same year, she was considerably unwell, and exhausted by fatigue; and this debility continued through the winter. She was again absent from home for several weeks in the spring of 1809, and returned so far improved as to be able to join her friends in their public assemblies for Divine worship; but, as the winter approached, the gradual decay of nature rendered it necessary for her to confine herself very much to the house. The following extracts, from a few memorandums left behind, exhibit the humility with which her mind was clothed. "I have had some precious seasons of Divine overshadowing during my illness; which have been better than all the cordials administered by my medical attendants." — "I am sometimes strengthened to speak well of His name, who lives and reigns, and is forever worthy. I have cause to be thankful for strength being granted to sit with my friends, though often in much poverty of spirit."—"I have little to remark, my allotment being often in suffering as to the body, and low in mind; yet I can say, God is good, and a strong-hold in the day of trouble."

She endured much bodily suffering previous to her dissolution, with exemplary patience and sweetness, remarking: "Unless the Lord has some further service for me to do, I could not wish to stay much longer, I suffer so much; but all in his ordering is best." And at another time, when in great pain, said, "It would be a great favour to have a little ease once more before I leave you; I should like to be a little cheerful, for I have nothing but the pains of the body to make me otherwise." After having been greatly exhausted by seeing some of her nearest relatives, she said to a friend sitting beside her, "The Lord be praised. He is wonderfully good, even now." The evening before her death, when in extreme suffering, one of her attendants, who thought she had asked for something, said, "Can we do anything for thee?" to whom she replied, "Rejoice evermore, and in everything give thanks!" and shortly afterwards said, "The Lord's will be done." She seemed to be engaged in supplication for some time after this, although her expressions could not be understood.

Thus was this faithful disciple enabled, in the closing days of her earthly pilgrimage, to confide in the Almighty, and to evince that her soul was prepared to unite in that song of praise and thanksgiving, which is the blessed employment of those redeemed spirits who stand before the throne of God and of the Lamb, for ever and ever.

THE END OF THE THIRD VOLUME.

www.ingramcontent.com/pod-product-compliance
Lightning Source LLC
LaVergne TN
LVHW021131110826
845150LV00005B/994

* 9 7 8 1 4 2 5 5 5 0 3 0 1 *